AS Citizenship Studies for AQA

Tim Holden-Rowley, Mike Mitchell, Richard Seymour & Hazel White

HODDER
EDUCATION
AN HACHETTE UK COMPANY

The Publishers would like to thank the following for permission to reproduce copyright material:

Photo credits
p.3 T © rgbdigital.co.uk/Fotolia; C © doraemon/Fotolia; **p.5** © Pool Photograph/Corbis; **p.7** © Photos 12/Alamy; **p.18** 1st column (T to B) © Mark Scott/Fotolia; © Stan Kujawa/Alamy; © Todd Keith/Istock; © Christopher Nolan/Fotolia; **p.18** 2nd column (T to B) © Rupert Hartley/David Hartley/Rex Features; CL © c/Fotolia; CR © Mark Matysiak/Fotolia; © Carolyn Clarke/Alamy; © Bettmann/Corbis; **p.23** © Miroslav/Fotolia; **p.36** © Rex Features; **p.40** © Neil McAllister/Alamy; **p.41** © Janine Wiedel Photolibrary/Alamy; **p.47** © Philip Brown/Rex Features; **p.50** © Steve Maisey/Rex Features; **p.53** © HBO/Everett/Rex Features; **p.61** © Rex Features; **p.62** © Argus/Fotolia; **p.78** © Mike Egerton/EMPICS Sport; **p.100** (T to B) © Andrew Wiard/Alamy; © Rex Features; © Fiona Hanson/PA Archive/Press Association Images; **p.102** © Image Source/Rex Features; **p.114** © Sylvia Cordaiy Photo Library Ltd/Alamy; **p.115** PA Archive/Press Association Images; **p.121** © Stockfolio/Alamy; **p.127** © BL Remy De La Mauviniere/AP/ Press Association Images; BR © Gareth Fuller/PA Archive/Press Association Images; **p.139** © moodboard/Fotolia; **p.151** © Elmtree Images/Alamy; **p.152** © Mike Abrahams/Alamy; **p.160** © Simply Signs/Alamy; **p.191** © Rex Features; **p.200** © Julio Etchart/Alamy; **p.209** © David Jones/PA Archive/Press Association Images; **p.221** © ITV/Rex Features; **p.222** © Nils Jorgensen/Rex Features; **p.228** © Scott Hortop Travel/Alamy; **p.229** © John Giles/PA Archive/Press Association Images; **p.249** © Rob Wilkinson/Alamy; **p.250** © ICP/Alamy; **p.259** © Gareth Fuller/PA Archive/Press Association Images; **p.268** © Dima/Fotolia; **p.276** © Stan Kujawa/Alamy; **p.283** © Jeremy Sutton-Hibbert/epa/Corbis; **p.287** © Janine Wiedel Photolibrary/Alamy; **p.289** © Rex Features; **p.291** © Andrew Wiard/Alamy

Acknowledgements
Crown copyright material is reproduced with the permission of the Controller Office of Public Sector Information (OPSI); **pp.9–10** Extract from www.dosta.org reproduced with permission of The Council of Europe's DOSTA campaign; **p.48** 'On the margins' article © Guardian News & Media Ltd 2007; **p.50** 'Stereotyping is leading to terror' article reproduced with permission of the *Daily Mail*; **p.52** 'The mean Scot' cartoon reproduced with permission of the *Hertfordshire Mercury* and Don Mann; **p.65** 'I was called names like slut and whore' article © Guardian News & Media Ltd 2007; **p.70** Logo reproduced with permission of the Disabled Citizens Advice and Support Services; **p.83** Case study reproduced with permission of Robin Landman and the Network for Black Professionals; **p.127** Cartoon reproduced with permission of Martin Rowson; **p.134** 'Welsh councils refuse to answer nearly one in ten freedom of information requests they receive' article reproduced with permission of the *Western Mail*; **p.155** Logo reproduced with permission of the Legal Services Commission; **p.157** 'Parents get legal aid to sue health chiefs over radiation death of Lisa Norris' article reproduced with permission of the *Daily Record*; **pp.224–25** 'Kerry Katona' and 'Boris Johnson' complaints reproduced with permission of the Press Complaints Commission; **p.229** 'Ray Mallon takes control of Grove Hill revamp' © *Evening Gazette* and www.gazettelive.co.uk; **p.248** UKIP policies in brief reproduced with permission of the UK Independence Party; **p.250** '50 reasons to love the European Union' reproduced with permission of *The Independent*; **p.271** 'Animals in research – Directive 86/609' reproduced with permission of the Royal Society for the Prevention of Cruelty to Animals; **pp.277–78** 'The campaign that changed the eating habits of a nation' article reproduced with permission of *The Independent*; **p.284** 'NSPCC ads target child cruelty' article © Guardian News & Media Ltd 2006; **p.287** 'Invasion of the Commons: Five protestors storm chamber' article © Guardian News & Media Ltd 2004; **p.290** 'Fathers 4 Justice campaigners climb onto Harriet Harman's roof' article © Telegraph Media Group Limited 2008; **p.292** 'We didn't stop that war, but may have stopped the next' article © Guardian News & Media Ltd 2008

Every effort has been made to trace all copyright holders, but if any have been inadvertently overlooked the Publishers will be pleased to make the necessary arrangements at the first opportunity.

Although every effort has been made to ensure that website addresses are correct at time of going to press, Hodder Education cannot be held responsible for the content of any website mentioned in this book. It is sometimes possible to find a relocated web page by typing in the address of the home page for a website in the URL window of your browser.

Hachette Livre UK's policy is to use papers that are natural, renewable and recyclable products and made from wood grown in sustainable forests. The logging and manufacturing processes are expected to conform to the environmental regulations of the country of origin.

Orders: please contact Bookpoint Ltd, 130 Milton Park, Abingdon, Oxon OX14 4SB. Telephone: (44) 01235 827720. Fax: (44) 01235 400454. Lines are open 9.00–5.00, Monday to Saturday, with a 24-hour message answering service. Visit our website at www.hoddereducation.co.uk.

Cover photos: main image © Andrew Stuart/PA Photos; BL Ryan Pierse/Getty Images for Laureus; © David Cheskin/PA Photos; BR © Mode Images Limited/Alamy.

Illustrations by Barking Dog Art and GreenGate Publishing Services

Typeset in AGaramond 11pt by GreenGate Publishing Services, Tonbridge, Kent

Printed in Italy

A catalogue record for this title is available from the British Library.

ISBN: 978 0340 958 407 A 434606
N 323.60941

Contents

Introduction

This book has been designed to support the AQA AS Citizenship Studies specification. It is written by experienced examiners and is designed to encourage you to build your citizenship knowledge and skills, as well as skills in examination technique. Chapters 1 to 6 relate to a key question in the specification content and Chapters 7 and 8 give you some guidance on the assessment.

Chapters 1 to 6 have the following features in order to aid your learning:

- **Introduction**
  The introductory page gives you an overview of the main issues that are covered in each chapter.

- **Issues and topics**
  The chapter is then broken down into two sections which reflect the two main issues related to the key question in the content outline of the specification. These are further divided into three topics.

- **Sources**
  There is a range of visual and text-based sources throughout the chapter to extend knowledge and understanding of each issue.

- **Activities**
  Each chapter has a range of activities which encourage you to develop your skills in knowledge and understanding and in analysis and evaluation – these are the skills outlined in the Assessment Objectives (see pages 301–2).

- **Glossary**
  At the end of the book is a glossary containing key terms for each chapter.

The AQA specification requires students to complete an Active Citizenship Profile, on which they also answer questions in their Unit 2 examination. Chapter 7 provides some ideas on where to start with active citizenship. Chapter 8 gives advice on how to answer the examination questions for AQA AS Citizenship Studies.

IDENTITY, RIGHTS AND RESPONSIBILITIES

SECTION 1: IDENTITY

Chapter 1: What does it mean to be British?

In this chapter we explore two main issues which examine the key question 'What does it mean to be British?'

ISSUE 1: What is a citizen and perceptions of being 'British'
This issue is explored through the following topics:

- what is a citizen?
- is there agreement about what 'being British' means?
- how do individuals and groups define their identity/identities and where are these definitions drawn from?

ISSUE 2: How socially diverse is Britain?
This issue is explored through the following topics:

- how much change and continuity is there in migration patterns?
- how far is Britain a multicultural society?
- what is stereotyping?

ISSUE 1: WHAT IS A CITIZEN AND PERCEPTIONS OF BEING 'BRITISH'

In this section we explore the following three topics:

- what is a citizen?
- is there agreement about what 'being **British**' means?
- how do individuals and groups define their identity/identities and where are these definitions drawn from?

1 What is a citizen?

In this topic we define **citizenship**, explore the nature of citizenship, including active citizenship, and look at citizenship in a modern society, in particular the idea of citizens as subjects.

We then go on to look at different views of citizenship, including individualist and communitarian views, before examining citizens' legal, social, moral and political **rights** and duties.

Definition of citizenship

Citizenship is a term which means being a member of a state; in other words, a person belongs to that state or country. In the past the term used to mean belonging to a city but we now use it to mean belonging to a state or a country. A person belonging to a country is referred to as 'a **citizen**'. A citizen is protected in various ways by the country of which they are a citizen. The protections provided by a country are called rights and these vary from one country to another. A country has a wide range of organisations responsible for the running of the country and the protection of citizens' rights. Collectively these organisations are referred to as 'the **state**' and they include local and national rules and decision making bodies (government), a legal system and welfare systems, such as the national health service, police and emergency services and armed forces.

Alongside their rights protected by the state, citizens also have duties or **responsibilities**. These duties or responsibilities vary from one country to another. For example, in Germany, Switzerland, Israel and France citizens have to undertake a period of national service – which is no longer the case in Britain.

ACTIVITY 1

1) Identify one main benefit of being a citizen.
2) Identify one right and one responsibility of being a citizen.

Responsibilities in Britain include obeying laws laid down by the state, respecting other citizens' rights, voting and contributing to society, for example through employment or as a parent. (We discuss rights and responsibilities further in Chapter 3.)

Citizenship can therefore be viewed as a kind of agreement between the citizen and the state to which they belong. In return for the protection of rights by the state, the citizen has duties and responsibilities to uphold. Citizenship thus is a two-way term which includes the responsibilities or duties of a citizen as well as those things a citizen expects from the state – protection of rights.

The image on page 3 is of a passport of a UK citizen (the UK is part of the **European Union**). Many people see their citizenship as symbolised by the passport they carry. The passport symbolises the belonging of that citizen to a state and the passport declares that the state will expect its citizen to be treated appropriately. Otherwise the state to which the citizen belongs will take action to protect them. But citizenship in modern Britain means more than just holding a passport and enjoying the protection of the state. Citizenship means participation in duties and responsibilities as well as being in possession of rights.

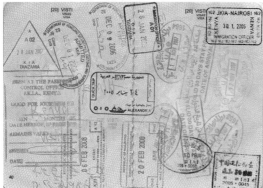

Passports are regarded by many people as a symbol of their citizenship

The passport is a powerful document. The bearer of the passport shown above is a citizen of the UK, which is part of the European Union.

1) What is the purpose of a passport?
2) What protection does a passport offer?
3) Who is requesting that the bearer be protected and allowed to pass freely?
4) Why do you think a passport should be kept safe at all times?

The nature of citizenship

Central to the notion of being a citizen is the aspect of belonging. As we explored on the previous page, the nature of citizenship is about duties and responsibilities of the citizen. We now go on to briefly explore some of those duties as a citizen. We give specific focus to a term which is frequently used and much debated – 'active citizenship'.

People (citizens) are very different – lifestyles do not just vary from individual to individual but also throughout an individual's lifetime. Given this diversity the activities a citizen is involved in at different stages in their lifetime are numerous and varied.

Therefore the nature of citizenship and what is meant by the term active citizenship is very complex. Some people may be working and paying taxes; this is a type of active citizenship as they are acting on duties to work and pay taxes. Others may be family members looking after younger brothers or sisters, older relatives and dependent relatives and some may be raising children. Some citizens are active outside the home beyond being employees, for example taking part in voluntary work such as running a local football team, or volunteering in a charity shop. Others may be local representatives who give up their time to serve on local residents' committees or on parish councils. Some people may show neighbourly concern by looking in on local residents or lending an ear to a friend or helping a person in need; others may organise or take part in local residents' associations such as neighbourhood watch, local history associations, after-school clubs and other hobby related activities. Some may fund raise, for example by taking part in Red Nose Day or Children in Need. Active citizenship could involve local community work, such as local environmental tidy schemes, reading with children at a local school, participation in political parties or campaigning to raise awareness of local or national issues. Many citizens are active church members attending church or mosque, temple or synagogue, which contributes to community togetherness and unity.

Clearly there are numerous ways in which active citizenship participation can take place. There are no rules on how much or how little someone should take part and studies in citizenship are not about judging other people's active citizenship. However governments (national and local) encourage citizens to take as active a part in community life as is possible.

Although a citizen's active contributions or participation is varied, it is possible to categorise active citizenship into two broad areas:

- citizenship in the private sphere – the family and friends of that individual, and
- citizenship in the public sphere – outside the individual's family area in communities and beyond.

Within these two broad areas active citizenship often fits into one or more of five types of role:

- citizenship as an employee
- citizenship as an employer
- citizenship as a volunteer (charity work, membership of community organisations, political campaigning)
- citizenship as a family member
- citizenship as an active neighbour or friend.

Many people see active citizenship as unselfish acts giving up free time for no financial gain. This is frequently the case, but active citizenship can be paid or unpaid and does not necessarily require the same amount of time for any specific period. For example, a citizen may be active simply by paying their taxes directly out of their monthly or weekly wages – no further action is

required other than remaining in employment. Alternatively the unemployed could be fulfilling active citizenship by actively looking for work.

Most people take part in unselfish active citizenship of one kind or another in addition to expected citizenship activities, such as attending school and lessons or working and paying taxes.

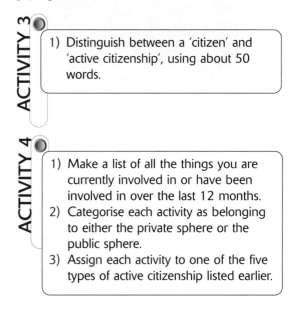

ACTIVITY 3

1) Distinguish between a 'citizen' and 'active citizenship', using about 50 words.

ACTIVITY 4

1) Make a list of all the things you are currently involved in or have been involved in over the last 12 months.
2) Categorise each activity as belonging to either the private sphere or the public sphere.
3) Assign each activity to one of the five types of active citizenship listed earlier.

If you are young and live with parents or older adults, ask them to carry out Activity 4. Explore how active citizenship participation differs for different age groups.

Citizenship in a modern society

We have so far explored what citizenship means for individuals, but they have not always enjoyed the rights that they do today. Now we must explore when the term citizenship emerged and contrast it with another type of belonging to a state – as a subject. There is some debate about whether British people are subjects or citizens and it goes to the core of our relationship with the state that we belong to in modern Britain.

A large turnout greets the Queen on her visit to Huddersfield. Citizens of Britain have a variety of different identities. How many different identities can you identify in the photograph?

Although the term citizen dates back to Roman times, it is only relatively recently that British people have been referred to as citizens. There is no clear date as to when the term citizen first began to be applied to British people but it is mainly over the last 100 years which in historical terms is modern times. In the last 10 years however, the term citizen has become much more commonly used but in modern Britain it can be argued that we are both subjects and citizens.

A subject is someone who is directly controlled by the rulings of a monarch – a king or queen. In modern Britain this is currently Queen Elizabeth II. A subject has very little or no say in whether or not the monarch is right or wrong and originally a subject was required to obey without question – they did as they were told! Although no monarch since 1215 has had absolute power, the monarchy's power was *almost* absolute for centuries. But since 1215, rights have gradually been secured for people leading to our system of democracy and accountability in modern Britain.

In contrast to a subject a citizen has a say in who will be their leader and whether to accept the rules. If the citizen does not wish to follow the rules they can change them if they make their legal case to parliament or the courts which make and enforce our rules. Citizens agree to obey laws because they have had a say in what the rules state we must or must not do. In short, citizens have a say because citizens have rights which hold their leaders to account and the right to challenge or question the law. The law is not fixed permanently because citizens always have the right to challenge it; we call this modern British system of decision making, rule and accountability a **democracy**.

Britain is different from countries such as the USA, Russia or France in that it has both a monarch and a legal parliamentary democracy. France had a revolution which decided that a parliament would rule and not a monarch. Britain had a civil war and got rid of monarchy rule for a period only to reinstate the monarch with a parliament running alongside. Other countries such as Denmark or Holland have a similar system to Britain. But unlike Denmark or Holland, Britain does not have a written constitution to clearly set out the powers of the monarch and the powers of the parliament. Therefore in effect we remain subjects in theory but citizens in practice. It is further complicated for those serving in the armed forces: they have to swear allegiance to the monarch rather than to parliament!

It is reasonable to conclude that modern Britain has not clearly defined our belonging as subjects or as citizens. We still have this strange peculiarity of remaining subjects to 'Her Majesty', yet are also subject to the rule of law in which we have a say, which therefore makes us citizens. The reality is, however, that slowly over the centuries we have secured more and more rights such as freedom from false imprisonment, a right to a fair trial, freedom of speech and belonging to faith, to define our sexuality etc. These rights have undermined the monarch's control and given rise to the term citizen. More recently, the term active citizenship is used which refers to conscious citizenship where we have rights and belonging as well as duties and responsibilities.

Differing views of citizenship

Some academics believe that citizenship means a series of rights that set the individual free to do as they choose within the law. This is the **individualistic** view of what citizenship means. In contrast the **communitarian** view from writers such as Etzioni sees citizenship as more than just a duty to follow the laws of society and rules of conduct. It sees citizenship as also requiring participation – an active contribution to society. The communitarian view sees society as stronger through active participation for two main reasons: 1) because unity builds between citizens and the law and 2) decision makers are held to account and therefore do a better job on behalf of all of us.

Citizenship is not merely a matter of personal morality, of learning not to steal or beat people up in the street. Nor is it simply a matter of political effectiveness, of knowing which buttons to press in order to get a government grant or to claim a benefit. If you are going to be an active citizen, involved in doing things on behalf of the community as a whole, then you must have an understanding of what that community stands for. And that in turn, having yourself a member of a historic community in whose positive achievements you can justifiably take pride, and of whose shortcomings you feel ashamed.

Millar, D (2000) 'Citizenship: What does it mean and why is it important?' in *Tomorrow's Citizens: Critical Debates in Citizenship and Education* (Pearce and Hallgarten), IPPR, London, p31

ACTIVITY 5

1) Identify the ways in which the extract opposite is referring to a *communitarian* view of citizenship.

Citizens' rights

Belonging to a society carries with it rights and responsibilities and citizens have different types of rights and duties. In Britain, which considers itself a liberal society, the rights of citizens are built around the notion or principle that every adult citizen should have equal access to some basic civil, political and social rights. This is referred to as a liberal model of citizenship which has at its heart freedom and equality for all adult citizens. It must be noted that not all societies will have such ideas of equality for all. Some countries, for example Saudi Arabia, do not allow women equal rights in all areas. Also note that rights are not the same for all ages. For example in Britain young people are not allowed to vote until they are 18 or stand for parliamentary elections unless they are over 18.

The sociologist T H Marshall explored the changing nature of British citizenship. He set out a model of **three** stages in the development of citizens' rights in a liberal society, starting from the 1700s leading to more views of citizenship rights.

STAGE 1 CIVIL RIGHTS

These citizens' rights were what many people now take for granted. They are often called basic human rights but they did not always exist for everyone. At this early stage in the development of citizens' rights emerging in the seventeenth and eighteenth centuries, citizens were guaranteed rights such as freedom of speech, a fair trial and justice, freedom to practise a faith of their choice and to own a property. In theory the state would protect these rights for every citizen.

STAGE 2 POLITICAL RIGHTS

In the 1800s and early 1900s political decisions increasingly involved wider numbers of people and organisations. For example trades unions were becoming more powerful and workers were granted rights to represent their views to management in key decisions, such as wage agreements and safety issues.

Throughout this period political rights were gradually extended through a series of reform acts so that by 1928 all women and men aged over 21 had the right to vote and stand for parliamentary and local elections. The voting age was lowered to 18 in 1969 (although a person still has to be 21 to stand for parliamentary elections). Such political rights are now often considered basic rights in Britain.

Suffragettes demonstrating for women's rights to vote

STAGE 3 SOCIAL AND MORAL RIGHTS

By the mid-twentieth century notions of citizenship rights extended to a basic standard of living guaranteed by the state, such as a minimum standard of health care, social security, employment and education. This stage in the evolution of citizens' rights guaranteed by the state is called a **welfare state**. In a welfare state the citizens' rights are guaranteed by the state but in ways beyond having a say in the legal and political system. By this stage – the mature stage – citizens' rights extend to moral dimensions, such as the right to a basic standard of housing, with adequate health care support, life without poverty where possible and a basic income. In short, the social and moral rights of this third stage extend to having a fair stake in society and in the wealth of that society.

Much debate exists about what this basic welfare standard should amount to, for example what the Income Support and minimum wages levels should be. Debate also exists around how welfare payment should be organised, for example whether Child Benefit (guarantees all children have some financial support) should be universal (paid to all parents regardless of their income). However although there is debate about what the amounts or levels should be and about how it should be paid to citizens, the principle of basic citizens' rights to a minimum standard of welfare and social/moral security is established in this mature society. (We explore the debate about how far the welfare state is responsible for individual citizens' welfare in Chapter 2.)

In this third stage the area of social or moral rights is expanded to include a number of complex and controversial issues. For example protection of a citizen's right to

ACTIVITY 6

1) Identify one example of a civil right, a political right, a social right and a moral right.

2) Draw a timeline to illustrate how over the period mentioned on pages 6–7 the stages in citizens' rights have evolved. Allow plenty of space along your timeline to add further findings about citizens' rights as your studies of citizenship and related subjects progress.

3) Imagine you are a wealthy citizen living in a time of recession. Explain why you benefit as well as a poor person who is unemployed. In this answer you will explain why the rights of one citizen may benefit not just themselves but other citizens as well.

choose whether or not to continue with a pregnancy – abortion laws in the late 1960s – and areas more recently, such as the right to smoke-free air at work, the banning of smoking in public places in 2000 or the disability discrimination Acts of the 1990s which protect the rights for disabled people to access all public buildings. Recently there has been a complex debate on whether the citizen has the right to end their own life. These are social and moral issues about the rights of citizens which occur in the third stage of Marshall's changing stages of British citizenship.

Citizens' responsibilities

So far we have explored the area of rights associated with British citizenship. However in return for these rights, individuals have duties and responsibilities as well. These include a responsibility to be an effective parent or a duty to respect the rights of others and to uphold the law. There is also a duty to pay taxes – even if an individual's income is below the level where they pay income tax (as is the case with most part-time student workers) – because value added tax is charged on most consumables.

Adding to earlier explorations of the active citizen and the duties of a citizen, on pages 8–10 are two case studies intended to encourage you to consider the complicated balance between rights and responsibilities as a citizen.

CASE STUDY 1: Citizenship and belonging: the case of the Roma people

Roma people live throughout Europe. They are often called gypsies (and other unpleasant names) and they give valuable insight into the nature of citizenship and belonging to a state. This case study illustrates how different people feel a sense of belonging in different ways which leads to different types of lifestyles, differing relationships with a state and differing ideas of what makes a citizen and what therefore citizenship involves.

In the case of the Roma people they have a culture with long traditions of being nomadic (frequently moving from place to place). Traditionally the Roma did not recognise a sense of belonging to any one particular country or state and instead moved from place to place for work and to trade; they did not really recognise national boundaries. As a consequence, the Roma people have been viewed suspiciously for centuries as a stateless people, not fully accepted by other citizens. Many of the countries through which the Roma people move are hostile to them.

The Roma struggle to gain respect as a people with rights – many areas of Britain have frequently been hostile to Roma travellers treating them with suspicion, anger and misunderstanding of their culture.

CASE STUDY 1: The Roma people's campaign (DOSTA)

The Roma people have been in European countries since the fourteenth century and originated from Pakistan and Northern India. The Roma culture has a very diverse range of unique languages and is very much based on a nomadic lifestyle (constantly moving from place to place). The Roma have suffered persecution from various countries throughout their history, notably by Nazi Germany during the Second World War.

The vast majority of Roma people are now sedentary – settled in one area and no longer nomadic. Over generations most have become naturalised citizens to one country including many obtaining British citizenship. Roma people and their descendants live in most European countries and the largest number of Roma people live in southeast Europe.

A significant proportion of Roma people, however, still hold to the nomadic travelling way of life and move from place to place throughout Europe. Nomadic Roma make a living from, for example, selling small items (often home made) door-to-door, working seasonally in fields or selling services such as palm reading at fairs.

The nomadic Roma people are stateless in terms of belonging to a specific country. Although nomadic Roma do not have a distinct country to which they belong they are living in Europe and recently (around 2005) the European Commission recognised the rights of the Roma people and now considers them EU citizens.

Being citizens of the EU with full citizenship rights but being of no specific country causes problems in terms of providing education, health and social security services. EU member states or national governments tell or direct local governments to provide secure 'camps' or areas for travelling Roma to settle, but the Roma people often argue these are inadequate for their numbers. Consequently if the nomadic Roma people have no space on designated camps, sometimes and often very suddenly, groups of Roma settle in an accessible section of open land (often council land) and this causes hostility from local residents towards the 'invaders' and creates costs to councils to evict the illegal settlers.

ACTIVITY 7

1) Why do you think the nomadic Roma people's lifestyle causes suspicion among citizens of EU countries?
2) Briefly discuss the extent to which, as citizens primarily of the UK and then of the EU, we all have a responsibility to promote the rights of the Roma people.

Web action

To find out more about the Roma people go to **www.Dosta.org**.

ACTIVITY 8

1) Read through the *Yorkshire Post* article on page 10 and briefly explain how the Roma people and their culture came into conflict with the local people.
2) Using examples briefly outline what you think to be the article's opinion of Roma people.

CASE STUDY 1: Citizenship and belonging: the case of the Roma people

Massive bill as travellers set up 200 sites illegally

Taxpayers are forking out thousands of pounds a month for unlawful camps.

Thousands of pounds a month are being spent on legal fees, clean-up costs and increased security measures to protect council land.

Local authorities have also had to deal with more than 1,000 complaints from the public in the past year.

Authorities have had to deal with travellers on football pitches, school fields, at a church, business parks, lay bys and a country park.

The Conservative councillor responsible for the issue in Leeds hit out at the Government for pressurising councils across Yorkshire to come up with new sites.

There was uproar in Kirklees when the Gipsy Council submitted plans for two sites in Huddersfield. It later withdrew both following opposition.

A spokeswoman for the Gipsy Council said councils across the country were wasting money on evicting travellers when they ought to be creating legitimate sites which she claimed would reduce unauthorised camps.

Yorkshire Post, 14 May 2007

The article above from the *Yorkshire Post* indicates the anger and community unease resulting from nomadic Roma people settling in an area. The article emphasises hostility towards people seen as invaders, outsiders and with no right to be there.

In contrast below is an extract from a pamphlet from the Roma people seeking to raise awareness of their culture, identity and sense of belonging.

Dosta! means 'enough' in Romani. It is also the name of a Council of Europe/European Commission awareness-raising campaign which aims to bring non-Roma closer to Roma citizens by breaking down the barriers caused by prejudices and stereotypes.

Although Roma have been in Europe since the fourteenth century, they are not always recognised by the majority society as a fully-fledged European people. Many Roma communities today live in very difficult conditions, and their participation in public life is extremely limited.

… Roma are European citizens, they form a group of about 10 million people … Being European citizens means that Roma have not only duties but also rights and aspirations just like everybody else, and therefore their citizenship and human rights must be recognised. In addition Roma culture is a rightful part of Europe's cultural heritage.

www.dosta.org

1) Outline the key points the *Dosta* campaign leaflet makes which defend the Roma culture.
2) Write a paragraph to explain whether you agree or disagree that people should be allowed to be nomadic but also to have rights as citizens. In your response reflect upon the key value of freedom.

CASE STUDY 2: Should prisoners have the right to vote?

Britain is one of 13 EU countries that does not allow prisoners the right to vote (those on remand are allowed to vote, however, as are those jailed for contempt of court or non-payment of debts). This is based on the view that imprisonment as a punishment should do more than deprive a person of the right to liberty: prisoners should feel themselves to be excluded from other rights granted to law-abiding citizens.

Others would disagree with this view and would argue that prisoners are human beings and deserve human rights, including political rights and freedom from inhumane or degrading treatment. This view has been backed by the European court in Strasbourg, which has ruled in favour of UK prisoners looking to reclaim their right to vote.

1) Do you agree or disagree that British prisoners should have the right to vote? Explain your answer.
2) Discuss how this case displays difficulties with balancing rights and responsibilities as a citizen.

So far we have been exploring definitions of citizenship and what it means to be a citizen of a country such as Britain. Given this belonging, citizens have rights and duties which differ from country to country. They are however rights that we expect to be protected by the state to which we belong.

Britain considers itself a liberal society where one of the main values underpinning our rights is that of freedom; for example freedom to act as individuals, to express our own opinions, identities and religions. Our rights, then, reflect this fundamental core value.

In the next section we will explore what it means to be British. Is there a clear British identity? How much is this British identity changing and where does our British identity come from?

2 Is there agreement about what 'being British' means?

In this topic we explore different approaches to understanding the British identity.

First we briefly outline the historical events leading to the formation of the country now called the United Kingdom of Great Britain and Northern Ireland (UK for short). Note that citizens of the UK are called 'British'.

Second we emphasise different views on what ordinary people see as British.

Third we explore some of the things which may define or unify the British by exploring what we imagine to be Britishness, some symbols of Britishness and events that may unify the British people.

At the end of this topic we return to the question of whether we are in agreement about what it means to be British and ask the question – to what extent are we a united people in agreement about our Britishness and what it means?

Addressing the question of whether there is agreement about being British requires a definition of who the British are and what Britishness is. We may end up with more questions than answers because our nation like all countries is very diverse. Also remember this topic links closely with other topics in this chapter. For example two major concepts feature elsewhere – 'identity' is explored in topic 3 and 'multiculturalism' is explored in topic 5.

The nature of British citizenship

As we identified in the first topic (page 2), being a member of the UK means you are a British citizen subject to the laws of the land with the monarch as your head of state. However exploring a definition of Britishness and what people understand to be British is complex with a range of different opinions.

Types of citizenship status

British citizenship is complicated because of the colonial history of the UK, the fact that the UK still has 14 overseas territories and because of its membership of the EU. Below we set out three broad groupings which are types of British citizenship status.

British citizen

This is the most common type of citizenship status. A British citizen is someone who has full citizenship rights, including the right to live in, work in, vote in and be protected by the UK. Also since the UK is a member of the EU British citizens have the right to live anywhere within the EU, work anywhere within the EU, vote and be protected by EU law.

British Overseas Territories Citizenship (BOTC)

This form of citizenship is for people living in one of 14 small areas (often islands) across the world called British Overseas Territories. Since 2002 these people have full British citizenship rights. Examples of existing overseas territories are the Falkland Islands, British Virgin Islands and Gibraltar.

British citizenship and BOTC are the only types of citizenship to give you an automatic right to live in and work in, vote in and be protected by the UK and the EU.

Types of citizenship status for peoples in former colony countries

Once a country was granted independence from British colonial rule (this occurred mostly after the Second World War) the people became citizens of the former colonial country. However before the 1960s people living in countries that were colonies or former colonies of the UK (such as the West Indies, Kenya and India) had the right to live and work in Britain and adopt British citizenship. Following concerns about large numbers of immigrants moving to Britain and adopting British citizenship, changes were made to immigration law in particular in 1962, 1971 and 1981. These laws restricted or tightened controls on British citizenship but anyone moving to Britain before 1981 from the former colonial country was likely to have become a British citizen by January 1983.

Since 1981 broadly speaking people living in former colonies were allowed a kind of British citizenship. There are four different kinds depending on the country and the nature of the relationship with the UK:

- British overseas citizens
- British subjects
- British nationals (overseas)
- British protected persons.

These types of citizenship are now largely symbolic and do not allow a person to live in Britain or the EU. Any person wishing to become a British citizen must apply to the Crown (Passport Office).

Dual citizenship

If a person leaves Britain and is adopted by another nation as a citizen it does not mean they lose British citizenship. They have dual citizenship. Similarly many people formerly of other countries adopted as British citizens who live in the UK have dual citizenship.

ACTIVITY 1

1) Identify the type of citizenship status that allows a person to live in Britain.
2) Briefly explain why the Government decided to monitor and control the numbers of people becoming British citizens.

British citizens and citizenship of the EU

The UK is one of 27 member states of the EU which means British citizens are also citizens of the EU. Being an EU citizen means a person has various rights and freedoms which apply throughout the EU area. They are to:

- travel throughout the 27 countries of the EU (with a valid passport)
- work (or apply for work) anywhere in the EU
- live anywhere in the EU
- stand for election in EU elections (for example European Parliament)
- vote in EU elections
- be protected under EU law and security services.

Citizens of the 27 member states retain their original citizenship of the member state such that if you have a passport it will have European Union written on it and the name of the member country of which you are a citizen.

We discuss further the issue and influence of the EU in Chapter 5, pages 241–51 and also the influences on citizenship following devolution in the UK.

Becoming a British citizen

Today, generally speaking, a person may become a British citizen in one of five ways:

1) **Born in the UK**: since 1983 a person automatically becomes a British citizen if they are:
   - born in the UK, and
   - both their parents are married,* and
   - at least one of their parents is a British citizen, or settled in the UK.
   (*A person born in the UK, whose parents are not married, becomes a UK citizen if their mother is a British citizen or is settled in the UK.)
2) **Adoption**: a child who is adopted by a British citizen becomes a British citizen on the day of their adoption order.
3) **Descent**: if a child with a British parent is born outside the UK, then that child becomes a British citizen – as long as the parent did not acquire their citizenship by descent (e.g. their parents were British but do not live in the UK). If they did, then the child will have British citizenship only if that parent was working overseas for the UK Government or European Community.
4) **Registration**: a child born in the UK, but not registered for British citizenship, may, at the age of ten, qualify for British citizenship, as long as they have not spent more than 90 days a year outside the UK. A child may also

become a British citizen if their parent gains British citizenship.

5) **Naturalisation**: the process by which a person who is of another nationality applies to become a British citizen. The process requires the following:

- living in Britain for five years (three if married to a British citizen)
- showing understanding of English or Welsh or Gaelic language and British culture
- passing a language and knowledge test
- completing an application form and paying a fee (approximately £150).

Thorpe, T and Jarvis, R (2006) *Inside Britain: A guide to the UK constitution, Citizenship Foundation*, Hodder Murray, London, pp53–54

ACTIVITY 2

Exploring views on EU membership

1) Draw up a short questionnaire, with perhaps between five and ten questions, which ask about feelings of belonging and citizenship in the EU. For example you could ask about feelings on European integration, the effects of EU membership, understanding of rights as EU members. Using the questionnaire you could carry out short surveys on older generations, for example grandparents, parents and also your own generation. Once complete you will have collected data which could show patterns of differences between the generations about their feelings as citizens of the EU.

2) Using your questionnaire data briefly discuss your findings about British citizens and membership of the EU. Which of the views do you agree with and which do you disagree with?

The development of the UK and its constituent parts

The terms British and UK often get confused and here we try to clarify what they mean and where they come from.

In 1707 the kingdom of England, which at this time included Wales and the Channel Islands, (Guernsey and Jersey), united with the kingdom of Scotland to form a single kingdom called Great Britain. The new country was governed by a parliament in Westminster (London) with the monarch as head of state (Queen Anne at the time).

The kingdom of Great Britain extended in 1801 to incorporate the northern part of Ireland (mainly protestant at the time). Great Britain was then called the United Kingdom of Great Britain and Northern Ireland and is now commonly known as the UK.

Members of the UK are referred to as British citizens (British). All members of the UK are governed by the Houses of Parliament still in Westminster, London and have the same monarch as their 'head of state' (currently Queen Elizabeth II).

The Isle of Man is a slightly more complicated part of the UK. It was included into the new United Kingdom in 1765 but the parliament of the Isle of Man (Tynwald) kept independence from the new Westminster parliament. The people of the Isle of Man (Manx people) are British citizens and the UK parliament in Westminster is broadly responsible for the island and its security.

Devolution, British unity and the UK

Northern Ireland and Wales have *national assemblies* and Scotland has a parliament. Powers were transferred in the late 1990s from

Westminster to the assemblies and the Scottish parliament. It was felt that some decisions affecting the nations were best made in their locality where issues were clearer to the people locally. (England does not have its own parliament or assembly.) Some people regard this transfer of power as the first step to the break-up of the UK into nations once again.

It must be noted that not all powers have been transferred away from Westminster. Scotland, Wales and Northern Ireland are still subject to the decisions of Westminster UK Parliament for matters of national security, the economy and foreign policy and they remain subjects of the crown. We explore devolution in more detail in Chapter 5, pages 227–39.

ACTIVITY 3

In this activity you are exploring the issue of nationality within the UK.

Some citizens prefer to call themselves English, Scottish or Welsh rather than British. Many people prefer to associate with a region or nation within Britain rather than with Britain as a whole.

1) List what you consider to be the benefits of uniting the countries of Northern Ireland, England, Scotland and Wales. You may think about the economy, national security, influence in the world (sporting, cultural or political) and so on.
2) Using the same themes list what you think may be disadvantages or problems of being a united kingdom of four countries.

Colonial history and the ethnic diversity of the British people

Former Prime Minister Tony Blair says that 'blood alone' does not define national identity

and that modern Britain was shaped by a 'rich mix of all different ethnic and religious origins'. These views were reflected by the Queen, who talked about 'our richly multicultural and multifaith society' in her jubilee speech to parliament:

'The increasing ethnic diversity of British society means it is difficult to define what makes someone British.'

www.webritish.co.uk

As a result of the colonial history of England and the UK many countries in all continents of the world, in particular Asia, Africa and America (north and south), became subjects of the crown (colonies). Today most colonies have regained their independence, this process was called decolonisation. By 1983 most people from former colonies who had moved to Britain were granted British citizenship.

As a result in part of our colonial history the UK is a highly diverse population in terms of race (**ethnicity**), culture and countries of origin. If you have dual citizenship or your parents/grandparents were born in a different country and you are British there may still be a practical association (for example relatives still living in the country of origin whom you visit) or some feelings of belonging to the country of your or your family's origin. This issue of mixed feelings of belonging is evident in some of the definitions of what it means to be British on page 16. We explore racial and ethnic diversity in more detail later in this chapter in topics 4 and 5, pages 28–49.

ACTIVITY 4

1) What is a 'former colony'?
2) How has colonial history affected the ethnic and racial diversity in Britain?

The nature of British identity

Below are comments and opinions which indicate that the answer to the question of what it means to be British is very complex.

They are comments from the WeBritish website which are some ordinary people's attempts to define or describe British identity.

I have lived in Canada for 31 years but still consider myself to be British – and proud of it. I am proud to be a member of a nation that has offered so much to the world in the form of medical discoveries, scientific breakthroughs, world leadership, social reforms, a political foundation that is copied and envied the world over, whose people have a wry sense of humour and are able to laugh at their own quirks and foibles and above all else have a tolerance for others that has sometimes been stretched to the limit – but has not been broken.

Gareth J Green, Niagara Falls, Canada

Being British conjures up notions of fair play, rounded education, good driving, respect for laws, standing up for rights and against injustice, sharp humour (irony, self-effacement, puns etc.), sociability, appreciation of foreign people and customs (yes, I really mean that!), generosity in giving to charitable causes, invention and creativity, independence, tolerance and flexibility. We are certainly not perfect and perhaps we still cling too much to the 'glorious' past but we represent a lot of what is good in the world.

John Barry, Paris, France

British characteristics are contradictory – eccentricity with privacy, pride with self-effacement, pragmatism with tradition. We're a people of innovation, on a permanent nostalgia trip.

Tim Staddon, UK

Being British is being able to moan about anything and everything, and not truly appreciate anything. The weather, the NHS, the roads, the schools, the crime levels – no one can be satisfied with anything. Oh yeah, and there's the monarchy. Everyone seems up for ousting them, but I think for once we ought to be proud and more than content with our royal family. They are British – a unified family with moral values.

Shahid Hussain, UK

Being British is: applauding the other team when they score. It's being courteous to people serving me at a store. It's giving way at a roundabout (somewhat nerve-wracking here). It's helping my elderly nextdoor neighbour for the pleasure of it. It's respecting the values and traditions that were instilled into me by my parents along with a strong community spirit. It's feeling profoundly satisfied with a Monarch who has served us faithfully for over 50 years.

Linda, Sydney, Australia

All Indians who have lived here and taken British nationality feel British, live British and value British ways of life and justice. Britishness means tolerance, justice and fair play and practice of religion without harming others. The problem is for the indigenous population in accepting dark skinned people as Brits even if they are born, bred and brought up in Britain.

Sridhar Rao, Bromley, Kent, UK

www.webritish.co.uk

ACTIVITY 5

You may wish to carry out this activity with the whole class or in groups.
1) In 150 words compile your own definition of British and compare it with those in the box on page 16. Or select 150 words from the comments above and edit them to compile a definition which you feel most closely matches what you feel it is to be British.
2) Go to the WeBritish website at www.webritish.co.uk and post your definition.

What is it that unifies us?

To declare a nation of unified countries/regions does not mean that the people will be united. There are symbols and associations which unite the British people. Some of these symbols are visible, such as the flag; others things that unify us are invisible or imagined. What do we imagine to be typically British behaviour and identity?

Agreement may exist among the British people about what it means to be British through sharing images of the past or sharing feelings and thoughts about now. These thoughts or feelings are imagined impressions of what it means to be British. On the other hand agreement may exist about symbols which are used to signify 'the British' such as the Union Jack. Other impressions of British could emerge during events which British people participate in.

Imagined impressions of what it means to be British

Here we are exploring the ways that British identity can be described as a feeling not necessarily clear or visible – an imagined British identity.

If you go on holiday abroad or spend some time away from home, what is it that you miss, if anything? Imagine you have settled in another country: what images and feelings of 'home' (Britain) would you reflect on? Your thoughts would probably consist of impressions and feelings, rather than actual physical objects or clear signs. Also as part of our imagined Britishness, many people refer to the past in very nostalgic ways and romanticise about events of the past in ways that make them seem better or nicer or worse than in fact was true:

'things used to be better then', 'there was never as much crime then', 'people seemed happier then', 'families were more stable then', 'young people respected their elders then', 'it was miserable in the 1980s, everyone was unemployed', 'it was always sunny in summer, and snowed in winter then'.

The phrases above are used by some people when referring to the past. The opinions may well be true but often our images of the past and what Britain used to be like get distorted as time passes. The point however is that these images of the past or feelings about now, whether illusion or truth, are often shared by others which means they unite people in a shared identity or indeed a shared British cultural history.

It must be recognised that feelings or images can differ widely and may cause strong differences of opinion which divide rather than unite the British people – indicating a lack of agreement about what it means to be British.

ACTIVITY 6

1) Briefly explain how the two features of what we call 'imagined British identity' (feelings and thoughts of home, impressions of the past) can differ from person to person.

Symbols of British identity/unity

Rather than feelings and impressions, sometimes people define British and British unity in terms of symbols or signs. The photographs on this page give some suggestions.

What makes you feel British?

1) Think about the typically British things or symbols shown in the photographs on page 18. What images do they conjure in your mind when you think of them?
2) Do you think we all associate with the photographs in the same way? Think about people of different religions, different ethnic traditions, different languages, different ages.
3) Try to develop the list by adding further British signs or symbols to it.
4) Can pizza be British?

1) Try to add to the following list of places, people or things which have 'royal' in their name:
Royal Berkshire Hospital, Royal Dalton, Royal Worcester, Royal Oak, Royal Standard, Royal Mint, Royal Bank of Scotland, Royal Mail, Royal Berkdale, Royal Gala (type of apple).

Unity and language

In Britain, different regions have different accents or even dialects (variations of a language that have distinct emphasis, tone and words used). In the different countries of Britain languages are different especially in Wales which has its own language. However although there are variations, the official language of Britain is English.

Although in modern Britain we are officially subjects of the crown we see the royal family as more symbolic and we are now subject to the rule of law as set down by parliament which is run by elected representatives. However it is interesting to notice just how deeply engrained the royal family is within our culture. Centuries of royal rule have left their mark and continue to leave their mark on British and commonwealth culture. Activity 8 is an exercise exploring the way a culture can be shown through the language it uses. Our language incorporates a strong emphasis on monarchy which indicates the central role monarchy has played in the past and continues to play today, even if we do not believe in a monarchy.

Unifying events – 'British spirit'

Often events cause a noticeable outpouring of emotion across a nation which may create unity and give an indication of the nature of national identity. Many refer to such times as points when the British spirit shows through. The event may be a tragedy or one of celebration and joy.

The death of Diana Princess of Wales on 31 August 1997 is one such event. It is often referred to by people who remember it as a time when Britain was united in mourning and grief at the tragic loss of a figurehead whom many respected and saw as a symbol of British values. It must be noted, on the other hand, that many at the time of her tragic death saw it as a sad moment for her family but not necessarily an issue of concern for the nation, most of whom did not know her in person. Some refer to periods further back, for example during the Second World War, when Britain was united in the war effort. Often this period is referred to as a time when Britain united around a determination to support one another in the national struggle of wartime. More recently the celebration of the Queen's Golden Jubilee in June 2002 was seen as a typically British celebration of the monarchy. The winning of the 2012 Olympics for London was a period of national celebration and British pride. The day after the celebrations following the winning of the Olympic bid, the country was stunned by the terrorist bombings in London on 7 July 2005. At the time London and Britain as a whole joined in widespread condemnation of this attack on our freedoms.

ACTIVITY 9

1) Reflect on British periods of unity you have experienced. What feelings did you have at the time and what images were used, for example, by the media to symbolise the event? You might think of sporting occasions or charity days for example.

What does it mean to be British?

Read the four views below. Which one do you most agree with and why?

- Unity and agreement do not exist and the notion of British identity is an illusion or at least something which is so diverse that we can no longer find any agreement about it.
- Agreement is not shared by absolutely everyone nor in the same way at the same time, but there may be broad agreement about British identity.
- Some prefer to call themselves European or global citizens in a global world. British identity is no longer relevant.
- Some may feel so strongly about their British identity that it causes disagreement and conflict with other British people because they are considered to be betraying the 'way of life' by their actions.

ACTIVITY 10

1) Design a set of eight stamps which will be symbols of Britain. The stamps vary in value from first class and second class (the two most commonly used and widely seen stamps) to £1.00, £2.00, £3.00, £4.00, £5.00, £10.00. Each stamp has a different theme – diversity, culture and history, sporting achievements, social identity, political contribution, international influence, geographical location or places of geographical identity, scientific influence.
Does royalty feature in your stamp designs? What places or people feature? Which images get the highest value stamp? Which images were you putting on the most widely seen stamps and why? Do your stamps represent the nations of Britain? Should there be a different series of stamps for each nation of Britain?

2) Your stamp designs display a British culture and identity in a wide range of areas as you see it. Compare your findings with your classmates. It is also very revealing to ask younger children or older adults, such as parents or grandparents, to carry out this exercise to show how age differences cause variations in outlook of what is British.

3) Now create a set of stamps for the London Olympics 2012 or an Olympic flag which will be the flag behind the Union Jack carried by Team Great Britain at the 2012 London Olympics.

3 How do individuals and groups define their identity/identities and where are these definitions drawn from?

In this topic we define **identity** and explore the process of identity formation. We consider various influences on our identities and consider the debates about what forms our identity – **nature** or **nurture**? How as individuals do we link with others in a country or community? This section uses language which comes from social science, mainly from sociologists who study the social world.

Exploring identity and what influences our identity is very important to studies in citizenship because people's identity has a big influence on the extent of their participation in their country or community. Some groups or individuals have more influence than others. Also some groups or individuals have different values to the mainstream of a country or culture and are less or more able to participate in some areas than others. Therefore in understanding identity and what shapes it we are exploring the extent to which belonging, participation and influence (citizenship) are spread evenly throughout a country or community or what sociologists call a society.

Note: The specification gives a long list of ways that identity can be influenced. These areas are covered elsewhere in this book. See page 28 for a list. Also the exam questions on factors influencing identity should give you a choice of areas to focus upon. We focus on **social class** because it is widely relevant to all areas of the UK.

Culture

We can think about a **culture** as a collection of habits and customs. A culture is a collection of individuals sharing a common identity where we are able to relate to one another in that community.

As citizens of a country we share common features of behaviour which make us distinct or different to other countries or communities. As individuals we are able to relate to others in our country or community because we recognise similar patterns of behaviour and priorities in other people. As a result our country or community shares a sense of belonging, a common identity. Sociologists and social scientists explore these shared elements of our identity and they call this a culture or a society.

Cultural norms and values

A culture (or a society) is made up of **values** (key priorities) which drive or motivate patterns of behaviour (**norms**). The things we do (behaviour) are called norms, which are behaviour patterns associated with a particular culture's values. As a collection of individuals our identities are shaped by a set of dominant values in a society and a set of behaviour patterns linked to those values. Therefore sociologists argue that the dominant cultural norms and values of a society at the time shape our individual identity – what we believe and what we do is socially constructed.

We can consider norms and values in broad terms and in specific terms. For example society places very large emphasis on the value of work. Therefore much normal behaviour is shaped by the value of work. For example students at school are training for work; people tend to do their shopping on a Saturday because we structure the working week mainly around Monday to Friday, 9a.m. to 5p.m. The values of equality and unity in schools influence the fact that it is normal (even made into a rule) that school uniform is worn in most schools.

1) Define the following terms: culture, norm, value.

Socially constructed identity – nurture and nature

Are we products of our biological nature and natural instincts as animals or are we products of a culture or society teaching us what to believe and what to do? The nature/nurture debate is a very old discussion about our identity and where it comes from. Unique individuals we may be, but our identity is not something which develops in isolation from others in the social world around us. Most people agree that some of our identity is shaped by natural instincts and biological/ physical elements (nature) and some is shaped by social learning (nurture), but how much of each is debatable.

People eat because of the instinct of hunger, people procreate because of biological drives to reproduce and have sex. But what we eat, how we reproduce, how we have sex and what is seen as 'attractive' are different from place to place and over different periods of time. The behaviour associated with biological drives is shaped by the culture of the time and the place in which we live – it is socially constructed.

Sociologists believe most of our identity is learned and shaped by the culture of society in which we live (socially constructed). Key parts of a culture shape our identity and influence what we do. For example our home background, school experiences, wealth and income, how old we are, whether we are male or female, the region of the country we live in, type of job we do or our parents and their

parents before them do/did, our racial and religious background all shape elements of our identity. Although as individuals we are all very different, we are products of the way society views us, in particular in relation to our age, gender, ethnicity/race and social class. We explore each of these later on in the topic.

1) Define 'social construct' and explain how the concept links to identity.

Primary and secondary socialisation – how are our identities shaped by society?

Socialisation is the process of learning the social norms and values (customs, habits and priorities) of a culture. The process starts as soon as we are born and this early stage is most evident until we are about four or five years old. In these early (primary) stages of socialisation we are mainly influenced by close or immediate family members with whom we have frequent and direct contact. During this primary socialisation stage a child or baby is learning the basics of a social identity, how to understand language and authority, affection and trust, rules and mannerisms.

The secondary stage in socialisation develops as we begin to communicate with others outside our immediate family. The young child learning to share at a toddler group is learning the secondary stage of social integration by understanding how to interact with people not part of their own particular household. The process becomes hugely significant when at about four- or five-years-old we start school where we interact with teachers and other pupils and parents who become increasingly relevant to our lives.

Primary socialisation

In the secondary stage we are learning more formal systems of communication and social behaviour where the rules of conduct are often very different to the rules we have in our own home. As individuals we are learning our own identities and we become able to understand social rules for ourselves and make sense of the world around us with increasing independence from our parents.

During this secondary socialisation stage we encounter social interactions with others our own age (**peers**) and begin to develop our identity based on what we learn from others or what we are encouraged to do or not do by our peer group. This **peer group pressure** influences identity because many of the lessons and aspects of identity we learnt at home begin to be challenged by our peer group.

During the secondary stage of socialisation we develop our individuality and begin to express our 'selves'. We are developing a self confidence and our identity is modified by influences from our peer group. Many sociologists and psychologists believe our individual identity is formed through rebelling against external messages we receive. Often for example we may rebel or criticise some rules. We may rebel by directly challenging rules or rebel indirectly by expressing our identity in dress or preferences in eating habits. Peer group influences can be

both positive and negative. Many influences from peers can be hurtful or upsetting while others can be a boost to our self-esteem. As growing individuals we are increasingly able to accept and reject messages from peers but often this takes time or proves challenging.

A very important influence on identity at both primary and secondary stage is the mass media, for example TV, books, internet and radio. The mass media is of increasing influence in the primary stage of socialisation, especially TV where young children recognise language and images.

ACTIVITY 3

Research investigation: each family is different; each household has particular rules. Although each school has a different ethos or culture, schools tend to be more uniform in their rules.

1) Reflect on, or observe one typical main mealtime in your own home. Compare your own experiences with those of two or more of your classmates. List the things that are different and the things that are similar or the same.

2) Now compare the experiences of you and your classmates' to those of mealtimes at school. How similar are your mealtimes at home compared with those at school? Who does what? What are the school rules and how do they differ to those at home? How far does your behaviour differ from that at home?

Research investigation:

3) Ask your parents or parents you know the following question and reflect on their answer in terms of the primary and secondary socialisation process. 'To what extent do you believe watching TV is an important influence on the identity of the under five-year-olds?'

Secondary socialisation and role models

As we develop our identities and individual beliefs and priorities we may associate with significant individuals who have a strong influence on us. These personalities are role models who shape and influence us as individuals. Since we choose our role models we are making independent choices and are beginning to shape our own identities rather than others shaping them for us as is the case in primary socialisation. Some types of role models are people associated with good deeds; others are associated with attractiveness or humour; others are moral guides or creative guides, for example musicians and fashion symbols.

Other places or spaces where secondary socialisation takes place include religious organisations, community groups, on the sportsfield. The areas or places where socialisation takes place are sometimes referred to by sociologists as agencies or institutions, for example the institution or agency of the family, or of schools or of religious groups or of sports clubs.

STAGES OF SOCIALISATION – A SUMMARY

• Primary stage – within families, learning the basics of human interaction. Prepares the individual, sets foundation for the secondary stage. In this stage particularistic values and norms are learned – they are particular to the families we live in.

• Secondary stage – within schools, learning in areas where we interact with non-family members and develop understanding of the social world outside our own families. Here we are learning and adopting patterns of behaviour and codes of conduct. In this stage we are learning universal values and norms – those which exist throughout society but are not necessarily particular to any one family.

ACTIVITY 4

1) Under the categories listed on page 23 or any more you can think of make a list of the people you consider to be role models – people you respect and feel have had or continue to have a major influence on your life. Make an assessment of the extent to which you think others influence you.

ACTIVITY 5

1) List under each socialisation agency (or institution) some of the lessons about behaviour that we may learn. family   education   mass media   religion   community   group
2) Using examples describe why rules at home may be very different to rules in institutions outside the home, such as schools.
3) Look back at question 1 and now make two lists, one for girls and one for boys. How might the experience of the socialisation process differ for boys and girls?

Identity and subculture

Many sociologists use the term subculture when referring to groups of individuals developing distinct identities of their own that may be, but are not always, in opposition to mainstream culture. A subculture is a group of individuals who have established some norms and values (a culture) of their own which are different (deviant) to mainstream society. Some subcultures are deliberately hostile to wider society; others just behave in different ways. Some subcultures are short-lived while other subcultures last for long periods of time, perhaps for generations.

A youth subculture typically defines itself through types of music or style of dress.

When groups break the norms of a culture and use this difference to define themselves they are called deviant subcultures. Deviance comes from the word 'deviate' meaning to break away from regular pattern. Deviance does not necessarily mean breaking the law. Some subcultures however, may exist which define themselves by criminal activities (criminal subcultures) where the norm is to break the law.

Identity, gender, masculinity and femininity

Gender means the socially approved habits and behaviours of males and females. Gender is different to sex because our sex (male or female) is determined by biological differences. Gender on the other hand means the social behaviour associated with the sexes. For example we can be biologically male but act at times (or all the time) in a feminine way, as can also be the case with a biological female acting in a typically masculine way.

Identity and ethnicity

Ethnic identity can significantly vary from one person to another. Ethnic group is a category of identity which is built from a number of possible factors, for example racial background (black/white), religious background (Muslim/Christian) and national/cultural background. Some of these background identity characteristics overlap but they can also be considered in isolation. Often ethnic groups are in a minority from the majority ethnic group. The majority ethnic group in Britain is white protestant Christian. White, Irish Catholic is a minority ethnic group just as much as a Black Afro-Caribbean Baptist or a Black Asian Muslim Bangladeshi. One problem with such categories is that no one is actually white or black; some may strictly speaking be British but consider themselves to be Welsh; some may call themselves Christian or Muslim but are not actually practising. Therefore identity is more about our behaviour than labels for our ethnic groups. There is further discussion on this on page 41.

ACTIVITY 7

1) Make a list of some differences in family life between you and a person of a different ethnic group to your own. How do your experiences differ? How have these experiences influenced your lives?

ACTIVITY 6

1) Make a list of some typically masculine and typically feminine activities among school children aged 14 to 16. Think of sporting activity, TV programmes, social activities and relationships with friends. How far are the activities entirely dominated by men/women? Why are they typically associated with one particular gender group?

IDENTITY, SOCIAL CLASS, EMPLOYMENT, EDUCATION AND LIFESTYLE

Social class is an identity shaped mainly by the type of employment. The culture of an individual and group is heavily influenced by the nature of the employment that dominates it. The types of work in some areas have shaped family and community life over generations.

Social class groups are said to establish distinct norms and values such that a different culture exists for middle class individuals and groups in contrast to working class individuals and groups.

Web action

- Using an image search engine (for example Google Images) search for images of working life.
- Identify which images are more likely to be associated with middle class and working class lifestyles.
- Identify ways with which the different images indicate contrasting lifestyles for middle class and working class citizens.

ACTIVITY 8

1) Discuss as a class the extent to which you can identify a distinct area where you live that could be described as working class and a distinct area that could be described as middle class.
2) What criteria were you using to make the judgements? Were you focusing mainly on affluent/desirable areas and less affluent, lower income areas?

Does social class shape identity any more?

Many social scientists argue that social class differences have become less noticeable today than was previously the case. It is suggested that the working class jobs have declined as factories, mines and other traditional industries such as agricultural work, shipbuilding, mining and factory work in the motor industry for example have declined. Working class pay and conditions have improved meaning better conditions at work and shorter working hours. Therefore the traditional differences between middle class and working class have merged to form a larger middle class. Some aspects of class difference remain but are likely to decline further as generations pass.

Other social scientists argue that distinct social class cultures remain in Britain and our society still regards people as middle class or working class according to their lifestyles and tastes. The differences between middle and working class groups are more subtle and complex today as

the world of work and employment changes but essentially cultural differences remain. For example people from a working class culture are more likely to have relatives living in the same community, place less importance on university and read the tabloid press.

Read the article opposite about how class divisions in Britain continue generation after generation despite improved conditions for the working class.

ACTIVITY 9

1) Explain what the author in the blog on page 27 means by 'the British middle classes are operating ... a closed shop'.
2) How might networking help the middle class maintain their prominence in society?
3) In your view and with reference to the article suggest the ways in which type of school influences a person's identity.

Does class matter any more?

The 'Tory toff' campaign has prompted a series of articles and comments about whether class is still a major issue in this country.

The truth is that Britain remains a nation that is still dominated by class division. Last year an ICM poll for the *Guardian* found that 89% of those surveyed thought that people are still judged by their class – with almost half saying that it still counts for 'a lot'. Over 50% of people said that class, not ability, greatly affects the way they are seen. Despite more than a decade of Labour in power social mobility in Britain has decreased, in fact the British middle classes are operating what is, in effect, a closed shop. For example our top universities are still, in the main, the preserve of a rich, well-connected elite.

Often the real reasons why many send their sons and daughters to fee-paying schools are not based on the examination results of the local state schools but on a desire to ensure that their child has access to what the local comprehensive cannot provide: privilege, advantage and the opportunity to network.

British public schools have always been a production line of the class system. They employ some of the best-qualified teachers, select their pupils, offer some of the most impressive sporting and extracurricular activities in the country. What's more they now recruit from a middle class obsessed by perceived educational and social advantage.

http://mike-ion.blogspot.com/2008/05/does-class-matter-anymore.html

EXAMINER'S TIP

In the exam an essay asking you to assess, such as Activity 10, will require you to explore the theme from more than one angle. You should aim for 300–400 words, between a side and a side and a half of A4 paper. The statement in activity 1 is suggesting that in today's society social class differences are no longer relevant. It is suggesting that a clear working class culture or middle class culture is no longer evident. In your answer you will be expected to argue a case on both sides.

- Keep in mind cultural things which may still exist which are unique to working class or middle class people. Also you will need to think about traditions and whether some people you know or know of still see themselves as working class. For example Alan Sugar the wealthy business man still sees himself as working class because that is where his traditions and background lie. You may consider older generations who may still see class differences as clearly as was the case in earlier decades. In addition some images on TV often show stereotypical images of different class attitudes: you could use examples of these in your answer.
- You could choose to focus on a specific area, such as the education system – on one side you could explore the notion of equality in education: the idea that all of us regardless of background have equal access to education. In contrast you could explore why some argue that the more wealthy are able to exploit the education system to their advantage. For example it may be that the middle class is more financially powerful but also more powerful in terms of talking the language of schools, school teachers and examiners.
- Your answer will need to assess the strengths and weaknesses of the arguments on both sides and link this to 'today'. Try to do some assessment throughout your essay, not just at the end.

Activity 9 should help with your answer.

1) Assess the view that 'differences in income are the only clear differences between individuals today'.

As mentioned at the start of this section the specification refers to a range of areas that might influence identity including:

- Regionality (the area you live in)
- Ethnicity
- Religion
- Age

- Nationality
- Employment and education

These aspects of identity are interlinked and are addressed in the next section.

EXAMINER'S TIP

You may well wish to explore each section further but we have emphasised social class because it is widely relevant throughout the UK. Exam questions on this part of the specification will give you a choice of areas to choose from. It will be your choice as to how you answer the question – whether by focusing on one area or more than one.

ISSUE 2: HOW SOCIALLY DIVERSE IS BRITAIN?

In this section we explore the following three topics:

- how much change and continuity is there in migration patterns?
- how far is Britain a **multicultural** society?
- what is **stereotyping**?

4 How much change and continuity is there in migration patterns?

In this topic we focus on some key terms: **immigration, emigration, migration** and **net migration**. We outline and discuss some of the migration patterns since 1945 focusing on the city of London. Some UK government and EU policy on migration is explored and recent statistics on numbers of people migrating are looked at. We also examine some of the factors causing people to migrate and debate some of the perceived influences of migration focusing in particular on immigration and its impact on employment.

Immigration and emigration: factors influencing migration

Migration means movement of people. This movement of people may lead across national borders. If this is the case the people become emigrated from the original country and are then immigrants to the new country. Immigration means moving into a country. Emigration is moving away from a country.

People have always moved from place to place. Humans were originally nomadic (having no fixed place of living, constantly moving) and some ethnic groups are still nomadic today (see pages 8–9). The issue of immigration has become increasingly important in this century particularly as countries try to protect their borders and manage the movement of people in and out of their areas/countries. Managing people moving in and out of a country has proved very important for the country to protect the rights and standards of living of its citizens.

Most of us move around from time to time. For example a family moves to a new house or an individual moves to university. Some movement, such as travel for pleasure or moving to study, may be just temporary. Whatever the reason and purpose of people moving, it can cause both positive and potentially divisive consequences for the individuals and communities involved. Migration between countries causes most conflict of all.

Why migrate?

The most frequent and most likely reason to migrate is to find work. Most of us would consider moving to get a better job. A better job may involve more pay and so a better standard of living. Moving may be necessary in order to find a job in the first place. The area an individual lives in may have few jobs or prospects and so they have no alternative but to move in order to provide for their family.

Living conditions may be better in one place than another, for example a better climate or health service. Perhaps there are more childcare and educational facilities in a different area. Many of the reasons for moving are economic.

Other reasons for moving could be to flee from famine and hardship. Many areas of the world face famine after a poor crop yield or war and people have no option but to move in order to find food and water. This type of migration is usually mass migration and often causes major humanitarian crises. Sometimes on a mass scale or perhaps at an individual level people are fleeing from oppression or political persecution.

There may be emotional reasons for moving such as to be nearer to family members or to a place that has greater cultural appeal.

Some factors that cause migration 'push' people away from where they live, others 'pull' people from where they live to a seemingly better alternative. Migration has both push and pull factors.

ACTIVITY 1

> 1) Identify the causes of migration mentioned in the above paragraphs and list them as either 'push' or 'pull' factors. Try to add some more factors from your own ideas or experiences.

Movement may be long-term migration or temporary migration. The Government considers migration to be long term if it is intended to last for more than one year. Migration by people within EU member states is simple but for people emigrating from countries outside the EU into EU countries the process is much more complex. Therefore the experience of migration may vary greatly depending on the area you are moving to or from.

Who migrates?

As well as the various reasons for migration it is also possible to identify some typical characteristics of people most likely to migrate. These points mainly apply to people migrating for work (economic reasons) but do not necessarily apply to people forced by war or famine to migrate – in these cases there is a broad cross-section of people that tends to move.

The typical characteristics of people emigrating for work are that they:

- tend to be young (typically in Europe aged 25–35), some with young families back home, some single
- tend to be male
- tend to be post-education stage, in general good health
- tend to migrate alone.

ACTIVITY 2

1) Comment on the likely appeal of an emigrant worker with the above attributes to their new employer (assuming they have the skills to do the job the employer has a vacancy for).

Trends and patterns in UK migration after 1945

The UK has a long history of colonial activity and this legacy from its colonial past has been very influential to immigration and emigration. For example the coastal cities on the west of Britain such as Bristol, Cardiff, Liverpool, Glasgow have had very diverse mixes of people for centuries mainly as a result of their involvement with the slave trade. Many people from the UK have moved and continue to move to former colonies notably Australia, Canada, New Zealand and South Africa.

During the Second World War a huge range of people from different countries fought to help defeat Nazism and many of these people settled in Britain. For example many Polish soldiers and airmen were offered British citizenship because they had been living outside Poland in Britain fighting Germany (which invaded Poland in 1939) for six years. Afro-Caribbean, Indian and African people and people from

other countries also joined the war effort and many were also allowed to settle in Britain.

After 1945 during the rebuilding of Europe, Britain and other countries did not have enough people to do the work. There were labour shortages. Many people had been killed or injured during the war and as jobs were plentiful the solution was to seek labour power from former colonial countries. Many people from the Caribbean came to Britain, settling mainly in London, to work in the health service or on London transport (often low-skilled jobs).

Two major events linked to the colonial past of the UK led to migration from the so called Indian subcontinent into Britain. After the independence of India (1949) many Indian people were allowed to move to Britain. Also after Indian independence disputes in northern India between Muslims and Hindus erupted there was an immigration of Indian people to the UK. The disputes were resolved by the formation of the country of Pakistan from northern parts of what was India and many people from this region were allowed to move to the UK. Britain therefore experienced a large number of Pakistani and Indian immigrants during the second half of the twentieth century.

Recent trends and patterns in UK migration

A recent example of migration into the UK as a result of skills and labour shortages has occurred in the last ten years. A shortage of nurses in the NHS has been in part dealt with by the Government encouraging nurses from other countries to move to Britain and work in the health service. Therefore many nurses from Spain and other EU countries are now working in the UK NHS.

During the middle of the last century English speaking former colony countries were encouraging British people to emigrate into their countries from the UK. Australia and New Zealand encouraged British people to emigrate by paying their travel costs and providing some support to set up a home. The people with skills or a trade were most sought after. Once you spent a year in the country you were allowed to either return to Britain or stay. If you stayed then you qualified for citizenship of that country and other members of your family were allowed to move out to join you.

The same situation is occurring today where some countries that have skills shortages are encouraging British workers to emigrate. For example teachers, nurses and social workers are being encouraged to apply for jobs in Australia and New Zealand. Other countries such as Egypt and regions of the Middle East, such as Dubai, are encouraging construction workers to move to their area for work. Skilled people are more able to migrate than lower skilled people because they have more to offer the host country. Furthermore, when a skilled worker moves to a new country that country has not paid for the worker's training and has therefore improved the skill level of its workforce for free. Many Polish construction workers and land workers are now working in the UK because they are able to apply for work permits and jobs in Britain, and they offer employees cheaper wage demands and are often willing to work longer hours.

The total number of immigrants for any one year in the graph opposite should not be seen as permanent immigration in all cases. For example in 2007 the total number of immigrants was 577,000; people with permits for one to two years was 246,000, for three to four years was 118,000 and for more than four

ACTIVITY 3

1) Imagine you had a skill or a trade sought after by the Australian Government. The Government was willing to pay for your flight to Australia and allow you to work there for one year. Do you think you would choose to stay permanently in Australia after this period? Alternatively, what things would encourage you to return to Britain? Think about family, friends, lifestyle, climate and money. What would your decision be most influenced by – economic or family responsibility?

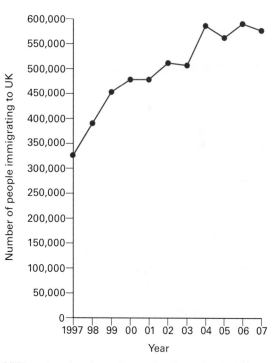

UK immigration (people staying for one year or more)

years was 174,000. For 38,000 immigrants it was not possible to state clearly on the permit how long their immigration was for. For example people granted asylum may be residents for a short or a long time.

ACTIVITY 4

1) Using the data from the graph on page 31 describe the pattern of UK immigration over the ten year period of 1997 to 2007.

2) Read the paragraph above about how not all immigration is 'permanent'. Assess the extent to which initial immigration is permanent for a lifetime.

ACTIVITY 5

1) Net migration is the difference between people entering and people leaving a country. Use the two graphs shown on pages 31 and 32 to calculate how many more people entered the UK than left in 2007.

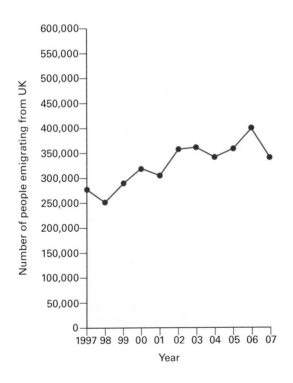

UK emigration (people moving out of the country)

IMMIGRATION TO UK IN 2007

Country/area of origin	Numbers of UK immigrants
Europe total*	215,000
• Europe 1	103,000
• Europe 2	112,000
Australia	31,000
Canada	6,000
New Zealand	10,000
South Africa	17,000
Indian subcontinent	95,000
USA	23,000
Middle East	23,000
Other countries worldwide	157,000
Total	**577,000***

*Europe is divided into two categories:

• Europe 1: From the EU15 (fifteen countries that have been members of the EU for some years including the UK) – Austria, Belgium, Denmark, Finland, France, Germany, Greece, Italy, Luxembourg, the Netherlands, Portugal, the Republic of Ireland, Spain and Sweden.

• Europe 2: From the A8 (eight countries that have more recently joined the EU) – the Czech Republic, Estonia, Hungary, Latvia, Lithuania, Poland, Slovakia and Slovenia – plus Bulgaria and Romania (joined the EU in 2007).

ACTIVITY 6

1) Identify some of the reasons why in 2007 over one third of all UK immigrants came from Europe.

2) Examine reasons why in 2007 over half of the total number of UK immigrants from Europe came from countries that had recently joined the EU.

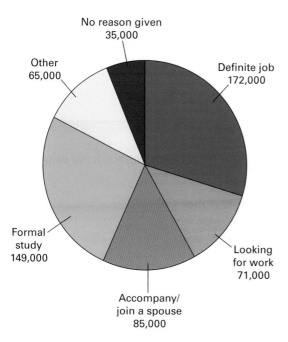

Formal study 149,000

No reason given 35,000

Other 65,000

Definite job 172,000

Looking for work 71,000

Accompany/ join a spouse 85,000

UK immigrants and reason for migration to UK

ACTIVITY 7

1) Three quarters of immigrants to the UK in 2007 were here for a specific job or to study. Using the data from the pie chart above examine some of the positive economic benefits to the UK resulting from immigration.

Government policy on immigration: foreign workers in the UK

The criteria that allow an individual to become a foreign worker in the UK are as follows:

- be a citizen of an EU member state which gives you the right to work anywhere in the EU. (Note that Bulgaria and Romania are the most recent members of the EU and there are restrictions on their freedom to seek employment in the UK.)
- for non-EU applicants successful application depends on a points system that has five tiers of entry status. Points are awarded depending on factors such as age, level of qualifications, type of skills, employment history/reference. The five tiers are:
  - tier 1: highly skilled
  - tier 2: skilled worker with a job offer
  - tier 3: worker in low skilled area where there is a shortage of workers in the UK
  - tier 4: students
  - tier 5: young people travelling seeking temporary work permits.

The higher the tier and the higher the points awarded within the tier the greater a person's chances of getting a temporary or long-term work permit.

Web action

Go to the website **www.uk-wp.com** which offers advice on how to get a work permit. The site has information on various types of work permits:
- business and commercial work permits
- training and work experience permit schemes
- highly skilled migrant programmes.

Explore the different types of work permits and then try a free test on the points calculator. You need to score 75 points or more in order to be successful.

Working in the UK – guidance for immigrants

If you are a national from one of the European Countries listed below, you have freedom of movement in the UK, as well as unrestricted access to the UK labour market. However, some EU Accession countries require permission to enter into, or change employment in the UK and will require a visa for this purpose.

Most nationals of the new member states (except Cyprus and Malta) who wish to work for more than one month for an employer in the UK need to register under the Worker Registration Scheme. You should apply to register with the Worker Registration Scheme as soon as you start a new job. If you do not apply within one month of starting a job, your employment will be illegal after that date. It will be illegal until you are issued with a registration certificate and you may have to stop working.

Iceland, Liechtenstein and Norway are not members of the European Union (EU). However, the European Economic Area Agreement gives nationals of these countries the same rights to enter, live in and work in the United Kingdom as EU citizens. Swiss nationals have the same rights as EEA nationals within the United Kingdom. They can work without a work permit.

www.globalpermits.co.uk

ACTIVITY 8

1) What happens if an immigrant to the UK does not apply for a work permit after working for one month?
2) Having access to the labour market does not mean an automatic right to a job. What things might limit a person's chances of getting a job in this country if they were applying for a job from any one of the above EU countries outside the UK?
3) There are agencies in the UK which help immigrants find work and also deal with the permit process. Suggest some positive and some negative experiences which may result from joining an agency. Consider the points that agencies often advertise with exaggerated images of a new life, that they may charge a fee, may take a cut of a person's wages and that not all agencies are trustworthy.

How do employers benefit from migrant workers?

Asked why they would employ foreign workers 50 employers surveyed by Dench, Hurstfield, Hill and Akroyd (2006)* revealed the following (note they also interviewed employers who did not employ foreign workers).

1) They were unable to find a skilled person in the UK.
2) Foreign workers are more likely to live in temporary accommodation and therefore be more able to move around the country to get work.
3) Reliability: foreign workers in many cases, such as in the hotel industry, are seen as more reliable and less likely to leave the job in the early stages.
4) Foreign workers are considered more willing to work hard and work long hours.
5) They are willing to work for lower wages or at least less likely to demand higher wages.

*Dench, J, Hurstfield, S, Hill, D and Ackroyd (2006) *Employers' Use of Migrant Labour*, Institute of Employment Studies, London.

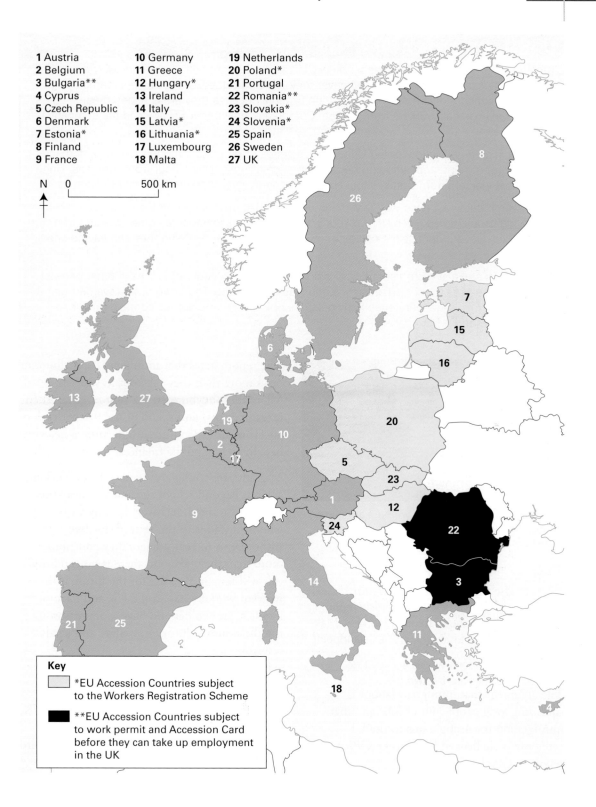

1 Austria
2 Belgium
3 Bulgaria**
4 Cyprus
5 Czech Republic
6 Denmark
7 Estonia*
8 Finland
9 France

10 Germany
11 Greece
12 Hungary*
13 Ireland
14 Italy
15 Latvia*
16 Lithuania*
17 Luxembourg
18 Malta

19 Netherlands
20 Poland*
21 Portugal
22 Romania**
23 Slovakia*
24 Slovenia*
25 Spain
26 Sweden
27 UK

N

0   500 km

Key

*EU Accession Countries subject to the Workers Registration Scheme

**EU Accession Countries subject to work permit and Accession Card before they can take up employment in the UK

CASE STUDY: Protests at TOTAL, February 2009

The French oil company TOTAL has a refinery in Lincolnshire that employs many overseas workers. The company can employ whoever they wish from the EU and has been employing increasing numbers of overseas workers (non-Britons) because they are cheaper. These increases in overseas workers from Eastern Europe are legal under EU law and the company has said that having an all British workforce is not realistic.

The protesting organisation, called Unite, held a series of protests throughout Britain, demanding that the Government stop large companies from increasingly using labour from overseas. Unite argues that workers from Britain should be given priority over workers from other countries.

The Government's response was that the company TOTAL had done nothing unlawful and when employing people it had given UK workers just as much consideration as other workers from the EU. Also the Government said it could not tell overseas contractors who they should and should not employ.

The unofficial strike and protest in Lincolnshire sparked other 'copycat' strikes in other parts of the country, such as Cumbria, Lancashire and Nottinghamshire. The Government warned that the protests over this issue were encouraging xenophobia which was not welcome in the UK, a member state of the EU.

Protesters demanding British workers are given priority over workers from other EU countries at TOTAL, February 2009

ACTIVITY 9

1) Use the information above to construct a newspaper article reporting on the issue of migrant workers. Make sure you justify the article's standpoint on the issue.

The argument that immigrant labour is squeezing local people out of jobs and that immigration is causing a loss to the UK economy is challenged by a Home Office report of October 2007.

The report states that immigrants contribute in taxes more than they take out in services. Migrants contribute 10 per cent of government taxes (receipts) and spend or use 9.1 per cent of government expenditures, indicating a net benefit to UK public finances.

Migrants are young and tend to be of working age but beyond school age and therefore the UK gains trained, relatively healthy workers who bring skills to the country for free. Although in the early stages they contribute more than they take out, there is no certainty this will remain the case for the future if the migrant workers stay in the UK and have families, grow older and have more reason to use the health, education, welfare and legal services.

The table on page 37 shows three groups which make up the whole of the UK workforce. The first group was born in the UK, the second group is foreign workers born in one of the European A8 countries and the third group is also foreign workers but those born

FOREIGN AND UK BORN WORKERS BY % IN VARIOUS TYPES OF OCCUPATION, 2006

Type of occupation	UK born, %	A8* foreign born, %	Other foreign born** %
Managers and senior officials	15	4	16
Professional occupations	27	9	35
Administration and secretarial	12	5	9
Skilled trades	11	15	8
Personal service	8	9	8
Sales and customer service	8	4	6
Process, plant and machine operatives	7	16	6
Elementary (low skilled)	11	38	12

*A8 countries are the new EU member states, excluding Bulgaria and Romania
**'Other foreign born' are original 15 member states of the EU or outside EU

outside the European A8. Each group is broken into different occupation types and the percentage of that category of the workforce (UK/Foreign A8/Foreign outside A8) employed in that type of occupation category is listed. Note each column adds up to 100 per cent.

The table above shows there is a much higher percentage of people working in the higher skilled occupations from 'other foreign born' category than the percentages from A8 and from UK-born. This reflects the emphasis given to allowing immigration to people outside the EU on a points system where the higher a person's skills level the higher their point score and the better their chances of gaining a work permit and visa. Newer migrant workers are probably lower skilled or filling the remaining jobs available which are those requiring less skill. The significance of this is that the economic power and skill status of migrants are not the same for all types.

The issue of migrant labour is developed further in the next topic, where we explore multiculturalism, migration and community unity through the case study of Wisbech, a rural area of the Fens in East Anglia (page 48).

Male and female experiences as migrants

Although we look specifically at employment rates, it is possible to explore the area of migration from the point of view of gender. Already mentioned is the predominance of male migrant workers but among long-term migrants numbers of males and females tend to be more equal.

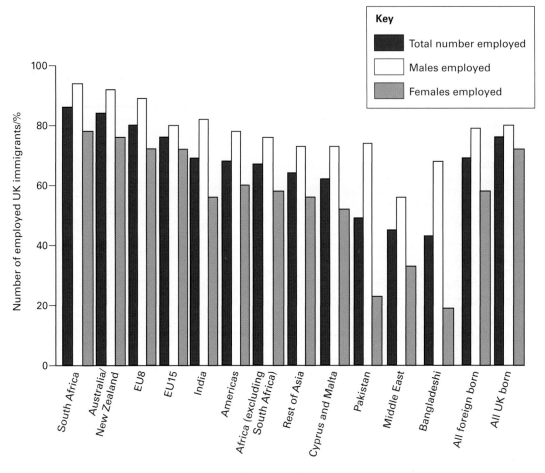

UK workforce - male and female employment rates by country of origin 2006

1) Using the data in the graph above describe how the pattern of immigrant male employment rates and female employment rates differ.
2) Using the data describe how the rates of UK born employment differ with those of foreign-born employment rates.

We can see from the graph above that the country of origin has an influence on how likely men and women immigrating to the UK are to have a job. It also shows that the percentages of each group's females and each group's males who have jobs vary enormously. For example 86 per cent of the workforce who came from South Africa have a job. However, looking more closely at South Africa, we find 94 per cent of male South Africans have a job whereas 78 per cent of females have a job. Note that many people without jobs may be 'housewife', sick, retired or unemployed.

CASE STUDY: Migration in Bethnal Green and East London

The East End of London has had a very long history of migrant workers. The main reason is that this area was (until the mid-twentieth century) the main area for shipping and freight export/delivery in and out of London which provided plenty of jobs. The docklands area of East London has a long history of people moving into the area looking for work on the docks. The Docklands and East London was a very important area economically, important not just to London but also to British and Commonwealth trade as well and it became a centre for immigrants from overseas looking for work.

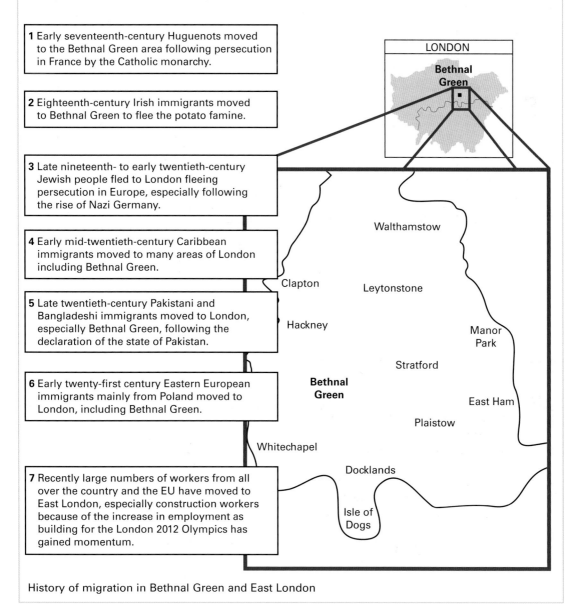

1 Early seventeenth-century Huguenots moved to the Bethnal Green area following persecution in France by the Catholic monarchy.

2 Eighteenth-century Irish immigrants moved to Bethnal Green to flee the potato famine.

3 Late nineteenth- to early twentieth-century Jewish people fled to London fleeing persecution in Europe, especially following the rise of Nazi Germany.

4 Early mid-twentieth-century Caribbean immigrants moved to many areas of London including Bethnal Green.

5 Late twentieth-century Pakistani and Bangladeshi immigrants moved to London, especially Bethnal Green, following the declaration of the state of Pakistan.

6 Early twenty-first century Eastern European immigrants mainly from Poland moved to London, including Bethnal Green.

7 Recently large numbers of workers from all over the country and the EU have moved to East London, especially construction workers because of the increase in employment as building for the London 2012 Olympics has gained momentum.

LONDON

Bethnal Green

Walthamstow

Clapton

Leytonstone

Hackney

Manor Park

Stratford

Bethnal Green

East Ham

Plaistow

Whitechapel

Docklands

Isle of Dogs

History of migration in Bethnal Green and East London

1) Look at the map on page 39 annotated with groups moving to London's East End over the centuries and identify why they moved.
2) Comment on the variety of different racial, religious and national groups to have moved into the East London area.
3) List some of the benefits and some of the potential problems for East London which may result from such a long history of migration into and out of the area.

Reasons for different rates of employment between immigrant males and females

Foreign-born women have far lower employment rates than UK-born women, especially women from Pakistan and Bangladesh. Some suggested reasons are linked to culture and language. For example women may be less likely to speak English because education may not have been as high a priority for females as for males in the family. The reasons could be linked to discrimination by employers preferring to employ males. Other cultural reasons could be that women are not expected to work outside the home. Many countries' cultures and traditions have a traditional view of the role of women keeping the household and caring for the children. Such views are often associated with Pakistani, Bangladeshi and Indian culture, yet India has a much higher percentage of female employment than Bangladesh and Pakistan (although it is still slightly below average for all foreign-born females).

Many argue that, as a result of prejudice at home and in the host country and restrictions in the workplace, foreign women migrant workers are very vulnerable and open to exploitation. The experience of migration therefore has different outcomes for males and females.

Many areas of London are associated with particular ethnic group clusters and these reflect the different patterns and trends of immigration over London's history. Stratford in East London is the most ethnically diverse region in the world. Brixton is well known to have a high Afro-Caribbean population and Palmers Green and Golders Green, in north London, are associated with Jewish and Greek populations.

1) In the city in which you live or live closest to, try to identify areas of the city associated with different ethnic groups. City council websites have ethnic diversity maps of various kinds which show percentages of ethnic group populations.

Pakistani women visitors to the Platt Fields Mega Mela in Manchester

5 How far is Britain a multicultural society?

In this topic we explore ethnic diversity in Britain and examine debates about **ethnic integration** focusing on models of ethnic integration – assimilation and multiculturalism. We outline some points of debate about the usefulness of the term multiculturalism and discuss whether multiculturalism has proved to be a successful model of integration. We highlight some issues of conflict or controversy emerging from ethnic diversity and multicultural Britain using a case study on tensions emerging in the Wisbech area of East Anglia following integration of Eastern European immigrants into the area. Note that themes from issue 1, topic 2 are relevant here – 'Is there agreement about what being British means?' (pages 11–20).

The degree of social diversity in Britain

Look back at the text on page 15. The former British Prime Minister Tony Blair said that 'blood alone' does not define being British; in fact over the centuries Britain has been made up of 'a rich mix of all different ethnicities and religions'. Also the Queen referred to our richly multicultural and multi-faith society in her jubilee speech.

What is social diversity?

Social diversity is the variety and differences in identities of British people.

The points from Tony Blair and the Queen refer to race and ethnicity and in particular religion. This topic focuses mainly on ethnic diversity but it is important to note that social diversity also includes differences in terms of social class, gender, age and region as well as race, religion and nationality.

Each ethnic group has differences within it, such as social class, income, gender, regional location, religion and nationality background. When exploring ethnic diversity we must not lose sight of the fact that variations in social background exist in all ethnic groups. Healthy citizenship recognises that we must never think about any ethnic group as if the group was all the same 'type' of identity.

The 2001 census identifies growing numbers of minority ethnic people in an increasingly wide range of groups which form the UK population today. Although the population is increasingly ethnically diverse, the vast majority of the population are 'white'. The table on page 42 shows the ethnic diversity of the UK.

Ethnically diverse crowd enjoying the music at the Notting Hill carnival in London

POPULATION OF THE UNITED KINGDOM: BY ETHNIC GROUP, APRIL 2001

	Total population (numbers)	(%)	Non-white population (%)
White	54,153,898	92.1	–
Mixed	677,117	1.2	14.6
Indian	1,053,411	1.8	22.7
Pakistani	747,285	1.3	16.1
Bangladeshi	283,063	0.5	6.1
Other Asian	247,664	0.4	5.3
Total Asian or Asian British	2,331,423	4.0	50.3
Black Caribbean	565,876	1.0	12.2
Black African	485,277	0.8	10.5
Black other	97,585	0.2	2.1
Total Black or Black British	1,148,738	2.0	24.8
Chinese	247,403	0.4	5.3
Other ethnic groups	230,615	0.4	5.0
Total minority ethnic population	4,635,296	7.9	100.0
Total population	58,789,194	100.0	

The majority of the UK population in 2001 were white: 54.2 million people (92.1 per cent). The remaining 4.6 million people (7.9 per cent) belonged to other ethnic groups.

ACTIVITY 1

1) What percentage of the 'non-white' population is Asian and British Asian?
2) What is this as a percentage of the whole population ('white' and 'non-white')?
3) What is the largest single ethnic group in Britain?
4) The data above comes from the most recent census – 2001. 'Asian' means born in Asia and moved to the UK. 'British Asian' means born in the UK of 'Asian' parents. Do you think the next census in 2011 will show increases or decreases for numbers of a) 'Asian' people and b) 'British Asian' people? Explain your answer.

Distribution of minority ethnic groups in the UK

The Government's statistics indicate that England is by far the most ethnically diverse UK country, as the piechart below shows.

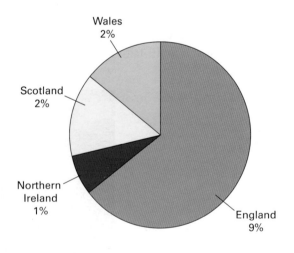

Percentage of ethnic minorities by UK country

One of the reasons for this ethnic diversity is that London, the capital city is the largest city in the UK and one of the largest in Europe. For a number of reasons London is a strongly attractive city for people seeking to move to the UK. Forty-five per cent of non-white people in the UK live in London.

- London has many jobs, both high and low skilled, as many companies have their international offices in London, and there are many positions in the hotel and catering industries, for instance.
- London is the centre of commerce (*the city*) for Europe, where high paying and specialist jobs are an attraction for skilled overseas workers, especially those working in the area of global finance.
- Another reason is historical. London was the place most Afro-Caribbean immigrants during the 1950s were encouraged to go in order to work in the health service and for London transport.

We explored a specific area of London (East London docklands) in topic 4 (see page 39).

Another reason that England has a much higher percentage of ethnic minorities is that it has more urban areas than any other country. London itself is a vast urban area and is home to high percentages of some ethnic groups:

- 78 per cent of Black African
- 61 per cent of Black Caribbean
- 54 per cent of Bangladeshi
- 32 per cent of White Irish
- 19 per cent of Pakistani.

From this list it is noticeable that White Irish and Pakistani groups have lower percentages living in London. In the case of White Irish they are dispersed throughout the UK, especially in Liverpool, Manchester and Corby. The White Irish have a long established migration pattern throughout the UK but many came in the first instance to build and work on the railways, which took them across all parts of the country.

In the case of Pakistani groups they are distributed mainly in the areas where textiles industries were strongest. For example 20 per cent of the Pakistani group live in Yorkshire – Bradford and Leeds areas – 16 per cent live in the North West – Manchester and Liverpool. Twenty-one per cent live in the West Midlands – Birmingham and Leicester.

ACTIVITY 2

1) Employment is the main cause of ethnic minority clusters in predominantly urban regions of the country. Given this situation for the first generation, for each of the ethnic minority groups below, where in the country would relatives wishing to move to the UK to join family members be most likely to move to?
   - Black African
   - Black Caribbean
   - Bangladeshi
   - White Irish
   - Pakistani
2) What will this do to the numbers of ethnic minorities in the future in these locations?

Rural/urban diversity and rural/urban difference

Less than 0.9 per cent of rural areas in southwest England, central Wales, Northern Ireland and Northern Scotland are made up of ethnic minorities. In contrast some cities, such as Leicester, are expected to have more than 50 per cent of its citizens from non-white backgrounds by Census 2011. Current census data for the whole of London identifies 29 per cent of the population to be non-white. Some areas, such as Tower Hamlets, have 70 per cent non-white.

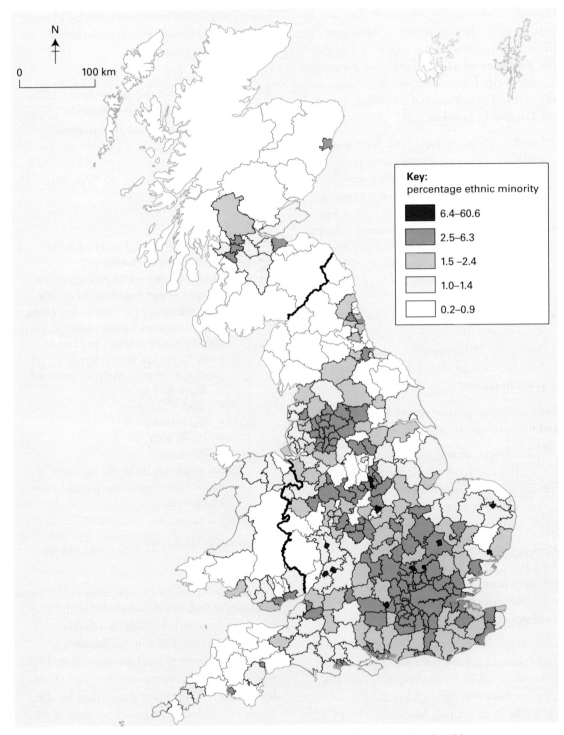

Map of British Isles showing percentage of region made up of different ethnic minorities

1) Imagine you are a student who has moved from your home in a rural area of the UK, such as central Wales, to East London (Tower Hamlets) to study. List and describe some of the lifestyle contrasts you might face in the context of the ethnic diversity of the city you have moved to.

2) Social diversity involves more aspects than ethnic group differences, for example social class and income differences. Still adopting this identity of a student moving from a rural area to East London list and describe some of these wider social differences you may notice and experience.

3) Given such distinct differences between urban and rural communities how might this influence cohesion and clarity about what is British?

Is Britain a multicultural society?

Citizenship involves awareness of our identity and we have explored the idea that British identity is very diverse. Citizenship also however involves participation and integration as well as awareness. Therefore the mere fact that Britain is diverse does not mean Britain is integrated. Knowing where people have come from and that people have various cultural identities is not enough for effective citizenship. We must also explore the extent to which integration has occurred – to do that we can use two different models of ethnic integration, the assimilation model and the multicultural model.

Models of ethnic integration

Two contrasting models – the assimilation model and the multicultural model – offer theories about how the integration of people with different ethnic backgrounds could be approached. The models also explore the impact ethnic mixing has on society and they address the question of how an ethnically diverse society should promote integration.

Assimilation into one identity model

In this model individual and group diversity exist but are absorbed into a collective national identity where individual identities are secondary to an overarching identity of nationhood. This model was said to exist in Britain after the Second World War where immigrant populations would become more like 'us' after a period of time and over generations. Immigrants' distinct ethnic and cultural backgrounds would fade away from being a central element of their identity as the minority group adapts by adopting more and more 'Britishness'. Generation after generation would become more and more British and less and less related to the identities of the country of origin. This is what the model means by assimilation – becoming as one.

Multiculturalism model

In this model a society is defined by its diversity of cultural backgrounds. No one culture is considered dominant, all cultures are celebrated and have a contribution to make in a society's evolution. People may live very different lives but these differences are encouraged and promoted which means that different ethnic and cultural groups live side by side sharing an understanding of one another but not necessarily following the same lifestyle patterns.

This multicultural model visualises ethnic integration to be more of a union of different cultures rather than a merging of cultural differences into one culture. In a multicultural society people are united by common values, not common cultures although some parts of culture do overlap and become similar. For example you were born in Britain and see yourself as British Asian; you are British but distinct because of your 'Asian' context of British – a British Asian.

All British people share some common values but may follow very different lifestyles. In effect Britain is a multi-faith, multi-racial and multi-ethnic society. All such differences should be celebrated and protected through anti-discrimination laws, for example making racial discrimination in the workplace illegal (see Chapter 2, topic 4).

ACTIVITY 4

1) Highlight the key differences between the two models of ethnic integration discussed on pages 45–46 on what happens to people's culture of origin generation after generation.

Having explored the theory through models of integration we now go on to examine some case studies which explore ethnic integration and diversity. The case studies focus on contemporary issues relating to living in a multicultural society.

CASE STUDY: The so-called 'cricket test'

An interesting study investigating sporting activity and support for national cricket and football teams among young British Asian males highlights the issue of which country the young South Asian males most identify with.

It is a strange sight to see British supporters with Pakistani or Indian or Bangladeshi backgrounds supporting not England but the country of their parents' origin. This does not necessarily mean that the South Asian males in the study saw themselves as British (or English); in fact the study finds that they are blending national associations between their country (country of birth) and their country of heritage (parents' country of birth).

The study revealed that many young British-born Asians would support the national cricket teams of their parents' origin (Bangladesh/India/Pakistani) for a number of reasons.

1) They did so as an act of protest or defiance, especially during the war with Iraq, when many young males saw support for their heritage country as a sign of rejecting English or British authority. This may be especially significant in cricket because many perceive (perhaps unfairly) that English cricket is for middle classes and many barriers are in place for young Asians to succeed in cricket. Similar situations to the South Asian support for country of heritage occurred and occurs with British born West Indian supporters.
2) The young men knew and idolised the cricketing superstars such as Sachin Tendulka from India or Shoaib Akhtar from Pakistan and identified with the iconic player, not necessarily the nation they played for.

ACTIVITY 5

1) Read the quotes from the Asian players and supporters below. To what extent might an individual from an ethnic minority feel they 'fit in' by supporting England?
2) Why might British-born Asians be more likely to support English football teams and not cricket teams?
3) Explain two possible reasons for not supporting England despite being English born.

Sachin Tendulka celebrates a hundred at Lord's cricket ground in London, the home of cricket. Sachin is adored by all cricketers, especially Indians and British Indians

Football

In football the situation was different because the South Asian nations are far less successful at football than British teams and the young males associated more with the England team and with English superstars.

Dagenham and Redbridge's Anglo-Asian defender in 2002 Anwar Uddin stated that: *'My mum's English (and white) and I was brought up in the East End [of London]. I think of myself as English and would be proud – so proud – to represent my country. I was asked to captain Bangladesh recently, but I turned it down, because if I played for them, I won't be eligible to play for England'.*

The researchers interviewed a number of professional footballers of South Asian origin and found in all cases they saw their country as England and it was the country they most wanted to play for also. For example Harpal Singh of Stockport County when asked which country he would wish to represent said *'England – no question'.*

More and more British Asians supported England in the last two football World Cups. *'I've spoken to a few people I know about this and all of us were actually up for England … And that's a first because in the past we've not really felt affiliated to England … I think people are realising that they're English or British or British Asians or whatever and want to fit in … I think more and more British-born Asian people are thinking that they are, or looking at themselves as, English and if they were given a choice in playing sport, they'd play for England'. (Interview with British Asian supporter, 2002).*

Burdsey, D (2006) '"If I ever play football, Dad, can I play for England or India?" British Asians and divided national sporting identities'. *Journal of British Sociological Association.* 40:1, SAGE.

Case study: Contemporary issues relating to living in a multicultural society

The following investigation reveals quite a number of challenges that ethnic integration poses, such as hostility over foreigners taking locals' jobs, perceived and real increases in crime, lack of community integration, i.e. divisions between people in communities.

On the margins

Fenland's farms and food factories are now powered by Portuguese and, more recently, Latvian, Lithuanian and Polish labourers. Rural life has probably not changed this rapidly since the agricultural revolution.

In Wisbech, the working market town known as the 'capital of the Fens', the migrants and the long-term residents are not rubbing along happily. But the Fens actually have a long history of absorbing outsiders. Locals such as Evan Hawkins, 79, who worked in Wisbech docks for 40 years, remembers boats from Russia, Germany and Holland regularly visiting the town. The Portuguese arrived in significant numbers a decade ago. Since the EU expanded in 2004, East Anglia has attracted Lithuanians, Latvians and Poles. Estimates suggest there are up to 80,000 East European migrants working in the region.

'You think you're in Russia,' says one local about the Sunday market on the edge of Wisbech. Most of the stallholders are British; the language of the buyers is Lithuanian, Latvian or Polish.

Racially aggravated violent assault and criminal damage in Cambridgeshire rose by 9% last year to 351 incidents – although migrant workers claim the authorities often ignore racist assaults. For some locals, attacking foreigners, known as 'fozzie-bashing', is a sport; there is a gang in Wisbech called the Friday Night Fighters that is devoted to the task.

Julie Spence the Chief Constable of Cambridgeshire says the police need more money to effectively police a community with large increases in immigrants. She said 'With the benefits comes complexity,' explaining the need to hire interpreters and the 'different standards' of the new arrivals. 'There were a lot of people who... because they used to carry knives for protection, they think they can carry knives here,' she said. 'We can identify a significant rise in drink-drive, which was down to people thinking that what they did where they came from they could do here. Their attitudes to drink-drive were probably where we were 20 years ago.'

Insecurity and a feeling of being unprotected by the police is a theme picked up by many migrants. Mykolas, a Lithuanian, is uncomplaining about the work. He rises at 4am, earns the minimum wage – £5.35 an hour – in a food factory and works seven days and 80 hours each week. (Like most migrants, he estimates that he earns between two and four times more here than he would in his skilled job at home.) Working these hours, he has had little time to learn English in his 17 months here, but he can say he is baffled by the lack of 'security' in Britain. This experience is supported by research for the Joseph Rowntree Foundation which found that working long hours in factories with mainly non-English speaking workers makes it very difficult for non-English speaking people to fit into the community.

After the drinking and kebabs and rowdiness of Saturday, the streets of Wisbech are desolate on a Sunday evening. The Kings Arms used to be more desolate than most until the owner took on a Latvian bar manager. Now, the pub is full on a Sunday night as a DJ plays Lithuanian techno and Latvian, Lithuanian, Portuguese and Polish workers take to the dance floor. Apart from a lack of long-term residents (there are about four British people in the pub, who are clearly welcome), it is a picture of integrated multiculturalism.

Patrick Barkham, *the Guardian*, 26 September 2007

Web action

Find the full article by Patrick Barkham at **www.guardian.co.uk** by performing an archive search using author name and date of the article.

ACTIVITY 6

Read the case study 'On the margins' on page 48.

1) Many areas have a long history of cultural mixing and immigration (for example the case study of East London on page 39 but why might Wisbech as a very rural town find immigration difficult to adjust to?
2) Explain why cultural differences can lead to increases in crime.
3) Discuss whether the rise in crime is likely to reduce as the immigrants adapt to British society.
4) Explain what the author means by 'a picture of integrated multiculturalism'.

6 What is stereotyping?

In this topic we examine the ways the media may shape perceptions of individuals and groups and how they may shape cultural identity. In particular we explore how **bias**, **labelling** and stereotyping influence cultural attitudes in society as a whole. We also explore the culture of the media industry itself and debates about the existence of an institutionalised built-in cultural bias within the various outlets of the mass media. Examples as illustrations are used to explore the themes.

Concepts of stereotyping and labelling

A stereotype is a generalised impression of a member of a social group which gives the impression that all members of that social group behave in the same way. A stereotype often emphasises a small element of a group's identity and exaggerates that above all other features of a personality or group identity.

The mass media are the focus of stereotype images and of much investigation into the processes and impact of stereotyping and labelling.

Labelling is a term which refers to processes which lead to an individual or group 'getting a name', for example being tagged as a 'deviant' or a 'criminal'. Young people wearing hoodies are often labelled as 'trouble makers' or 'trouble seekers'. The label reflects the media and public perception of an image but is not necessarily the reality. Many people argue that stereotypes in the media lead to labels being attached to groups and the labels often bear no resemblance to the group members' real identities. Some labels can be positive, such as 'clever' or 'good citizen', while other labels can be damaging or even dangerous, such as 'pervert', 'hooligan', 'waster', 'terrorist'.

Stereotyping is often an unconscious function and it can occur when we are being lazy in conversation and grasp for a simple and immediate character description. Stereotypes are challenged when we encounter people or members of a stereotyped group in real life and discover the truth about their character. Some people may fit the stereotype, other people may deviate from it. In most cases social encounters challenge stereotypes. Sometimes people are highly conscious of the stereotype of their group and make deliberate and obvious efforts to challenge the stereotype and be different.

'Stereotyping is leading to terror', says first Muslim Miss England

1) List the some stereotypical characteristics of a beauty queen.
2) List some stereotypical characteristics of a Muslim woman.
3) How does Hammasa Kohistani conform to the typical image of beauty queen?
4) How does Hammasa Kohistani break the stereotype of a typical Muslim woman?
5) In what ways has Hammasa Kohistani experienced hostility as a result of her role?

The first Muslim to be crowned Miss England

The first Muslim to be crowned Miss England has warned that stereotyping members of her community is leading some towards extremism. Hammasa Kohistani made history last year when she was chosen to represent England in the Miss World pageant.

But one year on, the 19-year-old student from Hounslow feels that winning the coveted beauty title last September was a 'sugar coating' for Muslims who have become more alienated in the past 12 months.

She said: 'The attitude towards Muslims has got worse over the year. Also the Muslims' attitude to British people has got worse.'

Born in Uzbekistan and raised in Afghanistan, Miss Kohistani divided Muslim opinion when she entered and won the Miss England pageant in Liverpool.

Several community leaders openly declared her to be betraying the laws of Islam while radical Muslims sent the teenager and her family death threats.

But after a busy year travelling around the world as an ambassador for England, Miss Kohistani said she feels Muslims are unfairly being branded as terrorists.

She added: 'For a Muslim to represent England is asking for controversy at the moment. I feel after everything that's happened Muslims are being stereotyped negatively. The whole community has been labelled and, whether they are guilty of crime or not, they are getting penalised for it.'

'I like being in the limelight because people can look at me and see I am a Muslim but good. Most of the people being pinpointed are judged by their outer appearances and people assume because they are Muslim and have a beard they have done something wrong.'

www.dailymail.co.uk

The nature of stereotypes: their origin and form

We now move on to explore the nature of stereotypes which requires investigating their origins, form and impact on us. Stereotypes which emerge in the media are shaped by the social world we live in.

The nature of stereotyping has its origins in the class and gender attitudes of society and its wider values which dominate, such as for example the roles of work and leisure. Some people regard the origins of stereotyping to be found amongst the rich and powerful in society, for example the positive image of an ideal worker or the negative image of a lazy student waster. Other people suggest stereotypes have their origins in males who dominate society, for example the stereotyping of women as sex objects and as housebound. Ethnic stereotyping, such as 'all black men play basketball' originates from a dominant white attitude with narrow perceptions of different ethnic identities.

Whatever the origins of stereotypes the common reason for their existence is that people find it convenient and easy to categorise others. This enables us to gauge what we might experience when/if we encounter that individual. This human social protection is heavily influenced by the media.

Examples of stereotyping are particularly obvious in advertising. When observing advertisements in magazines, newspapers or on TV, try to identify the stereotypes they contain.

Stereotypes are not always going to have a direct impact on an individual. Although we cannot be sure just how much stereotypes shape our outlooks, many people laugh at or disregard the stereotype as a total distortion of reality. Sometimes the media distort a stereotype to shock us and challenge what are established views. For example a shock

revelation in a soap opera when an individual turns out to be very different to what they normally are. Can you identify any examples of characters that confound their stereotypes?

It is very important to note that we all make general assumptions about categories of people. We pigeon hole individuals and groups into categories which allow us to make some sense or order out of a complex social world. These categories may be generalisations and at times may be wrong but they are an inevitable part of human behaviour. For example we see images of an individual and make assumptions about them and categorise them in certain ways. For example a stranger who we meet has an England rugby shirt on – we make assumptions about that individual based on our knowledge of what typical rugby union followers do. Another stranger with a Leeds United football top on would be similarly categorised by us as a football fan, from Leeds, probably working class and male. We use these categories to make judgements when we meet strangers because they allow us to make sense of the situation or person and the messages they are giving off. The categories or assumptions may be correct or they may be wrong; however we must recognise that our first impressions may be heavily shaped by the media images of that category and that these judgements may shape our interaction with that individual.

What impression might we have of the following individual? 'Believes in God, primary school teacher, aged 30, drives a mini, owns their own house.'

We are most likely to categorise this individual in our thoughts as middle class, reasonably wealthy, probably caring and pleasant, female, by this age may well have started a family but probably married, may well have grown up in a middle class, emotionally stable home. All such categories may well be right, they may well be wrong (some probably will be) but it gives us a basis of understanding of the character and therefore some ammunition (information background) to use in a social encounter with the individual. The issue of stereotyping begins to become problematic when we assume all individuals in a particular character category fit the stereotype. We can act in ways as to be blind to diversity and difference within particular groups.

The media often deliberately stereotype by giving us typical characters to associate with in films, books, magazines or in news programmes. The issue of stereotyping becomes damaging to citizenship inclusion when we stick rigidly to the categories or apply the images to all individuals and groups we encounter of that type. The mass media are accused of encouraging the impression of some groups as a narrow reflection of reality which encourages and spreads myths about those groups and also builds prejudice (pre-judgements) of particular groups – especially of groups we do not encounter on a regular basis. For example all drug users are 'down and out on the street, criminal and young males'. Or 'all HIV sufferers are gay males recklessly irresponsible in their sexual habits', or 'black men are good at sports, black women are good dancers', or 'terrorists are young Muslim males of Pakistani origin with dark features, possibly having a large beard'.

'The mean Scot' © *Hertfordshire Mercury*

ACTIVITY 2

1) Identify some of the stereotypes of the characters in the cartoon above. Think in terms of nationality, age, class and gender imagery. Suggest where these stereotypes originate from. You could think about social attitudes towards femininity, masculinity and social class.

How do stereotypes impact on attitudes and behaviour?

Little Britain characters play on stereotypes for fun and amuse us with their exaggerated characters.

Most of us laugh at the images and behaviour of the characters. These categories in themselves may be very beneficial by making people happy watching the programmes and possibly encouraging us to reflect on some of our own behaviour which may be similar. They become damaging however when we see the category only in that light as if all transvestites were the same as the characters 'The ladies' for example.

Most of us are aware of diversity and sometimes we anticipate the categories people place us into and try to act in ways that surprise our audience in order to challenge their impression or to confound them. Therefore most of us do not blindly believe the categories we are exposed to in the mass media. However many categories are so dominant and frequent that we become saturated with the image and unaware of alternatives. For example images of skinny models are so widespread that we believe it would not be possible to become a model if we were of average shape and did not fit the stereotype of a model. We may not be fully aware of how influential the media stereotypes are and we may not be aware of how different a group can be if we do not know much about that group or social category. When we know little about individuals and groups and the ways they vary we are more likely to be influenced by stereotypes than if we know about a category or a group. In effect the influence of stereotyping on us varies according to our social awareness of different categories of people.

Role of the mass media

Mass media are organisations communicating to large (or mass) audiences at any one time. The most recognisable examples are radio, TV, cinema and newspapers.

The mass media are a major influence on how we see others in society. Therefore an understanding of stereotypes requires an understanding of the ways the mass media influence us and society in general. We can explore the impact of the mass media by exploring three **models of media influence**.

Andy and his carer, Lou.
Characters from *Little Britain*

1 MARXIST, MANIPULATIVE MODEL

As a way of controlling the workers the mass media are used as a tool to shock, spread fear and suspicion about deviant groups. The media works to encourage conformity with the rules of capitalist society – work hard, avoid confrontation with your superiors/bosses and follow the expected patterns of behaviour associated with your role in the workplace and as men, women, children, old and young. This model assumes we simply receive messages and believe them. It also overlooks the fact that in an increasingly diverse media-driven society an individual on the street is able to contribute to the content of the media, meaning all sorts of views can be expressed. Also we are able to choose from a very wide range of images and view points. In other words we do not have to believe all we see, hear or read in the media and we have a far wider choice of things to consume in the mass media meaning that the influence of stereotypes is much more varied and less directly likely to manipulate us.

2 CULTURAL DOMINANCE OF MEDIA INDUSTRY

Unlike the previous model, the mass media do not operate as a tool to directly manipulate the masses. This model sees the industry as made up of a narrow range of identities causing a narrow range of content and imagery. Topics covered and how they are covered/dealt with in mass media are not a reflection of what society as a whole wants but a reflection of what the professionals working in the industry think is important. The way they create the messages reflects not a general reality but the reality of this narrow range of professional backgrounds.

The mass media are dominated by middle aged, middle class, males, educated to degree level probably living in the South of England. Such a dominant demographic identity in the media industry creates a dominant set of values and images in the programmes, stories or films the industry makes.

3 PLURALIST MODEL

We don't watch what we don't want to, we choose what to consume from the media. Content in the mass media only exists because the public demand it. The industry creates materials which would appeal to an audience and that audience has a direct influence on how the material is constructed. We are likely to see a new Indiana Jones film not because it is thought to be a good thing by the industry but because the public are likely to want to see the film. In 2007 the BBC was cutting many jobs because fewer people were watching their broadcasts and so we as consumers are directly influencing the content of the mass media, regardless of the background of the media industry professionals who run it. Demand for content is the basis of content being produced. Here any stereotyping is not the industry's creation but the public's categories that the media industry knows we would recognise and so they provide it for us. Any stereotypes existing in the media content reflect the stereotypes of the public.

CASE STUDY: Race and stereotyping in the media and the news

In his book *Race In the News* Ian Law explores the way race is covered in the media, especially in the news. He refers to the way the media represent race in typical categories. For example crime coverage often emphasises racialised crime for example rioting, mugging, drugs. Black Afro-Caribbean and Asian groups become associated with types of crime and the label 'dealer' or 'terrorist' criminal becomes associated along racial lines. Also as important is the not reporting of events, for example the lack of emphasis on positive stories associated with racial minorities and giving less coverage to racial minority actors at award ceremonies.

Law quotes Ross (1996) to emphasise his point.

It is the poverty of black images rather than the frequency that is the real problem, images constrained and constructed within a narrow band of character types in comedy and drama, or … [demonised] in factual programming.

Law argues that this systematic categorising of racial minority groups allows the stereotypes to continue and become reinforced in society.

Ross (1996) in Law, I (2002) *Race in the News*. Palgrave, Macmillan, p41

ACTIVITY 3

1) Using the article in the case study above which types of crime are associated with which ethnic groups?
2) Explain using examples what the article means by 'the poverty of black images rather than the frequency that is the real problem'.
3) Define what is meant by the term demonised.
4) Using the article and your own ideas, draw up a short list of racialised characteristics of ethnic minority groups. Using your list try to identify mass media characters or images you know of which fit these categories.

Web action

Soap watch
1) Using an on demand download service, such as the BBC's iPlayer, ITVplayer or Channel 4's 4oD, locate two episodes each from three soap operas. The soaps should be ideally from three different channels, for example EastEnders, Coronation Street, Hollyoaks.
2) When you watch the soap opera for the first time note down any characters you think display 'typical' feminine, masculine, middle class, working class and racial stereotypes and any that are breaking 'norms' of femininity, masculinity, middle class and working class and racial stereotypes.
3) Watch these characters closely in both episodes from each soap and clearly explain why you think their character conforms to or subverts stereotypes.

Note: you could carry out this activity by focusing on one specific category rather than them all.

Exam questions

SECTION A: IDENTITY

Answer Question 1 and **either** Question 2 **or** Question 3.

This section carries 30 marks.

1 Read the extract below and answer parts (a) and (b) which follow.

Some view citizenship as belonging to a state where you have rights in return for duties. Legal rights include basic human rights, such as the right to a fair trial or the right to own property. Other rights are political, such as the right to vote in elections and the right to join a trade union. More recently rights have been described as welfare or social rights – the right to live free from poverty on a basic income and access to a basic standard of health care. In return for these rights citizens have duties where they are expected to actively participate in society. Active citizenship could involve paying taxes, working or parenting appropriately, volunteering and showing respect for the environment and understanding your identity in an ever diverse and ethnically mixed society.

Your answers should refer to the extract as appropriate, but you should also include other relevant information.

(a) Briefly explain what is meant by the term 'active citizenship'. (*5 marks*)

(b) Examine some of the ways that British identity is shaped through the socialisation process. (*10 marks*)

Either:

2 Assess the view that referring to citizens as either working class or middle class is outdated and no longer appropriate in modern Britain. (*15 marks*)

Or:

3 Immigration into Britain has inevitably caused community tensions in the short-term but has also contributed huge amounts to the social identity and economic prosperity of Britain. Assess the evidence which supports this view.

(*15 marks*)

IDENTITY, RIGHTS AND RESPONSIBILITIES

SECTION 1: IDENTITY

Chapter 2: Are we all equal citizens?

In this chapter we explore two main issues which examine the key question 'Are we all equal citizens?'

ISSUE 1: Prejudice, discrimination and disadvantage
This issue is explored through the following topics:

- prejudice and discrimination
- disadvantage: how are life chances distributed among different social groups?
- to what extent does poverty exists in Britain?

ISSUE 2: How can discrimination and disadvantage be reduced?
This issue is explored through the following topics:

- the problem of defining equality in a diverse and changing society
- what steps can governments take to reduce discrimination and disadvantage and what policies have been implemented?
- how effective have these policies been?

ISSUE 1: PREJUDICE, DISCRIMINATION AND DISADVANTAGE

In this section we explore the following three topics:

- prejudice and discrimination
- disadvantage: how are life chances distributed among different social groups?
- to what extent does poverty exist in Britain?

1 Prejudice and discrimination

In this topic we define and illustrate the terms **prejudice** and **discrimination**. We explore the basis of prejudice and discrimination by examining **sexism**, **racism**, **homophobia** and **Islamophobia**. We examine how discrimination is based on prejudiced views by exploring forms of discrimination such as **antilocution**, **bullying**, **physical abuse** and **genocide**.

Definitions of prejudice and discrimination

Prejudice is a set of views or opinions about people or groups of people which consider them to be inferior to or below/lower than other groups. For example the view that men in general make better workers than women or that women are in need of protection from men. Other examples could be that blacks are better dancers than whites or that gay activity is morally wrong. Here the term is mainly referring to people's beliefs.

It may be possible to act differently from what you believe but if you act on the prejudiced beliefs then the action is discrimination. Discrimination is therefore the act of treating someone or a group of people differently because of prejudiced beliefs.

If a teacher has prejudiced beliefs they may act on them and treat the student or group of students differently. If this occurs it is discrimination because the teacher has acted upon their prejudiced beliefs. On the other hand a teacher may have beliefs that a particular student is a bad student but may well be able to hold back from acting on those views and behave consistently and fairly towards the student. In this case prejudice exists in the teacher's beliefs but does not develop into action (discrimination) because

the teacher has not acted upon their prejudiced beliefs. It must be noted however that if someone holds a belief it is very difficult to avoid acting upon them, even unintentionally.

Different types of discrimination

Discrimination can be direct or indirect, it can also be positive (affirmative) or negative. To illustrate these different types of discrimination we could stick with the teacher example. The type of discrimination depends on the type of action the teacher takes.

Direct discrimination
This is discrimination that is obvious and deliberate, such as deliberately abusing someone or treating someone unfairly, for example disregarding their religious beliefs or mocking someone because they have a disability.

Indirect discrimination
This is discrimination which is not directly intended but where actions lead to a person or group being restricted in taking a full part in the school. For example the school may try to be inclusive for all students but may not have the resources to provide for a student's needs. In this case the discrimination is indirect because it is not fully intended.

Positive discrimination
This is sometimes called affirmative action, meaning actions which are intended to improve a person's or group's situation and directly counter the prejudice they face. The teacher may be aware of their prejudice and act in a way as to encourage that individual. For example the teacher may give a student more time than others in extra lessons because the student is struggling. For example giving school boys more time in English than girls because boys as a whole do less well in English than girls. Here treating the student differently is discrimination but it is hoped the outcome is

positive or results in affirming the student's standing in the class and in achievement.

Negative discrimination

In contrast the teacher may act on their prejudice in such a way as to result in negative discrimination simply by treating the student unfairly, for example correcting them more or being harsher in marking. Here discrimination occurs and the outcome is most likely (not necessarily) to cause negative outcomes. Negative discrimination often causes harm or creates a situation that limits or restricts an individual or harms an individual/group in some way, in this case in terms of their educational progress.

Responses to discrimination

Individuals and groups are different and may respond to discrimination differently. For example a teacher being negative in their discrimination may cause the student to try harder to prove the teacher wrong. Others may find the discrimination unsettling and unfair and stop trying because they feel the teacher will always treat them unfairly so why should they make much effort?

ACTIVITY 1

1) Explain the difference between prejudice and discrimination.
2) Identify one example for each of the four types of discrimination.
3) Explain why some discrimination can have a positive outcome.

The bases of prejudice

As we have been exploring, prejudice is based on our views and these may or may not lead to discrimination. However it is sometimes difficult to clearly distinguish between a personal preference and a prejudiced view because often they can be the same.

The key aspect which makes preference different to prejudice is that prejudice is more a set of beliefs about a group in society (for example women, men, ethnic groups, religions, the elderly, disabled), whereas preference is personal and tends not to be based on a wider view about a group. The basis of preference is not founded on a theory but from personal experience.

JULIA AND JOHN

The year 12 end-of-term party is coming up and Julia wants to ask John if he will come with her to the party as her date. All of Julia's friends think John is a nice person and encourage her to ask him. Eventually Julia plucks up the courage and waits for John after school.

Julia *'Hello John.'*

John *'Hello Julia.'*

Julia *'John, have you got a ticket for the party next week?'*

John *'No I am not sure if I am going, none of my mates are going.'*

Julia *'Will you come with me?'*

John *'Erm, not sure, dunno.'*

Julia *'Why not sure? Is it that you don't like me? Does it matter if your friends aren't going?'*

John *'Well I would go with you as a friend but not on a date.'*

Julia (upset) *'What have I done wrong?'*

John *'Nothing, I like you but I don't like you in a girlfriend way because I only fancy girls who are taller than you.'*

Julia walks away to rejoin her friends.

John follows but Julia's friends all turn away from John because they could see he had upset their friend Julia.

ACTIVITY 2

1) Role play the characters on page 59 to explore how prejudice can be a simple preference which may or may not lead to harmful discrimination.
2) Now discuss the following questions with the class.
   - If John had said yes, Julia and her friends would be happy. But he said no and therefore John's actions made them upset. Did John do the right thing?
   - In what way was John showing preference or prejudice?
   - Did John discriminate against Julia in an unfair or offensive way?

ACTIVITY 3

1) Using sensible and realistic language, rewrite the role play so that it shows prejudice and discrimination.

Prejudice takes many forms but it is usually based on a set of ideas which are often based on stereotypes (perhaps shaped by mass media). We can explore prejudiced views by focusing on some set ideas about specific groups. Some of the generally held opinions which underpin prejudice are sexism, racism, homophobia and Islamophobia.

In the example on the previous page, John did not discriminate against Julia because she was shorter than he would prefer, he simply made a choice based on his preference. John did not cause deliberate harm by intentionally humiliating Julia in front of her friends nor did he say anything prejudicial other than his own preference for taller girls. If John had said 'I only date tall girls because short girls are silly and less intelligent' then he would be showing unfair pre-judgement which is prejudice. John may have thought this (prejudiced thoughts) but did not say it so his actions were neither prejudiced nor discriminatory.

ACTIVITY 4

1) Answer the questions in the survey on page 61. The questions are designed to explore your beliefs about men and women and to assess the extent to which you may hold prejudiced views perhaps without realising it. The activity is best done individually within a group of both males and females so that answers can be discussed and compared. Decide the significance of your scores; the lower your score the less sexist you are.
2) Discuss the degree of 'sexism' in each of the questions – were some more clearly sexist than others? Did the males and females in your group agree? Did you find any differences within the group on the answers and scores between the females and the males?

Sexism

Sexism is a prejudiced view that sees women as inferior to men or men inferior to women. Inferior means weaker or less capable and the prejudice we may hold is our attitudes to that gender group, for example, that women should be beautiful to the eyes of men.

66 unnervingly changing hairdos 99

66 uppity woman 99

66 would you be in this position were it not for your husband? 99

Do you think the media headlines above referring to Hilary Rodham Clinton are evidence of sexist attitudes in journalism?

1. Every man should have a woman whom he adores.

Disagree strongly					**Agree strongly**
0	1	2	3	4	5

2. Men should be the protectors of women but should also cherish women.

Disagree strongly					**Agree strongly**
0	1	2	3	4	5

3. Men without women are complete men.

Disagree strongly					**Agree strongly**
0	1	2	3	4	5

4. Most problems women have at work are exaggerated.

Disagree strongly					**Agree strongly**
0	1	2	3	4	5

5. Once a man agrees to commit to a woman she then starts to keep him under tight control.

Disagree strongly					**Agree strongly**
0	1	2	3	4	5

6. In an equal contest when women lose to men they frequently claim this was because of discrimination.

Disagree strongly					**Agree strongly**
0	1	2	3	4	5

7. A man has a responsibility to present his good woman for all to see.

Disagree strongly					**Agree strongly**
0	1	2	3	4	5

Web action

Go to **www.understandingprejudice.org**. The website offers interesting interviews and questionnaires about prejudice. Many aspects of racial and sexual prejudice are explored. Rather than outlining cases of discrimination this site is useful because it explores prejudiced views that we may possess as individuals. Try the full survey on sexism or an interview on racial prejudice. Also a test on personal prejudice shows images of faces and asks you to identify whether they are 'Black' or 'White' – here our stereotypical images of different racial groups are exposed.

Racism

Racism is prejudice based on the belief that someone's skin colour or religious/ethnic identity is somehow better or weaker than someone else's.

Web action

Go to **www.srtrc.org**, which is the Show Racism The Red Card website, and explore the activities the group is involved in. Many of the activities are aimed at young people. Explore the site and find the schools competition. You and some friends could enter with the chance of winning a signed shirt, free tickets and a trip to Wembley.

1] Why do you think the group's activities focus on young people?
2] How effective do you think the group is?

Now try the quiz on the **www.prejudice.org.uk** website. It has an answers section so that you can learn more and check your answers against the facts.

Homophobia

Homophobia is the irrational (not based on reason or facts) fear of homosexuality and the hatred, disgust and prejudice that fear brings. Oppression of lesbians and gay men, as well as bisexual women and men, is based on homophobia.

Heterosexism

Heterosexism is institutionalised (part of a person's or organisation's everyday belief) homophobia: the assumption that being heterosexual is inherently better or more moral than being lesbian, gay or bisexual. Like racism, sexism and other forms of oppression, heterosexism awards power to members of the dominant group (heterosexuals) and denies privilege to members of the subordinate group (lesbians, gay men and bisexual women and men).

Web action

Go to **www.endhomophobia.org**. Use the 'what we do' section to compile a brief report for the other students in your class that lists the activities of the organisation and comments on its effectiveness in challenging homophobia.

The Rainbow Flag, a symbol of gay pride for the gay and lesbian community

Homophobia is not restricted to any one area of society. Homophobic action is found in all walks of life both private and public. Some organised groups have viciously attacked homosexuals using physical threat and violent language (**abuse**) in an attempt to intimidate, humiliate and in their eyes even 'punish' homosexuals.

Discrimination against homosexuals comes in many forms. Homophobic beliefs may show up in people's behaviour at work, or at schools, in clubs and pubs, on the street and in many other areas. Frequently it seems that prejudiced views about homosexuals are based upon the belief that homosexuality is immoral. Being homophobic allows those people to feel they are stronger than, or more in control of homosexuals. Also being anti-gay seems to be more accepted than being anti or biased against any other such minority group which suggests that being anti-gay is more institutionalised as part of everyday life than other prejudices.

ACTIVITY 5

1) What is homophobia a prejudice of?
2) Explain how and why fear may lead to prejudice.
3) Give one example of how homophobia may be experienced in:
   - the workplace
   - at schools
   - at clubs
   - on the streets or in a shopping centre.

Islamophobia

Islamophobia is the irrational fear or prejudice towards Islam and Muslims.

British Muslims are a diverse and a vibrant community and they form an essential part of Britain's multi-ethnic, multicultural society. Despite their contributions to British society,

Muslims suffer from various forms of alienation, discrimination, harassment and violence. These actions of prejudice are rooted in mistaken and misunderstood stereotyped impressions of Muslims and of what Islam means – this has become known as Islamophobia. Islamophobia has now become recognised as a form of racism.

MUSLIM FACTFILE

- A significant presence of Muslims in Britain has been evident for over a century

- Today Islam is the fastest growing religion ever

- The UK 2001 census shows that there are more than 1.6 million UK Muslims which amounts to 2.7 per cent of the UK population

- Islam is now the UK's second largest faith after Christianity.

Intolerance, misguided and stereotypical views of Muslims and of Islam frequently show themselves in a number of ways. For example verbal abuse and written abuse, discrimination at schools and in workplaces, psychological harassment/pressure in public and in secret and outright violent attacks on mosques and individuals in the street.

Web action

1] Go to **www.fairuk.org**.
- What does FAIR stand for?
- Identify the aims of the organisation.
- Identify and describe the issue in the latest press release on the home page .

2] Go to **www.muslimnews.co.uk/news/index. php**.
- Explore the issues of the day which affect the Muslim community.
- Describe the range of countries mentioned in the stories.

3] Go to **www.ihrc.org.uk/file/report02sep06b acklash.pdf**.
- Referring to the types of discriminatory abuse described in these research findings, identify whether each one is verbal, physical or psychological.
- Identify the three stereotypical beliefs in the article which may underpin prejudice.

Forms that discrimination may take

Most commonly discriminatory actions take the form of one of the following: antilocution, bullying, physical abuse, genocide. Each type of discrimination links to different types of group. For example antilocution, bullying and physical abuse are types of discrimination which usually affect an individual or small group and are most often carried out by another small group or individual. In contrast genocide is a wider scale of discrimination carried out by a government (state) on a whole group in society.

Genocide

Genocide is most often based on racial prejudice. The term genocide was first used in 1944. It comes from the Greek word 'genos' (race) and the Latin word 'cide' (killing). Genocide as defined by the United Nations in 1948 means any of the following acts committed with intent to destroy, in whole or in part, a national, ethnic, racial or religious group, including a) killing members of the group; b) causing serious bodily or mental harm to members of the group; c) deliberately inflicting on the group conditions of life calculated to bring about its physical destruction in whole or in part; d) imposing measures intended to prevent births within the group; e) forcibly transferring children of the group to another group.

MAJOR GENOCIDES OF THE LAST **100** YEARS

- Bosnia-Herzegovina: 1992–1995 – 200,000 deaths
- Rwanda: 1994 – 800,000 deaths
- Pol Pot in Cambodia: 1975–1979 – 2,000,000 deaths
- Nazi Holocaust: 1938–1945 – 6,000,000 deaths
- Rape of Nanking: 1937–1938 – 300,000 deaths
- Stalin's Forced Famine: 1932–1933 – 7,000,000 deaths
- Armenians in Turkey: 1915–1918 – 1,500,000 deaths

www.historyplace.com

ACTIVITY 6

Web action

Go to
www.historyplace.com/worldhistory/ genocide. Select any one of the list of genocides listed above and explore the events surrounding these mass murders by governments. Be aware that the material you will encounter is very disturbing and you need to be prepared for this before you take part in the activity.

1) How do the themes in the article below link sexist views (prejudice) with bullying (discrimination)?
2) Using the article explain how the language and actions of some boys towards girls illustrate antilocution.
3) In what ways does the article show that bullying often goes unreported and that it is covered up?

Bullying, sexism and antilocution

'I was called names like slut and whore'

A survey for the National Union of Teachers showed that half of teachers had witnessed sexist language and bullying, and that, where it occurs, it occurs frequently… a study by the American Association of University Women found that four out of five girls and boys (because it affects boys too, especially boys who are, or are perceived to be, gay) had suffered sexual bullying at some point.

A 16-year-old girl in Cornwall was repeatedly called a 'slapper' because she had a large bust; she eventually had a breast reduction in the hope that the bullying would stop. A 14-year-old girl in Essex endured months of being called a 'slag' and a 'skank' and contemplated suicide; one day about 30 teenagers set on her, pulling her top down and exposing her breasts. She was beaten up so badly she was in hospital for three days.

Sexual bullying can be used to describe anything from sexualised comments about appearance and name-calling, such as 'slag', to spreading rumours about someone's sexual behaviour, to criminal offences such as assault and rape.

Like any kind of bullying, it can ruin the lives of the victims, but the sexual dimension of gender bullying means it can be even harder to talk about and so is rarely addressed. Sarah, 17, was bullied by a group of boys as soon as she started secondary school. 'I was called names like "slut" and "whore" – those were terms most boys used against girls,' she says. 'I was shy and I wore clothes that covered me up… A group of boys would grab me in corridors – it was embarrassing and I felt disgusting, but I couldn't do anything back. I just froze until they left. There were other girls they would touch too. I feel really guilty and embarrassed about it all,' she says. 'It changed me – I didn't look forward to going to school.'

Emine Saner, *the Guardian,* **30 November 2007**

2 Disadvantage: how are life chances distributed among different social groups?

In this section we explore the following themes:

- the nature of life chances
- an awareness of different life chances in relation to education, income, employment and health
- the relationship of life chances to gender, social class, age, disability, sexuality and ethnicity.

The nature of life chances

Life chances vary between different social groups, they also vary from time to time through different stages in our lives – a person's circumstances frequently change at various points throughout their life.

A chance in life refers to the opportunity to achieve a goal, ambition or desire. The ambitions or visions we have for our futures are just dreams unless we find a way of making them a reality. The ingredients required to achieve our ambitions in life can be called life chances.

Any examination of life chances must consider the issue of access or lack of access to opportunities that influence our life chances. Exploring life chances we focus on the key theme of **meritocracy**. Meritocracy is a term referring to the view that society mainly allocates jobs, positions and roles according to an individual's ability and/or hard work – not according to preference, prejudice or nepotism. Nepotism means favouring family members, for example, in appointments for jobs.

ACTIVITY 1

1) Make two lists. The first list is all those things you want to achieve as part of your career or future at work. The second list is all those things required in order to achieve your list of aspirations.
2) Having made your lists identify any things you think may act as barriers to your plans. How would you overcome these problems/challenges/barriers?
3) To what extent do you think the barriers you face are barriers most people face or are they specific to yourself?
4) Having completed questions 1 to 3 above, to what extent do you feel you have equal opportunities compared with others?

In this activity you have been exploring the issue of **equality of opportunity** – a term for this is meritocracy.

Factors influencing life chances

Some people are lucky – not just lottery winners – but also people being in the right place at the right time or being born to the right parents or being able to go to the 'best' schools, or live in an area or country with a stable economy, free from natural disasters. However UK society in theory has four key aspects which influence life chances:

- education
- income
- employment
- health.

These four themes vary across the country and from person to person. Therefore life chances are relative to where a person lives and their personal circumstances according to the four themes above.

Many social scientists argue that life chances vary in UK society because it is possible to link variations in them to social group. Achievement in education, levels of income, types of employment and level of health are all life chances influenced by a citizen's gender, social class, age, disability, sexuality or ethnicity. It is these identity criteria which determine life chances.

We now go on to explore the idea of equality of opportunity in life chances – meritocracy.

Meritocracy

Many social scientists and policy makers hold the view that our society is a meritocracy. Meritocracy is the idea that everyone in society has a fair chance to achieve their goals. Therefore differences in status, wealth and power in society are earned. According to this view, the rewards people enjoy such as high standards of living reflect people's hard work, and/or ability. Thus people in better paid jobs have achieved their position and have a justifiably higher status and higher pay.

In short we get what we deserve; status and rewards are achieved not ascribed. (Achieved means gained yourself, not given at birth which is ascribed.)

The idea of meritocracy assumes an equal chance to access and take advantage of factors influencing life opportunities. Access to education and employment as well as health and welfare support services are all vital to success in society.

Many social scientists point out that although individuals and groups do have access to services in theory, in reality access is not available to all to an equal extent. For example:

- many individuals have less choice of the type of school they attend

- others have fewer job opportunities in their areas
- some people's access to health services varies because health services are not evenly distributed throughout society, for example, some health services and treatments are available in some authorities and not in others
- also prejudice and discrimination influence people's life chances, for example, discrimination by employers favouring non-disabled people.

Life chances and opportunities may differ for different people for reasons beyond their control. As a result life chances vary from person to person for a variety of reasons, some within the control of the individual, others caused by society beyond the control of the individual. Consequently achievement of a position of status in society whether at work, at school or elsewhere is not always something all people can do simply by working hard and exploiting their ability because factors beyond their control may intervene.

The barriers to achieving goals can be imposed by yourself. For example negative attitudes to school and fatalistic views of your future or poor approaches to the values of responsibility and punctuality/reliability leave many people's potential undeveloped. And so opportunities are unfulfilled due to factors imposed by the individual themselves. We discuss these themes when we explore poverty and the concept of 'the underclass' in topic 3, pages 78 and 80.

ACTIVITY 2

Exploring equality of opportunity and barriers to it – self-imposed or otherwise – can be done through this activity.
Make a list of any celebrities you know of such as film stars or business leaders under the following categories:
* people who have worked their way up from 'the bottom'
* people who have a position given at birth (for example a title)
* people who have been restricted in the opportunities through no fault of their own.

We now go on to explore features of life chances according to some specific social groups and therefore examine the extent to which life chances are equally distributed.

Education and life chances by social class

Successive governments for generations have emphasised the importance of education to a healthy society, to the economy and to an individual's personal enrichment. Education is also vital for developing skills that employers want and are willing to pay for.

Many sociologists have provided evidence that achievement in education is heavily influenced by the social background of an individual. In particular the social class position of an individual as determined by their or their parents' occupation (see below) has a major influence on a person's chances and likelihood of succeeding in education.

SOCIAL CLASS CATEGORIES (BASED ON OCCUPATION)

1) Higher managerial and professional occupations:
   * manager or employer in a large organisation (100 employees or more), for example, company managing directors, chief police officers, senior military officers
   * higher professions, for example, barristers, senior solicitors, doctors, teachers, social workers, politicians.

2) Lower managerial and professional occupations, for example actors, nurses, police, soldiers (not officers), journalists.

3) Intermediate occupations, for example secretaries, Sky and telecommunications fitters, driving instructors, sales people, community wardens, personal assistants.

4) Small employers and own-account workers (self-employed), for example painters and decorators, builders, farmers, taxi drivers, school learning assistants, electricians.

5) Lower supervisory, craft and related occupations, for example bus drivers, train drivers, lorry drivers, butchers, plumbers, shop fitters, hair stylists.

6) Semi-routine occupations, for example traffic wardens, postal workers, farm/nursery labourers, factory workers, shop assistants.

7) Routine occupations, for example catering assistants, refuse collectors, road sweepers, cleaners, delivery men/women, call centre operators, crop pickers/field workers.

8) Never worked/long-term unemployed.

1) The Government's social class groupings are listed on page 68. Each group is based on occupation. Identify and explain one problem of measuring social class using occupation alone.
2) For each of the groups 1 to 8 identify and explain one advantage and one disadvantage students may face in school as a result of their parents' occupational background.
3) In 150 words assess the extent to which you feel home background is important to a student's achievement.
4) Draw up two lists, one of material factors influencing educational achievement and the second of cultural factors (such as language and parental attitude) influencing educational achievement.

Age and life chances

Average life expectancy is increasing – people are living for longer than ever before – and the number of elderly people in society is growing. For instance the number of centenarians (people who are 100 years old or more) has increased dramatically. The issue illustrated by the article to the right suggests that life chances are affected substantially as we get older.

A number of key issues apply as listed below.

- Many elderly people are retired and live only on their savings and pensions which tend to be lower than average earnings. This results in many elderly people living on low incomes and being reliant on the Government to protect their standard of living.
- There is prejudice in society which sees young people in the prime of their physical lives as most valuable and not people with experience and life skills. Consequently many elderly people face direct and indirect discrimination, such as being passed over for employment or promotion because they are seen as less skilled or less likely to take advantage of training. Also the perception of many is that the elderly are less likely to be employees for as long as young people will be.
- Issues of health affect the elderly as a group more than many other groups. The older a person is the more likely they are to need health services and we rely increasingly on health services to maintain our health and lifestyle. With increased demand for services it has to spread further and inevitably its resources become stretched.

Rise of the 100-year-old people

The number of people living for over 100 years in England and Wales has risen to its highest ever level, highlighting the need for good care of the elderly.

Official figures released by the Office for National Statistics show that 9,000 people in England and Wales have exceeded their 100th birthday and the figure is expected to rise to 40,000 by 2031.

Improvements in healthcare, housing, diet and cleanliness are being cited as the main factors that have contributed to the 90-fold increase in centenarians since 1911.

Dr Lorna Layward, a spokeswoman for Help the Aged, told the BBC: "It's hard to know whether these extra years are providing extra years of good health.

'Hopefully, with better medical provision, these extra years can be happy and healthy.'

There are concerns that NHS care services in England and Wales will be unable to cope with the growing number of elderly people, with a number of recent reports pointing to substandard conditions and standards of care.

Care of the Elderly News, 1 October 2007

1) From the article above identify some of the reasons for life expectancy rising.
2) Using the article and your own ideas list some of the 'problems' faced by increasing numbers of elderly people and list some of the benefits of growing numbers of elderly people in England and Wales.
3) In about 100 words explain why you agree or disagree with the phrase 'numerical age is irrelevant, all that matters is how you feel'.

Web action

Go to **www.ageconcern.org.uk** and identify the current issues raised on the main page. Click on the campaigns icon and identify some of the campaigning strategies and issues age concern is involved in.

Disability and life chances

Being disabled does not mean you cannot achieve your ambitions.

The Disabled Citizens Advice and Support services logo

Many positive role models exist for disabled people indicating disability is not necessarily a barrier to realising goals and dreams. There are, however, various indicators suggesting disabled people experience social exclusion and restricted life chances.

Educational outcomes of disabled and non-disabled 16 and 17 year olds

Research by the Joseph Rowntree Foundation explored how the issue of disability among 16 and 17 year olds influences educational and employment opportunities.

The research found that of the 16- and 17-year-olds:

- 71 per cent of non-disabled people were in full-time education; whereas 62 per cent of disabled people were in full-time education
- six in ten non-disabled people reported that they got the education or training place or job they wanted; whereas just over 50 per cent of disabled youngsters said they had received the education or training or job they wanted
- 13 per cent of disabled young people were out of work or 'doing something else'; whereas 7 per cent of non-disabled young people were out of work or 'doing something else'.

The gap between the proportion of disabled and non-disabled young people out of work widened as they got older. At 18 or 19 years of age:

- 25 per cent of disabled young people were unemployed or 'doing something else'; whereas 9 per cent of non-disabled people were unemployed or 'doing something else'
- among those who were in employment, earnings were lower for disabled than for non-disabled employees. At age 26, disabled young people were earning 11 per cent less than their non-disabled counterparts with the same educational qualifications.

The Education and Employment of Young Disabled People, **Joseph Rowntree Foundation, November 2005, ref. No. 0565**

ACTIVITY 5

1) Explain why ten per cent fewer disabled people than non-disabled people in full-time education is a cause of restricted life chances.

2) Suggest reasons that may explain why the patterns of inequality between non-disabled and disabled people exist. In your answer reflect on employers, the education system and public perceptions of disability.

Ethnic group, social class and gender and life chances

In this section we link together themes of ethnicity, social class and gender. The aspects of different social groupings have specific influences on life chances but also the issues faced by the groups can be linked.

The most important influence on life chances for the vast majority of people is their educational achievement. Many researchers point to the significance of ethnicity which impacts on educational experience and achievement. The group most likely to achieve least are Pakistani, Bangladeshi and white ethnic groups especially the male members.

An investigation for the Joseph Rowntree Research Foundation in 2007 investigated achievement by social group. The key findings of the research *Tackling Low Educational Achievement* (Cassen and Kingdon, 2007) is summarised below.

Achievement by social group

- Eligibility for free school meals is strongly associated with low achievement, but significantly more so for White British pupils than for other ethnic groups.
- Boys outnumber girls as low achievers by three to two. The gender gap is larger for some ethnic groups – Bangladeshi, Pakistani and Black African – among those not achieving GCSE grade C and above.
- Chinese and Indian pupils are the most successful in avoiding low achievement; African-Caribbean pupils are the least successful on average, though their results have been improving, and when compared with White British pupils of similar economic backgrounds, they achieve at a similar level.
- Not speaking English at home is only a short-lived handicap for most pupils – they commonly catch up by secondary school.
- Schools do impact on educational achievement. About 14 per cent of the incidence of low achievement is attributable to school quality. Good schools – those that are particularly effective in helping students to avoid low achievement – are not uniformly distributed across local authorities; they are concentrated in some local authorities more than others. There is considerable variability in school quality between local authorities.

The report indicates that the relationship between students' characteristics and low educational achievement is complex. For instance, the educational achievement of Black girls in receipt of free school meals is said to be significantly higher than that of Black boys in receipt of free school meals.

www.jrf.org.uk

ACTIVITY 6

1) List some of the reasons why being on low income (measured by qualifying for free school meals) might influence achievement in education.
2) Using the last section of the report on page 71 identify one reason why using the measure of free school meals does not show the whole picture of causes for low educational achievement.
3) The report states that there is considerable variability in school quality across regions. How might variations in school 'quality' influence educational achievement across a community?
4) Boys outnumber girls as low achievers in all ethnic groups. Suggest some possible reasons for the gender differences between boys and girls. Think about factors within a school, the individuals themselves and the influences from home backgrounds.

Factors which may influence educational experience/achievement are numerous and vary by region and from person to person. It could be argued that the three most influential factors other than an individual's ability and the school they go to are language used at home (both the accent and style of language as well as whether English is the first language used at home), household income and parental attitudes

Language

If English is not a person's first language or the first language used at their home they will face considerable difficulty compared to people using English as a first language. Many students go home to a different language to that used at school. Here limited parental help with homework and practice in English will be the two most obvious challenges.

Language is also variable among speakers of English as a first language. Different speech styles may mean some groups are better able to understand the teacher and the language of education and therefore achieve advantage over other students. For example teachers use complex language and jargon or language specific to schools and the subject being studied. If similar language is used at home then the student will be at a significant advantage over other households which may use less elaborate language and therefore be at a disadvantage.

Household income

Although all students have a right to free education, differences in income of the household often restricts chances in a number of ways. For example inadequate housing which is cold or cramped means many people turn out for school un-rested and less healthy and ready to learn. Also some households struggle to provide resources to buy revision guides and other such extras to help with school work.

Parents' attitude to education and schooling

Parents' experience of education and their approach to the school can have a major influence on achievement. What did your parents or older siblings achieve? And how does it impact on your motivation? The aspirations, self belief and focus of a student depend very much on the role model offered by their parents. Parental influence as support and guidance is also vital. Therefore in various ways parents have a major impact on students' learning, this is why governments and schools make so many efforts to encourage parents to get involved in the education of their children. Therefore variations in parental attitude and experience of education causes variations in achievement.

ACTIVITY 7

1) Taking each of the three factors above – language, household income and parents' attitude/experience try to write a short outline of how the three areas of ethnicity, social class and gender could be linked by the factors.

which makes the discrimination more difficult to manage. Facing homophobic discrimination at school for example, such as bullying, can cause significant impact on life chances.

Sexuality and life chances

www.eachaction.org.uk is an award winning website which aims to challenge homophobia and discrimination because of sexual orientation. The site offers a wide range of support, advice and fact sheets on issues facing gay and lesbian people. There are also various terms defined with useful links for further information. Also useful is the Directgov website www.direct.gov.uk which has fact sheets on sexuality and homosexuality.

The clear message from these and other sites is that gay and lesbian people face significant barriers to their life chances mainly due to prejudice and discrimination. Notice this theme links with the first topic where we explored prejudice and homophobia. We return again to this theme in topic 4 (issue 2, topic 1, page 00) in this chapter when we explore action dealing with direct and indirect discrimination.

www.eachaction.org.uk quotes data gathered by a survey of 18,000 gay and lesbian people in 2006, commissioned by Channel 4. The findings are outlined in the box on the right.

The specific difference between homophobic discrimination and other forms of discrimination is that it is a very personalised type of discrimination often carried out on young, vulnerable and often confused people facing identity dilemmas. The individual is facing challenges to their own personality

OUTRIGHT 2006 SURVEY

- 40 per cent of gay and lesbian people in the UK said they had experienced unacceptable discrimination because of their sexuality.

- The type of abuse 16 to 24 year olds are most likely to experience is verbal or physical abuse.

- Over half of the sample said they experienced verbal and physical abuse in the workplace from fellow workers and frequently from managers.

- Over 60 per cent of the sample said they had been targets for verbal and physical abuse on the streets.

- 64 per cent had faced verbal abuse and 35 per cent said they had suffered both verbal and physical abuse.

1) Suggest ways that facing homophobic bullying may affect an individual's or group's:
   • self-esteem
   • studies and success in school
   • friends and peer group (not just you but your friends may be facing difficulties because they are associated with a 'homo').

3 To what extent does poverty exist in Britain?

In this section we explore the following four themes:

• social distribution of poverty in Britain
• relative and absolute poverty
• explanations of the causes and consequences of poverty
• notions of underclass and poverty cycle.

Social distribution of poverty in Britain

In order to investigate **poverty** we must have a start point or basis upon which to measure whether people are in poverty or not. We must also explore what poverty is, for example what income do you require in order to maintain a lifestyle you consider matches your expectations? Some households have higher costs than others, for example a household with lots of children and dependents (for example a non-working disabled member) will have higher costs than a household with no children. However the former would qualify for more government benefits (such as child benefit and tax credit and disability benefit) than a childless couple.

We must also bear in mind that government spending on services, such as the health service and education, is something all households benefit from. Also paying taxes like VAT (value added tax) is something everyone has to do and thus affects every person the same if they buy something. For example, the VAT on a chocolate bar is paid by everyone who buys a chocolate bar regardless of income.

The graph below indicates one of the most frequently used measures of poverty – average household income. The preferred term the Government uses for poverty is low income.

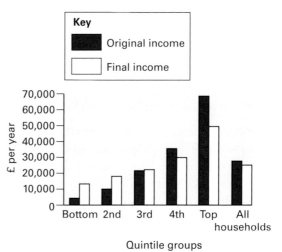

Average household income in the UK for 2005/6

1) From the graph shown above what happens to the right-hand bar for the bottom fifth?
2) What happens to the right-hand bar for the top fifth?
3) Using your answers to questions 1 and 2 what can you conclude about the Government's efforts to tax and redistribute wealth more evenly?
4) What is the average household income in the UK?

Some types of household gain more than others from this redistribution of wealth shown in the graph above. Retired households pay less in tax than they receive in benefits and so gain overall. Among non-retired households, single adult households with children also gain. Most other non-retired households pay more in tax than they receive in benefits. However households with children do relatively better than households without children due to cash benefits and benefits in kind (including health and education services).

Web action

Go to **www.ifs.org.uk/wheredoyoufitin**. On this site you will be able to measure your household income with that of the rest of the country. You will need details on household income from your parent/s and the amount they pay in council tax. The other questions relate to number of people in the household. When you have completed the questions your household income is plotted alongside that of the rest of the population and you can see at a glance where you fit in and how you compare.

Cash benefits, such as Income Support, Pension Credit, Child Benefit, Incapacity Benefit and the State Retirement Pension, play the largest part in reducing income inequality because they go predominantly to households with lower incomes. Cash benefits make up 61 per cent of gross income for the poorest fifth of households, 39 per cent for the next group and 2 per cent for the top fifth of households.

The graph below illustrates the percentage of people on household incomes below national average. If your household income falls below national average then your household is classed as a low-income household. Some of the low-income households are working households where one or both/all adults work but earn a wage which leaves their household below the national average income. Other households are non-working households because of unemployment or reliance on disability benefit or other benefits. Therefore being in a low-income household does not necessarily mean being unemployed. The proportion of households in rural areas which have below average earnings is higher than the proportion of households on below average wages in urban

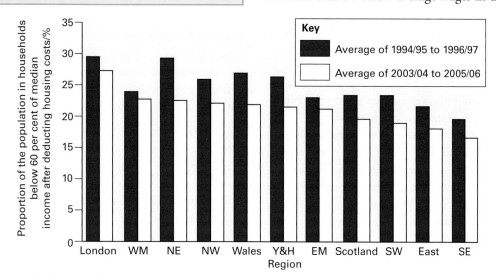

Regional distribution of low income

areas. In summary if you live in an urban area your wages are likely to be higher but it could be argued that your living expenses are also higher. Therefore using measures based on income must be done with caution because different areas have different costs of living.

ACTIVITY 2

1) From the graph on page 75 work out the average percentage of people living on low income in the UK.
2) Identify the area you live in and compare the percentage of people living on low income in your area to that of the national average. Is your area above or below the national average?
3) Which area has the highest decrease in percentage of people living on low income?

Web action

Go to **www.poverty.org.uk** and click on *rural England* then *view by age group* and click on *children*. What is the percentage of children living in low income families (poverty) in Britain?

Relative and absolute poverty

Investigating poverty and discussing the extent to which it exists involves identifying a definition of what poverty is. Many social researchers refer to types or levels of poverty. They refer to relative and absolute definitions of poverty. The debate is vital because what some consider to be poverty, others consider to be low income.

The disagreement about what poverty is leads to different views on a number of related factors, such as how to measure poverty, for example what should be used as a measure of whether someone is in poverty, should average household income be used as the Government does or should other factors, such as whether a person is able to afford a holiday once a year or whether they are able to choose where to go on holiday or whether they are able to buy what some call luxuries such as a TV to measure poverty? Given different measures of poverty we will find different views on how many people are in poverty.

Also, debate revolves around what comparisons should be made, should we compare our individual positions in the UK to the position of individual people in other countries? Should we think of poverty as lacking basics for survival such as shelter, clothing and food? Large numbers of people in less developed countries experience poverty to the extent that they face starvation; very few people experience this level of poverty in the UK. Others suggest we should disregard poverty as a term and refer to income difference where those on the lowest incomes are economically challenged but are not in poverty. It could be argued that the only people with a genuine claim to be in poverty are people sleeping on the street.

It is possible to use two broad models of defining poverty; absolute poverty and relative poverty. The two models give us a basis towards defining poverty and a working framework within which to measure poverty:

- absolute poverty – a lack of the very basics for healthy living – shelter, clothing, food and medicine
- relative poverty – possession of the basics for maintaining health but a lack of other resources to adequately participate in a given society. For example it could be claimed that a TV is vital to participate in today's society or a home computer with internet access.

Relative poverty allows a more varied understanding of poverty and offers a wider definition. If we use this wider definition the factors which cause poverty can be adapted to fit different societies or communities. For example a person living in a rural area may have specific difficulties travelling to local towns. This type of poverty is less of a problem in urban areas. However in urban areas difficulties arise, such as finding housing which is suitable or affordable, because the costs are often higher for renting accommodation. Also different age groups experience poverty in different ways. Children for example may live in a poor household which is poorly heated with little food but they go to school on the free bus and have free school lunches in a heated school. In contrast some elderly people may find poverty hits them because they are unable to heat their home adequately or cannot get a bus because the bus stop is a long way away or they may feel isolated because few people visit. Therefore the definition of poverty is a very subjective and debated issue.

The Government prefers to use a relative definition of poverty (rather than absolute) because few people in UK face absolute poverty other than those experiencing acute problems, such as sleeping on the streets. Given the government uses the relative model it prefers to use the term low-income families because this allows more variety of individual and personal circumstances to be considered.

Explanations of the causes and consequences of poverty

When exploring poverty, researchers and policy makers tend to focus on two main themes.

- What causes poverty in the first place. Here social researchers and policy makers are seeking to understand why poverty exists and

therefore can offer strategies which attempt to stop poverty at source.
- What effects poverty has for individuals, that is the consequences of poverty.

Dividing poverty into these two main themes allows social researchers and policy makers to develop strategies to tackle the worst effects of poverty.

Causes of poverty

The views on what causes poverty can be placed into two broad categories – first the structural model and second the individual behaviour model.

Structural model

The structural model argues that causes of poverty are beyond the control of individuals. The general cause is a lack of effort by society to solve the problem of poverty. The majority of the wealthy population is not willing to pay more taxes in order to provide resources and jobs for communities which are suffering decline. Frankly the problem is too costly.

Others who adopt the structural model point out that some areas have severe social and economic problems, such as high unemployment or decayed housing, which mean individuals and communities are faced with huge difficulties to overcome in order to avoid poverty. Areas where the main industry has recently declined often take generations to resolve. For example old mining regions in West Yorkshire where the vast majority of the workforce found themselves unemployed because of pit closure or rural regions where agricultural employment has declined leaving few opportunities for work. In regions with such extreme difficulties poverty becomes part of life and getting out of poverty for many is a long process.

Decayed housing is an indicator of poverty

ACTIVITY 3

1) The middle house in the photograph above seems occupied, the others are boarded up to stop intruders. In what ways can this image be seen as depicting poverty?
2) Make a list of some of the difficulties the residents may face to avoid poverty when living in the building and area such as the one shown in the image.
3) Suggest some strategies local and national governments could adopt as an attempt to break the decline of communities such as this.

Individual behaviour model

The individual behaviour model agrees with the structural model to an extent by accepting that some regions do pose difficulties for individuals; however this model also differs from the structural model. The individual behaviour model argues that the individuals themselves are more often than not the cause of poverty and furthermore, the individuals themselves are the solution to poverty.

The individual behaviour model argues that those individuals who stay in poverty do so because they have failed to adopt appropriate attitudes to avoid poverty and also the individuals have poor approaches to resolving the problems and challenges, in particular avoiding them in the first place. This individual behaviour model believes a culture has formed over generations which creates and breeds a cycle of poverty passed on from generation to generation. This model can be applied to some regions in the UK more than others.

The individual behaviour model can apply to both the causes of poverty and the consequences of poverty because to the individual behaviour model the attitudes of the poor are both the cause of the poverty in the first place and the culture which develops as a consequence of the poverty. Breaking the cause of a poverty cycle requires changing the culture of the poor themselves. We explore this cycle of poverty and the term associated with it, '**underclass**', later in the topic.

Consequences of poverty

Shelter, a charity that tackles homelessness and poverty, presents statistics that make grim reading. The details on page 79 indicate that the consequences of poverty are extensive – even in a country as wealthy as the UK.

Poverty statistics for the UK

- More than one million children in Britain live in bad housing – enough to fill the cities of Edinburgh, Bath and Manchester.
- Today, nearly 100,000 households in England will have woken up in temporary accommodation – more than twice as many as in 1997.
- Nearly one in ten children in England lives in overcrowded housing – enough to fill the new Wembley Stadium ten times over.
- Over 260,000 households in England are on waiting lists for properties with three or more bedrooms. Only about 5,000 social rented homes of this size are built each year.
- Black and minority ethnic households are six times more likely than white households to be overcrowded.
- More than one million homes in Britain are unfit for human habitation – and yet more than 90 per cent of these are occupied.
- One in 12 children in Britain are more likely to develop diseases such as bronchitis, TB, or asthma, because of bad housing.
- Homeless children living in bed and breakfast hotels are twice as likely to be admitted to A&E with burns and scalding.
- On average, homeless children miss out on a quarter of their schooling.

www.england.shelter.org.uk

The article below highlights some of the problems poverty brings and gives specific focus on children who can be regarded as the innocent victims of poverty and the people who suffer the most and in greatest numbers. The article also shows the divisive consequences poverty can have on communities, in this case London.

The consequences of poverty for the children and community of London

Towards the end of the first decade of this century London's is a tale of two cities. One is a rich economic powerhouse that is home to big businesses making billions, a vibrant and fashionable world capital to which millions of tourists flock each year. The other is a place where more than 600,000 children grow up in poverty, where parents go without so that they can feed and clothe their children.

It's shocking to think that in a city as rich and prosperous as ours, poverty can be so prevalent. In Outer London 30 per cent of children live below the poverty line, while in Inner London this rockets to more than 52 per cent.

Right across the capital, there are thousands of children who are malnourished, in poor health or living in squalid housing because they are in poverty. Thousands more miss out on things that others take for granted like a warm winter coat, going on school trips or having friends round to play.

London also has a high proportion of the groups of children who are at the very greatest risk of poverty, namely black and minority ethnic children, children of lone parents and children in large families.

Poverty seriously damages children's life chances and opportunities. While school standards overall are up, the poorest children who are entitled to free school meals are still half as likely to get five good GCSEs as those who are not. All too often today's poor child becomes tomorrow's poor parent, so it makes both moral and economic sense to tackle poverty.

Tackling Child Poverty in London, **North West London Newspapers, 2006 by Kate Green, Chief Executive of the Child Poverty Action Group and a member of the London Child Poverty Commission.**

www.cpag.org.uk

Read the article on page 79.
1) Briefly define the term 'poverty line'.
2) List the consequences of poverty for children identified in the article.
3) Referring to the article and your own ideas explain how poverty might be a cause of division within the London community.

Web action

Go to **www.londoncouncils.gov.uk** and select *London Child Poverty Commission*, then *poverty the facts*. Here you can compare London to other areas of the country. Also there is detail on the specific concerns over poverty faced by black and minority ethnic groups in London.

Notions of underclass and poverty cycle

When exploring underclass and the poverty cycle we can refer to the two models we examined earlier in this topic – the individual behaviour model and the structural model.

As the individual behaviour model which we explored earlier suggests, lifestyle is blamed for the continued existence of poverty. Here the suggestion is that individual behaviour is in large part the cause of their poverty.

Some of the attitudes and behaviours referred to by this model include poor attitudes to education, negative and fatalistic outlook on futures, disregard for the law, sexual promiscuity, dependence on welfare for income and irresponsible parenting. These attitudes and behaviours effectively place an individual behind self-constructed barriers to their chances of lifting themselves out of poverty.

Such a set of attitudes or values runs counter to mainstream society and merely causes the individual and sometimes whole communities holding these values to be socially excluded.

The term underclass is used by the individual behaviour model to refer to a group in society now deeply entrenched in their culture of poverty, unemployment and poor approach to education and the law. Some go so far as to say that an underclass is a lawless group unwilling to work – a stubborn segment of society which generation after generation is increasingly isolating itself from the normal values of society and living in increasingly deprived communities.

In contrast the structural model sees the cycle of poverty to be a trap and an underclass to be a product of society not of the individual cultures of one group or another. The structural model prefers to avoid over-generalised observations and suggests that the individual causes and experiences of poverty are different for everyone. The initial causes of poverty are more often beyond the individual's control. For example not finding work or growing up in a household with only one income and few resources. The attitudes of individuals may become fatalistic when facing problems associated with poverty but they are changeable through schools and support systems such as Sure Start. The poverty cycle which causes an underclass of neglected communities can be broken if resources and support systems are put in place to allow the individual to lift themselves out of poverty and avoid a depressed culture from emerging.

Web action

Go to **www.timesonline.co.uk/tol/news/uk/article438356.ece** or search *The Times* archive for the article 'Meet the "Neets"' by Robert Winnett.

This article looks at the Neets: '**n**ot in **e**mployment, **e**ducation or **t**raining', an underclass in the UK which is thought to have a marked impact on crime, public health and antisocial behaviour.

1) Why are the 'Neets' supposedly going to cost the tax payer £15 billion by 2060?

2) Has the author adopted a structural or individual behaviour model of causes and consequences of poverty? Explain your answer.

3) What reasons do you think Murray has for suggesting that an underclass is caused by unmarried mothers? Explain to what extent you agree or disagree with his view.

4) Explain what Murray means when he says "these people have never been socialised".

ISSUE 2: HOW CAN DISCRIMINATION AND DISADVANTAGE BE REDUCED?

In this section we explore the following three topics:

- the problem of defining equality in a diverse and changing society
- what steps can governments take to reduce discrimination and disadvantage and what policies have been implemented?
- how effective have these policies been?

4 What steps can governments take to reduce discrimination and disadvantage?

The problem of defining equality in a changing and diverse society

Equality does not mean everyone should be treated in the same way. Equality means ensuring as far as possible that everyone is treated fairly and has equal opportunity to participate fully in society and does not suffer discrimination. Specific groups face different types of discrimination – gender, ethnicity, disability, sexual preference, social class and age – this discrimination causes inequality. In a diverse society the idea of equality means to value and celebrate our differences rather than favour one group or identity over another and socially isolate people who seem 'different'.

For example our society has changed in approach to disability. Language to describe disabilities has changed, laws and policies have changed and images on television and the mass media have changed. In such a changed society, perception of difference changes and recognition of difference includes a wider range of identities. Once understanding of equality develops and we promote greater diversity we extend laws and policies to protect the rights of all citizens of an increasingly diverse range.

In a complex society challenging discrimination becomes increasingly far-ranging. Some people see the increased expansion of **anti-discrimination policy** and law as political correctness going too far. Others see it as a reflection of a healthy and mature society which promotes the inclusion of all citizens.

Equal opportunities policy extends to all people. All citizens are protected from abuse and can expect fair treatment. There are however various different groups in society that face specific issues that limit the extent to which they are treated equally (fairly). In these cases, specific laws and policies have been introduced in order that discrimination and unfairness can be challenged.

We can explore the notion that equality does not mean everyone being treated in the same way by applying it to the context of school inclusion policies.

In order to promote equality in schools a student with recognised learning difficulties and a student without recognised learning difficulties should not be treated the same way at school. Being treated the same way will not meet the learning needs of both students. A person with a learning difficulty, such as dyslexia, has specific learning needs required to manage the condition. For example the student may need different colour paper, be allowed extra time in an exam and to spend time with a learning support worker to assist with reading and accessing dense texts.

Such measures are not needed for a student without specific learning needs although of course every individual learns in different ways and each student is unique. Thus in order to meet the rights of both the students to participate fully in the education system, students need treating in distinct ways that meet their individual needs.

Equality therefore in this case requires that people are treated differently in order to promote inclusion (at school). Being treated

differently allows the celebration of all people's achievements and so meets the right of all students to access the mainstream school curriculum. It is however the case that some people's learning needs are so profound that they need specialist schools because mainstream schools are unable to provide the necessary resources to cope.

ACTIVITY 1

1) Explore your school's equality policy and examine how your school or another school seeks to treat all students fairly and meet the needs of all learners where possible. You could examine the gifted and talented policies or inclusion policies for students with learning difficulties.

Anti-discrimination policies in relation to gender, ethnicity, disability, sexual preference, social class and age

We now move on to examine some policies and strategies employed by organisations to tackle discrimination. We look at a non-government organisation and two examples of local government policy designed to tackle discrimination and promote equality.

Many organisations exist with the intention of promoting and protecting equality and challenging discrimination. For example the Network for Black Professionals (**www.nbm.org.uk/news.asp**) is an organisation set up to promote the interests of black and minority peoples' representation in professional and managerial positions. Equality is increased by organisations such as this which can take the following actions to advance equality and challenge inequality and discrimination.

- Target professional and managerial roles in organisations seeking to promote and encourage the appointment of black and minority people to managerial posts. The idea is that if more black and minority people get managerial jobs and roles in organisations then the interests of these minority groups can directly shape the running of the organisation. In this way **institutionalised racism** and discrimination is directly undermined.
- Increase the number of black and minority groups in managerial positions to advance equality and to challenge cultures of discrimination because a more positive image of black and minority groups is presented. More positive role models may change perceptions and challenge negative stereotypes held by fellow employees or the general public. This will then also provide encouragement to young black and minority people to raise their aspirations.

- Advise organisations using specialist knowledge and suggestions on how to introduce equality policies and how the **equal opportunities legislation** should be interpreted.

ACTIVITY 2

Read the case study below. This activity asks you to reflect on how power can challenge inequality and discrimination, not just in the workplace, but in the wider society. It also illustrates ways that power can be achieved by BME groups.

1) What does the chief executive mean by 'releasing the untapped talent ...'?
2) Black and minority ethnic groups make up over 9 per cent of the population. To what extent are black and minority groups proportionately represented among college principals?
3) Evaluate the view of the Network of Black Professionals (NBP) that the best way to promote black and minority interests is by increasing their power and representation in the boardrooms.

CASE STUDY: Executive makes the business case for corporate social responsibility

The Network's Chief Executive Robin Landman today presented the business case for realising the untapped talent of the UK Black Minority Ethnic (BME) communities.

Speaking at the prestigious Corporate Social Responsibility 'Social Footprints, 2007' conference at the ICC in Birmingham, Robin outlined the global and national challenges facing the developed economies of Europe and the social and economic costs resulting from the exclusion of BME communities young and old from the 'good society'... Robin spoke of the 'untapped talent pool' in BME communities and the opportunities that lay in engaging with younger and dynamic minority communities who will occupy such a significant proportion in the growth of the UK workforce in the next decade.

The position of colleges today where only 8 Principals (2 per cent of all Principals) are drawn from BME communities contrasts with the national student population of nearly 20 per cent, implying a requirement for 75 BME college leaders.

www.nbm.org.uk

Local government can agree policy which puts equality at the centre of their activities and these policies require that equality applies to all members of the community and any decisions need to be made in the context of an equal opportunities context.

Below is an example of one local government's policy. Notice that it defines equality at the very start to ensure all are clear as to what definition or model of equality is being used.

ACTIVITY 3

Read the case study below.

1) Identify from the case study below the benefits of equality and diversity for both employees of the council and the citizens as consumers of Nottingham City Council services.

CASE STUDY: Nottingham City Council

What is equality and diversity?

Equality is about making sure people are treated fairly and given fair chances. Equality is not about treating everyone in the same way, but it recognises that their needs are met in different ways.

Equality focuses on those areas covered by the law, namely the key areas of race, gender, disability and, more recently, religion or belief and sexual orientation. Age will also be covered soon. A recent amendment to the Race Relations Act adds a duty for us to actively promote race equality and avoid race discrimination, by acting before it happens.

People must not be unfairly discriminated against because of any of these factors and we must all contribute to creating a positive workplace environment where discriminatory practices and discrimination no longer happen.

– And diversity?

Diversity is about valuing individual difference. So 'diversity' is much more than just a new word for equality. A diversity approach aims to recognise, value and manage difference to enable all employees to contribute and realise their full potential. Diversity challenges us to recognise and value all sorts of differences in order to make the Council a better place for everyone to work.

Why are equality and diversity important?

Diversity is also about recognising that our customers come from different backgrounds. If we welcome diversity as colleagues, value each other and treat each other fairly, we will work better together. In doing so we will provide a better service to the people of Nottingham.

It will help our customers to approach us and use our services if we have a diverse workforce that feels comfortable with and understands their different needs. So diversity will also contribute to improving the services we provide.

www.nottinghamcity.gov.uk

Below is another example of a council policy intended to promote equality of opportunity. It is a broad policy which challenges discrimination by promoting inclusion.

ACTIVITY 4

Read the case study below.

1) In one or two paragraphs discuss how trust, equality and tolerance are promoted by the council.

CASE STUDY: Armagh City and District Council equality scheme summary 'improving the quality of life for all'

Mutual trust, esteem, equality of outcome, tolerance
Council Mission Statement

Armagh City and District Council has adopted the following mission statement:

'By 2020, Armagh City and District will be an inclusive, progressive, outward looking area with a vibrant and diverse economy offering a high quality of life, within an attractive physical environment.'

Our equality duty

In order to fulfil our mission statement, we are legally required in carrying out all our functions, powers and duties relating to Northern Ireland, to have due regard to the need to promote equality of opportunity under Section 75 of the Northern Ireland Act 1998:

- between persons of different religious belief, political opinion, racial group, age, marital status or sexual orientation
- between men and women generally
- between persons with a disability and persons without and
- between persons with dependants and persons without.

(The above groups are commonly known as the Section 75 Categories.)

In addition, without prejudice to its obligation above, Armagh City and District Council shall, in carrying out its functions relating to Northern Ireland, have regard to the desirability of promoting good relations between persons of:

- different religious belief
- political opinion
- racial group.

This will:

- increase transparency and openness in decision making
- improve understanding of the Council's services and policies
- assist in promoting social inclusion, target disadvantage and promote equality of opportunity and good relations.

www.armagh.gov.uk

ROLE PLAY

Imagine you are the human resource manager for Armagh City and District Council responsible for equality among the workforce. The chief executive of the council has asked you to write a report following the two complaints listed below that were made by employees of the council.

- Accessing the training room is not possible for disabled employees because wheelchair users have no way of getting to the upper office since there is no lift.

- Some female employees have complained about sexist language used by some male employees towards some women employees.

The chief executive wants a short report of no more than 200 words which can be distributed and understood across all sectors of the workforce. The report should say why the two complaints are discrimination, why it is unlawful and what should be done to tackle it. In your report refer directly to the Armagh City and District Council's equality scheme.

ACTIVITY 4

1) Read the role play above and then carry out the task requested by your chief executive.

Dealing with direct and indirect discrimination

Earlier in the chapter (pages 58–65) we explored discrimination more in terms of defining and illustrating what it means. Here we explore challenges to discrimination by focusing on direct and indirect forms of discrimination and how they can be guarded against.

Direct discrimination

Direct discrimination occurs when in a comparable situation someone is treated less favourably because of their racial or ethnic origin, religion or belief, disability, age or sexual orientation. For example a job advertisement which states that men need not apply clearly and deliberately excludes some members of society. Equally a shop worker/owner cannot refuse to serve a person because they are a woman or of a particular racial appearance. This type of discrimination is usually easier to identify and is rare because employers are well aware of and well advised on the meaning of direct discrimination.

Direct discrimination is not just something employers have to guard against when, for example, advertising jobs. It was common in the 1980s for public houses (pubs) and shops to place signs in their windows saying 'no van dwellers'. These signs were aimed at travellers (gypsies) and were implying that people who lived in caravans were potential trouble makers and would not be served or allowed on the premises. Such signs are directly discriminating against a group of people based on the assumption and generalised view that the travellers were trouble makers. Such practice is unlawful because it treats one group less favourably than another without justification. An organisation can ban an individual for specific action but not whole groups who are innocent unless found guilty.

Indirect discrimination

Indirect discrimination can exist which is more subtle and occurs as an unintended result of actions. For example a job advertisement could state that people applying must be able to work until late evening (8p.m. for example). In this case the employer may want longer working hours and some people will be willing and able to accept this. It is however less likely that a woman will be able to apply for this job because it is reasonable to assume that women are most likely to have childcare responsibilities and so are probably less able to meet the job advertisement specification. Consequently women are being treated less favourably than men. However this is not directly stated in the advert but is an indirect result of the advert. Hence indirect discrimination.

Exceptions where discrimination is allowed/justified

There are exceptions where employers are allowed to directly discriminate in favour of one group over another if they make a reasonable case. For example an employer may need female employees in a women's shelter. Here it is acceptable to discriminate against men and stop them applying by stating only women should apply. Since the role focuses specifically on issues affecting women men would not be suitable. In a shelter supporting women fleeing domestic violence, doing so more often than not from violent men, a male presence in the shelter may well be perceived as threatening to vulnerable women.

It is also possible to advertise a role to only a specific ethnic or racial group because some organisations may have a role specifically focusing on aspects of an ethnic group.

Within the workplace some activity may be necessary to meet specific needs of some groups of employees. For example training directed specifically towards women or a specific age or ethnic group. In this case it may be necessary to offer training which is not open to all groups because there are specific issues the training wishes to focus upon.

Web action

Search online newspapers for recent examples of individuals winning or losing claims for discrimination/flexible hours. To get started, you could search the *Guardian's* online archive for the story 'House manager wins claim over flexible work' by Rachel Williams, 21 December 2007, which describes a case about an employer refusing a request to allow flexible working hours.

1) Describe the type of discrimination found in your example or examples: is it direct or indirect?

2) Which organisations are involved when people go to court over discrimination?

Discrimination and human rights

Discrimination can also occur against our human rights. Where a person's human rights are abused the Human Rights Act protects citizens and offers a framework of legal safeguards. Here discrimination is challenged by international law and there are increasing numbers of citizens using this framework to challenge discrimination. Chapter 3 looks at Human Rights and the Human Rights Act and how citizens can use it.

5 What policies and bodies have been instituted?

The UK Government has set out a number of policies in an attempt to challenge **disadvantage** and discrimination faced by some vulnerable groups in society.

In this section we use a casestudy approach so that policies can be considered in context:

- the unemployed – new deal
- low paid workers – minimum wage
- equal opportunities legislation
- Equality and Human Rights Commission.

The Government has set up a large organisation responsible for promoting equality and challenging social exclusion. The Neighbourhood Renewal Unit (formerly the Social Exclusion Unit) has responsibility for a number of New Deal policies which focus attention towards specific groups in society.

New Deal

New Deal systems are designed to focus resources mainly to support individuals in finding work and training programmes. Benefits are linked to individuals' efforts to find work (the deal) such that benefits are in effect tied to a responsibility the individual has to making efforts to change their own circumstances. The Government therefore is offering the deal that if an individual makes the effort to find work they will get support, both financial and professional – no effort leads to withdrawal of benefit payments.

GROUPS TARGETED BY THE NEW-DEAL SYSTEM

- New Deal for Young People
- New Deal 25 plus
- New Deal 50 plus
- New Deal for Lone Parents
- New Deal for Disabled People
- New Deal for Partners
- New Deal for Musicians

An example of a New Deal programme for young people is shown below.

Is New Deal for Young People for me?

If you are aged between 18 and 24 and have had a continuous claim to Jobseekers' Allowance for six months or more, then this is the New Deal for you. In some cases you may be invited to join the programme earlier if both you and your New Deal Personal Adviser decide that this is the best course of action for you.

What is New Deal for Young People?

The New Deal for Young People is a mandatory (compulsory) programme of help designed to address the problems of long-term unemployment in 18–24 year olds. The aim of New Deal for Young People is to improve young people's chances of finding and keeping a job.

Whilst on the programme, participants will receive the continued help and support from a New Deal Personal Adviser whose main aim is to meet your needs of finding and keeping a job, or becoming self-employed. New Deal for Young People gives you a chance to re-look at your situation, take the skills and experience you may have already and build on them to create better opportunities for work.

www.jobcentreplus.gov.uk

ACTIVITY 1

1) Reflect on the age groups for the New Deals listed on page 88 and identify some of the different issues the contrasting age groups may face in returning to work and coming off benefit. In so doing you are exploring the reasons for targeted support focused towards particular groups.

ACTIVITY 2

1) Identify the ways in which the New Deal programme acts to support young people.
2) In your view to what extent does the New Deal programme seem likely to be successful in all cases? Explain your answer.

Web action

Go to **www.jobcentreplus.gov.uk** and select the *New Deal link*. Find out more detail about the New Deal for 18–24 year olds by selecting *New Deal for 18-24 year olds* and then the link *more information about New Deal for 18–24*. What are the six main responsibilities of the New Deal personal advisor?
On the same site select New Deal 25 plus and identify what is meant by 'intensive activity period'.

Minimum wage

Most workers in the UK are entitled to a national minimum rate of pay. A national minimum wage was introduced on 1 April 2009. The law stated that a minimum rate of pay should apply to three different age groups. There is one rate for 16–17 year old workers,

one for those aged 18–21 and a third rate for those aged 22 or above. The minimum wage rate is reviewed in October every year which means it may increase or perhaps decrease depending on the decision of the review body. The rates have increased every year since 1999.

Many employers complained to the Government that a minimum wage would push their wage bills up so that they would lose profits and even go out of business. However the Government went ahead and introduced the law despite the protests from some employers but it did allow some exceptions, such as workers in catering organisations and the hotel businesses.

There is a set minimum wage rate for the following categories, by age.

- Those above school leaving age (sixteen years) but below eighteen. Note if you are sixteen you are not classed as a school leaver until September of the year you turned sixteen.
- Workers aged 18–21, 'development rate'.
- Workers aged 22 or older, 'full adult rate'.

Web action

Go to **www.direct.gov.uk** and key in *national minimum wage* into the search bar and carry out the following tasks.
1) Find out the rates of the national minimum wage for each of the categories listed above.
2) Some groups of workers do not qualify for the national minimum wage. From the same web page identify the six types of worker that are not entitled.
3) In what ways do pay arrangements for agricultural workers differ to other workers?

Equal opportunities legislation

Legislation

By far the most widespread government role in the promotion of equality are laws and regulations designed to ensure that access to rights is promoted for all citizens and that discrimination where possible is challenged.

Laws, for example the Equality Act 2006, extended the idea of equal opportunities to include religion or belief and sexual orientation, summarised below. The law also set up the **Equality and Human Rights Commission** which is a body intended to support organisations in advising on how the law affects them. It is also an independent organisation whose observations and opinions are respected and valued on, for example, social development events taking shape in policy and elsewhere. The commission's role is largely educational.

Equality Act 2006

An Act to make provision for the establishment of the Commission for Equality and Human Rights; to dissolve the Equal Opportunities Commission, the Commission for Racial Equality and the Disability Rights Commission; to make provision about discrimination on grounds of religion or belief; to enable provision to be made about discrimination on grounds of sexual orientation; to impose duties relating to sex discrimination on persons performing public functions; to amend the Disability Discrimination Act 1995; and for connected purposes.

From the White Paper, 16 February 2006
www.opsi.gov.uk

In October 2007 the Equality and Human Right Commission set out different legal contexts for different social groups.

Equality and discrimination

Age

It is unlawful for your age to be the cause of less favourable treatment in your workplace or in vocational training. An employer must ensure it avoids discrimination because of your age. There are sections of the law which relate to the under 50s and the over 50s. The older people may find they are indirectly discriminated against because an employer decides to make all part-time posts redundant. This is indirectly discriminating against older people because older people are more likely to be part-time.

Religion and belief

Your religion or belief, or that of somebody else, should not interfere with your right to be treated fairly at work, at school, in shops or while accessing public services such as health care and housing. For example schools and employers must make reasonable efforts to accommodate your religious or belief needs, such as days off for religious ceremonies.

Disability

If you have a physical or mental impairment, you have specific rights that protect you against discrimination. Employers and service providers are obliged to make adjustments for you. For example that there are adequate facilities such that your disability does not stop you doing your job.

Gender

Women, men and transgender people should not be treated unfairly because of their gender, because they are married or because they are raising a family.

Race

Wherever you were born, wherever your parents came from, whatever the colour of your skin, you have a right to be treated fairly.

Sexual orientation

Whether you are gay, lesbian, bisexual or straight should not put you at a disadvantage.

www.equalityhumanrights.com

Web action

Go to **www.equalityhumanrights.com** and select *equality and discrimination* to explore more detail on each of the categories above. For example in what areas do the laws apply? What exceptions are there for each category which means discrimination may be possible?

Government bodies designed to develop equal opportunities

In this section we focus on one specific but large organisation called the Equality and Human Rights Commission (EHRC). EHRC is a new organisation set up in 2007 which brings together various already existing bodies which were originally set up to challenge discrimination and promote equal opportunities, including:

• Commission for Racial Equality (CRE)
• Disability Rights Commission (DRC)
• Equal Opportunities Commission (EOC).

The EHRC also takes responsibility for groups which did not previously have commissions to promote their interests, such as gay people and different age groups, such as the elderly.

The EHRC provides legal advice to companies on how best to promote equal opportunities in the workplace. It also offers legal advice and support for employees who feel they have been bullied or discriminated against by an organisation or an employee. The commission has a vital role in informing the public of issues about equal opportunities by publishing reports and investigations into matters of equality and discrimination. In March 2009 the commission published a report which called for changes to the law on maternity and paternity conditions using discrimination against women as the basis for its argument.

For example in April 2009 the commission published a report into the way women employees in the financial sector of the economy – 'the city' – were being treated unfairly. The report found that average women's earnings were 50 per cent less than those of males in the same line of work. It also found that women find great difficulty securing promotion to the top jobs. Although the numbers of men and women in the financial sector are about equal, only 11 per cent of the top managerial posts are held by women. The findings of the report were published in the media and the Government has agreed to introduce measures to secure more equality and challenge discrimination in the financial sector.

The commission also supports legal cases of individuals. An example in April 2009 involved a black veterinary worker who was found to have been treated unfairly by his employer because of his race. The employer was told to pay costs of £50,000 to the individual victim. The case was heard at a tribunal where the commission was able to legally support the individual. The case was also interesting because part of the complaint involved the individual claiming he was victimised because he had brought a previous case to a tribunal in the past. The case illustrates the power and influence of the EHRC.

Web action

Go to **www.equalityhumanrights.com** and select *current projects* and explore the most recent activity of the commission. The site also includes distinct themes for the different countries in the UK and specific news events.

Vision, mission and priorities

Our vision

- The Equality and Human Rights Commission aims to reduce inequality, eliminate discrimination, strengthen good relations between people, and promote and protect human rights.

- The commission challenges prejudice and disadvantage, and promotes the importance of human rights.

- The commission enforces equality legislation on age, disability, gender, race, religion or belief, sexual orientation or transgender status, and encourages compliance with the Human Rights Act.

- In order to bring about effective change, the commission uses influence and authority to ensure that equality and human rights remain at the top of agendas for government and employers, media and society. We will campaign for social change and justice.

- Acting directly and by fostering partnerships at local, regional and national levels, the commission stimulates debate on equality and human rights.

- The commission gives advice and guidance to businesses, the voluntary and public sectors, and also to individuals.

- Developing an evidence-based understanding of the causes and effects of inequality for people across Britain, the commission will be an authoritative voice for reform.

Our priorities

- To build a credible and independent commission – The Equality and Human Rights Commission will be a robust and flexible organisation with an open and friendly public face. We will offer effective advice and complainant services. We will create a strong body of research for our work and an inclusive network of partners and champions.

- To target key equality battlegrounds – The Equality and Human Rights Commission will create a clear map of key workplace challenges, an ambitious response to the Discrimination Law Review, a comprehensive assessment of public service fulfilment of the positive duties and a programme of authoritative 'pathfinder' publications, preparing for our first 'state of the nation' report.

- To improve life chances and reduce inequalities – The Equality and Human Rights Commission will target the use of our legal powers swiftly and efficiently; we will launch a major, long-term campaign against prejudice, particularly engaging young people and a major campaign against hate crime. We will also undertake a drive to support independent advocacy for disadvantaged groups.

- To promote new understanding of the equality and human rights culture – the Equality and Human Rights Commission will put in progress a comprehensive human rights training programme for staff and partners and a grants programme promoting local human rights and good relations. We will also aim for leadership of the intellectual agenda, through lecture series and public and private debates.

www.equalityhumanrights.com

6 How effective have these policies been?

Challenging actions is complex and whether actions are discriminatory is open to interpretation. Despite good guidance and extensive examples of how laws apply there are still areas where indirect discrimination occurs without individuals being aware or where perhaps an employer may be careful to hide their discrimination.

Although actions may be difficult to alter, people's attitudes or prejudices are even more difficult to challenge or change. For example an employer may be well aware of the legal responsibilities but may be unwilling to change their prejudiced views and as a result find a way to avoid or get round the law. It must be noted that laws do slowly change society's views and people adapt following the laws bedding down. For example people are willing now to respect the role of women in most if not all areas of the workforce more so than was the case perhaps as little as ten years ago. This is not to say that prejudice no longer exists, but they are less likely to be so fixed and widespread throughout society. Such changes have in part their base in changes to the law as well as social and cultural changes.

Thus laws are less effective in changing prejudice, although they are more effective in challenging direct discriminatory actions. Similarly because it is less clear cut, indirect discrimination is less effectively challenged than direct discrimination.

We must recognise the extensive successes that anti-discrimination policies and laws have achieved. Since the introduction of discrimination laws there can be no doubt that citizens are now far more effectively protected in society and are as a result able to participate more fully in it. The cases illustrated in topics 4 and 5 indicate the changed culture of society towards discrimination, both in terms of understanding it and in challenging it. The various laws have promoted equal pay, challenged sex, age, racial and disability discrimination highly effectively and most recently have addressed issues of discrimination on grounds of sexual orientation.

Despite the notable successes and advancements brought about through anti-discrimination law many argue there is a long way to go before society can be seen as equal for all citizens and many argue the laws do not go far enough. Below are three case studies which indicate ways in which the law to some people does not go far enough.

This case study on page 94 is intended to show how the Government can be held to account by the equalities commission. The article indicates that the Government's plans for promoting anti-discrimination policies are welcome but do not go far enough.

ACTIVITY 1

Read the case study on page 94.

1) Identify some reasons why Mithran Samuel believes that bodies setting their own priorities may lead to neglect of some groups.
2) Define what is meant by 'entrenched inequalities'.
3) Identify and describe some 'entrenched inequalities' present in some organisations.
4) Why do you think the commission argues that by making equality standards 'voluntary' and not compulsory will mean it will 'fail to reverse entrenched inequalities'?

CASE STUDY: New equality commission slams government green paper

The new single equalities watchdog has made sweeping criticisms of government plans to reform anti-discrimination law in its first major statement on the issue. The Equality and Human Rights Commission made several objections to the Government's green paper on discrimination law – the precursor to a planned single equality act, designed to simplify existing legislation.

It followed predecessor bodies the Commission for Racial Equality, the Disability Rights Commission and Equal Opportunities Commission in criticising plans to reform existing duties on public bodies to promote race, disability and gender equality, under a single duty. The duties have proved powerful tools, including on social care. For instance, the CRE took enforcement action against the Department of Health for failing to comply with its duty to assess the race equality impact of a number of policies, including the Mental Health Act 2007.

But the Government proposed ditching requirements for bodies to have 'due regard to equality' in all they do – effectively removing the need for equality impact assessments. Instead, they would have to set their own priority objectives on race, gender and disability. The EHRC said the proposals would marginalise equality issues, adding: 'There is a real risk that less popular issues, such as discrimination faced by gypsies and Travellers, trans-gendered people or people with mental health difficulties, may never be a priority.'

It also backed extending the duty to the other three equality areas, age, religion and sexual orientation, something the green paper does not commit to.

The commission also said the Government's plan to issue only voluntary equality standards for the private sector, to tackle issues such as disabled people's low rates of employment, would fail to reverse entrenched inequalities. The EHRC called for 'limited compulsory measures', including making companies publish 'self-portraits' of their employment practices and devise improvement plans.

It also backed extending the ban on discrimination in the provision of goods and services to age, which the Government remains ambivalent on despite similar bans applying to the other five equality areas. Help the Aged's head of public affairs, Kate Jopling, said existing measures had failed to tackle discrimination in the provision of social care and health, making such a ban vital. She added: 'It's very good the commission has come out strongly against watering down the public sector duties.'

Mithran Samuel, *Community Care*, www.communitycare.co.uk

For some people the law has the wrong focus and equality is not being addressed because of a culture over generations of favouring one group over another. In the case study described below, the issue for the Fathers 4 Justice group is that the law favours mothers over fathers.

CASE STUDY: Blueprint for family law in the twenty-first century

The F4J [Fathers for Justice] *Blueprint For Family Law In The 21st Century* document is available to all registered supporters of Fathers 4 Justice. The document outlines the core principles of a new framework for the family law industry and a proposed Bill of Rights for the Family.

The Blueprint provides a foundation upon which a truly fair, just, open and equitable system of family law can be based. A foundation of rights intertwined with responsibilities, built for the twenty-first century that genuinely puts children first.

Fathers 4 Justice proposes three strategies to reduce conflict for children and their families in contact disputes and rebuild public confidence in the discredited family justice system:

Early interventions and mandatory mediation

Before couples seek legal recourse, the Government must recognise that *all* couples should be bound to enter into mandatory mediation, with appropriately trained mediators.

Presumption of contact and shared parenting

The best parent is both parents. The starting point after separation should be to maintain where possible what the status quo was before separation. Children currently have no right in law to see their parents. The principle of shared parenting creates a level playing field where conflict can be reduced, as opposed to the current 'winner takes all' scenario which generates maximum conflict.

Open justice

The current family justice system has been publicly discredited by organisations such as Fathers 4 Justice. Only a fully open, transparent and accountable system of justice can restore public confidence. The various half-measures currently being floated by the Government will only serve to fuel public unease and distrust of a secret system. There is not a shred of empirical evidence to support the claim that open justice could 'damage' children. If the Government is genuinely nervous of the consequences to children, why not submit open justice to a limited trial, and monitor the results?

Fathers 4 Justice believes these three core principles should be the foundation on which to build a new *Bill of Rights for The Family* as documented in our Blueprint, a legacy our children and their children's children will enjoy free of the injustices of the old law.

www.fathers-4-justice.org

ACTIVITY 2

Read the case study above.

1) Summarise the arguments made by the Fathers 4 Justice campaign group about inequality of access as parents.
2) Identify and explain the suggested solutions proposed by the Fathers 4 Justice campaign group.

The third case study on page 96 illustrates the difficulties the law has in reaching some groups. The law may exist but issues of inequality and discrimination in many cases such as this one are very complex and difficult to isolate.

CASE STUDY: Gypsy, Roma and Traveller children speak out over racism

The Children's Society called today for increased efforts to combat prejudice against gypsy, Roma and Traveller groups.

A report from the Children's Society outlines the abuse and disadvantage faced by young people from these communities.

It asked 201 children and young people in London about public attitudes towards them and their families. Of those questioned, 86 per cent had been racially abused and 63 per cent had been bullied or physically attacked.

Respondents also asked why their racist persecutors were not punished and why newspapers were not prosecuted for printing anti-gypsy stories. They felt that there were 'marked differences in responses to prejudice against them compared to the racism aimed at other minority groups'.

Half of those questioned had attended school at some point, but the average age of those who dropped out was just eleven and a half years old. Reasons given for leaving school included bullying, other children's attitudes, failure to act against prejudice by authorities and an irrelevant curriculum.

Penny Nicholls, strategy director for the Children's Society, said: 'The report highlights worrying levels of prejudice and discrimination, which have a corrosive effect on these young people's self-esteem and confidence. We hope this research will generate debate and encourage better understanding of gypsy, Roma and Traveller communities, who are rightly proud of their culture and traditions.'

The Children's Society also recommended that youth offending teams should receive cultural sensitivity training to work better with children and young people from those communities. It was found that 36 per cent of those surveyed had been in trouble with the law, which the charity called 'a high number from such a small sample'. Roma children were found to be more vulnerable than those who identified themselves as gypsies or Travellers.

Corin Williams, *Community Care*, www.communitycare.co.uk

ACTIVITY 3

Read the case study above.

1) Explain some of the issues of racism faced by Roma people.
2) Identify and evaluate suggested solutions to the problems of racism and prejudice faced by the Roma people.
3) The article above indicates that the issue of discrimination against the Roma people is complex and varied, meaning cases may prove to be a challenge. Using the article and your own ideas, what problems might be encountered when trying to challenge discrimination against the Roma people?

The changing perception of equal opportunities in the UK

Approaches to equality have developed to include a wider range of groups in society and towards a wider impression of equality.

The example of the changed status of women is a good illustration of how society has developed. Many refer to phases or stages towards equal opportunities.

- First phase – political and legal rights where women campaigned for and eventually secured, the right to vote and be represented fairly. Here the early advances were vital but then stage two was needed to make the power influence laws.

- Second phase – legal rights, such as fairness in divorce hearings, equal pay and sex discrimination laws. But having the vote and passing laws did not mean women automatically achieved equality, many residual attitudes of male dominance continued and these barriers needed to be overcome after the second stage.
- Third phase – social and cultural equality – where traditional masculine attitudes held by individuals and society as a whole place barriers to equality. In for example the workplace laws may exist to challenge sexist employers but the sexist attitudes do not go 'overnight'. True equality is only be established when such attitudes are changed and this is the stage society is in today to varying degrees across the UK.

Extending the definition of equality and laws on equality is an indication of how equal opportunities have been advanced. Equal rights legislation has a chronological development:

- Sex discrimination and racial discrimination legislation during the 1970s was adapted to include equal pay and institutional racism in the 1980s and 1990s.
- Institutional racism. A concept developed from the Macpherson report into the investigation into the police handling of the Stephen Lawrence murder in 2000. The report was strongly critical of the way the police force in London (Metropolitan police force) dealt with the case and said they were racist in their day-to-day practice within the institution. The perception of young black men was that they would be victims of murder, if not murderers, and that investigating yet another death was not new and procedures were slack and negligent.

Here a conceptual approach to equality required organisations to reflect on their policies and practices to screen for racial prejudice. The same has to be done to guard against sex, disability and age discrimination.

- Disabled. In 1998, access to public spaces and more recently to include the disabled in the workplace and as consumers of services.
- Homosexuals and transsexuals. For example, the state recognising the legal status of same-sex marriages in 2006.
- Age. In 2006, discrimination on grounds of age is no longer legal. Improved health and reduced birth rates change the age profile of the population and so social agendas change and with them perhaps the feeling that being 'old' is equal to being useless.

Other factors which broaden the context of equality

A changing world in terms of health awareness issues means we are more aware of reasons for health conditions and are less likely to discriminate based on ignorance. AIDS for example in the 1980s was approached with suspicion and fear based on ignorance which led to severe discrimination against people with HIV virus and AIDS. More recently awareness has improved socially and medically resulting in a more informed attitude to the virus. This is not to say that prejudice has disappeared.

Stronger powers of intervention through empowerment of citizens with rules, for example councils to consult with service users, allows more people of all backgrounds to influence agendas. Also legal changes have shaped attitudes from employers and emphasised a growing view in society that difference and diversity are richly rewarding and beneficial to companies seeking to survive in a globally competitive market.

Exam questions

SECTION A: IDENTITY

Answer Question 1 and **either** Question 2 **or** Question 3.

This section carries 30 marks.

1 Read the extract below and answer parts (a) and (b) which follow.

> The most effective way to challenge poverty is to allow the poor to tackle their difficulties themselves. Policies, such as the new deal for unemployed, life-long learning and homelessness strategies, are only effective if the public and those in poverty are willing to believe in them.
>
> Many media images of the poor are stereotypical generalisations about what poverty actually is and what it means for those who live in poverty. Images of people sleeping on streets on the one hand and drug habit fuelling thieves on the other distort the truth for most people who are struggling to feed themselves and their families.
>
> Not only should the poor be encouraged to challenge their own poverty but also the public perception of the poor needs to change if poverty is to be a thing of the past in Britain.

Your answers should refer to the extract as appropriate, but you should also include other relevant information.

(a) Briefly explain what is meant by the term indirect discrimination. (*5 marks*)

(b) Examine some of the ways that the mass media may be able to influence attitudes in society towards 'the poor'. (*10 marks*)

Either:

2 Assess the view that prejudice and discrimination no longer have any relevance to British citizens because measures to promote awareness of diversity and difference have been largely successful. (*15 marks*)

Or:

3 Assess the effectiveness of one or more government policies designed to promote equality of opportunity for all British citizens. (*15 marks*)

SECTION 2: RIGHTS AND RESPONSIBILITIES

Chapter 3: What are my rights and responsibilities?

In this chapter we explore two main issues which examine the key question 'What are my rights and responsibilities?'

ISSUE 1: What are rights?
This issue is explored through the following topics:

- concept of a 'right'
- relationship between rights and duties
- different types of rights.

ISSUE 2: What rights do I have?
This issue is explored through the following topics:

- human rights
- the right to know
- other rights of UK citizens.

ISSUE 1: WHAT ARE RIGHTS?

In this section we explore the following three topics:

- concept of a 'right'
- relationship between rights and duties
- different types of rights.

First we start with a brief introduction to the English legal system.

The English legal system

Any study of citizenship inevitably involves a study of law. This is because in citizenship we study, among other things, the relationship between the individual citizen and the state. Most relationships, other than purely social ones, result in a legal link between the parties and our relationship with the state is no different. Many of the issues raised by that relationship give rise to disputes that sooner or later end up in court.

ACTIVITY 1

1) Think of three ways in which we are involved with the state.
2) How might these involve a dispute?

These disputes can be important to each of us, because the way that they are resolved may change our lives. We do not need to become lawyers to understand what these disputes are about, but it helps if we understand some of the basic legal concepts.

What do we mean by law?

It is surprisingly difficult to define what we mean by law. It has been said that law is like an elephant – hard to describe but you would recognise one the moment you saw it.

The law that we learn about in this chapter and in Chapter 4 is the law that applies to England and Wales. Scotland and Northern Ireland have their own legal systems. These are, in many ways, very similar to the English legal system, but there are some important differences, especially in Scotland, although none of the differences will affect the areas of law that we are going to cover. One of the difficulties about law is that sometimes it differs from country to

a Potters Bar train crash

b *The Herald of Free Enterprise* took on water in Zebrugge Harbour

c The London bus after the 7 July bombing

What have all these disasters got in common? They all resulted in legal action being taken

country since each nation state has it own unique legal system.

Although it can be difficult to come up with a neat definition of law it is relatively easy to identify the features that a legal system must have.

1) **To be effective law must be binding on the whole of society.** A law that applies to one section of society but not to another is not fair – 'just'. We usually associate law with justice, but in fact they are quite different concepts. In the UK we have come to think of them as closely associated, but that is possibly because we have lived in what is a broadly 'just' society for many years.

2) **The law reflects the moral attitudes of society.** If it does not then people would not respect the law and it would be disobeyed. We can see this in the fact that those laws which do closely reflect our moral values are accepted by everyone – it is against the law to kill other people – no one questions that rule and everyone accepts it. The majority of people accept the ban on smoking in public places, and although many people do not like it most people do obey it. But other laws are not so generally obeyed – it is still common to see people using handheld mobile phones while driving.

3) **Because the law reflects our moral values it is constantly changing.** Our values change all the time and if the law is to be respected it has to change with them.

4) **We need the law to punish people who commit criminal offences.** This is because as a society we have decided that some types of behaviour are not to be tolerated or accepted and that people who do these things are to be punished.

5) **We also need the law to enable us to do some things.** We need to be able to make agreements that we know will be enforced. If you buy a ticket for the Glastonbury Festival you need to be sure that it entitles you to admission to the event.

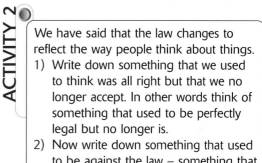

ACTIVITY 2

We have said that the law changes to reflect the way people think about things.
1) Write down something that we used to think was all right but that we no longer accept. In other words think of something that used to be perfectly legal but no longer is.
2) Now write down something that used to be against the law – something that we were not allowed to do – but that we are now allowed to do.

SO WHAT IS LAW?

There is no easy definition. It is:

- a series of rules

- made by society (usually by parliament, the EU, or the courts)

- it has to be obeyed

- it either enables us to do things that we need to be able to do to make society work, or …

- … that need to be prevented to make society work.

WHO MAKES THE LAW?

The 'rules' that set out our rights – in other words the law – are made by:

- parliament

- the EU

- the courts – the decisions made by courts are binding on lower courts and therefore become 'law'.

ACTIVITY 3

1) Write down something that the law enables you to do.
2) Write down something that the law would punish you for doing.

1 Concept of a 'right'

The fundamental nature of rights

As citizens we are interested in laws that enable us to do things. We often say that these laws give us the **right** to do something. (Laws that punish us for doing things that we are not supposed to do are considered in more depth in the A2 Citizenship course.)

WHAT ARE THEIR RIGHTS?

Amanda has just moved into Year 12 at St Tryhard's. She and three of her friends have gone out for the evening and they have gone into the Fox and Hounds for a drink. All four girls are aged sixteen. On the way to the pub they bumped into Bill who is eighteen and who works in the supermarket where Amanda has a part-time job. They all go into the pub together.

What rights do the girls have?

Do they have the right to:

- enter the pub?

- buy a drink in the pub?

- to have a meal in the pub?

- to have a drink with their meal?

The rights that people have are the building blocks that make up complex legal structures.

In the example on page 103 Amanda might say that she had the 'right' to go into the pub. But what does she really mean by that? She might mean that no one has the power to stop her going in. If you have a right to do something that would certainly imply that you were able to do it and that no one else could prevent you from doing it.

The Licensing Act 2003 says that under-sixteens can go into pubs, *if the management allow it and if they are accompanied by someone aged eighteen or more.* So does Amanda have the right to enter the Fox and Hounds? She is accompanied by Bill who is eighteen but since the landlord can stop her, then the answer has to be 'no'. If she needs someone else's permission, then she does not have the right to enter the pub.

So does she have the right to buy a drink? Here the answer is clearer. Assuming that she has been given permission to come into the pub she does have the right to buy a non-alcoholic drink, but the Licensing Act 2003 says that no one under the age of eighteen can buy an alcoholic drink, or drink alcohol in the bar. So she has a right to buy a drink, but it has to be non-alcoholic.

Amanda does, however have the right to have a meal and, at sixteen, she does have the right to have an alcoholic drink with her meal.

The Licensing Act 2003 sets out the law on most aspects of buying and drinking alcohol. We can see how it does this by determining what rights people have. The rights that Amanda has – and all the other rights set out in the Act – together make clear what the law is.

We have been looking at Amanda's right to buy a drink in a pub – important perhaps to her,

ACTIVITY 4

1) Can you think of any other rights that the Licensing Act 2003 would have to give to other members of the public and to the Landlord?
2) Can you think of any other aspect of your life where you need to know what rights you have? And what rights others have?

and it may have implications in relation to public order offences – but hardly a major issue. It is, however, important to see it as the practical end of legislation. The Licensing Act 2003 was an important new law – a statute that for the first time in many years revised the rules about drinking and pubs. It is made up of many rights like the ones we have been looking at in relation to Amanda.

The fact that Amanda has some rights in relation to her visit to the pub but that these are different from Bill's rights is more important than it might first appear. This is because the fact that Amanda and Bill have any rights at all means that:

- there is a legal system in existence that recognises their rights
- the legal system can enforce their rights
- no one else can stop them from exercising their rights (remember that we saw that Amanda did not have a right to enter the pub because the landlord could prevent her from doing that).

The mere fact that we have any rights at all is therefore immensely important – if we did not then there would be no legal system in existence and we would be living in complete anarchy.

The very existence of rights, however trivial, shows that we live under the rule of law.

Rights as building blocks in legal theory

The concept of rights would be of very little use if it only applied to Amanda's right to buy a drink in the pub. To be of any value the idea of rights needs to be applicable to a wide range of activities.

ACTIVITY 5

1) Can you identify the rights that you have in relation to:
   - getting a jacket dry cleaned
   - buying a T-shirt
   - voting in an election
   - being arrested
   - going to school?

You have rights in respect of all of these. All of these rights will be found in a **statute** just as Amanda's rights about going to the pub were found in the Licensing Act 2003.

Web action

The statutes where you will find your rights in relation to the issues in Activity 5 are set out below. See if you can identify which one will apply to each of the rights. Then go on the internet to find the various statutes and discover what your rights are.
- The Education Act
- The Supply of Goods and Services Act 1982
- The Police and Criminal Evidence Act 1985
- The Sale of Goods Act 1979
- The Representation of the People Act
- The Serious Organised Crime and Police Act.

[Note that one of the rights needs two statutes to deal with it fully.]

The rights we have been looking at above are all contained in statutes. Statutes are the most common source of law, but remember that we saw in the introduction that the law can also come from the EU or the courts. So although most rights come from statutes, some come from other sources.

The rights that we have looked at are quite simple, but some are more complicated. One of the most basic rights – and one that you will often take for granted – is your right to live in your house or flat. When you come to look at why you have that right the picture is much more complex.

Let's look at this more complex right in more detail. We need to think about what the right to live in our home implies.

- It implies that no one is able to stop you from living in your home. If someone could stop you from living in your house or flat, then clearly you would not have the right to live there.
- It implies that you can live there if you want to, but you do not have to live there if you do not want to. In other words you have a right to live in the house, but you do not have a duty to live in it.
- It implies that the law gives you the right to live in the premises – because either you rent the house or flat yourself or because your parents either own it or rent it and you live with them (although there are other reasons why you might have the right to live in a particular place).

BE SURE THAT YOU UNDERSTAND:

1) what a right is

2) where it comes from

3) what it implies.

Rights and duties

RIGHTS AND DUTIES

Chloe has a new iPod. She is sitting in a coffee shop showing it to her friend Davina. Edward pushes past her table with a tray of coffee and bumps into Chloe. As a result she drops her iPod into her latte. When she gets it out it is no longer working.

ACTIVITY 6

1) Do you think that Chloe has the right to be compensated by Edward for the damage to her iPod? Why?

When we look at this situation there are a number of things that we need to think about. Chloe has clearly a right to the iPod for it belongs to her and to no one else. But does that mean that she has a right to be compensated for damage to it? Read the following case study.

CASE STUDY: Donoghue v Stevenson 1928

In the case of *Donoghue v Stevenson* the **plaintiff**, May Donoghue, on 26 August 1928 went into a café in Paisley with her friend. Her friend bought ice cream sodas for both of them. These were brought to their table by Mr Minchella, the owner of the café. He placed a tall glass with a scoop of ice cream in the bottom in front of each of them. He then opened a bottle of ginger beer and poured some into May's glass. He left the bottle with the rest of the ginger beer in it beside May. He then opened a second bottle and poured some ginger beer into her friend's glass, leaving the second bottle beside her friend. May and her friend sat and chatted and drank the ginger beer, and ate the ice cream with a long spoon. When May had drunk some of the ginger beer her friend poured the rest of the ginger beer in the bottle into May's glass.

When she did that, the decomposed remains of a snail fell out into her soda drink.

The bottle was made of opaque glass and she could not have seen the contents. May developed severe gastroenteritis and had to be treated in Glasgow Royal Infirmary.

As a result of this she wanted compensation. The person who sold the ginger beer, Mr Minchella, did not know, and could not have known, that there was a snail in the bottle so she could not sue him.

The only person that May Donoghue could sue was the manufacturer of the ginger beer – James Stevenson. Before this time no one had succeeded in bringing a similar action against the manufacturer of goods that injured the eventual user of the goods unless there was a direct contract between the manufacturer and the user.

Notice that her friend had bought the drink – not May herself. Her friend could have sued the owner of the café, Minchella, for breach of contract. After all she had made a contract to buy a bottle of ginger beer and Minchella had broken the contract by supplying something different – a bottle of ginger beer with a snail in it. But the damages would have been limited to the difference in value between what was paid for (a bottle of ginger beer) and what was delivered (a bottle of ginger beer with a snail in it). The bottle of ginger beer had cost two pence and since a bottle of ginger beer with a snail in it has probably no value at all the maximum damages for breach of her friend's contract with Minchella would have been two pence. It was clearly not worth doing that.

The case of *Donoghue v Stevenson* started in the local court in Paisley and after a series of appeals it eventually reached the House of Lords – the final court of appeal. Interestingly the court did not talk about Mrs Donoghue's rights. Instead it focused on the duties of the **defendant**, Stephenson.

The House of Lords decided that a manufacturer owed a duty to avoid injuring persons who would purchase and consume his products without the opportunity of inspecting them.

In the House of Lords Lord Atkin delivered the leading judgment. He said: 'You must take reasonable care to avoid acts or omissions which you can reasonably foresee would be likely to injure your neighbour.'

He said that a 'neighbour' was any one that you could reasonably foresee would be affected by the action that you were taking and who you ought to think about when doing the action in question.

ACTIVITY 7

1) Look back to the example of Chloe's iPod on page 105.
   - Should Edward have foreseen the harm he did to Chloe?
   - Did Edward owe a 'duty of care' to Chloe?
   - If he did, was he in breach of the duty he owed her?
   - Does Chloe have a right to compensation from Edward?

Examiner's tip

Be sure that you can explain why rights are important.

2 Relationship between rights and duties

Rights and duties as the basis of legal relationships

In the previous section we looked at the idea of rights in some detail and we saw that they are the building blocks that go to make up the law. But we also saw that people have duties as well as rights. Remember Chloe had the right to compensation for her iPod because Edward had a duty not to harm Chloe (or her property).

In this section we need to look at how rights and duties fit together – at how they relate to each other. We need to do this because as we saw in the previous unit we have to use rights and duties to help resolve disputes.

Dispute resolution lies at the heart of our justice system. This is most obvious in civil disputes where one party is trying to assert a right against the other – for example Chloe's right to be compensated for the damage caused to her iPod by the negligent conduct of Edward. A right to be compensated might also arise for other reasons, for example as the result of the purchase of defective goods.

The **criminal law** is also concerned with dispute resolution, although sometimes this is not so obvious. As we have seen the **civil law** usually seeks to compensate the claimant for a loss he or she has suffered. The criminal law, on the other hand, is interested in punishing a person who has broken the criminal law.

Many disputes, both civil and criminal, will turn on the facts. The parties often agree on the rules to be applied, but disagree on the facts. For example if Chloe brought an action against Edward for compensation for the damage to her iPod, Edward might accept that he owed Chloe a duty of care, but deny that he had bumped into her.

Courts can resolve disputes about facts by deciding which view of the facts is correct. The losing party will probably not like the decision, but if the loser accepts the authority of the legal system and of the court then he or she will have to accept that the dispute has been resolved. So if the court listens to all the evidence and decides that Edward did indeed bump into Chloe as he pushed past her seat it will decide that he has to compensate her. Edward will be unhappy about that but he is likely to accept the court's decision.

In more difficult cases the parties may disagree about the rules that are to be applied.

This disagreement is likely to arise because the parties have conflicting interests. A manufacturer will not want a rule that imposes on him unlimited liability for his products, but the consumer will want just such a rule. A student renting a flat may want to be sure that she will be able to stay there for the time she is at university, but the landlord will probably want to be able to evict the student and get his property back if the student fails to pay her rent or annoys the neighbours.

> …[T]he law consists of certain types of rules regulating human conduct and…the administration of justice is concerned with enforcing the rights and duties created by such rules. The concept of a right is accordingly one of fundamental significance in legal theory.
>
> Salmond, J in Fitzgerald, P J (1966) *Jurisprudence*, Sweet and Maxwell, p215

Different views of rights and duties

The concept of rights and duties is fundamental to English law. But what, if any, is the relationship between rights and duties?

If we take the example of a debt owed by Fred to Gwyneth where Fred owes Gwyneth £25 we can say that Gwyneth has a legal right to be paid £25 by Fred. We can also say that Fred has a corresponding legal duty to pay Gwyneth £25.

It is tempting to think of the right and the duty in the example of Fred and Gwyneth as opposite sides of the same coin. But notice that it is Gwyneth who has the right, and Fred who has the duty. So they are not really opposite sides of the same coin, but the *same* side of *different* coins.

In the example we looked at above, where Gwyneth had a right to be repaid the money due to her and where Fred had a duty to repay the money he owed Gwyneth, we could see that the duty to repay was the corresponding duty to Gwyneth's right. But it is not always the case that a duty corresponds to a right.

RIGHTS AND DUTIES – PROBLEM 1

Some duties have a corresponding right. Some don't.

We all have a duty not to break the law, but where is the corresponding right? Some might argue that the community has the right to prosecute the wrongdoer who breaks the criminal law, but prosecution is a duty, not a right.

If the wrongdoer is prosecuted and convicted the judge has a duty to sentence him, but it would be strange to say that the accused had a right to be sentenced.

RIGHTS THAT DO NOT HAVE A CORRESPONDING DUTY

Austin, a nineteenth century legal writer, called duties that have a corresponding right (like Fred's duty to pay the debt we discussed above) **relative duties**. Duties that do not have a corresponding right (like the duty not to break the law) he called **absolute duties**.

RIGHTS AND DUTIES – PROBLEM 2

We are sloppy in the way we use the word right; there are different kinds of rights, but we just call them all rights.

We have looked at a number of examples of rights. We saw that:

1) Chloe has a right to be compensated for the damage to her iPod
2) Gwyneth has a right to have repayment of the money she lent to Fred
3) the community has a right to expect people to obey the law.

We have already seen that there are different types of duties – relative duties and absolute duties so it is not surprising that there are different types of rights too.

1) We have seen that Chloe claimed to have the right to be compensated by Edward and Gwyneth claimed to have the right to be repaid by Fred.
2) We have also discussed the right of a person to live in their home.
3) If Chloe tried to listen to her iPod in class her teacher might say that he had a right to confiscate it.
4) If Edward had contested Chloe's claim for compensation he would have had to give evidence in court. When giving evidence he could claim to have the right to say what he needed to say without the danger of being sued for defamation.

These are all rights but as we will see they are quite different from each other.

In 1913 Wesley Hohfeld, a law lecturer at Yale University in the USA, pointed out that the rights we have mentioned, and the duties that are associated with them, are so different that it is unhelpful to refer to them all as rights and duties. He argued that different types of rights attracted different types of duties. He said that the terms rights and duties were too broad and failed to explain the differences between the relationships that existed. He set out his own classification of what he called **jural opposites** and **jural correlatives**. These have been represented in the diagram below.

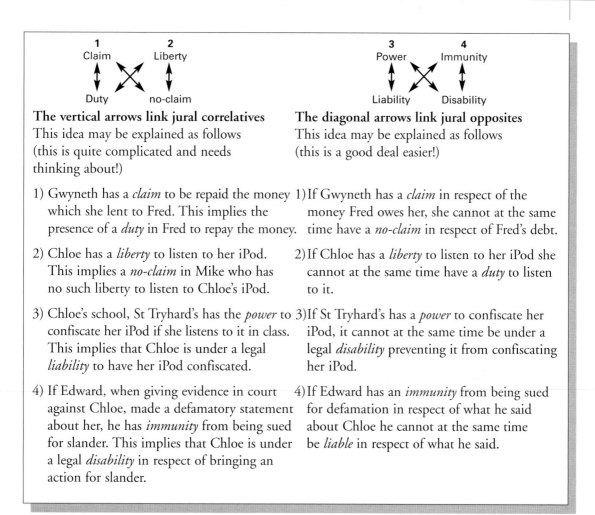

The vertical arrows link jural correlatives
This idea may be explained as follows
(this is quite complicated and needs
thinking about!)

1) Gwyneth has a *claim* to be repaid the money
which she lent to Fred. This implies the
presence of a *duty* in Fred to repay the money.

2) Chloe has a *liberty* to listen to her iPod.
This implies a *no-claim* in Mike who has
no such liberty to listen to Chloe's iPod.

3) Chloe's school, St Tryhard's has the *power* to
confiscate her iPod if she listens to it in class.
This implies that Chloe is under a legal
liability to have her iPod confiscated.

4) If Edward, when giving evidence in court
against Chloe, made a defamatory statement
about her, he has *immunity* from being sued
for slander. This implies that Chloe is under
a legal *disability* in respect of bringing an
action for slander.

The diagonal arrows link jural opposites
This idea may be explained as follows
(this is a good deal easier!)

1) If Gwyneth has a *claim* in respect of the
money Fred owes her, she cannot at the same
time have a *no-claim* in respect of Fred's debt.

2) If Chloe has a *liberty* to listen to her iPod she
cannot at the same time have a *duty* to listen
to it.

3) If St Tryhard's has a *power* to confiscate her
iPod, it cannot at the same time be under a
legal *disability* preventing it from confiscating
her iPod.

4) If Edward has an *immunity* from being sued
for defamation in respect of what he said
about Chloe he cannot at the same time
be *liable* in respect of what he said.

SOME PROBLEMS WITH HOHFELD'S ANALYSIS OF RIGHTS AND DUTIES

It is a complex classification, but many legal
relationships can be successfully pigeon-
holed under it. Notwithstanding that, it is
open to criticism.

- Some of the terms used (for example no-
claim) are not legally recognised (and
indeed are not even real words). They
were made up by Hohfeld because there
was no existing word that meant exactly
what he was trying to express.

- 'Power' can take many forms, for
example the power that everyone has to
make some sort of contract may be quite
different from some of the special powers
that police officers have.

- Civil law duties are quite different from
criminal law duties and arguably require
a more detailed analysis than Hohfeld
provides. Hohfeld died at the age of 26.
Had he lived longer he might have
developed his theories further.

Hohfeld's work is a significant help in resolving the problem of trying to explain the complex relationship between legal rights and legal duties. It does not solve all the problems that arise, but it can help in many cases and it is always useful to analyse situations where conflicts arise in Hohfeld's terms.

For example, schools will often tell students that they have a duty to wear their uniform to school. If we apply Hohfeld's analysis to the situation we can see that the school is clearly wrong. A student could only have a duty to wear his or her uniform to school if the school had a claim that the student should wear the uniform.

In fact the school does not have a claim right. It has a power to require students to wear uniform and so the students are under a liability to wear it. This is because a liability is the jural correlative of a power.

You may be tempted to say that it does not make any difference, because the outcome is still the same. The student has to wear the uniform. But in fact it can be important because if we can think clearly about the precise relationship between people with different perspectives in a dispute we are better able to understand their legal relationships.

Using Hohfeld's analysis it might be argued that David has a claim right – in which case the school would have a duty to accept him. But it does not make much sense to talk about a claim in this context.

DAVID AND EILEEN HAVE BEEN OFFERED PLACES IN YEAR 12 AT ST TRYHARD'S SCHOOL.

- David's father tells him that he has a right to attend the school.
- The Local Authority says that as it is funding the course David is taking he has a duty to attend school.
- David's tutor tells him that he has a right to learn.
- The maths teacher tells David that David has a duty to allow other students to learn.

Eileen's mother has given her a new mobile phone so that she can keep in touch with home when she is out.

- Her mother tells her that she has a duty to use the phone to tell her where she is.
- Eileen asserts that she has a right to take the phone to school.
- The Headmaster of St Tryhard's says that he has made a rule banning mobile phones in the school and that no student has the right to take a phone into the school.

It might be more satisfactory to conclude that he has a liberty right – he has a liberty to attend school. If that is the case the jural correlative is a no-claim and that is what someone who did not have his liberty to attend school would have. But the jural opposite of a liberty is a duty. If David had a liberty to attend school he cannot also have a duty to attend school. But, of course, he will have a duty to attend school, so he cannot therefore also have a liberty to attend; so he cannot have a liberty right.

ACTIVITY 1

1) Read the information in the following box. Can you work out what sort of a right or duty David and Eileen have?

He must therefore have a power right – he has the power to attend school. The jural correlative is a liability – the school is liable to accept him and teach him. The jural opposite is a disability – he cannot at the same time have a power to attend school and be disabled from attending school.

ACTIVITY 2

1) See if you can work out the rest. Ask yourself what sort of right or duty the person means and see if it fits with Hohfeld's analysis.

Hohfeld's analysis is very helpful in clarifying the issue of rights and duties and it certainly makes us think carefully about these complex issues.

But the system does not always work. This is because as we saw earlier some duties do not have any corresponding right – Austin's so called 'absolute duties'. The best example of an absolute duty is the duty of all citizens not to break the criminal law. We saw that there is no jural correlative for that. It just does not make sense to talk about the right to be punished.

Hohfeld's analysis is, however, very complex. It is certainly helpful in focusing our minds on the different types of rights and duties that exist. But modern writers have tended to take a different view of the relationship between rights and duties and these are explored in the next section.

3 Different types of rights

Determining the powers of citizens

The complexity of Hohfeld's analysis of rights and duties shows just how difficult it is to define the relationship between them. In the latter half of the twentieth century lawyers began to see that there was no need to develop an all-embracing definition of rights and duties. Instead they began to explore the idea (implicit in Hohfeld's analysis) that the meaning of the terms rights and duties is not fixed, but varies according to the context in which they are used.

It began to be seen that the whole concept of rights was too complex to enable them to be defined by words like claim, liberty, power or immunity. Instead of trying to define the concept of a right by looking for a number of other words that might define some types of right modern writers have tended to try to explain in more detail what a right is.

THERE IS BROAD AGREEMENT THAT THE STATEMENT 'GEORGE HAS A RIGHT' IMPLIES THE FOLLOWING.

1 There is a legal system in existence.

2 Under the rules of the legal system some other person, say Harry, is (in the circumstances that have occurred) obliged either to do something or to abstain from doing something.

3 This obligation on the part of Harry (i.e. to do something or to abstain from doing something) is made by law and depends on the choice of George – in other words George can choose whether Harry has to do the act in question or abstain from doing the act.

So the statement 'George has a right' means that we can draw a conclusion about what the law is in a case which falls under the particular rule that is involved in the situation.

This is quite helpful. It helps us to understand the background to the statement that George has a right. It is asserting that there is a law which says that in particular circumstances George can require Harry either to do something or to refrain from doing something. The only problem is that it suggests that the rule relating to George's right is clear and that there is no doubt as to either George's right or Harry's obligation. Unfortunately, this is not always the case for there are many situations where the law is far from clear about what right George has and what obligation Harry has.

As a simple example we can take an imaginary rule that says 'No vehicles are allowed in the park'. From this rule it is clear that no motor cars are allowed in the park. The owner of the park has the right to require that people do not bring motor cars into the park and if Harry were to drive his car into the park he would clearly be doing something that was breaking the rule and the owner of the park could use the law to enforce its right that cars do not enter the park.

But suppose that Harry comes into the park on roller blades or with a pram. Is that against the rule? This is not nearly so clear cut, especially if the rule was made 50 years ago, before roller blades were invented.

The rule that no vehicles are allowed in the park can be seen to have a core of certainty: under it motor cars are clearly prevented from entering the park. But it can also be seen that the rule has a grey area (sometimes called a 'penumbra') of doubt: it is not clear if the rule prevents roller blades and prams from being used in the park.

This grey area of doubt occurs frequently. In topic 1 we looked at the famous case of *Donoghue v Stevenson* (pages 105–6).

The important thing to notice about this case is that when May Donoghue started her case she was alleging that she had a right to be compensated for the illness she contracted as a result of drinking the ginger beer made by the defendant, Stevenson. She said that Stevenson had to compensate her because he had a duty to make sure that where he supplied ginger beer to consumers he did not allow it to become contaminated.

But when she started her case (remember that the snail appeared out of the ginger beer bottle in 1928) there was no clear rule that manufacturers owed such a duty to people who used their products. As a result of her case the House of Lords decided that a manufacturer owed a duty to the ultimate consumer of his products.

REMEMBER WHAT LORD ATKIN SAID?

He said that there was a duty:

- to take reasonable care to avoid acts and omissions
- that would be reasonably foreseeable
- as likely to injure anyone that should be in the contemplation of the person owing the duty.

So as far as May Donoghue was concerned the House of Lords found that Stevenson did owe her a duty. He had clearly broken that duty by allowing a snail to get into the ginger beer at some stage of its production. As a result Mrs Donoghue had a right to be compensated.

But, of course, none of the approaches to the question of rights and duties that we have looked at would have been able to predict that. They can only analyse situations where a right exists. Where no right is known to exist, however, they do not help to decide if such a right does in fact exist. Before Mrs Donoghue won her case in the House of Lords if you had asked, 'Does Mrs Donoghue have a right to compensation?' the answer would have been 'Maybe, and maybe not.'

We need to remember that one of the features of law in general is that it is never static. The law is always changing to adapt to changing social, political and economic conditions. So when we talk about our rights we need to appreciate that they will not always be the same. The word that is used to express this constantly changing aspect of our law is dynamic.

Our rights and duties are part of a continuing process of legal regulation. In this process our rights and duties will change and be modified. Because of the dynamic nature of our law they may be extended and developed or they may be extinguished altogether. We noted earlier that this change will be driven by social, economic and political factors that are also changing all the time. In this way the law remains focused and relevant to the needs of individuals and society.

All this helps to explain why the law changed to allow Mrs Donoghue to claim compensation

ACTIVITY 1

1) The box on the left shows some rights that have changed recently. Can you explain why these changes came about?
2) For each right state whether the reasons for the change were social, political or economic.

for the injury that she sustained by drinking Stevenson's ginger beer. Before her case it was not seen as necessary to have such a rule, but the facts of her case highlighted the need for people in her position to be able to claim compensation from negligent manufacturers in the situation that she found herself in. The House of Lords accepted her argument that she ought to have a basic right not to be injured through a manufacturer's negligence.

We saw at the very beginning of this chapter that the rights we enjoy come from laws made by parliament or by the courts or by the EU. In Mrs Donoghue's case the right came from the courts. But even when parliament creates a right it is often the job of the courts to consider the extent of the right and to decide whether or not the right applies to a particular situation.

In the case of *Donoghue v Stevenson* the courts decided that there is a duty to take reasonable care to avoid foreseeable harm to people that ought to be in the thoughts of the defendant when he or she is doing (or sometimes not doing) a particular act. When that was applied to Stevenson it was seen that the ginger beer manufacturer should have been able to foresee the harm that would happen to the people who drank his products if he did not take care to prevent them from becoming contaminated.

RECENT RIGHTS

- The right to smoke in a pub.

- The right to carry gels and liquids in your hand baggage on an aircraft.

- The right to have your bin emptied every week.

- The right to discriminate against older people in employment.

CASE STUDY: Home Office v Dorset Yacht Club Co Ltd 1970

A group of borstal[1] trainees were taken on a training exercise on Brownsea Island in Poole Harbour. They were supervised by three borstal officers who were instructed to keep a watch over the boys at all times and guard them in shifts at night. Contrary to these instructions the officers all went to bed one night, leaving the trainees unsupervised.

Seven of the boys escaped and went on board a yacht which they tried to sail away. It collided with another yacht owned by the Dorset Yacht Club. The boys boarded the second yacht and did considerable damage to it.

Brownsea Island

The Dorset Yacht Club sued the Home Office (the supervisors' employer) alleging that the negligence of the supervisors was the cause of the damage to their property and it claimed compensation.

[1] Borstals were abolished a number of years ago. The modern equivalent would be a Young Offenders Institute. The important point to note is that the trainees were in lawful custody.

But we have noted that the law never stands still and the duty (and the corresponding right to compensation for the complainant) established in *Donoghue v Stevenson* was soon being applied in other directions.

This can be seen in the case of *Home Office v Dorset Yacht Club Co. Ltd.* The facts were just about as different from those of Donoghue v Stevenson as it was possible for them to be.

In the above case the claimants were making a claim in a context in which the court, if it recognised and accepted the claim, would have to apply the law of negligence. The court agreed with the claimants that there was a claim in negligence and went on to apply the basic rules set out in *Donoghue v Stevenson*. The Court (again the appeal went all the way to the House of Lords) decided that the escape of the trainees was foreseeable and that the borstal officers had been negligent in allowing them to escape. The only way the trainees could escape

from Brownsea Island was by boat and so it was foreseeable that they might damage a boat. The Dorset Yacht Club had a right to be compensated for the damage done to its property and that damage was caused by the negligence of the defendants.

Conflicting rights

Hohfeld's analysis of rights and duties showed us that once we had determined what sort of right we were talking about we could identify what the jural correlative of the right was – the duty that was inevitably associated with it. But another difficulty that we need to consider is the problem where two or more people have a right in connection with the same matter but those rights, both valid in themselves, conflict with each other.

This problem is illustrated in the case of *Gillick v West Norfolk and Wisbech Area Health Authority.*

CASE STUDY: Gillick v West Norfolk and Wisbech Area Health Authority 1985

Area Health Authorities are the bodies responsible for employing general practitioners (GPs). The West Norfolk and Wisbech Area Health Authority was very concerned by the number of unwanted teenage pregnancies that were occurring and in an effort to reduce these told the GPs it employed that if they were satisfied that girls under sixteen (by which was meant girls of fifteen) were sufficiently mature and understood what was involved GPs could prescribe the contraceptive pill without their parents' knowledge or consent.

Mrs Victoria Gillick

Mrs Victoria Gillick was the mother of ten daughters. She was a strict Roman Catholic and had religious objections to birth control. She was very concerned that her GP might prescribe the contraceptive pill to her daughters without her knowledge.

She brought an application in the High Court asking for a declaration that the Area Health Authority was wrong in giving this advice.

She lost in the High Court but won in the Court of Appeal. The Area Health Authority appealed to the House of Lords.

By a majority of three to two the House of Lords agreed that the Area Health Authority was correct in advising GPs to prescribe contraceptives to fifteen-year-old girls without the knowledge or consent of their parents.

This case is interesting for a number of reasons.

- There was no clear rule about prescribing to children under sixteen years of age. Parliament had never made any rule about it and the courts had never been asked to consider it before. Children under sixteen normally need their parents' consent before having medical treatment as at that age they are unable to give consent themselves. But the issue here was whether that rule should apply in this case or not.
- Mrs Gillick was asserting that she had a right to be informed. By implication she was also asserting that children under sixteen had no right to give consent themselves.
- The criminal law clearly provides that girls under sixteen cannot consent to having sexual intercourse. Any man, irrespective of his age, who has sexual intercourse with a girl under sixteen commits a very serious criminal offence.

MRS GILLICK'S CASE RAISED A NUMBER OF ISSUES:

1) Was the parents' right to know more important than the children's right to privacy?

2) Was allowing fifteen-year-old girls to consent to contraception encouraging them to have sexual intercourse and so encouraging breaches of the criminal law?

This was a difficult decision for the members of the House of Lords to make. It illustrates the problems that arise when the courts have to 'make' law. Two of the law lords adopted the moral arguments advanced by Mrs Gillick. But the other three did not argue along moral lines at all, although it may well be that they accepted that not allowing fifteen year olds to have contraception would not stop them having sexual intercourse but that giving them the pill would certainly prevent them from getting pregnant.

ACTIVITY 2

There were always five judges in the House of Lords. In this case they were all white men. The oldest was 74 and the youngest 69.

1) Do you think that five grandfathers were the best people to decide if fifteen-year-old girls should make decisions about contraception rather than their parents?
2) If senior judges should not make this sort of decision, who should decide issues like this?
3) What do you think the judges should take into account when making up their minds?
4) The Government could easily have passed a statute or made a piece of delegated legislation to clarify the powers of the Area Health Authority. Why do you think that it did not do this and deliberately left it to the courts to decide?

Note that the Supreme Court has now taken over the role of the House of Lords as the final appeal court in the UK.

In the event the Law Lords decided that GPs should be able to prescribe the contraceptive pill to fifteen-year-old girls without the knowledge or consent of their parents. So the majority of them thought that the right of fifteen year olds to privacy out-weighed the right of their parents to be informed and to make decisions for their children. One of the reasons that they gave was that they thought that fifteen-year-old girls were mature enough to make such decisions.

When the rights of one section of society conflict with the rights of another section (as in the *Gillick* case) it is always difficult for judges to decide whose rights should prevail. In *Gillick v West Norfolk and Wisbech Area Health Authority* there was a temptation to make this decision on the basis of morality. Indeed the two minority judges did expressly base their arguments on the same moral grounds that were advanced by Mrs Gillick. The majority, however, said that they did not make the decision on moral grounds, but that they merely applied the rules of common law as they interpreted them.

ACTIVITY 3

1) Do you think that it is true that the three judges in the majority ignored concepts of morality in making their decisions?
2) If they had decided to insist that parents were involved in the decision do you think that would have prevented some fifteen-year-old girls going to their GP about contraception?
3) Would not giving the girls the pill reduce the chances of them having underage sex?
4) Allowing the girls to choose to have the pill would clearly have reduced the chances of unwanted pregnancies. Would that be a good thing?
5) What is the moral thing to do? Choose from the following.
   - Accept that the girls are likely to have underage sex anyway but try to reduce unwanted pregnancies by allowing them to have the pill.
   - Refuse to give the girls the pill in the hope that it would stop them having underage sex.

It is very hard to separate moral and legal issues in cases like this.

1) Can you think of any other situation where the interests of the state conflict with our personal interests?
2) In the examples that you have suggested, does the public interest or the private interest usually prevail?
3) Are the rights of individuals more or less important than the rights of society or of the state?

ISSUE 2: WHAT RIGHTS DO I HAVE?

In this section we explore the following three themes:

- human rights
- the right to know
- other rights of UK citizens.

4 Human rights

Residual freedoms and the principles of human rights

In Issue 1 we looked at some of the different types of rights and duties that make up our legal environment. In this issue we are going to focus on some specific rights and duties.

The first set of rights that we are going to investigate is the area of law that is often collectively referred to as human rights.

We need to start this by explaining that in most democratic countries the rights of the citizens are defined in a written **constitution**. A written constitution is a collection of rights that have been formally recognised by the state and which cannot easily be changed. Probably the best known written constitution is that of the USA, because it is frequently referred to in films and other forms of media. But the vast majority of democratic countries has a written constitution. The constitutions follow different patterns and adopt different approaches to what they are setting out to do. For example the Indian constitution is a very long and very complex document. The Irish constitution is a model of brevity and simplicity.

All these very different constitutions provide a statement of the rights that can be claimed by the citizens of the country in question. If a particular right is enshrined in the constitution, then the citizens are able to enjoy and exercise that right. If it is not in the constitution, then the citizens do not have that right.

We need to be clear that in the UK there is no written constitution. We often say that in the UK there is an unwritten constitution, but in some ways that is misleading. There is a very large area of law known as constitutional law and clearly that has all been written down. The law of the constitution is concerned with how the country is governed – for example, how often elections must be called, how they are conducted, the power of the cabinet and rules that apply to cabinet ministers. These rules are all clearly known. Some of them are embodied in statutes, some in the decisions of the courts and some have come about because of long custom and practice. Most people would accept that they are binding.

But the important thing for us to remember is that they are all, at best, just ordinary laws that can be changed at any time. There is no single document that sets out the rights of British citizens.

REMEMBER

We said that the special thing about a written constitution was that it was difficult to change.

In the UK, because we do not have a written constitution, any law can be changed by parliament at any time.

To understand these rules we need to understand two important terms (see the box below) that we will refer to as we deal with the issue of human rights.

THE SOVEREIGNTY OF PARLIAMENT

This means that in the UK parliament is the final and supreme law maker. This involves several important issues:

- parliament can make any laws it wants to

- parliament can overrule any laws made by the courts

- parliament can change any laws made by a previous parliament.

Traditionally the UK has approached the issue of the rights of its citizens by assuming that every citizen is free to do whatever he or she wants to do – provided that it is not against the law. In other words our courts have taken the view that rights are not something that are given to citizens by government, but are something that everyone has automatically. Sometimes, of course, this absolute freedom has to be restricted. This might happen if parliament passed a statute prohibiting certain conduct – for example when it passed the statute banning smoking in public places. The courts might also consider that some particular conduct by an individual had to be prohibited in order to protect the rights of other individuals. We will see an example of that in the case of *Miller v Jackson* on page 177.

THE RULE OF LAW

This is a basic principle of our legal system. Everyone is governed by the same law that is administered in the coronary courts. There are no special courts for parliament or government matters as there are in some other European countries. This means that the Government is bound by the same law that binds you and me:

- no one can be punished unless he or she has been convicted of breaking a law by an ordinary court

- everyone, irrespective of status, rank or office is equal before the law

- if a law has been broken, then justice will ensure that the law is enforced

- the rights of individual citizens exist as a result of the decisions made in the ordinary courts of the country. The fact that every accused person has the right to appear before these courts safeguards the liberties and freedom of the individual.

We usually refer to this as a system of **residual freedoms**. By this we simply mean that UK citizens cannot point to a written constitution to define their rights, because they have the right to do anything that has not been made illegal.

We can see how this system of residual freedoms works by considering the right to freedom of speech. We are free to say whatever we like unless there is a specific law preventing us from saying or communicating specific things.

WE ARE RESTRICTED IN WHAT WE CAN SAY BY THE FOLLOWING:

1) The law of defamation: we are not allowed to publish (i.e. pass any information on to a third person) things that are untrue and would lower the person about whom they are made in the estimation of right thinking members of society.

2) National Security: there have been restrictions on what information can be disclosed ever since the first Official Secrets Act was passed in 1911. In recent years this has been considerably extended to deal with the threat that is perceived to be posed by terrorist activity.

3) Censorship: local authorities have the power to decide if a film is suitable for showing to the public in their area. They may, but do not have to, follow the guidance given by the British Board of Film Classification.

4) Obscenity: there are rules that prevent the publication of material that is likely to corrupt those who have seen, read or heard it.

5) Race relations: it is an offence to say (or do) things that would stir up racial hatred.

There are many other restrictions on what we can say or write, so although we cherish our right to freedom of speech it is not an absolute right. For very good reasons it has had to be restricted in order to ensure that individuals are not unreasonably treated and that society itself is not put at risk.

ACTIVITY 1

Americans tend to talk about 'civil rights'. In the UK we tend to call these 'civil liberties'.
1) How is this difference between the use of the two terms related to the fact that the USA has a written constitution and the UK does not?
2) Go back to the section on rights and duties (pages 106–11) and remind yourself of the difference that Hohfeld saw between a claim and a liberty. Write a brief explanation of this difference.

Does this system of residual freedoms work? In theory it should work well, and indeed it has served the UK very well for about 300 years. But in the last twenty years it has come under increasing pressure.

You will recall that we talked about the rule of law earlier (pages 102–4). This rule provides that everyone is subject to the same rules and that the rules are applied in the ordinary courts. This means that the state (i.e. the Government) is subject to the same rules as you and I are. Therefore just as we have residual rights, so does the Government. That in turn means that the Government can interfere with the freedom of individual citizens provided that there is not a law preventing it from doing so. It does not need a specific law permitting it to interfere with the rights of the citizen.

CASE STUDY: Malone v Commissioner for the Metropolitan Police (1979)

In this case the police tapped Malone's telephone without any authority to do so. There was no law which forbade such conduct and therefore the police action was not against the law and so Malone's case against the police failed.

This case illustrates how the Government was prepared to use the concept of residual rights to interfere with the personal liberty of its citizens.

In the 1970s and 1980s successive governments showed that they were prepared to use their residual rights in a way that they had not done previously. This made UK citizens uneasy about relying on residual freedoms in the way that they had done in the past. As a result there was increasing pressure for a written constitution that would guarantee certain freedoms and rights to individual citizens.

The European Convention on Human Rights

The European Convention on Human Rights (the convention) was created in the aftermath of the Second World War. It was recognised that one of the causes of the Second World War was the way in which the Nazi Government of Germany had abused the human rights of the Jews and other minority peoples. It was thought that if there were safeguards in place that would prevent similar abuse in the future the overall security of Europe would be improved.

The convention is in effect a treaty made by the countries who signed it agreeing that they would give the basic rights set out in the convention to all their citizens. The convention created the European Court of Human Rights (the ECHR) to deal with claims about breaches of the convention.

The convention was signed in Rome in 1950. It was ratified by the UK in 1951 and it became binding on all the countries that ratified it in 1953. It has now been signed by 45 European states (including all the members of the EU).

The fact that a state signed and ratified the convention did not, however, mean that the terms of the convention became part of the state's domestic law. It was an international agreement and as such provided an international obligation on each signatory to maintain the rights laid down in the convention, but it did not change the domestic law of the states that signed it.

Although the UK was one of the first countries to sign the Convention and ratified it in 1951 it did not incorporate the terms of the convention into UK law until 2000. That meant that between 1953 and 2000 UK citizens could not rely on the terms of the convention in cases before the UK courts as the convention was not part of UK law.

This meant that until the year 2000 if a UK citizen believed that his or her rights under the convention had been abused the only way the matter could be brought before a court was to issue proceedings in the European Court of Human Rights. This court sat in Strasbourg and no case could be taken to it until all possible appeals had be made in the domestic UK courts so it took a long time to get a case before the ECHR and it was also very expensive.

The European Court of Human Rights, Strasbourg

ACTIVITY 2

1) Discuss the benefits to citizens which may result from having rights written down in this way. Consider the general public's understanding of their rights when they are written in this list.
2) Refer to articles 2, 8 and 14 on the next page and give a brief example to illustrate how these rights may promote a citizen's freedom and equality.

Examiner's tip

Don't confuse the European Convention on Human Rights with the EU. They are quite different.

One important difference is that although the convention did not become part of the domestic law of the states that signed it, treaties between members of the EU do usually become part of the domestic law of the member states.

So what rights does the convention protect? Remember the following:

1) most of these rights were enjoyed by UK citizens long before the convention was made
2) the convention helps to ensure that these rights are not taken away by legislation
3) the convention rights are guaranteed and so cases like that of *Malone* would be prevented
4) states have the right to derogate (i.e. to decline to carry out their obligations under the convention) from most of these rights in times of emergency.

Since the convention was made a number of additions have been made to it. These are known as 'protocols'. The most important of the protocols are shown on page 123.

It is very important to remember that the European Convention of Human Rights gives individuals rights against the Government and local authorities. It does not give one individual rights against another individual.

Examiner's tip

Make sure that you understand what the articles in the convention mean.
Very common mistakes by students in the exam are to state that the convention guarantees the right to trial by jury (it doesn't) or to suggest that it made murder illegal. It doesn't do that either.
Remember that the convention gives citizens rights against the Government and public authorities. It does not give citizens rights against other citizens.

It is also important to note what the convention does not do. It does not cover the whole field of human rights.

It makes no provision at all for what we can call social and economic rights. For example it makes no provision for:

• housing
• a minimum income
• free health care.

ARTICLES

1) The right to life. There are limited exceptions where it is acceptable for the state to take away someone's life, for example where a police officer acts justifiably in self defence.

2) Freedom from torture, inhuman or degrading treatment. No derogation is allowed from this article.

3) Freedom from slavery or forced labour.

4) The right to liberty and security of the person. No one can be arrested or detained except in the circumstances described in the article. It is, for example, permitted to arrest and detain a person suspected or convicted of a crime where this is justified by a clear legal procedure.

5) The right to a fair trial. This applies to both civil and criminal cases. Hearings must be independent and impartial. Under Article 6 the public can be excluded from the hearing, but not from the judgment. Anyone facing a criminal charge is presumed innocent until proved to be guilty. There are rights guaranteed by the article allowing the accused persons to defend themselves.

6) The prohibition of retrospective criminal laws. This article gives people the right not to be convicted of an offence arising out of actions by the accused that were not criminal at the time the accused carried out the actions.

7) The right to respect for a person's private and family life, home and correspondence.

8) The right to freedom of thought, conscience and religion.

9) The right to freedom of expression. People are allowed to express views that they hold, even if these are unpopular or disturbing. But the convention provides that there are exceptions to this, and so, for example, it is not a breach of the convention to prohibit the making of statements that would incite racial hatred or terrorist acts.

10) The right to freedom of peaceful assembly and association, including the right to join a trade union. This right can be restricted in specified circumstances.

11) The right to marry and have a family. Each member state can make its own rules about how, and at what age people are able to get married.

12) This article deals with technical legal issues applicable to the remedies available in the European Court of Human Rights. It has not been incorporated into UK law.

13) The right to enjoy the rights protected by the convention without discrimination. Restrictions which can be reasonably justified are allowed.

14) The right to an education.

15) The right to participate in elections (subject to age restrictions).

16) The right not to be subjected to the death penalty.

Protocol 1 Article 1	The right to peaceful enjoyment of private possessions. Public authorities cannot usually interfere with things that we own or the way we use them except in specified limited circumstances – for example it can limit ownership and use of firearms and knives
Protocol 1 Article 2	The right not to be denied access to the educational system
Protocol 1 Article 3	The right to fair and free elections by secret ballot. States can place restrictions on those who are allowed to vote, for example a minimum age
Protocol 4	The right to move freely within a state. This provision has not been ratified by the UK
Protocol 4 Articles 1 and 2	These provisions abolish the death penalty. There can be limited exceptions in time of war

These are things which many people would argue should be a basic right in a modern civilised society. They are issues about which it might be difficult to obtain agreement among all the signatories of the convention. British citizens have these rights, but they are not protected by the convention.

The Human Rights Act (HRA) 1998 and the impact of human rights legislation

The Human Rights Act (HRA) 1998 came into force on 2 October 2000. It incorporated the convention and its first protocol into UK domestic law.

We saw above that the convention was not part of UK law until the Human Rights Act 1998 came into force. Before then UK citizens had to takes their cases to the European Court of Human Rights in Strasbourg if they wanted to establish that their rights under the convention had been violated. That was because UK judges could not apply the convention as it was not part of UK law.

The HRA provided that the convention became part of UK law. We usually express that by saying that the HRA incorporated the convention into UK law. The most obvious and important effect of this is that the terms of the convention can now be enforced and applied in UK courts and that there is no longer a need for UK citizens to take their cases to the European Court of Human Rights in order to have the terms of the convention applied. The right to take a case to the European Court of Human Rights has not, however, been abolished. If a UK court made a decision on an issue about human rights it would still be open to the loosing party to appeal to the European Court of Human Rights.

ACTIVITY 3

1) Using points 1, 2, 3 and 4 on the next page discuss the extent to which the HRA has become a central aspect of UK law.

The most important changes made by the HRA are as follows:

1) The rights of UK citizens have been strengthened by making the convention part of UK law and so enabling citizens to use the rights given by the convention in UK courts.

2) UK courts must, wherever possible, interpret all legislation in a way that makes it compatible with the rights given by the convention.

3) It is unlawful for the Government or a public authority to act in a way that is incompatible with the rights given in the convention.

4) When a new bill is introduced the Government must publish a statement as to whether or not it is compatible with the convention.

CASE STUDY: Douglas v Hello! 2001

The courts are a public authority and so the HRA applies to them. It has been argued that if a court failed to apply a convention right in a civil case between two individual citizens that it would then be in breach of its obligations under the HRA. In the case of *Douglas v* Hello! Michael Douglas and Catherine Zeta-Jones argued that their right to privacy had been breached when the magazine *Hello!* published photographs of their wedding without their permission. Although no public authority was involved in the action the court held that the claimants were entitled to compensation from *Hello!* under the HRA.

ACTIVITY 4

1) Refer back to the list of 16 articles in the HRA on page 122 and identify which one most applies in this case. Explain how the article applies.

The HRA gives citizens rights against the Government and public authorities. The term public authorities includes local authorities and organisations such as the NHS and the police. It extends to any organisation that fulfils a **statutory obligation**, so would include schools and the railway companies. Because the HRA applies to government and public authorities it is sometimes said to have 'vertical effect'.

It does not extend to individuals or limited companies. So it does not have 'horizontal effect'. It therefore appears that an individual can breach the HRA with impunity.

We noted earlier that the courts must try to interpret all statutes in such a way as to make them compatible with the HRA and the convention. But it is important to note that under the HRA the courts do not have the right to refuse to apply a statute that is not compatible with the convention. This is because of the rule that parliament is sovereign and that it cannot be dictated to by any other body.

ACTIVITY 5

1) Using the strengths and weaknesses points in the table on the next page write a brief assessment of the impact of the HRA.

If a statute does not comply with the convention:

- A court cannot refuse to apply it.
- The court must apply the statute in the usual way.
- The High Court or the Court of Appeal or the House of Lords Court can, however, issue a declaration of incompatibility.
- The relevant minister can then use a form of delegated legislation to amend the statute without the need for going through the full parliamentary process that would normally be required.

Advantages of HRA	Disadvantages of HRA
<ul><li>It has made it easier and cheaper to enforce one's rights under the convention.</li><li>The remedies that a successful litigant can obtain are more suitable as now all the usual remedies that are available through the courts can be given to people whose human rights have been infringed.</li><li>It makes the law on civil liberties in general more accessible and simpler.</li><li>It avoids conflict between domestic and international law.</li></ul>	<ul><li>It has been argued that it gives too much power to the judges; although not everyone would agree that that was undesirable.</li><li>The Human Rights Act 1998 is not entrenched and could be repealed by parliament at any time.</li><li>So it cannot be seen as a bill of rights or as a form of written constitution.</li><li>The HRA seems to be enforceable only against the Government and public authorities and not against individuals or limited companies.</li></ul>

Contemporary debate about the impact of human rights legislation

CASE STUDY: The right to a fair trial extends to everyone but many believe 'that the HRA is misused by convicted criminals'

In May 2009 the man found guilty of the murder of 'Baby P' was also found guilty of the rape of a two-year-old girl. At the trial of the man who was convicted by a jury, the prosecution used evidence given by the victim of rape who by the time of the trial was four years old. The four-year-old victim was interviewed in a separate room and cross examined via video link. The jury believed the girl's evidence and found the defendant guilty.

A few days after the trial the defence lawyers, arguing that the evidence given by a four-year-old girl was not reliable enough to be used in court and that the rights of the accused were breached because he did not have a fair trial, filed an appeal. They argued that the verdict was unsafe because it relied so heavily on what they considered unreliable evidence.

This was the first case where evidence in court was allowed from someone so young. The girl faced a difficult cross examination and many people believed this was unfair because it expected too much from a young child.

ACTIVITY 6

1) What article in the HRA is being referred to by the defence lawyers of the man convicted of the rape of the girl?

2) The problem for some people is that the right to a fair trial (including the right to appeal) extends to all human beings even if you think they are 'monsters' as the *Daily Mail* described the convicted man in the 'Baby P' case (4 May 2009). Why is it important to ensure the rights to a fair trial of all citizens regardless of their crimes?

3) Identify arguments for and against the use of evidence in court by small children such as the four-year-old girl in this case. Consider the protection of the child and the reliability of a four-year-old child's testimony.

Sometimes it can be argued that the right to live life free of torture and the right to have a fair trial, for example, can at times be seen as not in the public interest. Some people argue that HRA works to protect the criminal, especially terrorists, more than it works to promote the interests of society as a whole.

ACTIVITY 7

1) Phil Woolas wants the HRA to be reviewed. What are the restrictions imposed by the courts (i.e. the HRA)? What does Phil Woolas fear most?

2) To what extent do you agree with the Conservatives that the HRA protects criminals too much and should not apply in the same way to convicted criminals as it does to law abiding citizens?

3) Define the term 'deportation'.

4) Suggest some ways the law could be overhauled to deal with deportation regulations.

5) Why might individuals wish to avoid deportation?

Criminals to face easier deportation

Human rights legislation that prevents ministers from deporting foreign criminals is to be overhauled under new government plans.

The 1998 Human Rights Act, which incorporated the European Convention on Human Rights into UK law, has been used successfully by lawyers to stop foreign criminals from being deported to countries where, they claim, they might be tortured or face other threats to their lives.

Phil Woolas, the immigration minister, said that, because of restrictions imposed by the courts, 'my biggest fear would be if Osama Bin Laden was arrested in London and we found that we were not able to deport him'.

The Conservatives have claimed that at least 4,000 foreign criminals convicted every year of offences such as theft, burglary, benefit fraud and drug dealing are allowed to remain in the UK after they are released from jail.

Jonathan Oliver, www.timesonline.co.uk, © *The Times*, 3 May 2009

5 The right to know

Article 10 of the Convention on Human Rights sets out the right to freedom of expression. That has to be the starting point for any discussion about the 'right to know'.

It is interesting to note that the convention uses the term 'expression' and not 'speech'. This is because speech (even if taken in the widest sense to include writing articles and broadcasting) is limited in the sense that the media is controlled by a very small number of people and so the opportunity of using speech to influence opinion is, for most of us, very limited indeed.

If you or I want to influence opinion we have little direct access to the media. But we can attract the media's attention by staging a demonstration.

From a practical point of view the best opportunity that most people will have of making a point and getting publicity for it will not be by speaking or writing, but by doing something and it is therefore right that the latter should be protected by Article 10 just as much as the former.

The term 'expression' will, of course, also include such things as photographs, cartoons and other forms of art. It is important that these should be protected. They can influence opinion and make a point just as effectively as other forms of expression.

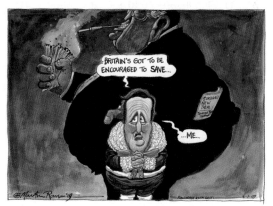

A political cartoon mocking Gordon Brown's efforts to tackle the credit crunch. How important is the role of cartoon in political debates?

Greenpeace's campaign to ban genetically modified food production. The building is a famous landmark in Paris – the Arc de Triomphe

TV celebrities Trinny and Susannah posed naked with a number of volunteers to promote their TV show and to celebrate the variety in Britain's body forms. The stunt and the TV show were raising awareness of body diversity in Britain

CASE STUDIES

Should giving money to support a particular cause be regarded as an 'expression' within Article 10?

In the case of *Bowman v UK* the European Court of Human Rights held that restrictions on the amount of money that non-candidates could spend on an election in the UK were a breach of the claimant's freedom of expression under Article 10.

Should a terrorist act (for example causing an explosion which killed or injured people and damaged property) be regarded as an 'expression'?

Would the damage to people and property justify making this an exception to the meaning of 'expression'? Or is the act itself so wicked that it could not be regarded as a justifiable form of conduct?

ACTIVITY 1

1) With reference to the case study above and any other themes you are aware of make a case for and against the restriction of extremist views from publicity and election funding.

Why is freedom of expression important?

The right to freedom of expression is protected by most constitutions. It is the subject of the first amendment to the USA constitution and is in the first section of the Canadian Charter of Rights and Freedoms. This would suggest that the freedom of expression has particular significance. There may be three reasons for this.

1) The argument from truth

No one has a monopoly on truth and the fact that one particular view is widely accepted does not justify preventing the views of those who disagree from being known. The minority may eventually be shown to be right. After all, at one time the majority of people thought that the world was flat and the centre of the universe. Even if the majority view is correct it is always better that it should be tested and debated rather than just accepted.

2) The argument from self-fulfilment

The right to express ideas is an important part of an individual's self-fulfilment. This is wider than the argument from truth – for example it includes artistic expression. Inherent in this argument is the idea that the ability to express our ideas is tied up with the nature of humanity. What makes us different from animals is our ability to communicate and express our feelings and emotions in a variety of ways. If we are unable to do that we lose something of the very nature of humanity itself.

3) The argument from democracy

This argument starts with the assumption that democracy is itself valuable and desirable. This is not the place to examine or develop that argument. In a democratic system the wishes of the people are taken into account by those in government. It follows therefore that for a democracy to work it is essential for people to be able to express their opinions on all relevant issues. It also follows that in order for people to be able to form opinions they need to have access to all the factual information that is available.

Restrictions on freedom of expression

Article 9 (the article in the convention that provides for freedom of expression) allows for the freedom to be restricted for a variety of reasons (look back at page 122 to see some of the reasons for restricting freedom of expression explained in more detail). These include the following:

1) national security, territorial integrity or public safety
2) the prevention of disorder or crime
3) the prevention of disclosure of information received in confidence
4) the protection of reputation.

Governments have for many years tried to keep the public from knowing some of the things that they were doing. It is clear that there are some activities that governments have to keep secret. When our armed forces are involved in conflict it would clearly be counterproductive to make public their long term strategies or their immediate plans. In the same way it would not be appropriate for the discussions of government ministers about these issues to be made public either. We have to accept that in some circumstances the Government needs to keep some things secret.

The problem arises about where to draw the line. Over the years governments have developed an ethos where the general attitude to any official information was one of secrecy. The approach has been that unless there is a good reason for disclosing information it should be kept secret. This approach has been fostered by a series of Official Secrets Acts 1911–1989 which criminalised the disclosure of 'official secrets' by anyone with access to them.

Against this background there was a movement for greater access to official information. In 1993 a white paper (a statement of government policy) entitled *Open Government* was published and in 1994 a code of practice (*Code of Practice on Access to Government Information*) based on it was introduced. Although this was a step in the right direction it was unenforceable and there were so many

exemptions that it was easy for ministers and others who were asked to disclose government information to find reasons for not doing so.

Examiner's tip

Questions often ask why freedom of information is important.

Remember that freedom of information is about access to government-held information – it is not about access to information held by individuals.

Be sure that you understand why we need to have access to government-held information. The examiner may link the question to human rights in general so be sure that you can relate the need to know what the Government is doing and the information that it has with the exercise of other democratic rights.

The purpose of the Data Protection Act (DPA) 1998

The Data Protection Act has two main purposes:

1) to protect the information held on an individual. Any organisation has a responsibility to keep records held on an individual safely. The loss or misuse of personal data can lead to prosecution under the law
2) to allow access to that information held on the individual if he or she requests it.

The Data Protection Act (DPA) 1998 came into force in 1999. The act tells all organisations such as businesses (large and small), schools and hospitals to allow the public free access to information the organisation keeps on them. If for example a credit card company held details on your credit history the DPA allows you to request a copy of the data.

If you make a request to your employer you must do so in writing stating what you require and the employer must reply within 40 working days. In the case of schools the Data Protection Act is very important because schools hold lots of data on both staff and students. In the case of a parent asking for data on their children the school must provide this within fifteen working days.

Why might you request information held about you?

It may be there are errors on your credit history which you would like to correct or check. Or you may simply be interested to know what an organisation knows about you; the data may simply be of interest. It may be that a school has reports on a child's conduct and progress and a parent wishes to know about this; they therefore have the right to access it as legal guardian of the student. Students can access data held on them such as references and reports. The point here is that for whatever reason you have the right to scrutinise any data an organisation holds on you. If you are able to access what a company holds on you that company is held more accountable to respect the rights of the employee or citizen's identity. Also your data is protected under the DPA where organisations have to show they are making every effort to keep your information secure. In the age of identity theft this should become more and more important.

Note the DPA is different from the Freedom of Information Act (FOIA) because the FOIA allows the public access to official documents and documents held by organisations which may have a public interest. An individual for example will be granted access to public documents such as the records of a health authority's budget through the FOIA but that individual would not be granted access to data held on individuals other than themselves under the DPA.

Web action

Go to the Information Commissioners office at **www.ico.gov.uk**. Click on *Data Protection Act* and then select the subsection called *for the public*, then the subsection called *crime*. You should be able to find out how the act applies to you and any records held on you by the police. As well as a section on crime there are also links to other sections such as education, health, housing, junk mail and marketing calls. Also, under the FAQs for the public there are a range of interesting areas where and how the act may apply. For example how to request information, whether you can request information on a deceased relative, and what your rights are under the act if a neighbour has a CCTV camera overlooking your garden.

Web action

Search online archives of national or regional newspapers and the BBC for recent cases involving the Data Protection Act. Two examples to get you started are as follows:

- In April 2009 hospital trusts were found to have breached the Data Protection Act in regard to safeguarding patient data – examples included losing memory sticks full of unencrypted patient data and having computers stolen that were full of patient records.
- In May 2009 a policewoman working in Edinburgh used police computers to illegally obtain personal information on dozens of Chinese people living in Scotland.

1) With reference to the cases you have found, assess the extent to which the DPA is an effective protection against misuse of personal details.

2) In what ways might personal details be used for criminal purposes?

The Freedom of Information Act (FOIA) 2000

After the general election of 1998 the new Labour government introduced legislation to deal with the issue of access to government held information and this resulted in the Freedom of Information Act (FOIA) 2000.

In broad terms the FOIA provides that an individual may make a request for information to a 'public authority' and that the authority must then tell the applicant whether or not it holds the information and, if it does hold the information requested, it must then provide that information to the applicant.

This is an encouraging start. The FOIA sets out in detail what is meant by a public authority. The definition of a public authority is very wide and it stretches to over seven pages. It includes central and local government and organisations such as the police, the National Health Service, maintained schools, FE colleges and universities. It also includes non-governmental organisations such as the National Lottery Commission and the Tate Gallery.

ACTIVITY 2

1) Look up the Freedom of Information Act 2000 on the internet and list five non-governmental organisations that are covered by it.

Applications for information under the FOIA

The FOIA sets out the procedures to be followed when a citizen makes a request for information under the act. These can be summarised as follows:

1) the application must be made in writing to the public authority believed to hold the information that is requested

2) the authority may charge a fee for dealing with the request

3) the authority is entitled to request more information from the applicant before dealing with the request

4) the authority should deal with the request within twenty days of the receipt of the request or the further information needed to deal with the request

5) if the authority supplies the information requested it will usually do so 'in permanent form'.

> Anyone can apply for information under the act. There is no need to show any reason for applying.
>
> If the information is supplied there is no restriction on what use can be made of it – it is a common mistake to think that it must be kept confidential.
>
> Remember that the obligation under the act is to provide 'information' – not documents. There is no need to supply copies of documents.

ACTIVITY 3

1) Given there is only the obligation to supply 'information', not actual documents, imagine you were a campaigner who needed details on a particular issue from a public organisation. Explain why it is vital to ask the right questions or make realistic requests for information from public bodies.

The act contains a long list of exemptions setting out circumstances where a public authority to which an application for information has been made does not need to supply the information that has been requested. These fall into five broad categories.

EXEMPTIONS TO THE FOIA

1) **Administrative reasons for refusing to supply information:**
   a) It would cost an unreasonable amount of money to supply the information
   b) The request for information is vexatious or has been made by the same applicant before.

2) **The request is unnecessary:**
   a) The information that has been requested is reasonably accessible by other means
   b) The public authority intends to publish the information in the future.

3) **Exemptions based on the nature of the subject matter that has been requested:**
   a) The information requested comes from the security or the intelligence services
   b) Disclosure of the information requested would prejudice national security
   c) Disclosure of the information requested would prejudice international relations
   d) Disclosure of the information would prejudice relations between England, Scotland, Wales and Northern Ireland
   e) The information is held for the purposes of a criminal investigation or prosecution

   f) The information is held for the purposes of law enforcement and the disclosure of it might prejudice the prevention of crime etc.

4) **Exemptions relating to the way the Government operates:**
   a) The information requested relates to the way in which government policy is formed and/or developed
   b) Disclosure of the information requested might prejudice the way the Government works or the way in which public affairs are conducted.

5) **Specific exemptions**
   a) The information requested relates to Court records, communications between the Government and the Queen, or material that is legally privileged
   b) The information requested relates to personal information or to private or commercial confidences.

This list of reasons is not exhaustive. There are other reasons for refusing to provide information. The above list is only intended to convey the broad general reasons for refusing to supply information that has been requested under the FOIA.

ACTIVITY 4

1) For each of the five exemptions listed above try to identify an example where each may apply – either real situations or hypothetical ones you make up.

You might think that there is not much information that is left to be disclosed and that on the basis of this list most requests could be turned down under one or other of the exemptions. It is certainly a disappointing feature of the Act that there are so many exemptions.

There is, however, a redeeming feature. Section 2 (S2) provides that information in most (but not all) of the exempt categories should be disclosed unless the public interest in exempting it outweighs the public interest in disclosing it. This does not apply to information from security or intelligence services or information which is exempted on the basis of being personal information, or of being covered by parliamentary privilege or to information from court records.

It does, however, apply to information that comes into the general categories of national security and defence.

If a public authority is asked to supply information which is exempted, but to which S2 of the FOIA applies, then it has to decide if the public interest in disclosing the information outweighs the public interest in keeping it secret.

The Information Commissioner

The Government has issued codes of practice to be followed by public authorities when making decisions in relation to applications for information under the FOIA. The operation of the act in general and the codes of practice is supervised by the **Information Commissioner**.

Any member of the public can complain to the Information Commissioner if he or she believes that a public authority has failed to deal properly with a request for information made under the act. The Information Commissioner has powers to investigate such complaints. In some circumstances he can obtain a search warrant and search the premises of the public authority complained about.

At the end of his investigation he will issue a decision notice. Either party can appeal to the **information tribunal**. A further appeal can be made to the High Court.

The Information Commissioner can also issue an enforcement notice specifying the action that has to be taken by the public authority if he believes that it has failed in its obligations. As with a decision notice, the public authority has the right to appeal to the information tribunal with a further appeal to the High Court.

The FOIA contemporary debate

Contemporary debate about the FOIA often revolves around two areas:

1) whether or not organisations are complying with the law or dodging their responsibilities
2) whether citizens are effectively more empowered because of the act.

CASE STUDY: Welsh councils refuse to answer nearly one in ten freedom of information requests they receive

Wrexham AM Lesley Griffiths said last night: 'The Freedom of Information Act was a landmark Act of Parliament that gave private citizens the right to know and I don't think some public bodies have embraced that ethos yet.' The Government introduced the Freedom of Information Act, which came into force in January 2005 and forced public bodies to disclose vital information.

'Whether those in the political world agree with it or not, there's no doubt the extra scrutiny on public bodies is welcomed by the taxpayer. Obviously, some requests can simply not be answered as they may be too general, are too time-consuming to deal with or jeopardise public safety. However, everything must be done to make sure people feel they have the adequate means to find out public information they feel they are entitled to.'

A total of 14,158 requests were filed to Welsh councils, with 1,315 turned down either partly or fully. Another 336 remain unanswered. Common reasons for refusing applications include claiming processing them would take too long and cost too much money, or that information can be kept secret under the Act.

Freedom of Information campaigner Heather Brooke said: 'One of the most important things for an informed electorate is that you have information. It sounds obvious, but a lot of public bodies don't understand that. Freedom of information is answering questions the public want to know, not what councils want them to know.'

A Welsh Local Government Association spokeswoman criticised the way the latest figures were compiled. Pointing out that there are 26 legitimate reasons for not providing information under the Act, she added: 'This research highlights over 14,000 freedom of information requests received across Wales but it would be interesting to know how many of these are officially freedom of information requests.'

'Hundreds of the requests sent to councils on a daily basis are neither legally nor officially defined as freedom of information requests. Many of them are covered by the Data Protection Act meaning there is no legal requirement on councils to provide this information.'

Ben Glaze, _Western Mail_, www.walesonline.co.uk, 4 May 2009

ACTIVITY 5

1) What reasons are most frequently used for rejecting a request for information from the public?
2) Why might the figures which were published by the Labour group in the Welsh Assembly be misleading?
3) Explain what Heather Brooke means by her statement 'Freedom of information is answering questions the public want to know, not what councils want them to know'.
4) Evaluate the contribution of the FOIA to an informed electorate.

There is no doubt that the FOIA represents a great step forward and brings the UK closer to the position of most other western democracies by giving its citizens much greater powers to obtain information about the workings of the Government of the day. But the legislation is complex and there is plenty of scope for public authorities to avoid giving information that they want to keep secret.

6 Other rights of UK citizens

In this chapter we have been considering the way in which the concept of rights has affected the law. We have seen that the law consists of a series of rights that citizens and others can exercise and that these rights create duties that oblige other citizens or the state to do something or to refrain from doing something.

We have seen how the Human Rights Act 1998 incorporated the European Convention on Human Rights into UK law and how this strengthened the protection of the rights of UK citizens as it made it possible to enforce the Convention rights in the UK courts.

We have also seen how the Freedom of Information Act 2000 has, to a limited extent, improved the access that citizens have to information held by public authorities that was previously kept secret.

But, of course, UK citizens enjoy a wide range of rights, many of which are not protected by the existing human rights legislation. The Human Rights Act 1998 has, however, very wide ramifications and its scope and effect are the subject of constant expansion by the courts.

The purpose of this topic is to look briefly at some of the other rights that UK citizens have.

There are quite a lot of rights that come into this category. We do not have to use the examples from the specification. But they are good examples and so we will use them first.

Welfare rights

When we looked at the Human Rights Act 1998 we saw that it does not deal with social or economic rights. It focuses on what we might broadly call political rights. That is because it would be very difficult to find a consensus

among the countries that have signed the convention as to what social or economic rights should be protected or how that protection might be given.

In the UK the welfare state provides support for its citizens in a number of ways. The NHS provides health care that is usually free at the point of delivery. This includes primary health care in the form of GP surgeries and a range of hospital facilities.

It must also be remembered that there is considerable overlap in the provision of 'welfare' as both social services and education link in to a number of other services provided by the state for its citizens.

The state also provides a series of allowances payable to citizens in a variety of circumstances. Examples are as follows:

- Job Seekers' Allowance is payable to those who are unemployed and who are actively seeking work
- Child Benefit is payable to the parents of all children under the age of sixteen

- Disability Living Allowance is paid to citizens who are unable to perform certain essential tasks for themselves
- a state pension is paid to all citizens of pension age.

The examples listed above are only a tiny proportion of the provision made by the state for the welfare of its citizens. The law relating to the provision of welfare is very complex and it is beyond the purpose of this book to discuss or explain it. It is sufficient to note here that the provision is almost entirely created by either statutes or delegated legislation and that a series of tribunals ensure that it is fairly and correctly administered.

Clearly UK citizens rely heavily on the welfare services provided by the state. It would be very hard to imagine what life without them would be like. But there is nothing in the European Convention on Human Rights that protects them.

They are, however, indirectly protected. Any government that abolished the welfare state (or a significant number of the advantages it provides) would be so unpopular that it would be likely to be voted out of power at the next general election. The HRA protects the right to free and fair elections by secret ballot, so no party could abolish the welfare state and then try to avoid holding an election in order to remain in power.

Many people would argue that this is a serious weakness in the HRA. The right to the welfare benefits to which UK citizens have for so long been accustomed is largely taken for granted, but as previously noted, there would be no consensus among the other signatories of the convention about how such provision should be made. It is for that reason that there is no reference in the HRA to the welfare rights we have been discussing.

EDUCATION AND THE HRA

We usually consider education to be part of the general welfare provision and in the UK there is free education for all under sixteen year olds.

The right to an education was not mentioned in the original convention, but Article 2 of the first protocol provides that there is a right not to be denied access to the educational system.

In the UK this system is free to all. Under UK law everyone of school age is entitled to a free education and the right to participate in the system is protected by the first protocol. But, if there was a root and branch change to the system so that everyone had to make a direct contribution in order to access it that would not be a breach of the first protocol as long as there was no discrimination about who could access it.

The right protected by the HRA is not to be denied access to the system. The HRA could not prevent changes to the system, for example it could not prevent the introduction of a charge.

ACTIVITY 1

Our rights to free medical care may not be protected by the HRA, but they are nevertheless fairly safe. It is unlikely that any government would take the political risk of interfering with them. But is this enough?

1) Do you think we should have a separate bill of rights that includes things such as free medical care? Explain your answer.

2) Is it desirable that welfare rights should be 'fixed' in some way, or is it better that they should be flexible and able to change and adapt to the needs of society? Explain your view.

The right to defend oneself

The defence of self defence usually arises when a defendant is charged with assault and argues that the force used was necessary to protect himself or herself from an attack by the victim. We all have a right that is well recognised in criminal law to use reasonable force to defend ourselves from an attack by another person.

There is no mention of this right in the HRA or in the convention. But this is a very different situation from the welfare rights that we have just considered.

The welfare rights are specific rights given by statute and/or delegated legislation to UK citizens. They are entirely outside the scope of the convention and therefore of the HRA.

The convention is drafted in a typically European fashion – it tends to set out general principles rather than deal with details. It makes no mention of issues such as self defence. To that extent one could argue that the right to defend oneself is not protected by either the convention or the HRA.

Suppose for the sake of argument that the British Government abolished the right to self defence. Would that be a breach of the convention – and therefore of the HRA?

We have seen that the convention does not mention the right to defend oneself. But it does, however, protect the right to a fair trial. It would certainly be open to a defendant charged with assault to argue that if a person charged with assault was not allowed to produce evidence that he was defending himself agaainst an unjustified attack then he or she would not have a fair trial. If the court took a broad view of the convention then this approach would certainly be arguable. If X attacked Y and Y used reasonable force to defend himself and in doing so injured X then one could certainly argue that it would be unfair to convict Y of assaulting X.

If a narrow view of the convention was taken, then the position might be different. It could be argued that the right to a fair trial relates only to the procedures adopted at the trial. It might be argued that if the procedures were fair, then the fact that a particular defence was not available would not be relevant. The trial itself would still be fair.

This narrow view seems unacceptable. Before the Second World War Nazi Germany passed laws allowing the Government to send people to concentration camps because they were Jewish. The laws were passed in accordance with the then German constitution and were valid laws. In accordance with those laws Jews were sent to the concentration camps. It was legal under the existing laws of the time. But it was unfair because the laws themselves were unfair.

In the same way it could be argued that a law that took away the right to use reasonable force to defend oneself would effectively take away the right to a fair trial and so would be in breach of the convention.

We saw in the previous section of this chapter that the courts would have to apply such a law, but the High Court, the Court of Appeal or the House of Lords can make a declaration of incompatibility allowing the Government the opportunity of adopting a fast track procedure to change the law to bring it in line with the HRA and the convention.

So this is a right which, although it is not mentioned in the convention, does seem to be protected by it.

ACTIVITY 2

1) Can you think of other situations where a right is not specifically mentioned in the convention, but is covered by a general provision in the convention?

The right to trial by jury

The right to be tried by one's peers is often said to date back to Magna Carta in 1215 and indeed juries have been used in trials in England since Norman times. Today juries are rarely used in civil cases.

Juries are usually found in criminal cases, but even here they are only used in a very small percentage of cases.

Juries are used in the Crown Court to decide if the accused is guilty or not guilty. Juries do not have any role in deciding the sentence – that is done by the judge. If the accused pleads guilty then a jury will not be involved as the accused has admitted his or her guilt and the judge will pass sentence.

Juries are only used in about 1 per cent of all criminal cases – but that is still about 30,000 cases every year. These are the most important and serious cases.

TRIAL BY JURY IN CIVIL CASES

Under the Supreme Court Act 1981 the right to trial by jury in civil cases is limited to cases relating to:

- defamation (that is cases of libel or slander)
- fraud
- malicious prosecution
- false imprisonment.

In all of these cases the court can refuse trial by jury if the Judge believes that the case will involve:

- prolonged examination of documents or accounts, or
- scientific or local examination which cannot conveniently be done by a jury.

From a practical point of view trial by jury in civil cases is usually limited to cases about libel and slander. Cases involving fraud, malicious prosecution and false imprisonment are very rare indeed.

Juries can only be used in other types of civil case in exceptional circumstances where the court permits trial by jury.

TRIAL BY JURY IN CRIMINAL CASES

All criminal cases are divided into three categories. These are:

- summary cases
- cases triable either way
- indictable cases.

Summary cases are usually the least serious type of cases. They are tried only in the magistrates' courts. The majority of offences are summary offences and, because in general they are the least serious type of offence, they tend to be the most commonly committed type of offence. Juries have no role in trying summary offences. About 95 per cent of all criminal cases will be tried summarily in the magistrates' courts without any involvement of juries.

Indictable offences are the most serious type of criminal case. They will always be tried in the Crown Court and will therefore be tried by a jury as juries are only used in the Crown Court.

Cases triable either way are cases where the accused has the right to choose trial in the magistrates' courts or the Crown Court. If the accused elects to be tried in the magistrates' courts then he or she will have a summary trial (where there is no right to a jury) but if the accused elects for trial on indictment the trial will be in the Crown Court where a jury will be involved.

Juries are only used in certain types of cases

We have seen that the HRA and the Convention do protect the right to a fair trial. But in 95 per cent of cases there is no right to trial by jury and it is not suggested that trial in the magistrates' courts is in any way unfair. There is no suggestion that a jury is the only way to ensure a fair trial – it just happens to be the way that serious cases are tried in the UK.

There is no doubt therefore that it is not protected by the HRA. As long as the trial process is fair that is all that is required. In most people's view trial by jury is the fairest way to try serious criminal cases, but it would have to be conceded that it is not the only fair way to try them.

The jury has a central role in our criminal justice system. It is used in relatively few cases and it may be argued that its significance is symbolic rather than real.

But the issue we need to consider is whether or not it is protected by the HRA.

ACTIVITY 3

This topic is designed to get you thinking about what sort of rights are protected by the convention and the HRA – and why some things are not protected while others are.

1) Make a list of four or five rights that are protected by the convention – and four or five that are not.
2) What was the convention trying to do?
3) Has it got it right, in your opinion?
4) Do we need to protect the issues that are not covered by the convention in some other way?
5) Do you think this is possible?

Exam questions

SECTION B: RIGHTS AND
RESPONSIBILITIES

Answer Question 4 and **either** Question 5 **or**
Question 6.

This section carries 30 marks.

4 Read the extract below and answer parts (a)
and (b) which follow.

> The Human Rights Act 1998 is a complex law which professional lawyers still debate today. Although the law is part of English legal system it usually requires solicitors to advise citizens on how it applies in law.
>
> The Human Rights Act 1998 includes the various parts of the European convention (agreement) on human rights such as the right to an education, the right to marry who we choose, the right to a fair trial, the right to express our own faith, to vote in free elections, etc.

Your answers should refer to the extract as
appropriate, but you should also include
other relevant information.

(a) Briefly examine the meaning of the
term 'human rights'.   (*5 marks*)

(b) Examine some of the ways the Human
Rights Act 1998 has impacted upon
the rights of British citizens. (*10 marks*)

Either:

5 Assess the difficulties in balancing both
duties and rights in legal issues.
    (*15 marks*)

Or:

6 Assess the impact of the Data Protection
Act 1998 and the Freedom of Information
Act 2000 in protecting the rights of all
British citizens.   (*15 marks*)

SECTION 2: RIGHTS AND RESPONSIBILITIES

Chapter 4: How are my rights protected and supported?

In this chapter we explore two main issues which examine the key question 'How are my rights protected and supported?'

ISSUE 1: The legal framework: protecting the citizen
This issue is explored through the following topics:
- civil and criminal law
- legal representation
- alternative methods of resolving disputes.

ISSUE 2: How do the courts protect my rights?
This issue is explored through the following topics:
- the role of the courts
- the courts and the Human Rights Act
- judicial review.

ISSUE 1: THE LEGAL FRAMEWORK: PROTECTING THE CITIZEN

In this section we explore the following three topics:

- civil and criminal law
- legal representation
- alternative methods of resolving disputes

1 Civil and criminal law

In the introduction to Chapter 3 we looked at what we mean by the idea of law. Look at this introduction again (pages 100–2). In particular look at the section that asks to you think about what the law does.

There are many different ways of analysing legal rules. Sometimes it is useful to think of them in terms of the way in which they were created. You will remember that in Chapter 3 we saw that some law is made by Parliament, some by the courts and some by a variety of forms of delegated legislation.

More often it is useful to classify legal rules by what they do. When we do this we usually think about the law in terms of civil law and criminal law.

ACTIVITY 1

1) List the elements of justice mentioned in the statement of goals by the HMCS opposite.

W e b   a c t i o n

It would be very useful for you to explore the website of HMCS, **www.hmcourts-service.gov.uk**, at regular intervals. Also of use is the site **www.direct.gov.uk**, click on the *crime, justice and the law* section.

Criminal law and punishment

HER MAJESTY'S COURTS SERVICE

Her Majesty's Courts Service (HMCS) is an executive agency of the Ministry of Justice (MoJ). Our remit is to deliver justice effectively and efficiently to the public.

Our goal is that:

'All citizens according to their differing needs are entitled to access to justice, whether as victims of crime, defendants accused of crimes, consumers in debt, children in need of care, or business people in commercial disputes. Our aim is to ensure that access is provided as quickly as possible and at the lowest cost consistent with open justice and that citizens have greater confidence in, and respect for, the system of justice.'

www.hmcourts-service.gov.uk

When people think about law they usually think of a series of rules. It is a good deal more complex that that suggests, but nevertheless it is a very good starting point. When we think about the law as a series of rules we usually think of rules that prohibit us from doing a variety of things, for example 'don't kill', 'don't steal'. Most Western societies trace these particular basic rules back to biblical times and the Ten Commandments set out in the Book of Exodus in the Old Testament.

In our modern society these rules prohibiting certain types of conduct are usually quite complex and in addition to proscribing certain behaviour they usually carry a penalty for doing the acts that are forbidden. So the Theft Act 1966 not only prohibits theft, but it lays down penalties for those who steal. This area of the law is known as criminal law.

The main purpose of the criminal law is to regulate and control society by punishing what society regards as unacceptable behaviour. Not every form of wrong doing will be punished. Adultery is not a crime and neither is smoking in the open air. We saw in the introduction to topic 3 in Chapter 3 that the law is not static and as society changes its mind about certain types of behaviour so it will change its mind about what should be punished and what should not.

SOCIETY CHANGES ITS MIND!

For many years it was an offence for two people of the same sex to have a sexual relationship together. As society became more tolerant of people's personal preferences this rule was abolished.

At one time it was not an offence to smoke in public places. As society became more aware of the harm caused by passive smoking this rule was changed and it now is an offence to smoke in enclosed public places.

Some forms of conduct are clearly unacceptable – most people would agree that murder, rape and theft are all unacceptable and no one would seriously suggest that they should not be crimes. But there is a range of other forms of conduct where there is less agreement. Many people, for example, would argue that abortion should be a crime whereas others may argue that the smoking of cannabis should not be a crime.

ACTIVITY 2

1) Identify two other things that are crimes but that you think should not be considered as criminal. Explain your reasons.
2) Identify two things that are not crimes at present but that you think should be considered as criminal. Explain your reasons.

When it is believed that a crime has been committed the **police** are usually called in to investigate. They have to decide if a crime has been committed and if so they then have to try to find out who committed it.

Once the police have found out who committed the crime they send the information they have collected to the **Crown Prosecution Service (CPS)**. The CPS decides if there is enough evidence against the suspect to obtain a conviction in court. It also decides if it is in the public interest to prosecute the suspect. If the CPS decides to prosecute, a member of its staff presents the evidence against the accused in court.

CASE STUDY: What is the difference between punishment and compensation?

Hussain drives his car carelessly and knocks Yasmine down and injures her. There may be two consequences:

1) Hussain may have committed a criminal offence (for example careless driving). If he has, then he may be prosecuted by the state and be punished.
2) As Hussain has injured Yasmine she may want compensation.

WHERE IS THE CASE HEARD?

1) Serious criminal cases are tried in the Crown Court where a jury decides on the facts of the case and if the accused is guilty or not guilty of the offence with which he is charged. Serious cases (called 'indictable' cases) include cases where the accused is charged with murder, attempted murder, manslaughter, rape and serious assault.

2) The least serious cases (called 'summary' cases) are tried in the Magistrates' Court.

3) Cases that may or may not be serious depending on the facts of the particular case (such as theft) are called 'cases triable either way' and these are tried in either the Crown Court or the Magistrates' Court.

THE CASE AGAINST HUSSAIN

If the case against Hussain is successful the court finds him guilty and it **convicts** him.

After a person has been convicted by the court the court then **sentences** them.

The sentence is the punishment that the court orders. It can be:

• a fine

• imprisonment

• a community sentence, for example an order to do unpaid work for a number of hours.

We have seen how the state will deal with the criminal issue set out above. The police will investigate it and will pass their file to the CPS who will make the final decision about whether or not Hussain should be prosecuted. If he is to be prosecuted, then the CPS will bring the case against him in the Magistrates' Court – as most motoring offences are summary offences.

In the example we looked at Hussain has injured Yasmine, so she may want compensation for her injuries and any loss that she has had as a result of the accident. Yasmine will have to rely on the civil law to get damages for the injury that Hussain has caused her.

Web action

Go to **www.direct.gov.uk/en/index.htm** and select from the menu *crime, justice and the law*, then from the *'judicial system'* section select *sentencing and appeals*.

1] Identify the three main types of sentence and briefly explain each of them.
2] Identify three of the twelve types of community sentence available for use by the courts.
3] Using the same area of the web page define what is meant by 'community payback'.

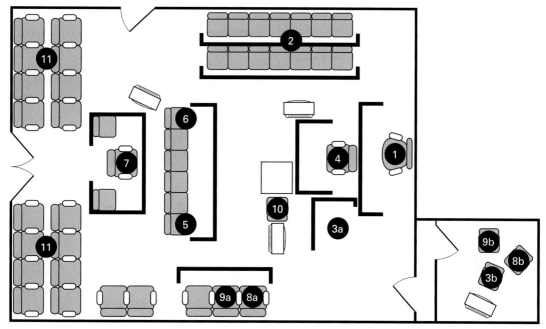

Inside an English Crown Court

Key to inside an English Crown Court

1 **The judge**
The judge ensures all the rules are kept and that the defendant has a fair trial. If the defendant is found guilty the judge will pass the sentence on them, or tell them they're free to go if found not guilty.

2 **The jury**
The jury is made of twelve men and women. They do not know the details of the case beforehand; their job is to listen to all the facts and decide whether the defendant is guilty or not.

3a **Witness box**
This is where the witness will stand or sit to give their evidence.

3b **Witness video room**
A room where the young/vulnerable/intimidated can give evidence. The video is shown in the court room, on small screens.

4 **The clerk**
The clerk takes care of the papers that are needed during the trial.

5 **The prosecutor**
The prosecutor is a lawyer for the Crown Prosecution Service. They will present the evidence and show how the defendant may have broken the law.

6 **The defence lawyer**
The defence lawyer's job is to persuade the jury that the defendant is not guilty by cross examination of prosecution witnesses and calling witnesses to support the defendant's case.

7 **The defendant**
The defendant is the person who the police believe broke the law. An officer from the prison service will sit next to the defendant.

8a **Witness service**
8b If you want the witness service to assist you and to sit with you in the court, here is where they will do that.

9a **The usher**
9b The usher will wear a black robe. They will tell witnesses when to come into the court and will ask them to swear an oath.

10 **The note taker**
This person writes down everything that's being said, so witnesses must speak clearly. The judge may also take notes.

11 **The public**
The court is open to the public, people may sit and listen in the background. If this worries a witness the court may be closed to the general public

Adapted from www.info-court.org

ACTIVITY 3

1) Which body makes most of the decisions on what should and should not be a law?
2) What is the main purpose of criminal law?
3) Name two acts that are wrong-doings but are not punished by law.
4) Distinguish between 'burden of proof' and 'standard of proof' in criminal law.
5) Briefly explain the role of the Crown Prosecution Service (CPS).

Civil law and compensation

Civil law differs from criminal law in many ways, but the most obvious is that it does not involve the state. It is sometimes said to be 'private law' as it involves actions by one private individual (or company) against another. The purpose of the civil law is to sort out disputes that arise between individuals or organisations.

Look back at the case study on page 144. Yasmine was injured when Hussain knocked her down. It is unlikely that she will want compensation for her injuries. This is a very typical example of the sort of problem that has to be sorted out by the civil law, but there are many other situations where one person has a dispute with another.

Other examples of civil disputes:

- one person has borrowed money from another and has not repaid it in accordance with the agreement they made
- one individual has damaged the reputation of another
- a buyer has purchased goods from a seller and either the seller has not handed over the goods or the buyer has not paid for them
- a person is annoying his neighbour by having regular late night noisy parties that keep the neighbour awake.

In the situations outlined above the person bringing the action (the **claimant**) will usually be wanting compensation from the person he brings the action against (the **defendant**).

In some limited circumstances a claimant may want the court to make a defendant do something – or in the case of the noisy neighbour, to stop doing something!

The civil courts are usually asked to make the defendant pay compensation to the claimant. Cases where other remedies are required are relatively rare and the court only grants alternative remedies in special circumstances.

THE COURT SYSTEM: APPEALS AND FUNCTIONS

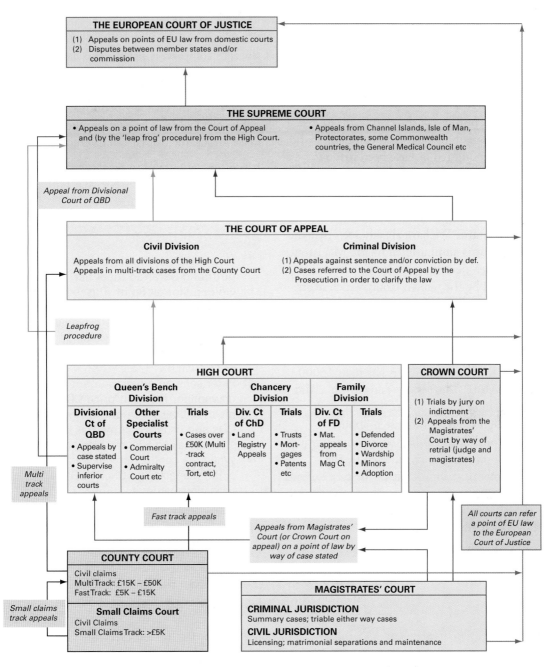

THE EUROPEAN COURT OF JUSTICE
(1) Appeals on points of EU law from domestic courts
(2) Disputes between member states and/or commission

THE SUPREME COURT
- Appeals on a point of law from the Court of Appeal and (by the 'leap frog' procedure) from the High Court.
- Appeals from Channel Islands, Isle of Man, Protectorates, some Commonwealth countries, the General Medical Council etc

Appeal from Divisional Court of QBD

THE COURT OF APPEAL

Civil Division
Appeals from all divisions of the High Court
Appeals in multi-track cases from the County Court

Criminal Division
(1) Appeals against sentence and/or conviction by def.
(2) Cases referred to the Court of Appeal by the Prosecution in order to clarify the law

Leapfrog procedure

HIGH COURT

Queen's Bench Division

Divisional Ct of QBD	Other Specialist Courts	Trials
• Appeals by case stated • Supervise inferior courts	• Commercial Court • Admiralty Court etc	• Cases over £50K (Multi-track contract, Tort, etc)

Chancery Division

Div. Ct of ChD	Trials
• Land Registry Appeals	• Trusts • Mortgages • Patents etc

Family Division

Div. Ct of FD	Trials
• Mat. appeals from Mag Ct	• Defended • Divorce • Wardship • Minors • Adoption

CROWN COURT
(1) Trials by jury on indictment
(2) Appeals from the Magistrates' Court by way of retrial (judge and magistrates)

Multi track appeals

Fast track appeals

Appeals from Magistrates' Court (or Crown Court on appeal) on a point of law by way of case stated

All courts can refer a point of EU law to the European Court of Justice

COUNTY COURT
Civil claims
Multi Track: £15K – £50K
Fast Track: £5K – £15K

Small Claims Court
Civil Claims
Small Claims Track: >£5K

Small claims track appeals

MAGISTRATES' COURT

CRIMINAL JURISDICTION
Summary cases; triable either way cases

CIVIL JURISDICTION
Licensing; matrimonial separations and maintenance

NB The diagram does not show all the work carried out by the High Court. The various divisions of the High Court all perform a number of other functions, but there is not enough space to show these.

It is important to remember that civil law and criminal law are very different. We have already seen that they have different purposes:

- the main purpose of the criminal law is to regulate society by punishing those who are found to have broken the rules that society has laid down
- the main purpose of the civil law is to compensate individuals and companies who have been injured or have been made to suffer in some other way by the conduct of other individuals.

Civil law and criminal law are administered in different courts. We have already seen that the criminal law is administered by the Magistrates' Court which hear the 'summary' or less serious crimes and by the Crown Court which hears the 'indictable' or serious crimes.

Civil cases are heard in either:

1) the **Small Claims Court** if the value of the claim for compensation is less than £5000
2) the **County Court** if the value of the claim is over £5000
3) the **High Court** if the case is about:
    - personal injuries (i.e. about compensation for a physical injury suffered by the claimant) and the value of the case exceeds £50,000
    - any other matter where the case is particularly difficult or where the parties agree that it should be heard in the High Court
    - one of the issues that must be heard in the High Court, for example defamation or a complaint against the police.

Most appeals will be heard in either the Court of Appeal or the Supreme Court irrespective of whether or not the case involved civil or criminal law.

How the law enables citizens to make appropriate arrangements

We said that the main purpose of the criminal law is to compensate people who have suffered a loss or injury as a result of the conduct of another individual. There is, however, another purpose that the civil law performs and this must not be overlooked. The civil law allows people to make arrangements that can be enforced.

It is often very useful to be able to make an agreement with someone else that both parties know will be carried out.

CASE STUDIES

1) **Nick makes an arrangement with his girlfriend Sarah to meet her in the Golden Lion at 8p.m.** This is just a simple agreement. If Sarah did not turn up Nick might be very annoyed (and he might not make another arrangement to meet her) but the law would not be involved in it.

2) **Peter sees an advertisement in a newspaper for a cut-price CD and gives his credit card number to Xtra Cheap CDs and orders a copy.** This is the first step in making a legally binding contract. When the contract comes into existence both Peter and Xtra Cheap CDs will have obligations under it.

Making contracts

Every day people buy and sell things and every such transaction is a contract. We do not need to worry about the quite complex rules about how contracts are made, or about the consequences of making a contract, but we do need to appreciate that every time anyone buys or sells something there is a contract between the buyer and the seller.

In many cases there is no time lapse between making the contract and completing it. If

Emma goes into a shop to buy a lipstick, selects it and takes it to the checkout to pay for it she makes a contract with the shop (the checkout operator represents the shop that is selling the lipstick). When Emma pays for the lipstick she performs her part of the contract. When the checkout operator gives it to her the shop performs its obligations under the contract.

CONTRACTS

Contrary to what most people believe contracts do not usually need to be made in writing. Most contracts are made orally. It can, of course, be useful to put the terms of the contract in writing to avoid any argument about what they are. A few contracts (for example contracts for the sale of land and contracts about consumer credit) must be made in writing.

Not every contract is as simple as the one above. If you buy goods on the internet you don't get them the moment you pay for them. But the same rules apply. Every contract for the sale of goods has an obligation on the part of the buyer to pay for the goods he or she purchases and the seller has an obligation to hand the goods over to the buyer.

CASE STUDY

Hamish goes to get his hair cut in 'Clippers' the barbers. He is making a contract with the hairdresser to cut his hair in the fashion that he has asked for. The obligation on the hairdresser is to cut Hamish's hair the way Hamish has asked for it to be cut. The obligation on Hamish is to pay the agreed price, or, if no price has been agreed, a reasonable price.

The law of contract makes it possible for us to transfer ownership of goods from one person to another in a wide variety of circumstances. The law of contract also makes it possible for us to purchase services from someone else.

If we were not able to make such arrangements life would be very difficult. You need to be confident that when you get on a bus and pay your fare that the driver would then take you to your destination and not just take you part of the way and then say that he did not feel like completing the journey.

ACTIVITY 4

1) Make a list of three very simple contracts that you make every day.

Making a will

As people get older they start to think about what will happen to their belongings when they die. The law provides a list of rules about how their property will be divided up. These rules are quite complex. They are contained in the Administration of Estates Act 1925.

Often people want to make their own decision about what will happen to their property after their death. The Wills Act 1837 and the Administration of Justice Act 1982 allow a person to bypass the state's rules and (with some limitations) make their own decisions about what will happen to their property when they die.

If a person makes a valid will he or she has made arrangements that they know will have legal effect after their death.

This is another aspect of the civil law. It is called the law of succession and it is another example of how the civil law allows us to make legally binding arrangements.

Other aspects of the civil law

We have seen how the civil law enables people who have been injured or who have suffered some other kind of loss or damage to get compensation and how it allows us all to make arrangements that will be legally binding.

The civil law does many other things too; in fact it influences every aspect of our lives. For example it:

- sets out the rules about marriage and divorce
- sets out the rules about making companies and partnerships
- protects creative work that we produce by the laws of copyright
- allows us to manage our business and family affairs by creating trusts
- makes provision about the ownership of land and houses.

Cafcass

Cafcass is an organisation that uses the court system to resolve disputes.

It helps children and their parents sort out their differences if problems arise that they cannot sort out themselves.

Cafcass advises parents and children of all ages on how and what the family courts do.

ACTIVITY 5

1) How does standard of proof differ in criminal law proceedings compared with civil law proceedings?
2) What are 'summary cases'?
3) Where are 'summary cases' tried?
4) What is the key difference between civil law and criminal law?
5) Distinguish between agreements and contracts using examples to illustrate your points.

Web action

Go to **www.cafcass.gov.uk** and click on the section *about Cafcass*.
1) What does 'Cafcass' stand for?
2) What things does cafcass do?
3) What are the three main areas that the courts ask Cafcass to assist with?
Go back to the Cafcass home page. Click on the *information for children* image and explore the role of family courts.
4) What are the main areas that the courts will make decisions about you and your living arrangements if your parents cannot agree between themselves?
Now click on the *what happens in court* image to activate the flash player information presentation.
The website has a wealth of information about all sorts of issues involving family and children's law and the site is well worth exploring further. For example click on *publications* to find leaflets for children.

2 Legal representation

The legal professions: solicitors and barristers

We have seen in topic 1 that some aspects of the law can be quite complicated. Most people rely on lawyers to advise them when they are involved in legal matters. We are all familiar with footballers consulting their **lawyers** before making a contract to join a new club and most people get help from their lawyer when they come to buy a house or a flat.

The term 'lawyer' is a general expression without much clear definition. It just means 'a practitioner in the law ... a person learned or skilled in the law ...' (*Chambers Dictionary*).

In the UK, unlike in most other countries, there are two distinct legal professions – **barristers** and **solicitors**.

Historically, the distinction between the two professions was very clear, but in recent years this has reduced considerably. Both professions do broadly the same sort of work. They:

- advise clients about the law and their rights
- draft legal documents
- represent clients in court.

The two professions still have some differences but today these are principally in the proportion of time they spend doing the various tasks that they perform. They are, however, two separate professions and so we consider each of them separately here.

Solicitors

The Law Society's offices

There are nearly 100,000 solicitors in England and Wales. Scotland and Northern Ireland have their own legal professions. The body which regulates the solicitors' profession is the Solicitors Regulation Authority. It was set up in 2005 to deal with concerns that the profession did not pay enough attention to the needs of its clients. The Solicitors Regulation Authority has sixteen members, nine of them solicitors, but seven of them are **lay people**.

The Law Society is a trade association for solicitors and looks after their interests.

Solicitors spend much of their time doing office-based work. This includes:

- conveyancing (buying and selling houses and other property)
- drawing up wills and contracts
- giving oral and written advice to clients on legal topics.

In the past, all solicitors had the right to represent clients in the magistrates' courts and the County Court, but only barristers could represent clients in the Crown Court, the High Court, the Court of Appeal and the House of Lords. We have seen in the last topic that about 98 per cent of all criminal cases are heard in the magistrates' courts and here the **advocate** (the name given to a lawyer who represents a client in court) is usually a solicitor, so solicitors have traditionally done the bulk of criminal advocacy, but were restricted to appearing in the lower courts.

The Courts and Legal Services Act 1990 and the Access to Justice Act 1999 have given solicitors the same rights to appear in court and represent a client as barristers, but they have to complete additional training in order to exercise these rights. A solicitor who has done the additional training and has the right to appear in all courts is called a **solicitor-advocate**. Approximately 1000 solicitors have become solicitor-advocates and the number is growing all the time.

Most solicitors work in partnership with other solicitors. Firms of solicitors are found in most towns across the country.

Barristers

A barrister outside court

There are far fewer barristers than there are solicitors – only about 11,500. The barristers' profession is collectively known as 'the Bar'. The governing body of the Bar is the Bar Council. It acts like a trade union, protecting the interests of barristers. It has created a Bar Standards Board to regulate the profession in the same way as the Solicitors Regulation Authority regulates solicitors.

In general a client cannot approach a barrister with a legal problem directly. They would usually take their problem to a solicitor and he or she would engage a barrister if it was necessary to do so. But just as solicitors have gained the right to appear alongside barristers in the higher courts, so barristers have now the right to accept work directly from the public, provided they have done a course qualifying them to do so. There is little evidence to suggest that many people do bring their problems directly to a barrister.

Barristers spend much of their time in court, or preparing for court. Until 1990 they had the monopoly of advocacy in the higher courts, but we have seen that that has now been lost as solicitor-advocates have the same rights of advocacy as the barristers. There are, however, still relatively few solicitor-advocates and so most advocacy in the higher courts is conducted by barristers.

Unlike solicitors, practising barristers are not allowed to form partnerships. They must be self-employed, but they usually share offices (called 'chambers') with other barristers, where they share the administrative costs of running the chambers.

Barristers operate a system known as the 'cab rank rule' under which if they are offered a case in their area of specialisation and at a fee commensurate with their experience, and they have no other commitments that clash with it, they must accept it. This is supposed to ensure that everyone, no matter how unpopular he or she is, gets proper representation. A person cannot be said to have had a fair trial if he or she was not properly represented.

Many people would argue that we don't need two different professions. It is certainly true that very few other countries have a similar system and that the reasons for having it are historical. In the 1970s there was a lot of argument about fusing the two separate professions into one, but instead the two professions have just become more similar, both doing similar things but from a slightly different perspective.

BARRISTERS AND SOLICITORS

Similarities	Differences
• Training is broadly similar.	• The two professions are quite separate.
• Both are practising lawyers.	• They are organised in quite different ways – solicitors usually work in partnership with colleagues; barristers are self-employed.
• Both are subject to strict professional rules.	
• Both do the same sort of work, but in different ways.	• It is difficult to move from one profession to the other.
• Both work for a client.	• Solicitors can sue for their fees; barristers cannot.

ACTIVITY 1

1) What do you think are the advantages of having two different professions and what are the disadvantages? (Use the table below to help you.)
2) Identify and explain two differences between the work/roles of solicitors and of barristers.
3) Identify the bodies that represent the interests of lawyers and barristers.
4) Explain how the so called 'cab rank rule' ensures all citizens get a fair trial.

ONE LEGAL PROFESSION OR TWO?

Advantages of having a single legal profession	Disadvantages of having a single legal profession
• It should be cheaper (one taxi is cheaper than two, so one lawyer should be cheaper than two) – but this is not as clear cut as some writers suggest. Barristers have much lower overheads than solicitors and can make more profit from lower costs than solicitors can.	• There is a need for specialised advocacy that is met by the present system.
	• The 'cab rank rule' guarantees independent representation for all.
• Avoidance of duplication of work.	• The Bar is needed by small firms of solicitors; without it they could not have access to the specialist services their clients need – only the largest firms could do without the services of the Bar.
• Waste of talent would be avoided.	
• Common in other countries – no other common law country is so rigid in the division of the profession.	• Because they are self-employed and do not have the responsibility for running a large office with a client base, barristers are better able to cope with the uncertain demands of court time.

In addition to the traditional professions of the barrister and the solicitor there is now a new, third legal profession emerging – that of the **legal executive**. Legal executives are usually found working in solicitors' offices where they perform many of the routine, and not so routine, tasks that have to be undertaken in every case. They are regulated by the Institute of Legal Executives. To qualify as a legal executive it is not necessary to have a university degree (as most barristers and solicitors do) and most legal executives study for the qualifying examinations at the same time as they work in solicitors' offices. They do not have to study the same wide range of legal subjects that a solicitor would have to cover in his or her route to qualification, but they study a narrower range of subjects to a similar standard as a solicitor.

Legal executives have limited rights of audience in the magistrates' courts and the County Court. They are almost the only non-graduates who are able to qualify as solicitors.

ACTIVITY 2

1) Identify and explain two advantages that may result from this new legal executive professional role to:
   - the general public
   - the legal system.

   In your answer you could consider costs of training, access to the profession by citizens of a non-academic background, solicitor's offices with heavy workloads, specific advice from specialists who are perhaps industrially experienced.

Web action

For more information about the legal professions look at:
- Law Society's website **www.lawsociety.org.uk**
- Bar Council's website **www.barcouncil.org.uk/index.asp**
- Institute of Legal Executives' website **www.ilex.org.uk**

- The Institute of Legal Executives (ILEX) controls the newest branch of the profession.

- Legal executives work in solicitors' offices where they are responsible for much of the work done by the practice.

- Candidates study for exams at degree level, but they study fewer subjects.

- Legal executives have the same depth of knowledge as solicitors, but over a narrower range of legal issues.

- Once a legal executive has completed the examinations and obtained the appropriate experience he or she can become a Fellow of the Institute of Legal Executives.

- There are special arrangements for Fellows of ILEX to become solicitors.

Paying for legal services

It is not enough to have a good legal system and well trained and capable legal professionals working in it. People who need to use the system have to be able to access it. People with legal problems usually need help from a professional lawyer. Some people need only advice, but others need to be represented in court by a solicitor or a barrister.

This raises the problem of cost. In a civil case this is made more complicated by a rule that the losing party has to pay the winning side's costs in addition to his or her own costs. In a case in the High Court this can easily run into hundreds of thousands of pounds and even in a much smaller case in the County Court the costs can be more than the value of the case itself.

If a person cannot afford to bring a case or defend a case that is brought against them, then they are being denied justice. In order to ensure that no one is excluded from the legal system on the basis of expense the Government introduced a system of **legal aid** in civil cases in 1949 and extended it to criminal cases in 1964.

The system of providing financial help to people who need legal advice or who need to bring or defend a case was changed by the Access to Justice Act 1999. This act set up two schemes:

1) the Community Legal Service for civil matters
2) the Criminal Defence Service for criminal cases.

Both these services are overseen by the **Legal Services Commission**. This body is responsible for managing the Community Legal Service Fund which is provided by the Government. The Minister of Justice is responsible for the Commission.

legal services
COMMISSION

The Community Legal Service and the Criminal Defence Service work in different ways and so we will look at them separately.

The Community Legal Service

The Access to Justice Act 1999 provides that the function of the Community Legal Service is to:

- provide general information about the law, the legal system and the legal services that are available
- provide legal advice
- help prevent, settle or resolve legal disputes
- help enforce the decisions by which disputes are resolved.

> The Government provides a set amount of money for the Community Legal Service each year. The Minister of Justice has to decide (within the Government's overall spending plans) how much this should be. This sum of money has to cover all the demands made on the fund in that year.

Most of the services provided by the Community Legal Service are **means tested**. Some are also **merits tested**.

- Applicants whose disposable income exceeds the maximum level (which can change from time to time) will not receive help from the Community Legal Service.

MEANS TEST

A means test is used to ensure that those being supported are unable to pay for the services they require out of their own funds. The means test looks at:

1) the claimant's 'disposable income' (i.e. the amount of money left after payment of rent or mortgage, tax, national insurance and deduction of an allowance for each dependant)

2) the claimant's disposable capital (i.e. his or her assets – such as money in the bank, stocks and shares, the value of the family home after deducting the outstanding mortgage).

MERITS TEST

A merits test means that the Legal Services Commission has to decide if:

1) the case is important enough to justify spending public money on pursuing it

2) there is a reasonable likelihood that it will be successful.

The merits test is flexible, so that it varies with the type of help a person wants. For example, the likelihood of success might be important in some cases, but not in others. It would not be important in a case about whether or not a child should be taken into local authority care.

- Applicants whose disposable income is below the minimum level will receive free help from the Community Legal Service. Applicants whose income exceeds a maximum level will not receive any help from the Community Legal Service.
- Applicants whose disposable income falls between the maximum and the minimum

levels will receive help from the Community Legal Service, but will have to make a contribution towards it. The amount of the contribution they have to make will depend on by how much their disposable income exceeds the minimum level.

It is important to remember that the Community Legal Service can be available either to those people wishing to bring a civil action (the **claimant**) or to those who need to defend a civil action (the **defendant**).

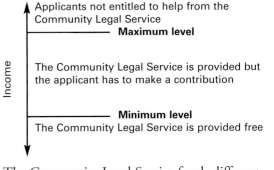

The Community Legal Service funds different levels of help for those needing its services.

- **Legal help**: this is the lowest level of service. It provides advice and assistance with any legal problem. It could include writing a letter. It does not cover representation in court. It is means tested, but not merits tested.
- **Legal representation**: this level of service provides funding for the applicant to be represented in court by a solicitor and/or a barrister. It is means tested and merits tested.
- **Help at court**: this level of service really comes somewhere between legal help and legal representation. It funds someone (a solicitor or some other suitable advisor) to speak on the applicant's behalf without formally acting for them in the whole proceedings. It is means tested, but not merits tested.

In addition there are two other levels of help available in relation to family matters.

> ### CASE STUDY: Parents get legal aid to sue health chiefs over radiation overdose death of Lisa Norris
>
> Tragic Lisa Norris's parents have won legal aid to sue health bosses for medical negligence over their daughter's death.
>
> Distraught Ken and Liz launched their landmark legal action claiming that medics caused her death through a massive radiation overdose.
>
> Lisa, sixteen, died of a brain tumour in October 2006 after being treated at the Beatson cancer centre, in Glasgow. Her dad Ken, 53, said doctors made another error when they halted Lisa's radiation treatment when the huge overdose was discovered after nineteen treatments.
>
> He added: 'We were really glad to finally get legal aid. We wanted to take legal action against the health board to make sure that this is not just allowed to happen. The health authorities should be called to account for what happened to Lisa. For too long, doctors have been able to close ranks and get away with making errors that cost lives.'
>
> Now her parents could get hundreds of thousands of pounds in damages from NHS Greater Glasgow and Clyde.
>
> The Norris's solicitor Cameron Fyfe said: 'The family have been granted legal aid to pursue an action in court on the basis that Lisa would have survived had it not been for the overdose of radiation.'
>
> A report by Dr Arthur Johnston, scientific adviser to the Scottish Government's health department, revealed the overdose happened after an under-qualified and under-trained staff member entered a wrong number on a form.
>
> Stephen Stewart, www.dailyrecord.co.uk, 20 April 2009

The facts of the case study above occurred in Scotland. The provision of legal aid in Scotland is similar to that in England and Wales, but it is administered by the Scottish Legal Aid Board. The outcome of the case would have been the same if the facts of the case had occurred in England or Wales. Northern Ireland also has its own system of legal aid, similar to that in the rest of the UK.

ACTIVITY 3

1) Outline the stages in which legal aid is granted.
2) What impact do you think the availability of the Community Legal Service has on people's attitude to the law?
3) What are the benefits for society of everyone having potential access to legal aid? Are there any disadvantages?

WHAT COMMUNITY LEGAL SERVICE DOES NOT COVER

1) Cases involving defamation.

2) Disputes arising in the course of the applicant's business.

3) Cases concerning companies, partnerships, trusts or boundary disputes.

4) Cases involving personal injuries.

(How these cases are funded is examined on page 161.)

The Community Legal Service is only available from selected firms of solicitors and advice agencies. These firms receive a **franchise** from the Legal Services Commission. In order to be awarded the franchise they have to demonstrate expertise in the particular service that they are franchised to provide. It is expected that this will make the provision of services more efficient and more cost effective.

Firms of solicitors and advice agencies that receive a franchise from the Legal Services Commission are allocated a pot of funds to pay for the work that they do on behalf of the Commission. When those funds are exhausted they do not receive any more funds until the next financial year. This means that a person wanting to use the service may be refused simply because the supplier he or she approaches has run out of money for the particular service that the client wanted to use.

The Criminal Defence Service

The system for applying for funding to defend a criminal charge is quite different from that of the Community Legal Service.

The state provides funding for criminal defence work on a demand led basis. This means that, unlike the Community Legal Service, there is no predetermined limit to the amount of funding that is needed and no one is refused state funding in a criminal case just because the money available has been exhausted. All cases which satisfy the merits criteria and the means test are funded.

The Criminal Defence Service funds criminal legal services in three ways:

1) duty solicitor schemes
2) direct funding to approved private practitioners for legal representation of those charged with a criminal offence
3) the employment of public defenders.

Each of these is considered separately below.

Duty solicitor schemes

There are two duty solicitor schemes – one in police stations and the other in the Magistrates' Court. Local solicitors who are approved by the Legal Services Commission to provide legal services to those charged with criminal offences are required to provide rotas to cover both of these services.

DUTY SOLICITOR SCHEMES IN POLICE STATIONS

A means test is used to ensure that those being supported are unable to pay for the services they require out of their own funds. The means test looks at:

1) The Police and Criminal Evidence Act 1984 provides that every person in police custody has the right to see a solicitor at no cost and in private. The duty solicitor scheme in police stations is designed to ensure that those provisions are complied with.

2) The function of the duty solicitor in police stations is to enable anyone in police custody to have free and independent legal advice and to assist persons being interviewed by the police.

3) The service is free to all and there is neither a means test nor a merits test.

DUTY SOLICITOR SCHEMES IN THE MAGISTRATES' COURTS

1) Solicitors operate a rota to attend all magistrates' courts in their area.

2) They provide advice, and, if appropriate, representation for anyone appearing unrepresented in the court.

3) The scheme is free to all and there is neither a means test nor a merits test.

ACTIVITY 4

1) Why do you think there is no means test or merits test needed to get help from the Duty Solicitor when in police custody?

2) Explain why when in police custody it is vital that the right to see a solicitor is complied with by the police. Consider the powers of the police and the fair treatment of people who are innocent until tried and convicted.

Directly funded schemes

Direct funding is where the state pays firms of independent solicitors in private practice to represent those charged with criminal offences. Only firms which have obtained a contract from the Legal Services Commission to undertake criminal work are able to offer state funded representation.

There are three levels of service where the state pays private firms of solicitors to represent those charged with criminal offences.

1) **Advice and assistance**: as the name suggests this is limited to giving advice and writing opinions about the case and negotiating with the prosecution. There is a means test, except in relation to advice given when a suspect is being questioned by the police.

2) **Advocacy assistance**: this covers the cost of a solicitor preparing a client's case and representing the client in the magistrates' courts, and (in relation to some matters) in the Crown Court. There is a merits test, but no means test.

3) **Representation**: this covers the cost of a solicitor to represent the suspect in the magistrates' court, and, if appropriate in the Crown Court. It also covers the cost of being represented by a barrister in the Crown Court and the costs of any appeal.

The decision about whether or not an individual should receive state funded legal assistance is made by the magistrates in the Magistrates' Court at the first hearing following the charging of the accused. It is granted where it is 'in the interests of justice' to do so.

It is in the interests of justice to grant state funded legal assistance where:

1) the case is so serious that the accused is, if convicted, likely to be sentenced to a term of imprisonment

2) there are substantial issues of law involved in the case (complex cases)

3) the accused is unable to understand the case against him or her or to explain his or her own case because he or she does not speak good enough English or is suffering from a psychiatric illness.

ACTIVITY 5

1) Identify two cases, hypothetical or real, for each of the above three categories which deem it 'in the interests of justice' to grant legal aid.

Public defenders

In 2001 a pilot scheme was set up under which the Legal Services Commission directly employs a number of criminal defence lawyers to defend those charged with criminal offences. These are called public defenders.

The lawyers working as public defenders receive a fixed salary and take on the cases of those individuals who are charged with criminal offences and represent them at all stages of the prosecution process, including any appeals where those are appropriate. The pilot scheme provided for them to operate in eight centres scattered across the country.

They operate to a strict set of guidelines ensuring their independence and guaranteeing a standard of service but have not proved to be popular with defendants. It is not thought likely that the scheme will be extended.

Other sources of advice and representation

When people think of obtaining legal advice or representation they usually go to see a solicitor who advises them and either represents them in court or instructs a barrister to do so. There are also other sources of advice and representation.

Community Legal Service Direct

The Legal Services Commission established Community Legal Service Direct in 2004. This is a national telephone and website service that is available 24 hours a day, seven days a week and can provide advice on issues relating to social security benefits, housing and debt.

COMMUNITY LEGAL SERVICE DIRECT

This can be accessed on **www.clsdirect. org.uk**. The site receives over 50,000 hits each month.

It is an alternative to receiving face to face advice through one of the other services.

Criminal Defence Service Direct

The Criminal Defence Service Direct provides telephone advice to people detained by the police for non-imprisonable offences. It handles about 200 calls per day.

Law centres

Law centres are funded by grants from central and local government. Some also receive money from large local firms.

They offer a free, non-means-tested service to people who work or live in their area. They usually stay open for longer than traditional office hours and usually provide a relaxed and informal atmosphere. Advice is given by both professional lawyers and suitably trained lay people.

There are about 50 in the whole of the UK and so they are usually found only in the larger cities. Their main areas of work are in housing, welfare, immigration and employment.

They are not restricted in the way in which they offer their services. As a result they often run local campaigns to make local people aware of their legal rights. They provide representation in the courts as well as giving advice.

Citizens Advice Bureaux

The 700 or so Citizens Advice Bureaux in the UK are funded directly by central government. They are staffed mainly by volunteers who are trained to high standards. They have a high profile and are easily accessible by members of the public. Their main expertise is in social security law and in dealing with problems created by debt.

They provide free non-means-tested advice to anyone who calls in to their offices. A few larger centres offer a limited amount of representation in their areas of expertise, but usually they refer clients needing representation to a firm of solicitors able to provide it using the state funded system.

Conditional fee agreements

In the USA many cases are brought by individuals who enter into an agreement with their lawyers that if they lose the case their lawyers will not charge a fee, but if they win, their lawyers will receive an agreed percentage of the damages. This is often referred to as a 'no win, no fee' agreement. Such arrangements are illegal in the UK where **conditional fee agreements** are used instead.

The Courts and Legal Services Act 1990, as amended by the Access to Justice Act 1999, allows the use of conditional fee agreements in cases which are not covered by the statutory scheme operated by the Community Legal Service (see page 155).

Conditional fee arrangements are often referred to as 'no win, no fee' but that is misleading. The term 'no win, no fee' really applies to contingency fees operated in the USA and not to the system in the UK.

Conditional fee agreements are not means tested. This means that they are available to any litigant. There is no cost to the state. They were introduced to help reduce the enormous bill for legal aid that was incurred year after year under the system that existed before the Access to Justice Act 1999.

CONDITIONAL FEE AGREEMENTS

These work in a simple way. If a client wants to use a conditional fee agreement to bring a civil action (they have no application in criminal cases) the claimant's solicitors can agree to take the case on the basis that they will take no fee (or a reduced fee) if they lose the case, but that if they win they will receive the usual fee plus an additional agreed percentage of the usual fee. The additional fee (which can be up to double the usual fee) is known as the 'uplift' or the 'success fee'.

Note that:

1) the success fee is calculated on the size of the risk run by the solicitor: if the risk of losing the case is small the success fee will be small, but if the risk of losing is great then the success fee will be larger

2) the loser in a civil action has to pay the winner's legal costs and so a litigant using a conditional fee agreement to fund a case will need to take out insurance to cover the winner's costs in the event of losing the case

3) if the claimant uses a conditional fee agreement to bring a case and wins the case the success fee (and any insurance premium paid to cover the possibility of having to pay the defendant's costs) will usually be paid by the losing defendant.

Advantages of conditional fee agreements

- There is no cost to the state – the costs are all carried by the solicitors or the losing party.

- Most people are able to use them.

- They encourage solicitors to perform better as they have a financial interest in winning their cases.

- They are available for defamation cases and cases before tribunals – these were never covered by state funded legal aid.

- They are popular with litigants.

- There are restrictions on the costs that state funded clients have to pay to the other side and this can be unfair if the other side is an individual who was unable to qualify for state funded legal support. These do not apply to conditional fee agreements.

Disadvantages of conditional fee agreements

- Solicitors are unwilling to take on cases that have little chance of success.

- Claimants are often misled into believing that they will not be liable for any expenses, but they often find that they have to pay for expensive insurance policies – and these can be more than the damages that they receive.

- There are suggestions that claims management companies offering conditional fee arrangements often mis-sell the concept to claimants.

- Where insurance companies are involved in cases they often put undue pressure on claimants to settle cases to ensure that no claim is made on them.

- Where lawyers have a financial interest in the outcome of a case there may be a temptation to recommend settlement even where more money might be obtained if the case went to trial as they would get no fee at all if the case went to trial and they lost.

ACTIVITY 6

1) Briefly explain the main differences between solicitors and barristers.
2) Identify arguments for and against having two legal professions.
3) Explain the difference between state funded legal services and the other methods of obtaining representation.
4) Identify the main differences between state funding of legal services in civil and criminal cases.
5) What are the sources of legal advice and/or representation that do not depend on state funding?
6) What are the different levels of state funding for criminal and civil cases?
7) Explain what conditional fee agreements are.
8) Identify the main advantages and disadvantages of conditional fee agreements.
9) Define and explain the following terms:
   - means testing
   - advocacy
   - rights of audience
   - solicitor-advocates
   - success fee.

3 Alternative methods of resolving disputes

In the last two topics we looked at how lawyers deal with disputes through the courts. In this topic we look at how some disputes can be resolved without involving the courts.

At the outset we have to make it clear that these alternative methods of resolving disputes are limited to civil cases.

In criminal cases there is no real alternative to the prosecution of offenders in the criminal courts. There are, however, two situations where offenders may not be prosecuted.

1) Sometimes the police may decide to **caution** suspects instead of prosecuting them. A caution is a formal warning given by the police to a person who is believed to have committed an offence. It is usually given when the suspect is young and/or the charge is not very serious. It can only be used
- where the police have enough evidence to prosecute successfully, and
- when the suspect agrees to be cautioned instead of being prosecuted.

2) Some criminal offences are dealt with by **fixed penalties**. This mainly applies to some motoring offences (speeding, parking and some minor traffic violations) where the offender is given the option of paying a fixed sum of money instead of being prosecuted. Failure (or refusal) to pay the fixed penalty results in prosecution in the traditional way.

Resolving civil disputes in the courts has been compared to playing a game of tennis. If Nick and Hamish cannot agree which of them is the better tennis player they can arrange a tennis match to find out. There will be an umpire to make sure that they both play by the rules and to keep the score and decide who has won. Nick and Hamish will battle it out on the tennis court and the best player will win.

If they have a legal dispute they can do the same thing in a court of law. The judge makes sure that they both keep to the legal 'rules' governing a trial and decides who has the best case. They will fight it out in court, each trying to present a better case than their opponent. The one with the best case wins.

Litigants often find that there are problems with this system.

SOME OF THE PROBLEMS WITH LITIGATION

- It is very expensive. The legal costs can sometimes exceed the value of the claim.
- It is conducted in public – anyone can go to court to listen to the arguments. Individuals don't usually mind this, but businesses like to keep their affairs secret and dislike the publicity that can ensue.
- It is slow. In recent years the process has been speeded up, but it can still take over two years to have a civil action heard in the High Court.
- The court dictates the procedure – including time and place of the trial. This can be inconvenient for busy people.
- The judge decides the outcome (who wins and who loses) and also decides what the loser has to do to compensate the winner. The parties themselves have no input into this. The loser will be unhappy because he has lost and the winner may not get what he wanted and so be unhappy too.
- It is likely that the parties will be unable to remain on good terms with each other because of the confrontational nature to court proceedings. This could be important if the dispute was between two businesses that had done business together successfully in the past and wanted to continue to do so in the future, but had an important matter to resolve between them.

ACTIVITY 1

Clearly as the points on page 163 indicate, there are disadvantages to litigation.
1) Briefly outline some of the reasons why despite these disadvantages people still decide to go ahead with litigation. In your answer you may consider moral, financial and accountability issues.

ACTIVITY 2

1) Suggest two or more reasons why a citizen may wish to continue and extend the negotiating process right up until the point of entering the courtroom.
2) Briefly explain why some citizens still wish to have their case heard in court despite the fact that it could be settled out of court.

Mediation, conciliation and arbitration

Because of these problems people in dispute with each other sometimes try to find ways of resolving their dispute without going to court. Over the years they have developed a number of alternatives to using the courts to settle disputes.

Negotiation

Of course, the parties have always been able to avoid litigation by settling their case out of court. This is known as **negotiation**. It simply involves the parties talking to each other and deciding how the matter can be resolved. This has always been available to the parties.

It is completely private. It is also the cheapest and quickest way of settling a dispute. If the parties are unable to resolve the issue and instruct solicitors to issue proceedings their solicitors usually try to negotiate with each other to find a way of settling the case without having to go to trial. The vast majority of cases are settled in this way. Only a very small percentage of the cases that are commenced ever reach court.

One of the problems with this is that often the parties don't reach an out of court settlement until they are literally 'at the door of the court' on the morning of the trial. It is to avoid this situation that many other methods of Alternative Dispute Resolution (ADR) have been developed.

Mediation

Mediation has its origins in divorce cases. Those cases often involve disputes over issues such as maintenance and the arrangements for the care of children. Voluntary mediation sessions are made available to the parties so that these issues can be settled amicably rather than haggled over in court.

Although mediation has its origins in matrimonial cases, it is now widely used in all sorts of other disputes. It can take several different forms. The simplest form of mediation is where the mediator is a neutral person who helps the parties to reach a compromise solution. The mediator:

- meets separately with each party to see how much common ground there is between them
- explores the position with each party, looking at their needs
- takes offers to and fro between them.

The mediator does not tell the parties his or her own views. It is important that the mediator is seen as a 'facilitator' who helps the parties to reach their own agreement and who does not give his or her opinion of how the dispute should be resolved.

<table>
<tr><td>

Advantages of mediation

- Mediation is much cheaper than litigation.

- It is entirely private.

- Because the parties have reached their own agreement, it tends to last longer than settlements that are forced on the parties by someone else.

</td><td>

Disadvantages of mediation

- If professional mediators are used it can still be quite expensive.

- It may not end in an agreement and so the parties may still have to litigate.

- It is only suitable for disputes where there is likely to be scope for negotiation and compromise.

</td></tr>
</table>

ACTIVITY 3

1) Identify a real or hypothetical dispute and describe the skills you think a mediator needs in order to facilitate the process of resolving it.
2) Identify examples of a dispute where mediation might not be appropriate or realistic.
3) What factors during the process of mediation might be difficult or uncomfortable for individuals to experience?

Sometimes mediation can take a different approach.

- The mediator is sometimes asked to give an opinion on the merits of the case. In this situation the mediation becomes more of an evaluation exercise, but the purpose of the evaluation is still to enable the parties to reach their own agreement.
- A more formal approach to mediation can take the form of a 'mini trial' where each side presents its arguments to a panel made up of the mediator and a representative from each party. After the evidence has been presented the parties' representatives try to reach an agreement, with the mediator acting as a neutral advisor.

Conciliation

Conciliation is very similar to mediation. A neutral third party helps to resolve the dispute, but the conciliator plays a more active role – for example the conciliator may suggest the grounds for a possible compromise.

Conciliation is widely used in employment disputes. Actions before the employment tribunal are automatically referred to the Advisory Conciliation and Arbitration Service (ACAS), which will contact the parties to see if their differences can be settled by conciliation. Over half of all claims filed in the employment tribunal are settled in this way.

Advantages of conciliation	Disadvantages of conciliation
• Like mediation, conciliation is much cheaper than litigation. • Like mediation, it is entirely private. • It has a good track record of success.	• It may not end in an agreement and so the parties may still have to litigate. • There is some evidence to suggest that claimants in employment cases feel under some pressure to settle their claims and may accept less than an employment tribunal would award.

Arbitration

In the context of ADR, arbitration refers to a process where the parties agree to submit their claim to a private arbitrator and to be bound by his decision.

WHEN ARBITRATION IS NOT AN EXAMPLE OF ADR

Arbitration can also refer to the more informal procedure adopted by the Commercial Court of the Queen's Bench Division of the High Court. Here a High Court Judge tries the case but in a more informal setting than in the traditional High Court. This sort of arbitration is not an example of ADR because it is not an alternative to the traditional courts. It is a decision made by the traditional courts, but without some of the more traditional trappings – for example neither counsel nor the judge wear robes and the procedures are a lot less formal. It is a very popular method of hearing important cases in commercial law.

However, private arbitration is an example of ADR. It is governed by the Arbitration Act 1996 which provides that:

1) the parties should be free to decide how their disputes should be resolved, and
2) the agreement between the parties to submit their dispute to the judgment of an individual, other than a judge, must be made in writing.

Many commercial contracts contain a clause which provides that if there is a dispute between the parties it is settled by arbitration and not by litigation. The contract between the authors of this book and the publishers contains the following clause:

ARBITRATION

'If any difference shall arise between the proprietor and the publishers touching the meaning of this agreement or the rights and liabilities hereto, the same shall in the first instance be referred to the informal Disputes Settlement Scheme of the Publishers' Association, and failing agreed submission by both parties to such scheme shall be referred to the arbitration of two persons (one to be named by each party) or their mutually agreed umpire in accordance with the provisions of the Arbitration Act 1996, or any amending or substituted statute for the time being in force.'

1) Briefly explain why a publisher might want to write into their contract with an author that if a dispute occurred that it be resolved through arbitration and not through litigation.

The clause shown above as part of the publisher/author agreement is known as a *Scott v Avery* clause. It was in the case of *Scott v Avery* (1856) that a court first held that such a clause was valid and enforceable.

But note that if:

1) the contract is a consumer contract (i.e. a contract made between a supplier and an individual who is going to use the goods that are the subject of the contract personally as distinct from reselling them or using them in his or her trade or business), and

2) the dispute involves an amount that could be dealt with in the small claims court,

then the consumer can decide whether to go to arbitration under the *Scott v Avery* clause or to bring the action in the small claims court.

The procedure at the arbitration hearing has to be agreed between the parties. It can therefore take many different forms.

Paper arbitration

It could be done by sending all the papers in the dispute to the arbitrator and letting him or her make the decision based purely on the papers provided.

Paper arbitration with oral submissions

This is the same as a paper arbitration, except that the parties can make oral submissions to the arbitrator.

Formal hearing

The parties can also opt to have a formal hearing where witnesses give evidence and are cross examined as in court. If this is done then the Arbitration Act 1996 allows witnesses to be summonsed to attend as in a court.

Advantages of arbitration	Disadvantages of arbitration
• The parties can select their own arbitrator and therefore decide if they want a technical expert, a lawyer, or a professional arbitrator.	• There is no state funding for legal assistance in an arbitration and so an individual can be at a disadvantage if he or she is against a large company that can afford legal representation.
• The parties can choose the date, time and place of the arbitration.	
• Having a technical expert as arbitrator can save on the cost and expense of expert witnesses.	• An unexpected legal point may arise which a non-lawyer arbitrator may not be able to deal with.
• The procedure is flexible.	
• The arbitration process is private.	• Professional arbitrators are expensive.
• It is dealt with much more quickly than a court hearing.	• A formal hearing with witnesses and lawyers on both sides is also expensive.
• It is often much cheaper than a court hearing.	• The rights of appeal are very limited.
• The award made by the arbitrator is usually final and it can be enforced through the courts.	• If a professional arbitrator and lawyers are used the delays can be nearly as great as in a court hearing.

The table below makes a useful comparison of the ADR methods and litigation.

Method of ADR	Decision made by:	Advantages	Disadvantages
Negotiation	Parties themselves	Quick, no costs, parties are in control	None – provided the parties have equal bargaining strength
Mediation and conciliation	Parties, with the help of mediator or conciliator	Cheaper than courts, parties agree to outcome	Decision is not binding and the process may not lead to a settlement
Arbitration	Arbitrator	Cheaper than courts, but more expensive than mediation; decision is binding	Can be formal, the arbitrator's fees may be high, not suitable if the dispute is on a point of law
Litigation in the courts	Judge	The decision is final and binding	Expensive, lengthy, formal hearing, adversarial, hearing in public

Web action

- Go to **www.i-law.com** which is a commercial organisation offering advice and support through alternative dispute resolution with all sorts of cases and types of ADR, such as arbitration for various areas as financial and buildings or insurance and maritime (shipping) disputes. Click on the various sections and look at the display showing what the company does. Additional displays, including an i-demo, are useful insights into various types of ADR.
- Go to **www.adviceguide.org.uk** which is a legal advice website run by the Citizens' Advice Bureau and if you key in 'alternative dispute resolution' you can select fact sheets on conciliation, arbitration, mediation and ombudsman schemes (we cover omsbudsman later in this section).

EXAMINER'S TIP

The term ADR usually refers to arbitration, mediation and conciliation. Even though tribunals are different from the traditional courts they are not 'alternatives' to them. An essay on ADR would not require discussion of tribunals unless the question specifically referred to them.

CASE STUDY: PCB issues legal notice to ICC for World Cup exclusion

In the first official response to the International Cricket Council's (ICC) decision to exclude Pakistan from hosting the 2011 World Cup, the Pakistan Cricket Board (PCB) has issued a legal notice to cricket's governing body, calling the decision to do so discriminatory and 'legally flawed.'

The ICC decided at a recent board meeting in Dubai to take away Pakistan's share, as one of four co-hosts, of the World Cup matches. The move came after terrorist attacks on the Sri Lankan team during their February–March 2009 tour. A number of teams since then had refused to visit in the wake of an unsettled and increasingly violent domestic backdrop. The meeting also said that international cricket was unlikely to return to Pakistan till 2011.

In particular, Pakistan's gripe, a sokesman said, was that the status of the 2011 World Cup was not on the original agenda of the ICC Board meeting on April 17 and 18 (when the decision was made). The implication is that Pakistan wasn't given a fair opportunity to defend its case as a co-host.

'This issue was not on the agenda.' The PCB explained: 'There was a discussion of the Sri Lankan attacks on the agenda and this topic came up. They never gave us notice and it was not on the agenda. We want to revoke the decision full stop.'

The legal notice has been sent to the ICC president David Morgan and under the ICC's constitution, the PCB is asking for the matter to be referred to the disputes resolution committee. 'The matter has been submitted to the president of the ICC's dispute resolution committee. He can either refer the matter to the dispute resolution committee which is made up of ICC's officials or to the independent arbitration before the Court of Arbitration for Sport. The PCB prefers impartial arbitration in the interest of justice, equity and fairplay.'

If the disputes resolution committee fails to come up with a satisfactory solution, the option to take the case further remains. 'There are two options with the disputes resolution committee,' Salim Altaf, the board's chief operating officer, told Cricinfo. 'Normally all disputes are resolved there. But if there is no satisfactory resolution, then the case can be sent to the Court of Arbitration for Sports (CAS), in Lausanne, Switzerland.'

Ratification of the ICC's decision was expected to take place at the annual board meeting in June, though now that no longer seems a foregone conclusion.

Osman Samiuddin, content.cricinfo.com, 9 May 2009

ACTIVITY 5

1) What does the PCB seek to achieve from the ICC?
2) What are the two options for the disputes resolution committee?

   This case is not alleging any criminal wrong doing. In this case the PCB is not arguing the ICC has damaged them; it is arguing the issue be dealt with again in a more acceptable way.

Adopt the role of chairperson in the arbitration case and address the following tasks.

3) Try to make some arguments on both sides of the case – for the ICC and for the PCB.
4) Assess which case you think is the strongest.
5) State what further action you believe should occur.

Tribunals

Tribunals are not a form of alternative dispute resolution. They are a recognised part of the legal system. They are inferior courts (i.e. courts below the level of the High Court) such as county courts and the magistrates' court.

The tribunal system deals with over a million cases a year, so it is clearly a very important part of our legal system.

Most tribunals were created in the second half of the twentieth century and most are linked to aspects of the welfare state. Many tribunals were created at the end of the Second World War when the first labour government created the welfare state. The welfare state gave many citizens rights to benefits that they had not previously enjoyed, but it also created the potential for many claims relating to an individual's entitlement to those rights.

These claims would have clogged up the traditional courts – and in any case the ordinary courts were not the best places to deal with the very specialised problems that the welfare legislation created.

To deal with these claims the Government created a number of tribunals. Each tribunal deals with a particular type of claim. So, for example, there is a Social Security Tribunal to deal with claims about entitlement to different forms of social security, an Educational Appeals Tribunal to deal with appeals about a child's entitlement to attend a particular school and an Employment Tribunal to deal with employment issues such as redundancy and unfair dismissal.

These are only examples of the different types of tribunals. There are about 70 different types of tribunals.

Web action

1) Find out the names of three other types of tribunal and state briefly what they do.
Go to **www.ajtc.gov.uk/links/tribunals-and-inquiries.htm** for help.

It is important to remember that whereas the parties decide to use mediation or conciliation or arbitration instead of the traditional courts they do not choose to use tribunals. If they have a claim that falls into the jurisdiction of a tribunal then they have to persue that claim through the appropriate tribunal.

Tribunals procedure

The Tribunals, Courts and Enforcement Act 2007 made many changes to the way tribunals are organised. In the past each of the tribunals was responsible for its own organisation, but they are now all administered by one tribunal service.

Most tribunals consist of a legally qualified chairperson (a solicitor or a barrister) and two lay people (people who are not lawyers) who have a special expertise in the subject area that the tribunal deals with – for example two doctors in the Medical Appeals Tribunal or representatives from both employees' and employers' organisations in the Employment Tribunal.

The lay members take an active part in the decision making process. Each tribunal decides how to manage it own cases, although since the Tribunals, Courts and Enforcement Act 2007 was passed all tribunals adopt very similar procedures.

TRIBUNALS

Advantages

- **Cost:** applicants are encouraged not to use lawyers and the winner usually has to pay his/her own costs so in general they are cheaper than the conventional courts.

- **Speedy hearings:** at one time tribunals were able to deal with cases very quickly, but now, as the volume of cases increases, they are becoming slower.

- **Simple procedure:** hearings before tribunals are more informal than in a traditional court and many are held in private, but some – such as the Employment Tribunal – sit in public. The procedure is more flexible and strict rules of evidence do not apply. It is still difficult for some applicants to present their own cases and statistics show that applicants who are legally represented are much more likely to win their cases.

Disadvantages

- **Lack of funding:** one of the reasons why many applicants represent themselves in tribunal hearings is because there is very little public funding for tribunal cases. If both sides were unrepresented that would not matter so much, but the defendant is usually an employer or a government department that will usually be legally represented. This puts applicants at a considerable disadvantage.

- **Procedural problems:** some tribunals do not give reasons for their decisions so it is not always clear why one side has won and the other lost. In addition, some tribunals follow precedent, but some do not. Appeal procedures may differ from one tribunal to another (although judicial review is always available).

- **Impartiality:** in the past there was some doubt about the impartiality of tribunal chairmen as some were appointed by government ministers responsible for the department into whose decisions the tribunal was inquiring. All chairmen are now appointed in the same way as judges and so this problem no longer arises.

Web action

- In 2000/2001 Sir Andrew Leggatt, a retired Court of Appeal judge, conducted a review into the tribunal system. His findings can be seen at **www.tribunals-review.org.uk**.

- For an up-to-date explanation of the tribunal system look at the website of the Administrative Justice Council, the body that administers all tribunals after the reforms made by the Tribunals Courts and Enforcement Act 2007 at **www.ajtc.gov.uk/links/tribunals-and-inquiries.htm**.

CASE STUDY: Employment tribunal decision: X v Brighton and Hove City Council

Council ordered to pay £34,765.18 for twice victimising and discriminating against a transgender ex-employee

In June 2007 the Brighton Employment Tribunal ordered Brighton and Hove City Council to pay compensation of £34,765.18 to a former employee, in a case supported by the Equal Opportunities Commission (EOC). The identity of the former employee, a teacher, is subject to a restricted reporting order by the Tribunal.

The compensation order followed the decision of the Tribunal in November 2006 that Brighton and Hove City Council, and one of its senior managers, had discriminated against and victimised the former teacher on grounds of gender reassignment.

In 2003 the teacher registered with a teacher recruitment agency in order to seek work and sought a reference from her previous manager at the Council. However she lost the opportunity to obtain work as a result of her previous manager revealing her change of gender to the recruitment agency, despite a request that this should not be disclosed. Her previous manager initially delayed responding to the request for a reference. When he did respond, he faxed a secret side memo that disclosed her former name, stated her previous gender, and referred to her as both 'he or she', 'him' and 'her'. This treatment was held by the Tribunal to amount to discrimination and victimisation of the teacher, for which the Council and her previous manager were liable.

It was only after the teacher had contacted the agency directly some months later, because the agency had refused to provide her with any work, that she discovered the existence of the secret fax. The Council had failed to reveal its existence when originally asked.

In 2005, in the absence of having received any employment, the teacher again approached her previous manager for a reference but again was refused. The Tribunal found that both the Council and the manager had further discriminated against and victimised the teacher by refusing the second reference request and by refusing to hear her grievance over the refusal. The Council also failed to adopt existing Criminal Records Bureau procedures for transgender people, and ignored EOC guidance on the employment of transgender people.

Although the Council applied for a review of the Employment Tribunal's findings of discrimination and victimisation, and then lodged an Appeal, both were unsuccessful. As well as awarding the teacher compensation of £34,765.18 for her loss of earnings and injury to feelings, the Tribunal made a recommendation that the Council provide any prospective employer or employment agency with a non-discriminatory reference.

www.pfc.org.uk

ACTIVITY 6

Read the tribunal case above and then answer the questions below.
1) Why did X bring this case before the Employment Tribunal?
2) In what ways did the tribunal find that X had been discriminated against?
3) Other than being ordered to pay compensation what else did the tribunal state should be done by Brighton and Hove City Council?
4) Comment on the view that tribunal findings benefit society as a whole, not just the people involved in a particular case such as this one.

Ombudsmen

The word 'ombudsman' comes from the old Swedish word umbuðsmann meaning a representative.

It is another way of resolving a complaint and so needs to be briefly examined here. Usually the term 'ombudsman' refers to an official appointed to provide a check on government activity in the interests of the individual citizen and to oversee the investigation of complaints of improper government activity against the citizen.

If the ombudsman finds a complaint to be substantiated:

1) the problem may get rectified, or
2) the ombudsman may publish a report making recommendations for change.

Further redress depends on the law relating to the circumstances of the particular case but normally involves financial compensation.

In the UK there are a number of ombudsmen with responsibility for different aspects of government activity but when we think of the ombudsman we are usually thinking of the Parliamentary and Health Service Ombudsman. These are in fact two separate posts, but are always held by the same person. This official is also known as the Parliamentary Commissioner for Administration but is usually referred to as the Parliamentary Ombudsman.

> The term ombudsman is also used to refer to a person appointed by a non-governmental organisation, such as a trade or profession, to investigate complaints made by the public about its members, for example the Estate Agents Ombudsman.

The Parliamentary Ombudsman can carry out independent investigations into complaints about government departments, agencies and some public bodies. If an individual has received poor service or has not been treated properly or fairly – and the Government department involved hasn't put things right where it could have – the Parliamentary Ombudsman can help.

> There are two major constraints on the powers of the ombudsman.
>
> 1) The ombudsman is unable to deal with any matter that could be dealt with through the courts. He cannot, for example, deal with complaints about government departments not honouring contracts.
>
> 2) Complaints to the ombudsman must be made through an elected representative – in the case of the Parliamentary Ombudsman this means an MP. An individual cannot complain directly to the ombudsman. This can create an extra hurdle for a complainant to overcome and may mean that some genuine complaints are not passed on to the ombudsman.

Ombudsmen have been appointed in the following areas:

- the parliamentary and health service ombudsman
- the local Government ombudsman
- the financial ombudsman service (see case study on page 174)
- the european ombudsman
- the legal services ombudsman
- the ombudsman for estate agents
- the housing ombudsman
- the prisons and probation ombudsman
- the energy supply ombudsman.

CASE STUDY: Fight back against refusal to pay out on chip-and-PIN fraud claims

As thousands of angry customers are left out of pocket by the banks, we explain how to seek compensation

Victims of chip-and-PIN fraud who are unable to recover their money have been urged to consider legal action against their banks. Under the Banking Code customers are only responsible for losses arising from fraud if they acted 'without reasonable care'. This could include writing down a PIN or allowing someone else to use a card.

Cathy Neal, of Which?, the consumer group, says: 'Banks are very reluctant to admit that there any flaws in the chip-and-PIN system. The Banking Code is not specific enough and there appears to be different approaches from banks on how to compensate fraud victims. In many cases, the issue of "reasonable care" of a PIN becomes the consumer's word against the banks, which can lead to months of stress and financial hardship as customers try to recover their money.'

If victims of fraud are unable to gain compensation for their losses through their banks, they can refer cases to the Financial Ombudsman Service (FOS), the independent body that settles disputes between banks and consumers. Cases typically take up to nine months to resolve.

Ms Neal says: 'If a consumer is unsuccessful with the bank and the ombudsman, the only other option is to take the bank to the small claims court. It does not cost a huge amount, usually about £150 in court fees, which will be refunded if you are successful and you can represent yourself. You would be expected to prove your claim, so you may have to pay for an expert's opinion. However, if the ombudsman has investigated your case, you should have a lot of evidence already. The court would be mindful that you are an individual and would try to be as helpful as possible.'

If you win your case, you will get the court fees back as well as the claim, and you can also ask for certain expenses. If you lose, you will not get the court fees back, but it is unlikely that you will have to pay any other costs.

www.timesonline.co.uk, © *The Times*, 9 May 2009

Web action

Go to **www.adviceguide.org.uk/index.htm** which is an advice website run by the Citizens Advice Bureau. Key in *how to use an ombudsman* and you will be able to explore the ways to contact and use an ombudsman. For further information about the Parliamentary Ombudsman go to **www.ombudsman.org.uk**.

ACTIVITY 7

1) What role would you expect the Financial Ombudsman Service to take in situations like those described in the case study above?
2) The Financial Ombudsman Service is designed to be impartial and to offer expert opinion on such cases. If impartial experts decide that the bank has not acted improperly in a particular case, do you think it is right that people can still take the bank to court?
3) Summarise the ways of resolving disputes described in this case study.

The table below gives an overview of how disputes can be resolved without using the traditional courts.

Alternative methods of resolving disputes	Comments
Negotiation	Very informal, cheap, private and successful in many cases
Mediation	Parties agree the terms on which the dispute is to be settled with the help of an independent mediator who acts as a facilitator
Conciliation	Parties agree the terms on which the dispute is to be settled with the help of a conciliator who actively promotes the terms he or she considers most suitable
Arbitration	Parties appoint a mutually acceptable third person to decide how the dispute should be settled
Tribunals	Parties have a hearing before an informal panel usually consisting of a legally qualified chairman and two lay persons with special knowledge of the area in dispute
Ombudsman	One of the parties refers his complaint to a person appointed to review the issues in question

ACTIVITY 8

1) What is a litigant?
2) What is the term used for the process of settling a dispute out of court?
3) Identify the three main roles of a mediator.
4) For what sort of cases is conciliation widely used?
5) What are the three forms of arbitration?
6) What is an inferior court?
7) Briefly explain the relationship between tribunals and the welfare state.
8) What is the role of an ombudsman?

ISSUE 2: HOW DO THE COURTS PROTECT MY RIGHTS?

In this section we explore the following three topics:

- the role of the courts
- the courts and the Human Rights Act
- judicial review.

4 The role of the courts

Balancing conflicting interests

On pages 114–116 we looked at the issues raised by the case of *Gillick v West Norfolk and Wisbech Area Health Authority* (1985). Look back at these pages to remind yourself of the facts of the *Gillick* case and in particular of the competing interests that the House of Lords had to decide between.

In *Gillick* we saw that there was a conflict between the rights of parents and the rights of children and we have seen how the courts resolved that conflict. We saw that parents and children had different interests in the issues. Parents wanted to have the right to know what their children (for whom they were legally responsible) were doing and children wanted the freedom and the privacy to make some important decisions for themselves. It was complicated by the fact that the Area Health Authority wanted to reduce the number of underage pregnancies. In making its decision the court had to try to balance these different interests.

Conflicts of this type arise frequently. It often happens when Parliament makes a new statute that changes the law. This often involves changing the rights and duties of individuals or groups of individuals and so could give rise to the sort of conflict seen in the Gillick case. In many cases, however, the conflict between the different interests is settled by Parliament when it makes new rules.

PRESSURE GROUPS

In many cases Parliament is influenced by the views of pressure groups. Much legislation is the result of the work done by pressure groups that exist to influence the views of MPs, ministers and in turn governments. Very often the law, and the way in which conflicting views or interests are managed, is the result of a compromise reached by parliament after taking different views into account.

Often Parliament leaves the precise line between the conflicting interests of those involved to be drawn by the courts. For example, the Unfair Contracts Terms Act 1977 provides that if a clause in a contract excludes the liability of one of the parties that clause is void if it is unreasonable. But the act leaves it to the courts to decide or define what is 'unreasonable', according to the facts of the particular case.

When courts are called on to try to balance the rights and duties of the parties in a case they are inevitably engaged in balancing the different interests of the parties.

DIFFERENT TYPES OF INTEREST

In the early twentieth century the American legal academic Roscoe Pound produced a detailed analysis of the types of interest that came before the American courts and the way in which those interests were balanced and resolved.

He divided interests into categories. His two main categories were:

- individual interests – such as the rights of individual citizens in owning property, making contracts and having personal privacy

- social interests – such as protecting the security of the state and its institutions, conserving resources and promoting public morality.

Pound argued that an interest could only be properly balanced against another interest in the same category. A social interest could be balanced against another social interest, but not against an individual interest.

This point is well illustrated in the case of *Miller v Jackson* (1977) opposite.

CASE STUDY: Miller v Jackson (1977)

A housing estate had been built next to a cricket ground. The claimants, Mr and Mrs Miller, owned one of the houses on the estate. Between 1972 and 1974 cricket balls had, on a number of occasions gone on to the claimants' property, causing some property damage but no personal injury. In 1975 the height of the fence was increased so that it stood nearly fifteen feet high, the maximum height possible because of the wind. Nevertheless cricket balls were still hit over the fence. According to the club's count balls had gone over the fence six times in the 1975 season and on eight or nine occasions in the 1976 season. And, according to the claimants, some of these balls had come on to their property.

The claimants brought this action against the chairman and secretary of the club in their personal capacity and as representatives of other members of the club. They sought damages for their negligence and an injunction restraining the defendants from continuing the nuisance.

By a majority of two to one the Court of Appeal (Lord Denning MR dissenting) held that the claimants succeeded in their claims for nuisance and negligence.

In his dissenting judgment Lord Denning said, 'There is a conflict here between the interest of the public at large; and the interest of a private individual. The public interest lies in protecting the environment by preserving our playing fields ... The private interest lies in securing the privacy of his home.' He thought that the claimants should not be granted an injunction since the private interest in the privacy of home and garden should be subordinated to the public interest in preserving playing fields. But in any case he found that no nuisance had been committed.

Lord Denning saw the issue in the case as the claimants protecting their private interest in preserving the privacy of their home and garden against what he called the public interest (Pound would have called this a social interest) in protecting playing fields.

Once he had analysed the problem in those terms it was almost inevitable that he would decide that the public interest should outweigh the private interest.

If both interests had been presented at the individual level (for example the claimants' interest in their privacy against the defendants' personal interest in playing cricket); or if both had been presented at a social level (for example protecting general domestic privacy against protecting the environment) then the court could have engaged in a genuine balancing exercise.

ACTIVITY 1

1) Do you agree with Lord Denning? Should public interest be put ahead of private interests?
2) Can you think of any other situations where the interests of the state conflict with our personal interests?
3) In the situations you have suggested, does the public interest or the private interest usually prevail?
4) Are the rights of individuals more or less important than the rights of society? Or of the state? Explain your answer.

Individuals can have different interests depending on the circumstances in which they find themselves.

CASE STUDY: The case of the murder of Maxwell Confait

In 1977 three boys were arrested for the murder of a man called Maxwell Confait. The boys were aged fourteen, fifteen and sixteen, and one of them had learning difficulties. They were questioned by the police and they all confessed to the killing. At their trial for Confait's murder the main evidence against each of them was his own confession. But their conviction gave rise to considerable public disquiet and an inquiry was set up to look into it. The inquiry concluded that none of the boys had had any connection with the killing.

There was considerable disquiet about the way the police had interviewed the boys and as a result the Government set up a Royal Commission to examine police procedures. The Royal Commission on Criminal Procedure reported in 1981. It concluded that it was necessary to have a balance between 'the interests of the community in bringing offenders to justice and the rights and liberties of persons suspected of crime.'

As a direct result of this case the Government passed the Police and Criminal Evidence Act 1984 (PACE). The purpose of the act was to try to balance, at all stages of a criminal inquiry, the powers of the police to investigate crime with appropriate rights for those suspected of crime.

As members of society you and I want the police to have sufficient powers to catch people who commit crime and bring them before the courts. We have an interest in seeing criminals caught, prosecuted and convicted.

But everyone has a right not to be wrongly convicted of a crime that he or she did not commit. We have a right to be protected against the police using unfair methods to collect evidence against us. So we also have an interest in seeing that the police do not abuse the powers that they have to be given.

It is the law's job to balance these conflicting interests.

PACE tries to achieve this balance by giving the police powers to investigate crime that other citizens do not have. These powers include:

- the power to stop and search people in public
- the power to search premises
- the power to arrest suspects (but note that the power of the police to arrest suspects is now contained in the Serious Organised Crime and Police Act 2005)
- the power to detain and interrogate suspects.

These powers are balanced by various rights that PACE gives to those suspected of crime; for example:

- strict rules about the length of time that the police can detain suspects without charging them with a crime
- rules about how suspects have to be treated when they are in police custody
- rules about the conditions in which suspects can be questioned
- the right of suspects to have their lawyer present during police questioning
- the need for the prosecution to show that there was no oppression used during police questioning
- the right to have interviews tape recorded.

In the A2 course we examine these rules in more detail to see whether or not PACE achieves this balance.

The judicial process

We now consider how courts deal with the cases that come before them. We have already seen in topic 1, Chapter 4 (pages 142–143) that there is a difference between criminal law and civil law.

ACTIVITY 2

Look back at pages 142–43 and write a brief summary of the following.
1) The purpose of criminal law.
2) The purpose of civil law.

We have seen that the civil courts are mainly concerned with deciding whether or not a loss suffered by the claimant should be compensated and to fix the amount of compensation that an unsuccessful defendant should pay.

The criminal courts are concerned with deciding if the accused has committed a crime and to fix the punishment if he or she is found guilty.

Although these are very different aims, the civil and criminal courts set about their work in similar ways – they reach their decisions by applying the law to the facts that are proved.

Step 1 The doctrine of precedent

Much of the law that has to be applied comes from Parliament in the form of statutes but a significant amount of our law comes from the decisions that the courts themselves make. Our courts have a strict hierarchy and the decisions made by courts are usually binding on courts below them in the hierarchy. The rules that

deal with which courts are bound by the decisions of other courts are known as the rules of *stare decisis*. (This is a Latin phrase meaning 'let the decision stand'.)

The reason for the doctrine of precedent is that it brings an element of certainty into the law. Given a certain set of circumstances, a solicitor can advise his or her clients what the law is likely to be in relation to those circumstances.

It has been argued, however, that too rigid a system of precedent can be disadvantageous, preventing the law from developing to meet changing conditions. For example, a wrong decision of a superior court continues to bind an inferior court until it is overruled or changed by Parliament.

Rigidity in the system is avoided, however, by the fact that:

- judgments can be overruled by superior courts
- Parliament can always change the law and the courts must then follow the statute made by Parliament rather than the previous precedent.

The hierarchy of the courts is explained in the diagram below.

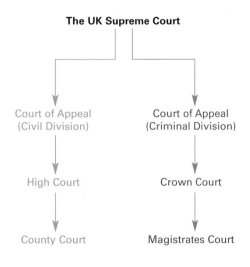

The UK Supreme Court

| Court of Appeal (Civil Division) | Court of Appeal (Criminal Division) |

High Court — County Court

Crown Court — Magistrates Court

The courts shown in green and linked by green arrows are those that deal with civil cases. The courts in red and linked by red arrows are the criminal courts. Until 1 October 2009 the House of Lords (as well as being the upper house of Parliament was also the highest appeal court in England and Wales. When it sat as a court it sat as a committee of the House and only the Law Lords (senior judges who were made life peers specially to be able to sit in the House of Lords) were able to take part in its proceedings. On 1 October 2009 it was replaced by the new Supreme Court which has taken over all the previous judicial functions of the House of Lords. All the existing Law Lords have become justices of the Supreme Court. The Supreme Court hears both civil and criminal cases.

Although the Supreme Court is the final court of appeal in the UK it is not by any means the busiest. Only about 70 cases will reach the Supreme Court each year. The Court of Appeal, on the other hand, hears about 10,000 cases each year – about 2000 in the Civil Division and about 8000 in the Criminal Division. The importance and influence of the Court of Appeal cannot, therefore, be underestimated.

The rules of *stare decisis* are set out in the table below:

THE OPERATION OF THE DOCTRINE OF *STARE DECISIS*

Court	Higher binds lower	Same level binds itself
UK Supreme Court	Decisions of the Supreme Court are binding on all other courts in England and Wales	• The Supreme Court will normally regard itself as bound by its own previous decisions, but • It has power to depart from a previous decision when it is right to do so NB: This power will be used very sparingly
Court of Appeal	Decisions of the Court of Appeal are binding on the courts below it – i.e.: • High Court • Crown Court • County Court • Magistrates' Court	The Criminal Division of the Court of Appeal is bound by its own previous decisions but can depart from them if it would be unjust to follow a previous decision
High Court	Decisions of the High Court bind all civil courts below it – i.e. County Court	The High Court is NOT bound by its own previous decisions
Crown Court, County Court and Magistrates' Court	The decisions of the Crown Court, the County Court and the Magistrates' Courts are not reported and so do not create any precedents	

PRECEDENT

Advantages	Disadvantages
• **Certainty:** the rules of *stare decisis* make it clear which courts are bound to follow which other courts and so make the law clear.	• **Complexity and volume:** there are hundreds of thousands of cases, some going back over 400 years, and it can be very difficult to find appropriate cases, although modern computerised methods have helped in this.
• **Detailed practical rules:** precedent is based on real cases so it gives a clear indication about how the law is to be applied.	• **Rigidity:** there is always a danger that old cases are followed and not updated – the law can get out of touch with modern needs.
• **Free market in legal ideas:** the courts adopt and follow good precedent, but find ways to avoid having to apply decisions which are unfair or unworkable.	• **Unpredictability:** there can sometimes be conflicting precedents on the same topic and it is impossible to tell which one a judge will favour.
• **Flexibility:** the courts are able to use a number of techniques to avoid precedents that do not suit the cases they are dealing with and the House of Lords is able to change bad rules.	• **Dependence on chance:** the judges have no control over which cases come before the courts and so they cannot control the time or speed at which they can develop the law.
	• **Lack of research about the social consequences:** the judges are unable to carry out research about the social consequences of any changes they make – they have to decide the cases they hear on the evidence before them.

The advantages and disadvantages of precedent are outlined in the table above.

ACTIVITY 3

1) With reference to the advantages and disadvantages of precedent above discuss the following conclusion.
   'There are more disadvantages than advantages, but there is no chance of precedent disappearing, because the arguments in favour of precedent, although fewer in number, are much more convincing than those against it.'

2) Define what is meant by the term 'precedent'.
3) What is an appeal?
4) What is the highest court in the land?
5) Which court hears more cases; the House of Lords or the Court of Appeal?
6) Which court's decisions are binding on all other courts?

Step 2 Interpreting statutes

Although the courts make a considerable amount of our law, most of it is made by parliament, in the form of statutes, or acts of parliament as they are often known. The two terms mean exactly the same thing.

The court has to interpret these and apply them to the situation before it can reach a decision. It has been estimated that courts spend approximately 80 per cent of their time interpreting statutes. One might imagine that this is a relatively easy task and that the meaning of statutes is always clear, but in fact that is far from the case. The problem is that when statutes are drafted it is just not possible to foresee all the circumstances in which they will be used. The problem that court usually has is to decide which of two possible meanings the statute should be given – it is not usually about trying to decide what the statute means in general terms.

The courts can approach the interpretation of statutes in a number of ways. A judge has a discretion about which of these methods he or she adopts and he or she uses the approach that gives the most suitable result in the case being tried.

In Victorian times judges tended to interpret statutes very literally, but this often produced absurd results since the statute was often being used in situations which were totally unforeseen when it was being drafted. Sometimes it just did not help – if a court was interpreting a statute which provided that no 'vehicles' were permitted on the platform of a railway station in order to decide that a person using a pram was in breach of the statute the literal rule would not be very helpful.

Nowadays the courts tend to use what is known as the purposive approach – the court asks itself what purpose the statute was intended to achieve and then tries to interpret it in such a way as to give effect to that purpose. So if the statute about vehicles on station platforms was intended to prevent passengers being injured by vehicles on platforms the court might well decide that a pram was not a 'vehicle' for the purposes of the statute, since it was unlikely to cause injury to other passengers. But if the case had been about whether or not a skateboard was a 'vehicle' for the purposes of the act then it might have reached the conclusion that skateboards could injure other passengers and so decide that a skateboard was indeed a 'vehicle'.

CASE STUDY

The Abortion Act 1967 was passed to achieve a number of objectives, two of which were:

1) to clarify the previous law and to make clear the reasons why a pregnancy could be terminated
2) to ensure that terminations were carried out skilfully and in safe and hygienic conditions.

The act provided that termination of a pregnancy was only lawful if it was performed by a 'registered medical practitioner' – in other words by a doctor. This was because in 1967 terminations were achieved by surgical intervention. By the 1980s most terminations were achieved by inducing premature labour by means of an intravenous drip. The drip was usually put up by a nurse and not by a doctor.

1) How might the purposive approach to interpretation be used in this situation?
2) Were nurses who put up a drip to terminate a pregnancy breaking the law?
3) How would you argue that a termination achieved by a nurse putting the patient on a drip was lawful under the act?
4) Have a careful look at the case of Royal College of Nursing v DHSS [1981] to see how the courts decided the issue.

The powers of the courts

Courts have different powers when dealing with civil and criminal cases.

We have learnt that civil law is about compensating the victims of accidents and those who have suffered other sort of loss. But it is also about establishing rights and duties and enabling individuals to claim those rights and perform those duties. The range of powers that the court possesses in order to do these things is considerable.

Civil cases

The courts have extensive powers to make orders in civil cases. The usual remedy is damages but a branch of law called equity allows the courts much wider powers to make orders that will be fairer to the parties involved in the proceedings. These powers are said to be 'discretionary'. That means that the court never has to apply them, but can do so when the judge applies a set of rules that indicate that these remedies have been used in similar situations in the past.

Damages

The award of damages is the usual remedy in tort and contract cases. Damages are intended to compensate the claimant for the actions of the defendant.

* In a breach of contract case they are intended to put the claimant in the same position, as far as money can, as if the contract had been performed by the defendant.
* In a tort case the intention is to put the claimant in the same position as if the tort had not been committed.

Damages are meant to restore the claimant to the position they would have been in if no wrong had been done to them.

Damages are said to be compensatory in nature. They should provide compensation for the wrong done to the claimant – nothing more and nothing less. Sometimes, however a court awards exemplary damages where the conduct of the defendant has been such that the court feels that they should be punished. The circumstances where exemplary damages can be awarded are very limited.

Specific performance

Specific performance is an order made by the court telling the defendant to perform the terms of a contract that he or she has made. It is a discretionary award – that means that the court is never bound to grant it, but only does so in accordance with rules that have been settled in decided cases over the centuries; for example it is never granted where damages would be a sufficient remedy or where the contract was for personal services.

Injunction

An injunction is another discretionary remedy which enables a court to make an order restraining the defendant from breaking a contract or from continuing to do an act that would constitute a tort. It is often used to stop the defendant from doing some act that would amount to the tort of nuisance.

There is a wide range of different types of injunction, for example a freezing order is an injunction that freezes a defendant's assets and prevents the defendant removing them from the country in an attempt to avoid having to pay damages to the claimant if he won the case.

Rescission

This is another discretionary order. It allows a court to order that a contract is set aside and the parties restored to the position that they were in before it was made. Like all discretionary orders it is only used in limited circumstances where damages would not be an appropriate remedy.

Rectification

This is also a discretionary remedy. It can be used when a written document does not express the true agreement of the parties, for example when there was a mistake in recording the agreed rent in a lease. It enables the court to amend the document to reflect what the parties had originally intended it to express.

Declaration

Sometimes a claimant asks the court to declare what the law is on a disputed point. This can often settle a dispute before the claimant's rights have been infringed in some way or can guide the claimant in his or her future conduct. Recently Debbie Purdy asked the court to clarify the law on assisted suicide as she did not want her husband to be prosecuted for helping her to go to Switzerland to an assisted suicide clinic. In that case it refused to make a declaration as it thought the law was already sufficiently clear.

ACTIVITY 5

1) Define the term 'discretionary remedy'.
2) Suggest six situations where each of the six discretionary powers listed above may be used as a suitable remedy.

Criminal cases

We have seen that in criminal cases the purpose of the law is to punish those who have been found guilty of a crime. Here too, the court has extensive powers.

When a criminal court passes sentence on an accused who has either pleaded guilty or who has pleaded not guilty but has been convicted after a trial it is required by the Criminal Justice Act 2003 to have regard to the following purposes of sentencing.

1) **Punishment of offenders**: the punishment must be appropriate to the seriousness of the crime committed by the accused.

2) **Reduction of crime**, including its reduction by deterrence: sometimes a severe sentence can reduce the amount of that particular crime, but as most crime is committed on impulse or by people who have not stopped to think about the consequences, the opportunities for reducing crime by deterrent sentences are very limited.

3) **Reform and rehabilitation of offenders**: reform and rehabilitation sounds like a very sensible aim, but in overcrowded prisons there is very little real opportunity for successful implementation of this aim, although drug rehabilitation programmes and courses on anger management seem to have some limited success.

4) **Protection of the public**: the public can be protected by sending offenders to prison, but this is very expensive and cannot really be justified except in the case of highly dangerous offenders. Prison is also where many offenders pick up new ideas and techniques and so can be counterproductive.

5) **Making of reparation** by offenders to victims of their crimes: this can take many forms – including various community sentences where offenders do unpaid work in the community.

Judges are unable to give effect to all of these aims in any one sentence, so they have to decide which aims they need to focus on in each case.

Examiner's tip

Sentencing is a very complex subject, and one on which many people have strongly held views. The examiner will not be impressed by students who 'rant' about sentencing. She or he will be looking for well argued and logical answers that examine all sides of the arguments.

Sentences fall into four broad categories:

1) fines and fixed penalty offences
2) custodial sentences
3) community sentences
4) other miscellaneous sentences.

Fines and fixed penalty offences

A fine is an order to pay money to the state – fines do not go to the victim of the crime. In the magistrates' courts the maximum fine is £5,000, but new legislation is planned to increase this to £15,000. There is no limit to the fines that may be imposed in the Crown Court, although many offences do specify a maximum fine. Fines are the most common sentences passed by the courts – in 2000, 75 per cent of all offenders were given a fine.

- Advantages of fines are that they bring income into the system; they do not have the disruptive effect of imprisonment and people who have been fined are less likely to re-offend than those given other sentences; although this may be partly explained by the type of offenders who are given fines in the first place.

- Disadvantages of fines are that there are high rates of non-payment and that fines may be unfair – the same fine could be a great hardship to a poor defendant, but could be insignificant to a rich one.

Fixed penalties are not really fines at all as they are not imposed by the judicial system, but are made by an official when, for example, a parking warden puts a ticket on a car that is unlawfully parked. In addition to being used for parking offences they can now be used by the police for offences such as being drunk in a public place and being drunk and disorderly. The similarity to fines is that they require the payment of money by the offender.

- Advantages of fixed penalties are that they allow minor offending that previously might have escaped any sanction to be punished without using police resources on court appearances.
- Disadvantages of fixed penalties are that they occur outside the framework of the courts and therefore there is a danger of abuse and corruption.

Custodial sentences

For adult offenders, a custodial sentence means a period spent in prison. Most prisoners do not spend the whole of their sentence in prison and it has been argued that a short sentence does not achieve any positive results. The Criminal Justice Act 2003 introduced the idea of 'custody plus' under which all prisoners sentenced to twelve months custody or less are released after serving a maximum of three months but are subjected to at least six months post-release supervision in the community. An offender who fails to comply with any of the conditions attached to the community part of the sentence is returned to custody.

Offenders sentenced to twelve month imprisonment or more spend half their time in custody and the remainder of their sentence under supervision in the community. The automatic reduction of the custodial part of sentences is currently being reconsidered by the Home Office as it is now felt that this may be inappropriate for serious offences.

Short custodial sentences can be suspended for between six months and two years. This means that the offender does not serve the sentence in custody but is required to undertake certain activities in the community. If the offender breaches any of the conditions of the suspension he or she is required to serve the remainder of the sentence in custody.

Committing a further offence at any stage of the period of suspension counts as a breach and is dealt with by the court dealing with the new offence.

Courts have no discretion about the sentence for murder and all persons convicted of this offence must be sentenced to life imprisonment. When passing sentence the trial judge must indicate the period of time to be served before the prisoner can be considered for release. Those convicted of particularly serious and heinous crimes (multiple murderers, child killers, terrorists) have to serve the whole of the life sentence. Those convicted of murders of police or prison officers, or of murders with a sexual, racial or religious motive have to serve at least 30 years. Others have to serve at least fifteen years. The Parole Board decides if release is appropriate once a life prisoner has served the minimum period. Those released are released on licence and can be recalled to prison at any time should their behaviour give cause for concern.

The last Conservative Government claimed that the advantage of a prison sentence was that 'prison works' in that offenders are not a risk to society while they are incarcerated. The current Labour Government claims that it can be made to work if proper use is made of the opportunities for rehabilitation.

One of the most obvious disadvantages of custodial sentences is that 60 per cent of prisoners are reconvicted of another crime within two years of release. This has led some writers to describe prisons as 'universities of crime'.

OTHER DISADVANTAGES OF CUSTODIAL SENTENCES

1) Budget cuts and overcrowding in prisons mean that there is very little opportunity for retraining, education or indeed any form of rehabilitation

2) Ex-prisoners often find it very difficult to get employment and so are more likely to drift back into criminal activity

3) It punishes the families of prisoners who suffer financial problems as a result of the breadwinner being in custody

4) It can lead to family breakdown

5) It is very expensive – it costs £36,000 a year to keep a person in prison. Three weeks in prison costs more than a lengthy community sentence

6) Many prisoners are serving sentences for non-payment of fines and other minor offences that could be dealt with more effectively in the community.

ACTIVITY 6

1) Using ideas of your own and those from the text assess the extent to which you agree with the statement 'prison works'.

Your answer should be about one and a half sides of A4 paper with reasoned arguments and using examples. Your answer needs a clear conclusion explaining your view. You should try to link your view with each point you explore.

In your answer consider the term 'works' in a wide context. For example you may think about prison 'working' for whom? The public? The prisoner's family? The prisoner and his or her future as a productive citizen? Is prison working financially? Does prison work as an effective deterrent from crime?

Community sentences

Community sentences leave the offender in the community but impose restrictions on his or her freedom. The Criminal Justice Act 2003 provides for a single community service order which can be applied to any offender over the age of sixteen. The order can contain a range of possible requirements that apply to the offender. These are set out below and are largely self explanatory.

COMMUNITY SERVICE ORDER REQUIREMENTS

- Do unpaid work for the community.
- Attend a programme of education or training.
- Attend an alcohol treatment/drug rehabilitation course.
- Refrain from doing a specified range of activities.
- Abide by a curfew.
- Live in a particular place (for example a hostel).
- Undergo mental health treatment.
- Be supervised by a probation officer.

- Advantages of community orders are that they do not have the disruptive effects of imprisonment; they are effective in reducing crime (for example by the imposition of a curfew); they can be used to achieve a variety of the purposes of sentencing, for example by providing for the rehabilitation of offenders, by restricting the movement of offenders and by protecting the public by requiring the supervision of offenders. They offer a real alternative to custody in many situations.
- Disadvantages of community orders are that they are seen by the public as a 'soft option' (although this is not the case). They are sometimes seen as degrading – for example tagging – although they are certainly less degrading than imprisonment. In some cases staff shortages mean that supervision is not effective and in some cases is almost non-existent.

Miscellaneous sentences

These involve a range of other sentences that do not easily fit into any other category.

Mental health orders

Under these the Crown Court can order that offenders suffering from a mental disorder are detained in hospital for treatment.

Binding over to be of good behaviour

This order dates back to the Justices of the Peace Act 1361 as amended by the Magistrates' Courts Act 1980. It can be made against any person before the court – not just the defendant, but also a witness – who has 'breached the peace'. People who are bound over must put up a sum of money (or find someone else willing to do so) which is forfeited if the undertaking to be of good behaviour is broken. A breach of the peace occurs when a person's behaviour is likely to provoke others to violence and the arrest and detention of the person so acting is not disproportionate to the aim of preventing disorder or of protecting the rights of others.

Absolute and conditional discharges

When a person is convicted of an offence (except an offence where the penalty is fixed by law) the court can discharge the defendant either conditionally or absolutely.

- Conditional discharge – no action is taken against the offender unless he or she commits another offence within a specified period of up to three years.
- Absolute discharge – no action is taken against the defendant at all. It is used where the defendant has broken the law, but where no reasonable person would blame him for acting as he or she did.

There are numerous other sentences in this category. Together they provide a useful and flexible method of dealing with a range of offenders where conventional sentences are, for some reason, inappropriate.

ACTIVITY 7

1) Identify two types of interest categories referred to by Roscoe Pound.
2) Why was the Royal Commission on Police Procedures set up?
3) What did the commission find?
4) PACE was set up as a result of the Royal Commission. What does PACE stand for?
5) What did PACE seek to achieve? And how did it seek to achieve these ends?
6) List the civil courts in order of hierarchy, starting with the most senior. List the criminal courts in order of hierarchy, starting with the most senior.
7) Identify and explain advantages and disadvantages of the following criminal court sentences: fines, custodial sentences, community sentences.

5 The courts and the Human Rights Act 1998

Civil actions to enforce human rights

In Chapter 3 we looked at the impact of the Human Rights Act 1998 (the HRA) on our legal system and what changes it brought and how we protect our rights. In this topic we look briefly at how we use the HRA.

ACTIVITY 1

1) Look back at pages 117–126 and write a brief summary of the changes that the HRA has made to our legal system.

In order to understand just how significant the HRA is we need to remind ourselves of the position before it was passed. We can illustrate the position by reference to the case of *A v UK Government* (1999) – a case that was heard by the European Court of Human Rights in 1999, before the HRA came into force.

CASE STUDY: A v UK Government (1999)

A was a nine-year-old boy. He was beaten with a garden cane by his stepfather. His stepfather was prosecuted for the assault in 1994, but acquitted on the ground that the punishment was a reasonable chastisement.

A then brought a case against the British Government in the European Court of Human Rights in Strasbourg alleging that the Government had breached his human rights by allowing his stepfather to beat him. The European Court of Human Rights held that A's rights had been infringed.

Note that although the HRA had been passed in 1998 it did not come into force until 2000.

This meant that although the UK had ratified the European Convention on Human Rights in 1951, the terms of the convention were not part of UK law until 2000. This produced the rather surreal situation that UK citizens were protected by the terms of an international agreement that was not UK law. This in turn meant that courts in the UK could not apply the terms of the convention. That was why A had to take his case to the European Court of Human Rights. A could not bring proceedings in the European Court of Human Rights against the person who had beaten him – he had to bring his case against the UK Government, alleging that it had allowed his stepfather to breach his human rights.

CONSEQUENCES OF THE CASE OF *A V UK GOVERNMENT* (1999)

1) The UK Government had to change the law to protect children against such treatment in the future.

2) The Government was ordered to pay compensation to A for its failure to protect him.

Note that it took five years for the case to come before the European Court of Human Rights. A was nine years old when his stepfather assaulted him, but he was nearly sixteen by the time the case was eventually heard!

However, while the HRA allows individuals to enforce their human rights against local and public authorities, there is some debate about the extent to which it allows individual citizens to enforce their Convention rights against other individuals.

SCOPE OF THE HRA

- Section 6 of the HRA states that any 'public authority' that acts in a way that is incompatible with a Convention right is acting unlawfully.

- The term 'public authority' is widely defined and includes central and local government and organisations such as the police, the NHS and the courts.

- Private individuals, private companies and businesses are not included.

Therefore if a citizen has his or her convention rights infringed by a public body (for example the police) in such a way as to amount to a **tort** the citizen can now bring a civil action in the UK courts.

In a case before the HRA came into force, *Hill v Chief Constable of West Yorkshire* (1989), the House of Lords held that the police were not liable in an action for negligence brought by a victim of the serial killer Peter Sutcliffe – the Yorkshire Ripper. The reason given for this decision was that as a matter of public policy the police should not be liable to individuals for the consequences of their strategies for the investigation and prevention of crime.

This can be compared with the view of the European Court of Human Rights in the case of *Osman v UK* (1999).

This decision has been criticised on the basis that it did not pay sufficient attention to the rules about the law of tort in the UK and the European Court of Human Rights has since acknowledged that that may be the case. The case illustrates that by using the rights given by the European Convention on Human Rights individuals are able to challenge the barriers to bringing civil actions to enforce their rights under the convention.

Although the HRA specifically provides that public authorities that breach the Convention are acting unlawfully the courts appear to accept that the Convention also applies, at least in a limited form, to individuals. This was illustrated in the case of *Douglas v* Hello! (2001) (see also page 124).

CASE STUDY: Osman v UK (1999)

A teacher had become obsessed with a fourteen-year-old boy in his school and as a consequence of the attentions he paid to the boy he was suspended. He made threats against the boy's parents and the school's deputy headmaster. As a result of these threats the police went to interview the teacher, but he had disappeared and they took no further action. Two months later he went to the boy's home, shot and injured the boy and killed his father. He then went to the home of the deputy headmaster and shot and injured him and killed his son.

The student and his mother then tried to bring an action for negligence against the police in the UK courts, but the Court of Appeal, relying on the decision in *Hill v Chief Constable for West Yorkshire* (1989), struck the case out. The claimants then appealed to the European Court of Human Rights

The European Court of Human Rights held that the decision in *Hill* breached the claimants' right to a fair trial under Article 6 of the European Convention on Human Rights. The European Court of Human Rights accepted that while public policy issues had to be considered the decision in *Hill* should not be seen as a blanket restriction on access to the courts.

CASE STUDY: Douglas v Hello! (2001)

This case related to photographs taken of the marriage of the Hollywood celebrities Michael Douglas and Catherine Zeta-Jones. The magazine *Hello!* had published photographs of the wedding without the claimants' authority. The claimants alleged that this was a breach of their right to privacy under the terms of the HRA.

Hello! magazine was not a public authority and so it was argued that the HRA did not apply to it.

But the Court held that as the Court itself was in fact a form of public authority it was therefore unable to ignore the provisions of the HRA and so allowed the claimants' case to succeed.

Sally Cartwright, publishing director of *Hello!*

Note that this area of the law is constantly developing – it is not clear how it will change in the future.

ACTIVITY 2

1) Explain why the activities of *Hello!* magazine were intruding on the privacy of the celebrity couple. Bear in mind the fact that although they may be celebrities they are still entitled to privacy and that a rival magazine was paying the claimants for the right to publish the photographs.
2) Why was there difficulty in making a claim through the HRA?
3) Try to identify other areas where this issue of privacy may become a human rights issue for other citizens. Consider other celebrities and non-celebrities.

Remedies for breach of rights protected by the European Convention on Human Rights

Rights are only worth having if they can be enforced. The existence of adequate remedies is therefore an essential part of any examination of an individual's rights.

Civil action

This remedy is discussed on pages 189–191.

Criminal proceedings

If the breach of an individual's rights is a crime then criminal proceedings may be brought against the person or organisation that committed the crime. This can be particularly useful where, for example, a citizen complains that he or she was assaulted as assault is both a crime and a tort giving rise to criminal and civil proceedings.

The criminal proceedings can be brought either by the state or by the individual as a private prosecution. Of course, if an individual successfully brings a private prosecution against an offender there is no guarantee that the individual will get any financial benefit from the action as any fine imposed will go to the state and not to the prosecutor. The individual would only benefit personally if the court made an order for payment of compensation.

European Court of Human Rights

We have already seen that, before the HRA came into force, the only way Convention rights could be enforced was by an action in the European Court of Human Rights. It is now cheaper, more convenient and usually more effective to bring proceedings in the domestic courts. But the right to go to the European Court of Human Rights in Strasbourg still exists and in some cases (for example, where the Supreme Court has created a precedent that it is unlikely to depart from) it might still be the better course to take.

Ombudsman

The role of the ombudsman was discussed in detail on pages 173–175. The ombudsman can investigate any breach of an individual's rights that falls within his or her remit and this includes rights under the European Convention on Human Rights.

Judicial review

Judicial review is a very important way of enforcing one's rights when it is believed that a public authority has acted outside the powers that it was given. It is discussed in detail on pages 195–204.

Habeas corpus

Habeas corpus is a Latin term which literally means 'let us have the body'. It is a very old remedy that dates back to the reign of Edward I and was already well established in 1482. It allows a person who is detained to challenge the legality of his or her detention. It is exercised by the Divisional Court of the Queen's Bench Division of the High Court.

It works by ordering the person detaining the applicant to bring the detained person before the court immediately. The court decides if the detention is lawful. If it decides that it is

unlawful it orders the immediate release of the applicant. It does not punish the person who unlawfully detained the applicant, but, once released, the applicant can then pursue an action for false imprisonment against the person or organisation that detained him.

Habeas corpus can be used by, among others: suspects held by the police during an investigation; convicted prisoners; those remanded in custody pending trial; and psychiatric patients detained in hospital under the Mental Health Acts. Applications for *habeas corpus* take priority over all other business.

Self defence

Every citizen has the right to use reasonable force to protect his or her person and/or property from unlawful interference by another. This is usually associated with protecting oneself from a physical attack by another, but it applies to any unlawful interference, either civil or criminal.

The citizen seeking to rely on self defence as a means of protecting a right needs to be careful to use only reasonable force. Use of excessive or unreasonable force results in the loss of the defence and may result in the conviction of the citizen.

Miscellaneous remedies

There are a variety of other ways in which the rights a citizen enjoys under the HRA can be enforced – for example an MP can ask questions in the House of Commons and the Criminal Injuries Compensation scheme provides state compensation for innocent victims of violent crime. Neither of these methods are without their limitations, but for many people they provide a relatively easy way of raising matters of concern or getting compensation that could not be paid by the perpetrators of many offences.

Imagine that you work in an advice centre and that you have been consulted by a number of people:

Nick tells you that he was assaulted by the police after he was arrested for a minor public order offence during a protest march.

Sarah tells you that the local authority has refused to give her child a place in a primary school because he does not speak English.

Craig says that he found a burglar in his house and hit him with a baseball bat, breaking his arm. The police have told him that they are considering reporting him for assault.

1) What advice would you give to each of them?
2) What action should they each take?
3) Write a brief note to your supervisor explaining the reasons for the advice that you would give.

The role of the UK Supreme Court and the European Court of Human Rights

When we consider the role of the UK Supreme Court and the European Court of Human Rights we need to be clear that before the HRA came into force the courts in the UK could not apply the rights contained in the convention. That was because although the convention was an international treaty to which the UK was a party it was not then part of the law of the UK.

Since October 2000 most of the provisions of the convention have been incorporated into UK law by the provisions of the HRA. As a result the UK courts are now in a position to deal with cases involving the provisions of the convention.

The use of the term 'Supreme Court' in this context may be misleading. At the time of writing it does not exist, but it is intended that on 1 October 2009 it will replace both the House of Lords and the Judicial Committee of the Privy Council as the final court of appeal for the cases that currently go to those two courts for their final appeal hearings. For the purposes of this book it can be regarded as synonymous with the House of Lords.

All cases in the UK courts, including those involving human rights issues, can be taken on appeal if either party is dissatisfied with the outcome of the original trial. Cases that start in the High Court and larger cases that start in the County Court (known as 'multi track' cases) go on appeal to the Court of Appeal and a further appeal is possible from the Court of Appeal to the Supreme Court.

That gives the Supreme Court a powerful position when it comes to shaping the law on issues arising from the HRA.

There is little reason why any case would need to go to the European Court of Human Rights now that cases can be dealt with in the UK courts. Apart from the convenience of having cases heard locally instead of having to travel to Strasbourg for a hearing, it is cheaper to have cases dealt with in the UK.

In addition it needs to be remembered that using the UK courts to enforce human rights issues have some other advantages:

- **Cost:** it is a great deal cheaper to bring an action in the domestic courts rather than have the expense of bringing an action in the European Court of Human Rights in Strasbourg.
- **Speed:** the case of *A v UK* (1999) took up to seven years to reach the European Court of Human Rights. Cases can be heard much more quickly in the domestic courts.

- **More convenient remedies**: in the European Court of Human Rights cases have to be brought against the Government on the basis that the claimant is alleging that the Government allowed someone to breach the claimant's rights. If the court finds that the claimant's rights were breached then the Government is deemed to have allowed it in the sense that it did not stop the breach from occurring.

   If the claimant is able to bring his or her action in the domestic UK courts the action can be brought against the person or body who actually breached the claimant's human rights. Of course, the defendant will need to be a 'public authority' as discussed at the beginning of this topic as only a public authority is acting unlawfully if it performs an act that is incompatible with a right protected by the Convention and the HRA (but this needs to be interpreted in the light of the decision in *Douglas v Hello!* (2001) as discussed on pages 190–91).

   It is obviously more satisfactory to bring an action against the organisation that has actually breached the claimant's rights than against the Government that has not been directly involved in the incident in any way. An added attraction is that success in the European Courts means the Government has an obligation under the convention to change the law, but no other remedy is guaranteed. Compensation may be available from the Government, but not from the organisation or person who breached the claimant's rights.

- **The wrongdoer can be made liable**: when a civil action is brought in the UK courts the winner can expect to be awarded compensation against the losing party. This is true in respect of actions alleging breach of the claimant's human rights and so the party who caused the breach has to pay – not the Government. Apart from being fairer, this should discourage further breaches by the defendant.

- **The incorporation of the Human Rights Act 1998 into UK law makes some areas of law more accessible**: the law on civil rights in the UK had long been confused and fragmented. The incorporation of the convention has made the law in this area much clearer as it provides a comprehensive statement of rights and freedoms in the UK.

On the other hand there are some disadvantages to having the Convention incorporated into UK law.

- **Potential for conflict between parliament and the courts**: before the HRA was passed the courts had to interpret and apply statutes made by parliament. They did not have to pass judgment on them. Since the passage of the HRA the courts are now frequently asked to decide if a statute is compatible with the HRA.

   That means, of course, that the courts are often drawn into a confrontation with parliament. The Government has often been unhappy when the courts declared that some of its anti-terrorist legislation is in breach of the HRA. The Government has contemplated changing the HRA to limit the power of the courts, but that would lead to people taking their cases to the European Court of Human Rights and so strengthening its position. It has therefore left things as they are.

- **The Human Rights Act 1998 is not entrenched**: because parliament is sovereign it can introduce any legislation it likes. No parliament therefore can limit the power of a future parliament and so a future parliament can repeal any legislation made by a previous parliament. This means that the HRA itself could be repealed by parliament in the same way as any other legislation can be repealed.

1) In what year did the Human Rights Act formally become part of UK law?
2) Briefly explain how the case of *A v UK Government* (1999) helped to improve the law.
3) Why would it be much quicker and simpler for A to have his case heard today than was the case when A was nine years old?
4) Using one or more examples explain how the HRA is not clear on the extent to which it applies to cases against individual citizens or private companies.
5) Briefly explain why there is less likelihood today than before 2000 that citizens will make use of European Court of Human Rights directly.
6) Briefly outline the roles of the Supreme Court.

There is a considerable debate between constitutional lawyers as to whether or not it would ever be possible to entrench legislation so that it cannot be changed or repealed without special procedures, such as a referendum or a weighted parliamentary majority – i.e. more than a simple majority as is the case at present. It seems unlikely that it could be done.

- **The convention is not drafted in the same way as a UK statute**: most European law is drafted in a different way to UK law. Statutes in the UK are drafted in a very detailed manner. In European countries the preference is to draft laws in much wider terms. The convention is drafted in the wide European style rather than in the detailed UK tradition. When it was incorporated into UK law it was, therefore in a different style to most UK law. UK judges, however, are used to interpreting law from the EU, and it is drafted in the same wide style, so this has not proved to be the difficulty that some commentators thought it might be. It may explain, however, why some provisions of the convention appear to be interpreted differently in the UK from other European countries.

6 Judicial review

What is judicial review?

The principal function of the High Court is to try important civil actions. But it has another role. It has the power to oversee the decisions of public bodies and officials such as:

- inferior courts and tribunals
- local councils
- members of the executive (including government ministers and police officers).

The power to oversee decisions made by such bodies is called 'judicial review'. It is exercised by two or more judges of the Queen's Bench Division of the High Court sitting together in a divisional court. It was famously defined by Simon Brown J (as he then was) in *Ex parte Vijayatunga* (1990), as the 'exercise of the court's inherent power at common law to determine whether action is lawful or not'.

There are certain bodies that are exempt from judicial review. Decisions made by the ombudsman (the Parliamentary Commissioner for Standards) cannot be subject to judicial review as he operates as part of the proceedings of parliament and the decisions of parliament are not subject to review by the court.

WHAT TYPES OF DECISIONS ARE CHALLENGED BY JUDICIAL REVIEW?

Judicial review enables a person who has been adversely affected by a decision of a public body (such as those mentioned above) that infringes a right protected by public law where there is no further or other right of appeal.

For example if a local council exceeded its powers and imposed a restriction on the lawful activities of a shopkeeper by preventing him from displaying legitimate goods in his shop window, he could challenge the decision of the local authority by asking for judicial review of the decision it had made.

A right protected by private law (a right arising under a contract or as a result of a tort) cannot be the subject of judicial review. The remedy of the person whose right has been infringed in such circumstances is to bring an action in private law for breach of contract or tort.

WHEN CAN A DECISION BE CHALLENGED BY JUDICIAL REVIEW?

In very general terms judicial review can be used to challenge actions and decisions in the following situations.

1) A public body makes a decision that it does not have power to make. This is known as substantive *ultra vires*.

2) A public body does not use the correct procedure for making a decision or shows bias or unfairness in the way it made the decision. This is known as procedural *ultra vires*.

3) A public body makes a decision that is unreasonable.

4) A public body makes a decision that is in breach of natural justice.

These points need to be considered separately. Note that *ultra vires* is a Latin term that literally means 'beyond the powers'. It is a way of describing the situation where a local authority or other public body has exceeded its authority.

In judicial review the court is not concerned with the merits of the decision. It is not concerned about whether the decision is good or bad – it is concerned about how the decision was made. It only quashes the decision if the decision was beyond the powers of the body making it or if it made the decision unreasonably.

Substantive ultra vires

When Parliament gives a public body power to make rules or carry out certain functions it usually sets strict limits on what the public body can do.

This is illustrated by the case study below.

CASE STUDY: A–G v Fulham Corporation (1921)

Legislation gave local authorities power to provide facilities where the public could wash their clothes. Fulham Corporation used this legislation to open a commercial council-run laundry where council employees washed clothes for residents. This was challenged by judicial review.

It was held that the council had exceeded the powers it was given. It had not been given powers to operate a commercial laundry. It had been given powers to provide a facility where residents could wash their own clothes.

This sort of conduct is described as substantive *ultra vires*. 'Substantive' indicates that it was the decision itself that was outside the power of the public body. It distinguishes it from the situation described below.

Procedural ultra vires

A public body is said to have acted in a way that is procedurally *ultra vires* when it reached its decision as a result of following the wrong procedure. The public body had the power to make the decision in question, but adopted the wrong procedure in making the decision.

An example of this is seen in the case of *Agricultural, Horticultural and Forestry Industry Training Board v Aylesbury Mushrooms Ltd* (1972).

Case study: Agricultural, Horticultural and Forestry Industry Training Board v Aylesbury Mushrooms Ltd (1972)

The Minister of Labour had been given the power by a Statutory Rule and Order to establish an industrial training board but required him to first '... consult any organisation ... appearing to him to be representative of substantial numbers of employers engaging in the activities concerned'.

The minister did not consult the Mushroom Growers' Association. It represented about 85 per cent of all mushroom growers in England and Wales.

The court held that the minister's failure to consult properly as he was required to do made his order invalid as it was procedurally *ultra vires*.

Unreasonableness

When parliament gives a public body the power to do something it expects it to exercise that power reasonably. It would be quite unthinkable to suppose that parliament would expect a power it granted to be used unreasonably. The problem is how to define 'reasonable'. This matter was addressed by the Court of Appeal in the case of *Associated Provincial Picture Houses Ltd v Wednesbury Corporation* (1947) (see page 198).

These conditions – now called the 'Wednesbury Principles' form the modern basis for deciding what is and is not reasonable. They have been used regularly to guide the courts in deciding when a decision is unreasonable and should be quashed.

Examples of unreasonableness include the following situations:

- **The public authority making the decision has taken into account matters that were irrelevant.** In *R v Somerset County Council, ex parte Fewings* (1995) the County Council had taken a decision to ban stag hunting on its land. It had a statutory duty to manage its land for the benefit of the authority's area. The Court of Appeal held that the ban was illegal. It considered that in exercising its discretion about how to manage its land the council may have given undue consideration to the moral issue that hunting was cruel; whereas its prime consideration should have been its statutory requirement to manage the land for the benefit of the County Council.

- **The public authority made the decision for an improper purpose.** A public body is acting *ultra vires* when it exercises its powers for an improper purpose. In *R v Derbyshire County Council, ex parte Times Supplements Ltd* (1991) Derbyshire County Council had

CASE STUDY: Associated Provincial Picture Houses Ltd v Wednesbury Corporation (1947)

Under powers granted to it in the Sunday Entertainments Act 1932, Wednesbury Corporation granted a licence to the claimants to open their cinema on Sundays. The act allowed for a licence to be granted with 'such conditions as the authority sees fit'. The corporation imposed the condition that children under fifteen were not to be allowed into cinemas on Sundays.

The company argued that the condition banning children was 'unreasonable' and therefore *ultra vires*, that is, beyond the powers of the corporation.

The High Court refused to grant a declaration that the corporation had acted unreasonably, and the company appealed.

The Court of Appeal dismissed the appeal. The leading judgment was given by Lord Greene, the Master of the Rolls. He said that where Parliament had entrusted powers to another body, such as a local authority, the courts could declare that some decisions were 'unreasonable', and thus *ultra vires*, but only in very limited circumstances. The courts could not simply substitute their own opinion for that of any other body.

He said that to be unreasonable the decision made by the authority would have to be one where:

1) the authority had taken into account matters which it ought not to take into account, or, conversely,
2) the authority had not taken into account matters which it ought to have taken into account.

Even if the decision making process passed that test, the decision could still be held to be unreasonable if:

3) it was one which 'no reasonable body could have come to'; for example a decision to dismiss a teacher because she had red hair.'

---

decided not to advertise its vacant teaching appointments in the *Times Educational Supplement* and the *Sunday Times*. It took this decision because *The Times* had published two articles about the Council suggesting that it had acted improperly and possibly illegally. Derbyshire County Council had the power to decide where to place its advertisements, but it had to exercise that power properly and impartially. In this instance it had been motivated by bad faith and vindictiveness. Its decision to withdraw its advertising was therefore *ultra vires* and was quashed.

- **Where a public authority has a discretion, it must exercise that discretion and cannot make a wide general rule to apply in all cases instead.** In the 1970s the Government operated a scheme under which the Ministry

of Trade was empowered to make grants to industrial firms to cover the cost of the purchase of large pieces of machinery. The Ministry developed a rule that it would not pay for any machinery that cost less than £25. The British Oxygen Co. spent £4 million buying gas cylinders which cost £20 each. It applied for a grant for assistance with this expenditure but the Ministry applied its £25 rule and rejected the application. British Oxygen Co. sought judicial review of this decision and in *British Oxygen Co v Minister of Technology* (1971) it was held, on appeal to the House of Lords, that where a public body had a general discretion it could only develop internal policies such as those in this case if it was prepared to listen to arguments for the exercise of discretion in individual cases.

1) For each of the three examples of unreasonableness on pages 197–98 explain why they could be deemed unreasonable. Refer to the Wednesbury Principles, in your answer.

1) Define what is meant by the term 'judicial review'.
2) Briefly explain the difference between substantive and procedural and define the three types of *ultra vires*.
3) Identify and explain briefly an example where a pressure group may apply for judicial review despite not having a direct interest in the matter.

WHO CAN APPLY FOR JUDICIAL REVIEW?

In order to make an application for judicial review the applicant must have *locus standi*. This is a Latin term that means that the applicant must have a sufficient interest in the matter to which the application relates. The applicant must, therefore, have a close connection with the subject.

The reason for this rule is to prevent time being wasted by vexatious litigants who want to raise issues, but have no direct involvement in the matters they are raising.

A *vexatious litigant* is someone bringing actions motivated by no other reason than to harass or cause effect with little directly relevant purpose to the case.

However:

● some interest and pressure groups are considered to have such an interest even though they are not personally involved in it

● the Attorney General (the chief law officer of the Government) always has an interest and can allow any action to go ahead under his name if he decides that it is appropriate to do so.

Judicial review and natural justice

Natural justice is an important concept in the legal systems of all democratic countries. It is based on the idea that certain basic rules are fundamental to any decision making process. The two main rules of natural justice are:

● no one should be a judge in his own case
● both sides have a right to be heard.

The rules of natural justice apply to the courts, tribunals and public authorities and ensure that powers and duties are exercised in accordance with the rules of 'fair play'. The usual remedy for a breach of these rules would be for the aggrieved party to apply for judicial review of the decision concerned.

This issue arose when the House of Lords heard an appeal by General Pinochet, the former dictator of Chile. Bow Street Magistrates had ordered his extradition to Spain to stand trial for human rights abuses alleged to have been committed when he was the Chilean Head of State. His appeal eventually reached the House of Lords. In this case no application was made for judicial review. The House itself decided that the court that heard his appeal might have been biased against him.

During his time as ruler of Chile between 1973 and 1990 thousands of people were killed or disappeared.

General Pinochet who died in 2006 aged 91

Unfairness by a decision making body is also evidence of a breach of natural justice and may be challenged by judicial review. In *R v National Lottery Commissioners, ex parte Camelot Group plc* (2000) the National Lottery Commissioners were held to have acted unfairly when they decided to negotiate only with Camelot's rival for the licence to run the National Lottery.

Even where a statute appears to rule out any kind of appeal or review of a particular decision, it is still often possible to challenge it by judicial review as it would be contrary to the rules of natural justice not to be able to do so.

The test for bias has been updated by the Court of Appeal in the case of *Director General of Fair Trading v Proprietary Association of Great Britain* (2001). When deciding if the court or body making a decision was biased the court should:

1) identify all the circumstances that had a bearing on the suggestion that the decision making body was biased, and
2) determine whether or not those circumstances would lead a fair-minded and informed observer to conclude that there was a real possibility that the decision making body was biased.

ACTIVITY 3

1) Explain what is meant by the term 'natural justice'.
2) Discuss ways that bias can be deemed to have influenced a decision.

The remedies available through judicial review

Most of the ordinary remedies available in any civil action are available through judicial review proceedings. These include:

- **Damages**: an order to pay compensation to the winning party.

CASE STUDY: R v Bow Street Metropolitan Stipendiary Magistrate, ex parte Pinochet Ugarte (No. 2) (1999)

In this case the House of Lords heard an appeal in connection with proceedings to extradite General Pinochet to Spain to stand trial for human rights abuses committed while he was the Head of State in Chile.

After giving its decision in favour of allowing the extradition it was discovered that one of the Law Lords who had heard the case, Lord Hoffman, had connections with Amnesty International, a human rights organisation that had supported the extradition proceedings. Lord Hoffman was a member of Amnesty International and his wife held office in the organisation.

Because it felt that this could indicate that the House had not been unbiased and that the decision might be seen as unfair, it decided to re-hear the case before a different bench of Law Lords. At the second hearing the House decided against allowing the extradition to proceed.

- **Injunction**: an order preventing the defendant from doing some act or from following some line of conduct.
- **Declaration**: a statement of the law and of the rights and responsibilities of the parties.

ACTIVITY 4

1) Identify and briefly describe one example where each of the three remedies above may have been granted. Try to identify real examples rather than hypothetical ones.

In addition to these remedies there are three remedies that are only available in judicial review proceedings. These are often called prerogative orders, because they originally belonged to the monarch and came from the idea that the monarch had the right to control what his officials did. From the fifteenth and sixteenth centuries these powers came to be exercised by the courts and not by the monarch.

The prerogative orders are:

- **Quashing order**: until the Civil Procedure Rules 1998 this order was known as *certiorari*. It quashes an *ultra vires* decision. This means that it makes the decision null and void. For example if the Social Services Department had made a decision not to pay welfare benefit to X and X sought judicial review of the department's decision and was successful, the court could make a quashing order nullifying the decision not to pay benefit made by the Department of Social Services.

  A quashing order is not available against the Crown. In cases against the Crown the Court makes a declaration and the Crown then complies with the law as the court has declared it.

- **Mandatory order**: this is an order to an inferior court or a public body telling it to

do something. It might arise in circumstances like these: suppose that a tribunal had decided not to hear a case because it thought that it did not have jurisdiction in it and the claimant then sought judicial review of the tribunal's decision in the Divisional Court. If the claimant was successful, the Divisional Court could make a mandatory order telling the tribunal that it had to hear the case. Sometimes an applicant seeks a quashing order and a mandatory order. He could get a quashing order to nullify an *ultra vires* decision made by a public authority and a mandatory order to force the public authority to hear his case according to its legal powers.

- **Prohibiting order**: this is an order that prevents a tribunal or a public authority from doing something that could, if carried out, be subject to a quashing order. It directs the public authority of the tribunal not to act unlawfully in the future. It could be used to prevent a tribunal from starting proceedings which would be outside its jurisdiction.

It must be noted that all prerogative orders are discretionary. Even though the applicant might win his or her case, the court is under no obligation to give him or her a remedy. It might refuse to give a remedy if:

- there was an alternative remedy available
- the applicant had brought the proceedings out of malice or vindictiveness rather than a need for justice
- the applicant had delayed unduly in seeking judicial review.

ACTIVITY 5

1) Briefly explain the differences between quashing, mandatory and prohibiting orders.
2) Explain what is meant by discretionary orders.

Criticisms of the judicial review process

Judicial review is a useful tool for a citizen who needs to challenge a decision made by a public authority that affects his or her rights. But it is not without its critics. The main criticisms are as follows.

'Wednesbury Principles' are too strict

The test for unreasonableness laid down in the *Wednesbury* case is much too narrow. This limits the court's powers to supervise the Government effectively. For example a ban on some activity might not be completely irrational, even though the reasons for it were not convincing. In such a case the courts would be unable to say that the ban was 'unreasonable' using the criteria laid down in *Wednesbury*. This was the case in *R v Ministry of Defence, ex parte Smith* (1995).

CASE STUDY: R v Ministry of Defence, ex parte Smith (1995)

The applicants sought judicial review of a decision to dismiss them from the army because they were homosexual. At that time it was the policy of the Ministry of Defence to ban homosexuals from joining the army. The ban was not completely irrational, but the reasons relied on to support it were very weak. However, the court had to accept that it was not *Wednesbury* unreasonable and so the application for judicial review failed.

The two soldiers concerned took their case to the European Court of Human Rights in Strasbourg. In *Smith and Grady v UK* (1999) the European Court of Human Rights held that the test for unreasonableness was set too high and was very critical of the English courts' attitude to it.

Powers given to public bodies are often very wide and discretionary

Legislation often gives very wide powers to decision making public bodies. In addition, these powers are often discretionary – the public body has a choice about whether or not to use the powers. The courts often try to imply limits on these very wide powers, but it can be very difficult to control their use.

CASE STUDY: R v Secretary of State for the Environment, *ex parte* Norwich City Council (1982)

The Housing Act 1980 gave the Secretary of State for the Environment power 'to do all such things as appear to him necessary or expedient' to enable council tenants to buy the houses they rented from the local authority. The Secretary of State for the Environment relied on these powers to take the sale of council houses out of the hands of councils that were not selling their housing stock as quickly as he wanted them to.

Norwich City Council challenged this decision by judicial review.

The court had to dismiss the application for judicial review. The powers given by the Housing Act 1980 were so wide that very little could be considered to be *ultra vires*.

Decisions made by judicial review are often of a political nature

Many of the decisions that are challenged by the judicial review process bring the courts and politicians into conflict. Many of the cases we have looked at involve the courts examining decisions made by ministers – for example in *R v Secretary of State for the Environment, ex parte Norwich City Council* the court was considering how the minister was implementing a key part of the then Conservative Government's policy about selling council housing stock.

ACTIVITY 6

1) Look back over this topic and list cases that involve the activities of central and/or local government.

Some critics have claimed that the courts are more reluctant to interfere with decisions made by a Conservative government than with a labour government. Others claim that the courts tend to favour the Government, irrespective of its political views. These arguments were convincingly advanced by an academic writer, J A C Griffith in *The Politics of the Judiciary*, London (1997) Fontana Press. In recent years the House of Lords seems to have become more critical of government decisions, but this may be influenced by the fact that the last three governments have been labour controlled.

CASE STUDY: R v Secretary of State for for the Home Department, ex parte Hosenball (1977)

In this case Mark Hosenball, an American journalist, used judicial review to challenge a deportation order made against him on the ground that his continued presence in the UK was not conducive to the public good. He claimed that the deportation order was contrary to natural justice as he had not been allowed to know any details of the case made against him.

The Court of Appeal ruled that although the proceedings had been unjust, the rules of natural justice did not apply to deportation decisions made on the grounds of national security.

Decisions relating to national security

Geoffrey Robertson QC, a leading human rights lawyer, has claimed that where issues of national security are involved the courts are reluctant to either assess the strength of the evidence relied on by the state or even consider whether decisions made on such evidence were made rationally. He asserts that where national security issues are raised the courts adopt a 'hands off' attitude.

ACTIVITY 7

1) To what extent does judicial review concern itself with the merits of a decision in the courts? What reasons can you give for your answer?
2) Using examples, examine the ways that judicial review can be used to challenge public bodies.
3) What reasons can you suggest to explain why the courts might be less willing to criticise Conservative governments than Labour governments?
4) Define what is meant by a 'hands off' attitude in issues of national security.

Exam questions

SECTION B: RIGHTS AND
RESPONSIBILITIES

Answer Question 4 and **either** Question 5 **or**
Question 6.

This section carries 30 marks.

4 Read the extract below and answer parts (a)
and (b) which follow.

> The legal system in this country has various
> courts with different powers. From the
> highest court in the land – The Supreme
> Court, county courts and magistrates' courts. Given
> this hierarchy of court system all legal cases however
> large or small that require court time can be fairly
> resolved.

Your answers should refer to the extract as
appropriate, but you should also include
other relevant information.

(a) Briefly examine some of the ways a
citizen's rights may be protected by a
solicitor.   (*5 marks*)
(b) Examine some of the differences in the
powers of civil and criminal courts.
(*10 marks*)

Either:

5 Assess some of the problems criminal **or**
civil courts face in balancing conflicting
rights when resolving disputes.   (*15 marks*)

Or:

6 Assess the ways that the process of judicial
review can be used to protect citizens from
misuse of powers by the state.   (*15 marks*)

DEMOCRACY, ACTIVE CITIZENSHIP AND PARTICIPATION

SECTION 1: MAKING A DIFFERENCE

Chapter 5: Who can make a difference?

In this chapter we explore two main issues which examine the key question 'Who can make a difference?'

ISSUE 1: Who holds power in the UK?
This issue is explored through the following topics:

- the concept and nature of power
- who has economic power in the UK?
- what is the influence of the media and how is its power controlled?

ISSUE 2: The citizen and political power in the UK
This issue is explored through the following topics:

- the nature of government and its impact on the lives of citizens
- local democracy
- what is the impact of the European Union on life in the UK?

ISSUE 1: WHO HOLDS POWER IN THE UK?

In this section we explore the following three topics:

- the concept and nature of power
- who has economic power in the UK?
- what is the influence of the media and how is its power controlled?

1 The concept and nature of power

Concepts of power, authority, influence, democracy and mandate

In order to understand who holds power in the UK it is important to understand what is meant by the term 'power', how we experience it and its relationship with politics. We also explore the concepts of influence, authority, democracy and mandate.

Power is the ability to achieve certain aims; and politics concerns the use of power in order to govern – in this way the two terms are inextricably linked.

However, power does not have to be held through an obvious position, for example a seat in the House of Commons; it can be attained in a number of ways. Examples of these are:

- socio-economic status
- personal charisma
- age
- expertise
- persuasion
- knowledge
- money
- force.

Power is present in many different situations, both privately and publicly. Privately, you might observe that certain members of your friends and family seem to have more 'say' in decision-making; in this sense, they hold a degree of power and are able to use it to **influence** decisions. Publicly, a citizen can gain influence by taking a recognised position of power, for example a seat on a student council, or a seat in the House of Commons. If a person or group has power they are able to influence decisions or events and thus affect other people's lives.

ACTIVITY 1

1) In small groups, complete the three 'power grids' below. In your group decide who or what you think is more powerful in each grid. You need to rank them 1–10 (1 = most powerful; 10 = least powerful). You need to reach a consensus. Some of the concepts you are asked to compare are quite abstract and so you may need to discuss them in depth.

POWER GRID 1	
Who is most powerful?	Rank
The Pope	
Richard Branson	
Steven Spielberg	
Robbie Williams	
Gordon Brown	
Victoria Beckham	
The Queen	
Chairman of United Tobacco	
Bill Gates	
Barack Obama	

POWER GRID 2	
What is most powerful?	Rank
Monogamy	
Alcohol	
Tobacco	
Private property	
Justice	
Freedom	
Social class	
Fear	
Cannabis	
Love	

POWER GRID 3	
Which is most powerful?	**Rank**
McDonalds	
Microsoft	
Television	
Cinema	
Coca-Cola	
British Telecom	
Royal Mail	
Knowledge	
Money	
Radio	

Authority, democracy and mandate

You may believe power and authority to be the same concept; however their meanings differ. Power is the ability to achieve certain aims, whereas authority is to the ability to exercise that power with legitimacy and justification. For example, a group of citizens may have the power to get together and paint the town hall bright green, in protest at a local council's environmental policies, but they do not have the authority to do so.

Before the English Civil Wars of the seventeenth century, the monarchy retained 'absolute power' – they had absolute authority to make decisions about the future of their **state**. However the UK now functions on the principles of **democracy** – a state should be 'ruled by the people'. This system of government is based on the belief that all people are free and equal, and therefore have the right to make collective decisions about the future of their state. However, trying to consult citizens on every single decision to be made is obviously not feasible. To allow citizens' opinions and wishes to be heard, but also enable an efficient forum for debate, representatives are elected to act on behalf of citizens.

Citizens theoretically have the ultimate power to govern themselves, as they are able to vote for the Government they believe will serve them most effectively. Every person can therefore choose a candidate that they think will act in their best interests and in doing so grant them permission to govern. This permission is essentially citizens giving government authority.

This permission is called the **mandate**. Democracies function on the principle that citizens grant governments a mandate to act on their behalf, by voting for them in the majority; thus giving them the authority and therefore power to make decisions and laws that affect their lives. There is often debate as to whether a mandate to govern has been granted if voter turnout has been low, as not enough citizens have actively given their consent via their vote.

Power and the state

The power of the state, within a democracy, is therefore derived from the people within it. In the case of the UK, the heart of this power lies in the Houses of Parliament where laws are created that the population have to abide by. The candidates elected by the population must consider their electorate's best interests, along with possible consequences, when debating those laws and finally agreeing them. The state has the power to enforce those laws via the judiciary.

By enabling a separate strand of government to enforce the laws that are created, another important principle of democracy is achieved – the 'separation of powers'. This notion ensures that the strand of government that creates laws – Parliament (or the legislature) – is separate from the strand of government that administers justice (the judiciary) and also the strand that manages the everyday running of the state –

in the UK this is the job of the controlling party in power (the executive). In this way, no single part of the state can become 'all powerful', as each strand keeps checks and balances on the other.

Within the UK there is a fusion of powers rather than a separation as the strands of government overlap – the executive (Cabinet and Prime Minister) consists of members that also sit in the legislature (parliament). Until a Supreme Court is established (see page 193), the judiciary also overlaps with the legislature as Law Lords sit in the House of Lords but also form the highest court of appeal in the UK.

LEGISLATURE HAS THE POWER TO MAKE LAW
Parliament (MPs) Examine, debate and vote on Bills which become Acts (laws).

EXECUTIVE HAS THE POWER TO PUT LAWS INTO ACTION
Prime Minister and Cabinet (ministers) Decide policy, draft Bills, enforce and administer Acts.

JUDICIARY HAS THE POWER TO MAKE JUDGEMENTS ON LAW
Judges Hear and decide cases by applying the relevant law to facts.

Citizens experience the power of the state at different levels; as some power from central government in Westminster is passed to local authorities so that they can better manage certain issues on a smaller scale. For example, a citizen might experience the power of the state when the law is changed to raise the age at which they can buy tobacco or at a local level via a council decision on planning permission.

Who holds political power in the UK?

This is dependent upon which political party has the greatest number of representatives elected by the public to take a seat in the House of Commons. There are approximately 25 political parties in the UK, but the three largest parties are Labour, Conservative and the Liberal Democrats.

These three parties hold the most seats in Parliament compared with other smaller parties, and therefore have the most influence in creating legislation. The party with the majority of seats in Parliament is obviously at an advantage when voting to pass a new law; with one vote per seat, they have the most votes. However, if other parties' members within Parliament decide to join together to vote against the Government, or MPs from within the Government's own party decide to vote against it, the Government may not be successful in achieving changes in law.

Those political parties that are not in overall control of the House of Commons can still be very powerful within local areas (constituencies), especially if the majority of people there regularly vote for them in general or local elections. In this way some political parties are said to have 'strongholds' in certain constituencies – they can almost guarantee that they will win a re-election. This can afford

Local people can also prove powerful by using a recognised position of power. An example of this is Dr Richard Taylor, a local doctor from Wyre Forest in Worcestershire. He was not a member of a political party and so campaigned as an 'independent' candidate.

Concerned by the proposed closure of the accident and emergency department at his local hospital, he campaigned on this single issue and was elected to Parliament. He felt this was the best way to raise awareness of the problem and place himself in a position of power that might allow him to fight the decision. It was also a means of allowing his fellow constituents the ability to publicly voice their opposition to the plans, by voting for him instead of a conventional party candidate.

Dr Taylor outside Kidderminster hospital which he campaigned for

those political parties with strongholds a long-term influence on the lives of citizens. Ultimately, however, they are still accountable to the electorate.

The leaders of these parties are often seen to be the most powerful individuals within the House of Commons, but there are other powerful 'players' within political parties in the House of Commons who can exert influence. If a political party loses faith in its leader, or its members feel that they are unlikely to win a future election

with their current leader, a leader may be forced to resign. Other members of a political party may want to be leader themselves or have influence over the leadership of the party.

David Davis was the Conservative shadow home secretary (the equivalent, in his party, to the Home Secretary within government) when he resigned his position. He claimed that he had done this to force a **by-election** in his constituency, which meant people in his constituency would have to vote again if they wanted to re-elect him as their Member of Parliament. Mr Davis disagreed with the result of a vote in the House of Commons on whether to change the law that allowed police to raise the amount of time a suspected terrorist could be detained, without charge, from a maximum of 28 days to 42 days. He also said that he was unhappy with the amount of invasion of privacy from the state in the form of increased CCTV surveillance, the DNA database held by police and the planned identity card scheme. His resignation was a

ACTIVITY 2

1) Imagine you are an independent candidate in a general election, trying to win a seat in the House of Commons.
   - Which issues most concern you?
   - How would you get people in your constituency to vote for you?
   - How would you target voters in your area?

very unusual step and attracted a lot of attention from the press and the public.

Mr Davis's decision to resign was made without consulting David Cameron, the leader of the Conservative Party, and raised the question of whether David Davis was exerting more power over the future of his party and was dictating its political agenda because his decision had created such **media** attention. Some commentators suggested that Mr Davis's resignation was a publicity stunt to raise his own public profile; whilst others declared it was a principled stand by an MP who wanted to reassure his electorate of his political values.

ACTIVITY 3

1) How might members of political parties, who are not leaders, gain power within their parties? Think about different types of power: influence, charisma, knowledge.

Private members bills

Members of Parliament also have the opportunity to propose their own bills, as potential new laws. In each session of parliament, twenty members are chosen by ballot to propose their own Private Members Bill and are then allocated time to debate it in the House of Commons. In theory, this affords MPs the power to create a new law on their own initiative. It also prompts groups or individuals to try to persuade an MP who they know has been selected to propose a new law or amendment that they would like to action. Past examples of Private Members Bills have been the Abolition of the Death Penalty Act 1964 and the Knives Act 1997. In practice, there is a limited amount of time given to debate Private Members Bills which means that only a few gain sufficient support to pass them as laws.

ACTIVITY 4

Think again about the 'power grids' in Activity 1.
1) Who in your group had the most influence on the group's final answers?
2) How did they achieve this?
3) Did one person speak more than others?
4) Who had the most convincing points of view – how did they communicate their arguments?
5) Why do you think people listened to their points of view?
Feed back each group's findings to the whole class.

Power of multinational corporations

A multinational corporation (MNC) is a company that operates in at least two countries. By manufacturing and selling products globally, as opposed to trading within a single country, MNCs are able to make large profits. Those MNCs with the highest profits can actually generate more money than that of many developing countries and employ hundreds of thousands of employees. By being able to locate in various parts of the world, MNCs can choose countries that offer low labour and property costs. These locations tend to be in developing countries, which means that MNCs can often face criticism on ethical issues for not providing the same wages or working conditions expected in a developed country.

In areas where an multinational corporation, such as Nike, Nestlé or Coca-Cola, is the main employer it has a huge impact on the lives of residents, whether it be through the wages it pays, the skills it teaches or its environmental impact. In many developing countries the prospect of an MNC locating to their region is very welcome as it offers jobs, training and skills to workers who might otherwise be unemployed. It also offers the promise of development and a rise in living standards in what may be an area of widespread poverty. In this sense MNCs can be very influential within communities.

The vast wealth of MNCs also makes them powerful 'players' in world affairs. Such companies have the power to influence government decisions in their favour because they have vast sums of money at their disposal to lobby government and fund large scale public relations campaigns. Whether large corporations wish governments to lower trading tariffs or alter environment policies, they have a significant influence on government decisions. However, this relationship works both ways as governments have the ultimate power to amend laws, which corporations must abide by.

Individual citizens also have the power to influence the behaviour of large corporations because they are the ultimate consumer of their products. Without the profits generated by sales of goods and services to the public, such corporations would not have the funds that afford them their power and influence.

In order to try to change the behaviour of multinational corporations or limit their powers, consumers are able to join together to boycott certain products with the intention of reducing a company's profits and raise awareness of the way companies operate. A number of student unions were involved in the boycott of Nestlé and Coca-Cola products – ensuring that their universities did not stock Nestlé or Coca-Cola products on campus. They were protesting against what they saw as 'unethical behaviour' by the companies.

Web action

1] Use the websites below to research specific examples of consumer power.
   - **www.blogs.guardian.co.uk** – article from *the Guardian* on the boycotting of multinational corporations.
   - **www.independent.co.uk** – article from *The Independent* on threatened boycott of Coca-Cola by the National Union of Students.
   - **www.markthomasinfo.com** – criticising the practices of the Coca-Cola Company.
   - **www.gettherealfacts.co.uk** – response from Coca-Cola regarding some of the criticisms levelled at the company.

2] In pairs, draft the following two pieces of writing.
   - Imagine you are trying to persuade a group of students at your school or college to ban similar products to those in the websites above. Draft a speech that lays out all the reasons this ban should go ahead.
   - Now imagine you are a delegate from a company selling the products that are being banned. You have been invited to speak to defend your products. Make a draft of your speech.

2 Who has economic power in the UK?

Concepts of economic power and control

Power is exercised in many different ways and citizens encounter it in different ways. This topic looks at how economic power is held by international bodies, the state, business and the citizen.

Economic power can be defined based on an assumption that 'those with most money have most power, and therefore control', but this fails to understand the complex system of power within the UK and worldwide. For example, it could be said that in the case of multinational corporations, their huge wealth and subsequent ability to influence politics, their role as a global employers and impact on developing countries equates to vast economic power – but this takes no account of the fact that their wealth and power are dependent on many citizens choosing to purchase their products.

When we look at the 'global picture' however, it is true that those countries with most power are those that are developed industrialised nations or those that are 'resource rich' (they have natural reserves of resources such as coal, oil and gas). This would suggest that a state's wealth is directly linked to its influence in global affairs. Although, as we have seen in recent times, this 'wealth' is increasingly based on complex interrelations between states.

As the economic power of a state becomes more **interdependent** on the power of other states it becomes difficult to try to predict and manage spending on its domestic affairs (education, health and welfare) as its government budgets can be affected by world events or changes in global markets.

ACTIVITY 1

Look at the pie charts on page 213.
1) Imagine you are the **Chancellor of the Exchequer**. You want to cut taxes as you know this will please voters – which area(s) would you cut them from?
2) Now imagine you have to raise taxes in order to increase government spending – in which area(s) would you raise taxes?
3) On what would you spend the increased revenue?

Economic power and the state

So that the UK Government is able to fund services required by its citizens it places taxes on income, services and products. Using the revenue from these taxes the Government creates a fund called the treasury. It uses this fund to pay for services such as the National Health Service, police forces, education, housing, transport and defence.

The Government does not manage all areas of spending but distributes it to local, regional, national and supranational organisations (such as local authorities, regional development agencies, devolved parliaments/assemblies and the EU) so that they may allocate money effectively to areas where it is most needed.

Role of government and the Bank of England

The Bank of England is the UK's central bank which, with the Government, is responsible for keeping the economy and financial system stable. It does this by maintaining the value of our money by setting interest rates to keep **inflation** low in an attempt to ensure steady annual growth in the economy. It issues banknotes and watches the financial system to reduce risk so it is safe and reliable.

Where taxpayers' money is spent

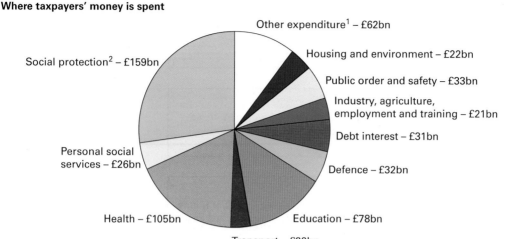

Total managed expenditure – £589 billion

1. Other expenditure includes spending on general public services; recreation, culture, media and sport; international co-operation and development; public service pensions; plus spending yet to be allocated and some accounting adjustments.

2. Social protection includes tax credit payments in excess of an individual's tax liability.

Source: HM Treasury 2007–08 projections. Spending is classified to functions using methods specified in international standards. Figures may not sum due to rounding.

Where taxes come from

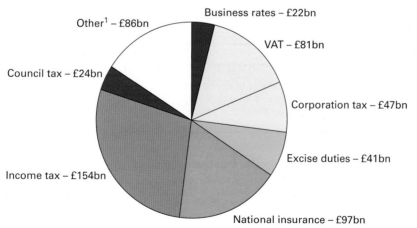

Total receipts – £551 billion

1. Other receipts include capital taxes, stamp duties, vehicle excise duties and some other tax and non-tax receipts (e.g. interest and dividends).

Source: HM Treasury 2007–08 projections. Figures may not sum due to rounding.

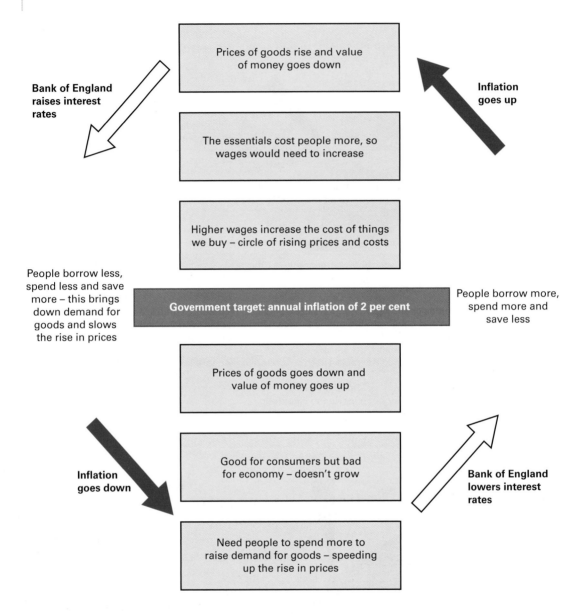

The way in which the Bank of England attempts to regulate inflation in order to promote growth and control prices

The value of our money depends on the prices we pay for goods and services. If prices increase the value of the pound in your pocket is reduced as it buys less. Inflation occurs when prices for goods and services increase in general reducing the value of the pound in your pocket, as everything is more expensive. High inflation is bad for the economy as costs and prices keep increasing, meaning your money has less value. To try to keep inflation under control the Bank of England lowers or raises interest rates. Interest rates influence the amount of money people spend and save.

The Bank of England is also responsible for issuing our banknotes. Although a banknote is only a piece of paper which costs a few pence to make it is worth more because we trust they can be exchanged for goods and services we want to buy. The trust that we can buy things with our banknotes gives them their value. The Bank of England makes sure notes are difficult to copy so 'fakes' don't undermine our real banknotes. Banknotes retain the words 'I promise to pay the bearer on demand' as it was once possible to exchange a bank note for gold of the same value.

The Bank of England works with the Financial Services Authority and the Government to try to keep the financial system stable and reliable. It does this by monitoring the system to identify weak points; providing extra money which has to be paid back to other banks if they need it, and regulating the system to avoid risk taking by individual institutions – as this undermines the overall safety and reliability of the financial system.

Since 1997, the Bank of England has been independent from government and is responsible for setting interest rates to keep the rate of inflation below the Government target of 2 per cent. The Bank's Monetary Policy Committee, which is made up of nine experts, meet each month to independently vote on what interest rate to set. The Government does not have an influence on this decision. However, if inflation is more than 1 per cent over this target the Bank of England's governor has to write a letter to the Chancellor of the Exchequer explaining why this has happened and what they plan to do to ensure inflation falls back below the Government target.

ACTIVITY 2

In small groups research the following:
- Who is the current Governor of the Bank of England?
- Who is the current Chancellor of the Exchequer?
- What is the current interest rate?
- What is the current rate of inflation?
- Why might there be concerns about the Prime Minister's influence over interest rates?

'CREDIT CRISIS' – WHAT IS IT AND HOW DID IT HAPPEN?

- The credit crisis started in the US, where US banks gave loans to people (who may not have been able to pay them back if interest rates rose) to enable them to get a mortgage to buy a home. These are called sub-prime mortgages.
- These loans were bundled together into complicated financial packages, which were sold to investors around the world.
- US interest rates rose considerably, from 1 per cent to over 5 per cent, which meant the US housing market suffered. House prices fell and repossessions increased as more and more people could no longer afford to pay their monthly mortgage payments.

- As more and more houses are repossessed, the debts which have been sold to investors around the world cannot be paid back. This undermines confidence in the banks, because they don't know the true value of their assets.
- As a consequence, banks stop lending to each other, major firms collapse and banks ask for financial support from the Bank of England, which is known as the lender of last resort.
- In the UK, the news that Northern Rock has asked for money from the Bank of England causes a 'run on the bank' – there are long queues outside of all of its branches as depositors withdraw one billion pounds in one day. This continues until the Government says it will guarantee all savings in Northern Rock.
- More and more banks announce major losses associated with the complicated financial packages that were originally sub-prime mortgages. Major global investment banks, for example Lehman Brothers, collapse.
- Governments across the globe spend billions of dollars on rescue packages to provide some financial stability in economy. The US rescue package is worth seven hundred billion US dollars.
- Many other well-known banks are nationalised or part nationalised as they struggle to survive in the crisis, for example Royal Bank of Scotland and Bradford & Bingley.
- The credit crisis continues to spread and confidence in economies across the globe collapses. Shares in global stock markets slump and prices in key commodities, such as oil, fall dramatically.

- Countries across the globe slash interest rates to encourage banks to start lending money again to ensure the economy can grow.
- End to risky lending and greater regulation of the financial system in the future to avoid a similar crisis.
- G20 summit meets to discuss reestablishing financial stability and avoiding a long period of global recession.

Globalisation

Globalisation is the term used to describe the process by which countries are becoming more interdependent and interconnected. More than at any other time in history, countries now rely on each other to ensure that their economies are stable and growing. Trade between countries is easier than ever before due to improved transport and communication links and the fact that businesses now often operate in more than one country. Businesses are therefore able to take advantage of cheaper labour and low government regulation. People can also move more freely between countries to work, which means they can relocate to areas with more employment opportunities. These factors mean that countries' wealth, labour force and industries are increasingly spread across the globe.

ACTIVITY 3

In small groups discuss what you know about the role of the banks and financial sector in the credit crisis.

1) Who do you think was to blame? Why?
2) How might it have been prevented?
3) Do you think that the banks had too much power?
4) Do you think government should have more power over banks?
5) Why was the credit crisis not confined to the US?
6) What role do you think globalisation played in the crisis?
7) How do you think governments might try to avoid a recession?

ACTIVITY 4

Read through the article on page 218.

1) How might citizens have been affected by the closure of the Woolworths chain as:
   a) employers
   b) employees
   c) customers
2) How might those citizens living in areas with Woolworths stores been affected by its closure?
3) How have citizens reacted to the 'new Woolworths' described in the article on page 218?
4) In which ways might citizens be viewed as economically powerful as:
   a) employers
   b) employees
   c) customers?

Economic power of companies and the role of the citizen as employer, employee and customer

We looked at the power held by multinational corporations in the previous topic. Local companies can also have a large impact on communities, especially if they are large-scale employers. Citizens also have economic power and this impacts on the power of companies. Woolworths, the high street store, had been in business for 99 years, with 800 stores on UK high streets employing 27,000 staff (and with 10,000 pension fund members) when, in the face of the credit crisis, it had to close in January 2009 due to the amount of money it owed its creditors.

Web action

Create a presentation to describe the roles of the Bank of England, Financial Services Authority and the Treasury and the ways in which they work together. Use the websites below to help your research.

- **www.bankofengland.co.uk**: Bank of England website which includes clear and concise explanations of money, prices and the workings of the economy.
- **www.fsa.gov.uk**: the Financial Services Authority, provides information on financial services aimed at the consumer.
- **www.hm-treasury.gov.uk**: the Treasury website which includes breakdowns of recent budget reports.

Woolworths to reopen online as Shop Direct buys name

Woolworths has risen from the ashes after a surprise deal with Shop Direct, the owner of Littlewoods, to revive the failed high street retailer in cyberspace.

A month after the shutters came down on the last Woolworths store, Shop Direct, owned by Sir David and Sir Frederick Barclay, is understood to have paid Deloitte, the administrator, between £5 million and £10 million for the Woolworths brand name. Shop Direct refused to comment on the price.

Woolworths, which was famed for its pick'n'mix confectionery, is to reopen as an online store in the summer. Shop Direct plans to focus its Woolworths offering on children's clothes and gifts, moving the business away from general merchandise and homeware. Ladybird, Woolworths' children's clothing range, was also included in the deal and its clothes will be sold through some of Shop Direct's other catalogue and online channels, which include Kays and Littlewoods.

Mark Newton-Jones, the chief executive of Shop Direct, said that Woolworths was an important part of Britain's retail heritage. 'The fondness there is for this business is underlined by the reaction we have had this morning,' he said.

Within hours of the announcement yesterday, 20,000 customers had registered with the woolworths.co.uk website, where they were encouraged to suggest what they would like the store to sell.

Mr Newton-Jones said: 'There have been lots of comments saying: "We don't expect you to sell ironing boards or washing-up bowls." That never sat comfortably with them.'

The Shop Direct deal has scuppered plans by Tony Page, the former commercial director of Woolworths, to rebuild the retail chain as a bricks-and-mortar store.

Woolworths was forced into administration in December after amassing debts of £385 million. Its collapse, which sent shockwaves through retailing, left 27,000 staff out of work and triggered the collapse of Zavvi, the music retailer, which relied on EUK, Woolworths' distribution division. The last of the Woolworths chain's 807 stores closed soon after Christmas.

Shop Direct cut 1,150 jobs last week, closing a call centre, as it transforms itself into a primarily internet-based retailer.

© *The Times*, **3 February 2009**

3 What is the influence of the media and how is its power controlled?

In this topic we will investigate the most common forms the **media** can take and explore their range, audience and impact.

What are the media (broadcasting, newspapers and other media)?

All forms of media together (TV, radio, newspapers, internet) are called **mass media**.

Newspapers

We come into contact with newspapers at both local and national levels. We either buy them or receive them free, in which case they are likely to be funded by selling advertising space. Although national newspapers often report the same news stories, they tend to report them in different ways and place emphasis on different topics. As we do not experience every news event personally, any news stories we read are via a third party and are therefore open to the interpretation of the journalists and media outlets reporting on them.

The format of newspapers is either tabloid (for example the *Daily Mirror* and *The Sun*) or broadsheet (for example *The Daily Telegraph*, *The Times* or *The Independent*). Although it may not be explicitly expressed most national newspapers can be seen to be on either the left or right of the political spectrum. This can be described as a political bias.

Those people that read a daily newspaper are likely to choose the same paper every day and they often express a strong allegiance to the paper they buy. This can mean that the articles they read, and therefore their perspective of the news, may be continually informed by the interpretation of the journalists reporting them and political bias of the newspaper they read. Of course, it may also be the case that consumers buy newspapers that they feel represent their existing political viewpoint. The table below shows how voting patterns vary depending on the newspaper a person reads.

	Daily Express /%	Daily Mail /%	The Mirror /%	Daily Telegraph /%	Financial Times /%	The Guardian /%	The Independent /%	Daily Star /%	The Sun /%	The Times /%	All /%
Conservative	44	57	13	64	36	7	11	17	35	44	34
Labour	29	24	66	14	34	48	38	53	44	27	39
Liberal Democrats	20	14	15	18	23	34	43	13	10	24	20
Scottish/ Welsh Nationalist	2	1	1	0	1	1	0	7	5	0	2
Green Party	2	1	2	1	0	7	4	3	1	2	2
UK Independence Party	2	2	1	2	1	0	1	3	3	2	2
Other	2	1	1	1	5	4	3	4	2	1	1
Total	100	100	100	100	100	100	100	100	100	100	100

Gather together a mix of several different newspapers, a mixture of local and national, broadsheet and tabloid newspapers.

1) Compare the local and national newspapers. For example, how do their formats differ?
2) Compare the broadsheets with the tabloids. For example, how are the stories they report different?
3) Choose a story and write a short review of all the papers exploring how it is reported in each.
4) Think about the tone of the article, the facts it quotes and the way the story is described. Discuss possible reasons for any differences in reporting you find. Can you find any evidence of political bias in the articles?

TV

Television (TV) is an incredibly effective medium by which to communicate entertainment, advertising, news or public information. Of the many providers of channels now available the BBC remains the only publicly owned, not-for-profit media outlet; the purpose of which is to provide information and education to the public (although Channel 4 does retain some government funding). Funded by the compulsory licence fee paid by all citizens who own a television, it contrasts with commercial television channels, such as ITV and Sky, whose funding is supplied by selling advertising time and/or through subscription fees.

As profit making organisations, commercial TV channels are concerned with viewing figures because this provides the main incentive to prospective advertisers. Therefore they produce and transmit those programmes that generate the greatest viewing figures in order to maximise profit. In contrast, although the BBC must compete with commercial media outlets in order to justify its licence fee, its priority remains programming 'to inform, educate and entertain', whilst remaining 'independent, impartial and honest'.

The advancement in digital and interactive television has revolutionised the functions and possibilities of television. It fulfils new and interesting functions, such as the use of digital TV to access NHS Direct allowing the viewers to access health information, possibly with the knock on effect of reducing waiting times at GP surgeries and accident and emergency departments. Interactive TV allows programmers to communicate directly with viewers and receive immediate feedback (for example via voting in opinion polls) but also enables greater scope for education and learning.

Although TV can be credited with keeping citizens informed, educated and entertained there remains debate as to whether violent programmes/films and negative images can have an adverse affect on behaviour, especially that of young people. It is argued that as TV channels become more numerous and films with adult content become more accessible (no longer restricted by a strict watershed) we run the risk of exposing young people to themes and images before they are mature enough to understand and process them in a healthy way.

Mary Whitehouse: right, after all?

A breast exposed on the BBC had her reaching for the smelling salts. She berated *Doctor Who* for scenes of 'strangulation – by hand, by claw, by obscene vegetable matter'. Even the puppets Pinky and Perky were slated for the 'callous' treatment of adults on their show. Hardly surprising that, in her Sixties heyday, most of us regarded Mary Whitehouse as a joke, said David Stubbs in the *Guardian*. Yet 40 years on, some are now saying that the 'disgruntled West Midlands teacher' may have had a point. Last week the BBC aired a drama about its old enemy – *Filth: the Mary Whitehouse Story* starring Julie Walters – which paid tribute to her stoicism and skill as a campaigner. And today there are many including former shadow home secretary Roy Hattersley, who feel we should have paid more attention to her warnings about the decline in standards. All the third-rate rubbish on TV – programmes such as *Wudja? Cudja?*, in which contestants drink beer through dirty socks and bathe in live worms – all this we might have avoided, says Hattersley, if Whitehouse had been given more of a hearing.

Of course Whitehouse had a point, said Stephen Glover in the *Daily Mail*. 'If violence is constantly portrayed as normal on the television screen,' she said in 1964, 'it will help to create a violent society.' Can anyone looking at the callous violence on our streets, boys stabbing each other on

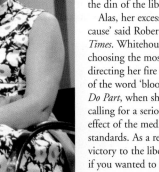

Whitehouse: 'ridiculous targets'

the slightest provocation, deny that this is just what has happened? Whitehouse may have 'sounded a little extreme' (it's hard to see what she objected to in the innocuous spy series *The Man from U.N.C.L.E*), but she had to be shrill to be heard above the din of the liberal consensus.

Alas, her excesses 'set back her cause' said Robert Whelan in *The Times*. Whitehouse had a 'genius for choosing the most ridiculous targets', directing her fire at Alf Garnett's use of the word 'bloody' in *Till Death Us Do Part*, when she should have been calling for a serious debate about the effect of the media on moral standards. As a result, she handed victory to the liberals. By the Eighties, if you wanted to argue that children should be protected from 'influences that sexualise them prematurely', you had to begin by saying: 'I don't want to sound like Mary Whitehouse but …' In my view, Whitehouse was wrong about sex, said Joan Bakewell in the *Independent*. At a time when it was still seen as 'secret and even dirty', greater openness was exactly what was needed. About violence, however, she was right. It now saturates our TV screens. It's hard to imagine what the benefits of such a liberal attitude to screen violence might be – even harder, sad to say, to imagine anyone doing anything about it.

***The Week*, 7 July 2008**

ACTIVITY 2

Read the article above.
1) Discuss whether you think it is right to be concerned about levels of sex and violence on TV.
2) Do you think that violence shown in video games has any affect on the individuals that play them?
3) Why might it be difficult to prove a connection between viewing violent images and violent behaviour?

Radio

Radio is associated with the broadcast of music, often providing the background noise of everyday life. However, it also plays a role as third party in the delivery of news and information. It is interesting to listen to the way in which various radio stations (BBC and commercial stations) report on news events. Each station has a target audience and therefore tailors its news stories to their interests. In the same way, the types of advertisements on commercial radio provide an indication of the audience tuning in.

The invention of the clockwork radio by Trevor Baylis, apart from creating an energy efficient alternative to conventional radios, has also enabled the media of radio to reach a much wider audience by allowing remote parts of the developing world to access radio in areas with no electricity supply. This promises improvements in communications technology as well as the prospect of improved education.

Trevor Baylis invented the clockwork radio

Magazines

Magazines are a popular form of media, with particular appeal to young people. However, the portrayal of male and female bodies in men's and women's magazines has been widely debated. It is argued that through such publications the media is projecting an unrealistic and unhealthy image of how people's bodies should look. By only showing images of very thin women or muscular men, magazines are accused of setting a standard in 'beauty' that is unattainable for much of the population. The use of airbrushing as a tool to remove imperfections in photographs of models and celebrities is also criticised for producing a false and unattainable representation of beauty. Such techniques have sparked debate about the link

between this and eating disorders in young men and women. There is also debate as to whether such magazines enforce gender stereotypes.

Internet

The greatest shift in the way the media communicates with people has most certainly been the arrival of the internet. The speed and efficiency with which it can convey messages, and the sheer breadth and depth of information has changed the way that news, entertainment and information are delivered to citizens across the world.

Not only can traditional newspapers create websites that reach a wider audience and can be updated instantly but citizens themselves can be empowered to publish and distribute information. In this sense individuals can find a wider choice of perspectives on events and information. Sites such as YouTube offer the public an opportunity to create their own media and distribute it, thus removing possible prejudice and bias of a third party media outlet.

However, although the internet provides an opportunity to create more diversity and greater freedom within the media, there remains an issue of authenticity and regulation. It is impossible to totally regulate the content of information on the internet. It is therefore important to be aware of information sources in order to verify its authenticity.

Globalisation and the media

Globalisation refers to the process by which trade and/or cultural influences become similar all over the world. For example, as it becomes cheaper to use the internet it therefore becomes available to a greater number of people worldwide. It offers the ability to read news stories almost as soon as they are reported;

when previously this was a process that could take weeks in some more remote parts of the world. The internet offers the opportunity to make the globe more connected.

In this way globalisation also allows the media to begin to align cultural influences, especially through advertising. Now, countries thousands of miles away are exposed to the same news, TV shows, advertising, music and images. It could be argued that people are becoming less 'citizens of countries' and more 'global citizens'.

Media ownership

Who owns media outlets and who decides their political or personal agendas? If an individual owns not just one media outlet but several they can prove very powerful, as they are able to exert their bias through several different media channels. The result is that an individual citizen can be exposed to messages with a particular bias from several different sources and perhaps be unaware that the same corporation or individual ultimately owns all of those outlets.

An example of a powerful media owner is Rupert Murdoch. He is the Chairman and major share owner of News Corporation, a company which owns approximately 175 newspaper titles across the world (including *The Sun, News of the World* and *The Times* in the UK), BSkyB (which dominates the UK's satellite TV market) and the Fox Broadcasting Company (incorporating 21st Century Fox and the Fox News Channel). His media empire has immense power to set the agenda for political campaigns and the capacity to influence citizens' political decisions. *The Sun* newspaper has been credited by some for winning the 1997 general election for Labour, as Rupert Murdoch controversially switched allegiance from its traditional support of the Conservative

Party. As a media proprietor he controls a significant proportion of the mass media, not only in the UK but worldwide.

Government and the media

The media and the workings of the Government have become so intertwined that neither could function in its current format without the other. Government is often assumed to be at the 'mercy' of the media when lurid stories appear about MPs' and cabinet ministers' private lives in the newspapers. It goes without question that the most important and useful roles of the media, within a democracy, are to scrutinise Government and investigate any possible misuse of power within it. However, the relationship between the media and Government is more complex than that, as the Government and political parties also uses the media to release information to the electorate. The way in which the Government package this information is

Web action

Go to **news.bbc.co.uk** and search for the 'Murdoch: I decide Sun's politics' article. Read the article and then answer the questions below.

1) Explain the ways in which a media owner can exercise power.
2) Outline the ways a media owner such as Rupert Murdoch might be able to influence the opinion of the public.
3) What arguments can you think of to counter the idea that media owners influence public opinion? Think about whether the media moulds public opinion or whether you think public opinion moulds the media. What evidence can you find to support your ideas?
4) Who has more power in terms of the media – citizens or media owners?

often a subject of debate itself and is often accused of containing 'political spin' (careful management of the timing, tone and content of information or responses released). The personnel employed to communicate these media messages are often known as 'spin doctors' as they are seen as experts in the art of manipulating the media to achieve the impression of events that they wish to portray.

Regulation of the media

Although UK citizens enjoy **freedom of the press** which allows for close scrutiny of the Government and individuals in other positions of power, it is important that the press itself is regulated to prevent or punish the publication of messages that are misinterpreted or untrue. It is also important that citizens are able to challenge anything that is reported about them in the media if it is false or creates an unduly negative impression of them.

The Press Complaints Commission (PCC) is an independent body that deals with complaints from members of the public about the editorial content of newspapers and magazines. The PCC does this with no cost to the citizen and aims to deal with complaints within 35 days. The PCC aims to resolve complaints by liaising with the publication that is the source of the complaint – this may be by the publication printing an apology or by removing the article from their website if it is online. If a resolution cannot be reached in this way – for example if the newspaper or magazine in question does not admit that it was at fault – then the PCC adjudicates and decides if the complaint should be upheld.

Below are examples of complaints that have been resolved by the PCC.

COMPLAINANT NAME: KERRY KATONA

Clauses noted: 1

Publication: *Reveal Magazine*

Complaint:

Kerry Katona complained through Max Clifford Associates Ltd about an article which suggested that she had been critical of her former husband's recent engagement. The complainant disputed the following claims in the magazine: that she believed he had proposed only to gain an advantage in the custody battle over their children; that she could not stand his fiancée; and that she could not accept their happiness together.

Resolution:

The magazine emphasised that the information under dispute had been obtained from a confidential source. However, the magazine agreed to publish the following letter from the complainant to give her the opportunity to deny the claims:

'Thank you for allowing me to respond to the article published in December. For the record I am drug free and have medical reports to prove this. I admitted to taking cocaine over 4 years ago at my lowest ebb and I have been accused of taking it ever since.

I am truly happy that Brian and Delta are getting married and I do not believe and have never said that the reason Brian proposed to Delta was to gain custody of our children.

Relationships end, I have moved on with my life as has Brian and we have two amazing little girls from the relationship. To suggest otherwise is hurtful and untrue. I am a committed mother and my children are my life.'

The complaint was resolved on that basis.

Source: www.pcc.org.uk

COMPLAINANT NAME: BORIS JOHNSON

Clauses noted: 3, 6

Publication: *Thelondonpaper*

Complaint:

The mayor of London, Boris Johnson, complained that the newspaper had intruded into the privacy of his children by publishing photographs of them on holiday. The images showed them walking in a street and sitting aboard a boat in a town in Turkey. Mr Johnson made clear that his children were entitled to a private life despite his own public profile.

Resolution:

The complaint was resolved when the editor of *thelondonpaper* sent a letter to the mayor and his wife apologising for publication of the pictures. He made clear that as soon as he had been made aware of their concerns, the photographs had been removed from the newspaper's website and internal archive. He assured them that *thelondonpaper* would abide by the Code of Practice regarding the family's privacy in the future.

Source: www.pcc.org.uk

The Office of Communications (Ofcom) is the regulator for the communications industry (including television, radio, telecommunications and wireless communications services). Its role is to ensure that the public are protected against any harmful or offensive material and it works to maintain high quality programming that is of wide appeal. It also monitors the industry to ensure it abides by any changes in law.

The Competition Commission is an independent public body, which helps to ensure that companies (including those within the media industry) offer the consumer a fair deal and do not restrict their choice of providers. Restrictions are in place to prevent any one company or individual owning too great a share in a particular market and therefore holding too much power.

Web action

Either:
1) Go to **www.pcc.org.uk**. Investigate two cases that have been brought before the Press Complaints Commission and create a presentation to inform your class of the cases and their outcomes.

Or:
2) Go to **www.ofcom.org.uk**. Research Ofcom's role in regulating the advertising of high fat, salt or sugar foods to children. Create a presentation to explain the issue to your class and Ofcom's role in regulation.

ACTIVITY 3

1) As a class, create a mind map to find as many examples as possible of each form of media. Can you think of any other forms of media?
2) How far do you think these forms of media influence young people's behaviour?
3) Do teenagers pay more attention to the media than other age groups?
4) Do you believe young people are more vulnerable to negative influences from mass media? Why?
5) Do you think the media is effectively regulated?
6) Do certain forms of media target certain social groups? How? Think about age, gender, race and socio-economic status.

ISSUE 2: THE CITIZEN AND POLITICAL POWER IN THE UK

In this section we explore the following three topics:

- the nature of government and its impact on citizens
- local democracy
- what is the impact of the European Union on life in the UK?

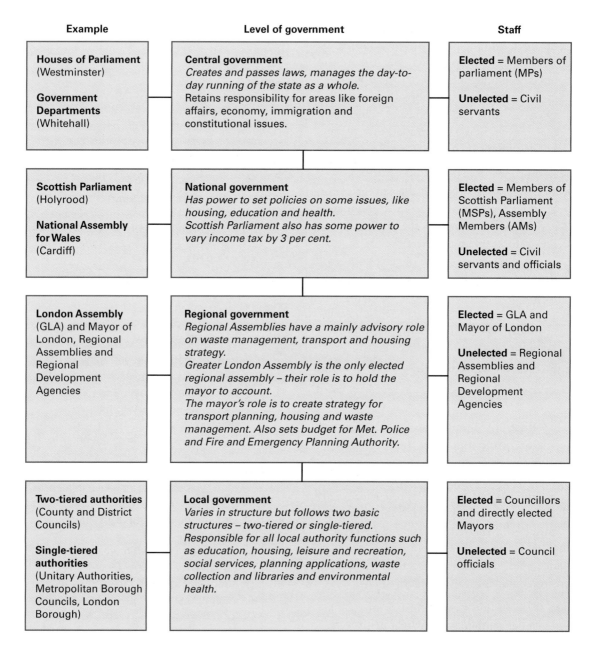

Example	Level of government	Staff
Houses of Parliament (Westminster) **Government Departments** (Whitehall)	**Central government** *Creates and passes laws, manages the day-to-day running of the state as a whole.* Retains responsibility for areas like foreign affairs, economy, immigration and constitutional issues.	**Elected** = Members of parliament (MPs) **Unelected** = Civil servants
Scottish Parliament (Holyrood) **National Assembly for Wales** (Cardiff)	**National government** *Has power to set policies on some issues, like housing, education and health.* *Scottish Parliament also has some power to vary income tax by 3 per cent.*	**Elected** = Members of Scottish Parliament (MSPs), Assembly Members (AMs) **Unelected** = Civil servants and officials
London Assembly (GLA) and Mayor of London, Regional Assemblies and Regional Development Agencies	**Regional government** *Regional Assemblies have a mainly advisory role on waste management, transport and housing strategy.* *Greater London Assembly is the only elected regional assembly – their role is to hold the mayor to account.* *The mayor's role is to create strategy for transport planning, housing and waste management. Also sets budget for Met. Police and Fire and Emergency Planning Authority.*	**Elected** = GLA and Mayor of London **Unelected** = Regional Assemblies and Regional Development Agencies
Two-tiered authorities (County and District Councils) **Single-tiered authorities** (Unitary Authorities, Metropolitan Borough Councils, London Borough)	**Local government** *Varies in structure but follows two basic structures – two-tiered or single-tiered.* *Responsible for all local authority functions such as education, housing, leisure and recreation, social services, planning applications, waste collection and libraries and environmental health.*	**Elected** = Councillors and directly elected Mayors **Unelected** = Council officials

4 The nature of government and its impact on the lives of citizens

Different levels of government in the UK

Ultimately political power is held by the Houses of Parliament at Westminster (known as central government). However, a great deal of responsibility is delegated to local government, regional governments and national governments. Each of these levels of government has different functions and responsibilities and impacts the citizen in various ways.

ACTIVITY 1

1) Reconstruct the diagram on page 226 using empty boxes to make your own personal diagram of levels of government for where you live. You need to complete examples of format, responsibilities and staff.

Central government has ultimate authority and in theory could remove all local government with a single Act of Parliament. This is unlikely to happen, not just because doing so would cause administrative chaos but because the principle behind transferring power in this way is to promote democracy. Government at local levels understands citizens' needs and problems and is best placed to deal with them. By giving responsibility for certain issues to local areas central government is better equipped to govern well. For example, there is a view that those in power in Westminster, a major urban area, cannot fully appreciate the issues faced by those in remote rural areas.

National government (devolved government)

Central government is the chief law and policy maker; but since the **devolution** of powers to the nations of Scotland, Wales and Northern Ireland some of those law and policy making

powers have been transferred to the Parliament in Scotland and the assemblies in Wales and Northern Ireland. Powers to make certain legislative and policy decisions were passed to the nations of the UK as a result of **referenda** to decide if citizens living there preferred it. This has given more say to the nations of the UK as to how they function; although there is opposition from some, who claim that devolution promotes inequality between the nations financially and politically. We explore these arguments in topic 5.

Regional government

In 1994, the then Government (Conservative) separated England into nine regional assemblies; these also act as the boundaries for Euro-election constituencies. The assembly is an unelected body with limited powers, which advises on overall transport, housing and waste strategies and has a role in the economic strategy of the region. Regional assemblies also prepare regional sustainable development frameworks.

County and borough councils appoint them as opposed to being elected by the public. The nine regions are as follows:

- Northeast
- Northwest
- Yorkshire and Humberside
- East Midlands
- West Midlands
- East of England
- London
- Southeast
- Southwest.

London is the only one of these regions to have an elected assembly. Under the Greater London Authority Act 1999, the Labour Government created a new Greater London Authority consisting of the London Assembly and the directly elected Mayor of London. The London Assembly has 25 elected members whose job it is to hold the elected Mayor to account. Boris Johnson was voted in as London Mayor in 2008, taking over from Ken Livingstone who had held the post since its creation. The mayor's role is to promote economic and social development in the capital, whilst improving the environment. They also set strategies for transport, planning and waste management; and decide budgets for various authorities, including the Metropolitan Police. London is unique in this respect as no other region has an elected assembly or directly elected mayor with comparable powers.

There are plans to abolish regional assemblies from 2010 and transfer much of their responsibilities to regional development agencies, which currently work to improve development and economic growth within the regions.

Boris Johnson, elected Mayor of London in 2008

Local government

Elected mayors

The Local Government Act 2000 gave local authorities (councils) with a population of 85,000 or more a choice in the ways in which to reorganise their structure so that it might be more efficient, democratic and less **bureaucratic**. One choice was whether or not to have a directly elected mayor. If councils wanted to introduce this form of government they had to first hold a referendum. Approximately 32 councils held referendums on whether to appoint an elected mayor from 2001 to 2002, with twelve councils voting 'yes'. However not all mayors are directly elected in England and Wales, as the quote below highlights:

'All authorities have chairman or mayors as leaders of local authorities, in some larger areas they may have Lord Mayors. Where an authority is called a District Council it will have a Chairman and where the authority is a Borough or City Council it will have a Mayor or Lord Mayor as the leader of the authority.'

www.lga.gov.uk

In 2002 Ray Mallon was voted the first directly elected major of Middlesbrough.

In his previous role as Detective Superintendent with Cleveland Police he was quickly dubbed 'Robocop' because of his tough stance on crime – the policing policies he introduced saw crime in the area fall by over 40 per cent. His success as a police officer made him very well known attracting accolades from high profile politicians such as Tony Blair (the then Prime Minister) and Michael Howard (the then Conservative Leader); plus a great deal of media attention. He was re-elected as Mayor in 2007.

Ray Mallon takes control of Grove Hill revamp

Middlesbrough Mayor Ray Mallon took control of a mechanical excavator to start demolishing homes in Pinewood Avenue.

Recently Mr Mallon called for action on the plans to demolish Erimus houses on the estate. The Mayor helped start the latest phase of the demolition programme which includes 24 homes in Pinewood Avenue and Fairfield Road.

The demolitions are part of a major revamp being undertaken by Erimus on the estate. It is aimed at boosting the popularity of Grove Hill as a place where people want to live.

Mr Mallon took the controls of the machine to start knocking down a block of homes and enjoyed the experience.

'The man in charge of the machine has offered me an application form for a job. I have now worked out what I will do for a living when I am no longer the elected Mayor!' said Mr Mallon.

He said the demolitions were good news for Grove Hill.

'It is important this area is demolished for future regeneration. Grove Hill, Saltersgill, and Beechwood are good areas overall but it is small segments that need to be dealt with.

'When this project is completed there may be less houses but those remaining will be in a much better area and the whole environment will be enhanced.'

www.gazettelive.co.uk, 14 December 2007

ACTIVITY 2

Read the extract from the article above. In small groups discuss whether you know of a directly elected mayor in your area. You may need to research this to find out.

1) If you do have a directly elected mayor, do you think they are doing a good job? Why?
2) What qualities do you think make a good directly elected mayor (DEM)?
3) What do you think the electorate in general want from their DEM?
4) Do you think it is easier to become a DEM if you have a high profile?

Structure of local authorities

Local government in Britain is structured in two ways:

- single tier 'all purpose council' which is responsible for all local authority functions

- two tier system, in which two separate councils divide responsibilities between district and county councils.

Within this framework there are some confusing classifications, as the system of government has evolved over many years and been altered by various government administrations. For example, although a council may have the word 'borough' in its title, its official classification may still be a 'district council'! The term 'local authority' is therefore used to describe the many different types of council.

This means that citizens may have very different council structures depending on where they live in the UK (see diagram on page 237). However in England, Scotland and Wales the services provided by local authorities – whether by a single or two tier structure –

are the same. Councils in Northern Ireland operate differently and do not have responsibility for education, housing or waste and recycling services, for example.

Although there have been attempts to realign the tiered system of local authorities so that all are single tiered (or unitary) this has not been achieved in England or Wales. Apart from the obvious administrative upheaval it would cause, such a revamp would essentially mean that citizens in some parts of he UK would be closer to their nearest level of government than others – closer not only geographically but also in terms of representation. Those living in a rural area, for example, with specific needs in terms of environment, education and waste collection may feel wholly alienated by a local government based in an urban area with priorities in housing and regeneration. The two tiered system allows local authorities to more easily give areas a say in the issues that affect them; and the ability to make necessary changes, therefore, promotes democracy.

So, in essence, citizens elect the representatives that they think will make decisions to make their lives better. Citizens evaluate how these decisions affect their lives and this informs how they vote in future elections.

How does government impact on a typical family's life?

CASE STUDY: A morning with the Clark family

Henry and Jan Clark live in a three bedroom house in Bromley, Kent. They have two sons, Jonathan and Harry. Henry works for an IT company and Jan is a secretary. Jonathan is sixteen years old and attends a sixth form college, where he is studying for his A levels. Harry is a university student studying for a degree.

This morning Henry is in a bad mood – he has heard on the radio that there is to be an increase in income tax. The telephone rings and he picks it up; he is pleased to hear his son Harry's voice on the phone but quickly realises that Harry is calling because he needs more help to pay for his university fees. Harry jokes that they should have moved to Scotland and Henry laughs. Henry finishes the conversation as he hears the postman arrive. He opens a letter with the London Borough of Bromley logo on the envelope. It is a council tax bill and as he starts to read through the bill Jonathan dashes past him to the kitchen. He is hurriedly making some breakfast before he goes to the local park to use a new basketball court before carrying on to college. Henry asks him if he needs any money for the bus and Jonathan rolls his eyes and reminds Henry that it is free for him to travel now, as long as he remembers his photocard!

Jan comes downstairs; she is just about to leave for work. She tells Henry that she will pick up the prescription for his mother who is unwell. He gives her a £10 note to pay for it. She jokes that he should ask his sister in Wales to pick up the prescription because she wouldn't have to pay for it there. As Jan heads for the front door she takes her cigarettes out of her handbag – she says there is no point taking them to work as it's too cold to stand outside the office to smoke. Jonathan walks past her to the door and says that his friends are not allowed to buy cigarettes any more because they are only sixteen years old.

As Henry leaves the house he takes the rubbish bins to the front of the house as it is collection day. They are particularly heavy as it is a fortnight since they were last collected. He makes a mental note to pay his congestion charge on the way to London before getting in his car and heading to work.

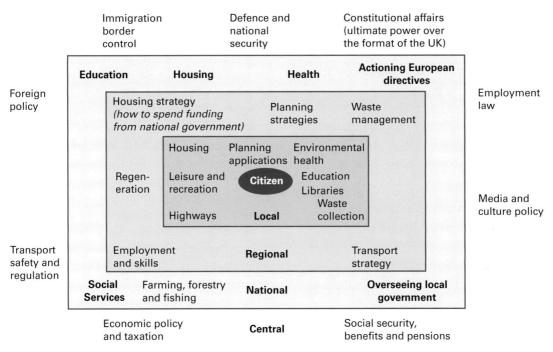

Levels and responsibilities of government

Read the case study on page 230.
1) In groups discuss which aspects of the story relate to central, national, regional and local government. It may help to use the diagram above.

2) Try to create your own example of a typical morning at home and highlight areas of your family's life affected by different levels of government.
3) What do you think a citizen could do to change any impact of government they are unsatisfied with?

Web action

Use the websites below to find at least five interesting facts about national government, regional government or local government to present to the rest of your class.
- **www.scottish.parliament.uk**: Scottish Parliament website which is a good overview of the role and format of the parliament.
- **www.wales.gov.co.uk**: good overview of the role and function of the National Assembly of Wales.
- **www.niassembly.gov.uk**: overview and general information on the workings of the Northern Ireland Assembly.

- **www.lga.gov.uk**: Local Government Association website which details the functions and latest news on local government issues. Includes a useful factsheet 'Types and Names of Local Authorities'.
- **www.englandsrdas.com**: Regional Development Agency website which gives an overview of its aims and partnerships.
- **www.communities.gov.uk/ citiesandregions**: provides a good synopsis of the role of regional assemblies.

5 Local democracy

The structure of government within the UK: central, devolved, regional, local

This topic looks at how levels of government are financed, the relationship between the centre and local government and the role of the **local representative**.

The responsibilities of the different levels of government are funded in part through income taxes, but there are other sources of finance that enable government to provide all of the services we enjoy as citizens. Each level of government usually receives grants on an annual basis from central government for each area of responsibility (for example housing and education). They can allocate their funding as they see fit, within those areas, but they must report to central government on the amount of money they have used. If they do not use their entire budget from Westminster it may be decreased the following year.

National (or devolved) government

The power of devolved government is derived or transferred from central government (Westminster), but under the UK system not all powers are passed to the nations of Scotland, Wales and Northern Ireland. The Scottish Parliament is often seen to have more powers than the assemblies in Wales and Northern Ireland as it has the ability to alter its own taxes (by 3 per cent) and therefore, to an extent, manage its own revenue, instead of solely relying on central government grants. It is also able to pass its own legislation (called primary legislation), whereas an assembly may only adapt legislation made by central government (called secondary legislation). Thinking again about the terms we used to describe power, the Scottish Parliament can be said to have legislative powers because it can create laws, but the National Assembly of Wales has only executive powers (the power to administer existing laws).

COMPARATIVE STRUCTURE AND POWERS OF THE DEVOLVED GOVERNMENT IN THE UK			
	Scotland	**Wales**	**Northern Ireland**
Location	Holyrood, Edinburgh	Cardiff Bay, Cardiff	Stormont, Belfast
Members	129 Members of Scottish Parliament (MSPs)	60 Assembly Members (AMs)	108 Members of Legislative Assembly (MLA)
Leadership	First Minister and Executive Cabinet	First Minister and Cabinet	First Minister and Executive Committee
Length of time between elections	Four years	Four years	Four years
Powers	Can alter income tax by 3 per cent; primary legislation – can create laws within the areas transferred by Westminster	Secondary legislation – can adapt **policy** within the legal framework set by Westminster	Can legislate in some areas, where power has been transferred.

MAIN SOURCES OF REVENUE FOR LEVELS OF GOVERNMENT

National	Devolved	Regional	Local
• Income Tax • Value Added Tax (VAT) • National Insurance • Corporation Tax • Fuel Duty	• Grants from central government • Ability to raise or decrease tax by 3 per cent (Scottish Parliament only)	• Grants from central government	• Grants from central government • Council tax • Non Domestic Rate Charge (charge to businesses) • Other fees and charges (e.g. parking)

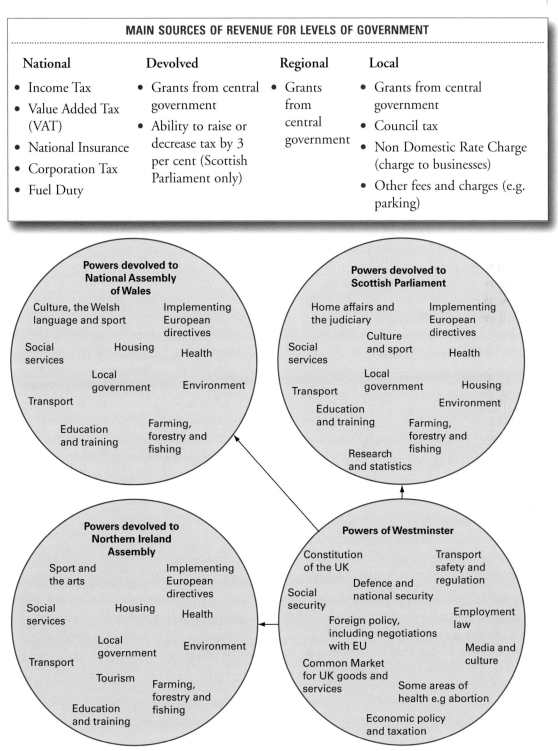

Areas of power devolved to national government in the UK

Scotland can create its own legislation but Westminster remains **sovereign** and therefore retains the power to overturn a law made by Scotland. As power is ultimately devolved from Westminster, it could abolish the Scottish Parliament entirely. However this would be highly controversial and unlikely to occur.

The table on page 233 illustrates the comparative structure and powers of the devolved governments in the UK.

Local government

A criticism of local government is that it is entirely administrative – it follows the orders of central government rather than debating and deciding on issues in its own right. However this may be the most effective role for local government as it frees it to get on with the business of delivering services to citizens.

Local Government Reform Act 2000

Many people argue that local government has been under constant reform throughout its life. In 2000 the New Labour government set out its Local Government Reform Act with the main aims of:

- better connections between local government and the electorate
- making the decisions more accountable
- making the system clearer and more efficient
- attempting to integrate greater scrutiny of decisions and decision making by citizens.

Before the Act, most local government involved a series of committees branching out from a central committee, often called policy and resources. The problem with this system was that it was considered confusing and complex and it was difficult to identify who had made which decisions.

Under the Local Government Reform Act 2000, all councils in England and Wales, except shire districts with populations of fewer than 85,000 people were required, after consultation with their local residents, to choose one of three systems. All of the three options were designed to make the decision making separate from policy execution. Each option was intended to make the system simpler to citizens.

Below is a brief outline of the three main options available to councils to select. Although councils have three options, they must abolish their existing systems and select one of the three.

- **Option 1**: leader and cabinet executive: leader elected by the full council (often in effect the largest party) plus between two and nine councillors with specific powers and responsibility for council policy. Council elections would happen as normal and then the councillors would elect a small number of senior councillors to become the cabinet. One of them would be elected as the leader. The remaining councillors would sit on committees chaired by the elected cabinet. Others would sit on scrutiny committees who would check that the procedures and policy of the council were being followed correctly.

Arguments in favour of option 1 are as follows:

1) speeds up decisions since the cabinet is a smaller single body making decisions
2) cabinet members would become well-known locally
3) non-cabinet members would no longer be tied down to a series of committees and would be able to communicate and work better with their constituents on, for example, residence committees
4) the policy of the council is rigorously applied by the scrutiny committee.

Arguments against option 1 are as follows:

1) alternative systems (for example, mayor directly elected) would be a quicker system of decision making.
2) the council is still complicated by a large number of committees.
3) it is not very different from the existing system.

- **Option 2**: mayor and cabinet executive: mayor directly elected by the whole electorate who appoints between two and nine councillors as executive members, much the same way as in option 1. All voters elect a mayor and all committees are abolished. The mayor selects a cabinet from the elected councillors. The remaining councillors scrutinise the council decisions and actions and are released for constituency work.

Arguments in favour of option 2 are as follows:

1) simple recognisable system where an individual becomes the focus for council policy and work, giving focus for public interest and elections
2) decisions are quick and responsibility is clear.

Arguments against option 2 are as follows:

1) too much power given to one person in choosing his/her cabinet and in decision making about policy
2) other elected councillors should have more say in decision making about policy
3) no guarantee it will increase citizen involvement and interest.

- **Option 3**: mayor and council manager: mayor directly elected by the whole electorate with an officer provided by the council to action the policy decisions of the council as defined by the mayor. Mayor elected as in option 2 and they would appoint a council manager and junior managers to run services.

Arguments in favour of option 3 are as follows:

1) as with option 2, except it would be even simpler and quicker with only two main people identified and responsible for decisions
2) councillors are free to work outside committees with their constituents directly.

Arguments against option 3 are as follows:

1) too much power to only two people, one of whom is not elected and therefore less accountable
2) limited role for other elected councillors
3) probably less open system for decision making since most decisions would be made behind closed doors with no open council meetings for decision making debate.

The scrutiny committee can ask for policy decisions to be re-examined by the executive, whether that be the mayor, mayor and cabinet or leader and cabinet. The scrutiny committee also has powers to ensure that no decision is made without having followed the correct procedure of being made in consultation with the residents. It also suggests, through reports and recommendations, areas for policy development that the council should consider.

ACTIVITY 1

1) To what extent do you believe directly elected mayors encourage voting and participation with local government?

The Government was very keen on elected mayors when it set out the act, but the general public seemed less convinced; although some areas did seem to support the idea strongly. The Department for Transport, Local Government and the Regions (as it was called at the time) commissioned a survey which found, among other things, the likelihood of people voting in an election for a mayor rather than an election for a local councillor:

- more likely 31 per cent
- less likely 13 per cent
- no difference 54 per cent.

As for the great majority of the councils, by May 2002 the leader–cabinet system was adopted (option 1).

Which model to adopt

The decision as to which model a council should adopt is made by the council itself. However it must show evidence that it has consulted their citizens by referendum, questionnaire, public meeting or focus group. If a community wanted a referendum on the issue of a directly elected mayor, they needed to secure a petition from 5 per cent or more of the constituents who fall within the council area. If secured, then a referendum of all citizens would have to be carried out. If a majority were in favour, then the mayoral system would have to be adopted by the council.

By December 2002, 30 councils held referenda, some of which were:

- Lewisham
- Doncaster
- Hartlepool
- Middlesbrough
- Brighton and Hove
- Sedgefield.

Most were done by postal ballot. There was also a referendum in Greater London on the mayoral issue. Of the referenda, eleven supported a mayoral system and nineteen rejected it.

Web action

Find your local council website by using a search engine and explore what type of council structure applies to it and you.

ACTIVITY 2

1) Which of the three options on pages 234–35 would you consider most democratic?
2) Assess the argument that more decisions in local government should be carried out through referendum of all constituent citizens.
3) Imagine you are elected as leader of a cabinet by the elected councillors. How far would you be free to select your cabinet from all the councillors elected if a) your council has a majority from one political party, or b) your council has no overall control (balanced)?
4) The Local Government Reform Act does not require electoral reform. Discuss the extent to which electoral reform to implement a system of proportional representation for local elections would a) enhance and encourage both voting itself, and b) include in council policy all constituent citizens.

Web action

Look at the diagram on page 237 of local government structure and the services it provides.

1] Research your representatives in each level of government and the structure of your local authority.

Use the following websites to help you:

- **www.theyworkforyou.com**: information on elected representatives.
- **www.writetothem.com**: contact information on your elected representatives.
- **www.lga.gov.uk**: contains factsheets on types of council and the services they provide.

Note: depending on the addresses of each member of your group, their local authorities may differ.

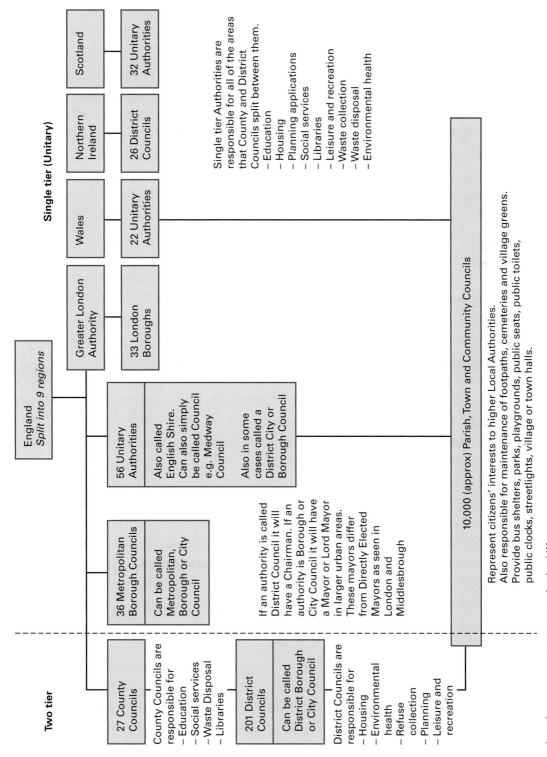

Two tier

27 County Councils

County Councils are responsible for
- Education
- Social services
- Waste Disposal
- Libraries

201 District Councils

Can be called District Borough or City Council

District Councils are responsible for
- Housing
- Environmental health
- Refuse collection
- Planning
- Leisure and recreation

36 Metropolitan Borough Councils

Can be called Metropolitan, Borough or City Council

If an authority is called District Council it will have a Chairman. If an authority is Borough or City Council it will have a Mayor or Lord Mayor in larger urban areas. These mayors differ from Directly Elected Mayors as seen in London and Middlesbrough

England
Split into 9 regions

56 Unitary Authorities

Also called English Shire. Can also simply be called Council e.g. Medway Council

Also in some cases called a District City or Borough Council

Greater London Authority

33 London Boroughs

Single tier (Unitary)

Wales

22 Unitary Authorities

Northern Ireland

26 District Councils

Scotland

32 Unitary Authorities

Single tier Authorities are responsible for all of the areas that County and District Councils split between them.
- Education
- Housing
- Planning applications
- Social services
- Libraries
- Leisure and recreation
- Waste collection
- Waste disposal
- Environmental health

10,000 (approx) Parish, Town and Community Councils

Represent citizens' interests to higher Local Authorities.
Also responsible for maintenance of footpaths, cemeteries and village greens.
Provide bus shelters, parks, playgrounds, public seats, public toilets, public clocks, streetlights, village or town halls.

Local government structure in the UK

Difficulties in the relationship between the centre and the locality

Local government

Some believe the local government system would benefit from further devolution of power from the centre, in order to fully govern local affairs rather than having to work within the framework of legislation and policy dictated by Westminster. If local authorities could govern comprehensively without being subordinate to Westminster they might better meet the needs of their citizens. Also, if local government must remain 'administrator' for central government, it has to continually adapt to changes in policy whenever a new political party is in power in Westminster.

However if all local authorities were to independently create policies to tackle social issues (for example access to education) citizens might receive unequal services depending on where they lived. Central government is therefore best placed to create a clear, single strategy that local authorities can deliver according to need at a local level.

Devolved government

The major criticism of the relationship between central and the devolved governments of the UK are that, between the nations, there are inequalities in funding and representation for citizens.

The amount of central government grants passed to Scotland, Wales and Northern Ireland is calculated through the use of a formula called the Barnett formula. It works on the premise that money should be diverted to the poorer parts of the UK – where it is most needed. The areas most in need tend to be outside of England as it is the wealthiest of the four nations. As the devolved nations vary in population size the level of funding also varies,

with England receiving less per head than other nations. England has the highest population of the UK with 50.7 million people. Scotland has a population of 5.1 million people, Wales' population is almost 3 million people and Northern Ireland has the smallest population, with 1.7 million people (Mid Year Population Estimate 2006, *Office of National Statistics*).

Another result of devolution of powers is that Scottish MPs continue to have a seat in the House of Commons (because their constituencies remain within the boundaries of central government) and continue to have a vote on matters that affect English citizens – when English MPs do not have the same privilege within the Scottish Parliament. Many people feel this is a fundamental injustice within the devolved system of UK government and some, including William Hague, former leader of the Conservative Party, have called for Scottish MPs to be prevented from voting on purely English issues. An alternative remedy suggested is the creation of a dedicated English parliament. However both of these suggestions would cause huge administrative and constitutional upheaval. Scottish MPs argue that as long as Westminster is sovereign and has ultimate power over their nation, its citizens should be represented in Westminster. This disparity is known as the *West Lothian Question*.

The variations in legislation that occur between the nations of the UK have also caused much debate. Since 1999 Scotland, Wales and Northern Ireland have introduced a number of new initiatives:

- no tuition fees for university students (Scotland)
- free prescriptions (Wales)
- abolition of school league tables (Wales and Northern Ireland)

- free personal and nursing care for the elderly (Scotland and Wales).

These policies have proved highly unpopular amongst those who see it as unfair that some nations are able to take advantage of certain benefits because they have the funding, per head, to do so.

ACTIVITY 3

1) Are some English people justified in feeling unhappy about the Barnett formula?
2) Is it fair that the poorest areas are given the most funding?
3) Should each nation be allowed to decide how it spends its allocated funding?
4) Do you think that each nation should raise its own revenue for public services? How might they do this?
5) Do you think the UK should attempt to support all of its citizens equally, regardless of their location?

THE GREAT DIVIDE

Scotland enjoys better health care and education funding than England – do you think it's fair?

The public services divide between England and Scotland has widened again as Scottish ministers pledge to abolish all prescription charges north of the border.

This comes after Scotland has successfully put in place free eye care and dental check ups, free personal care for the elderly, more wide-reaching heating grants and more expensive drugs that the NHS in England and Wales can't afford.

Not only that but under new plans Scottish students will receive free university education, as compared to the huge fees that English and Welsh students now face.

What's the big deal?

So what's all the fuss about? Shouldn't England and Wales be following their example and improving health care and education for their citizens? Unfortunately it's not that simple, and it's got a lot to do with something called the Barnett formula.

It's a mind-bogglingly complex formula that calculates how much the Government hands out to Britain's regions, and critics now claim that it's badly flawed.

Currently Scotland receives £1500 more per person than England every year. So opponents of the Barnett formula are arguing that English taxpayers are subsidising their Scottish neighbours, paying for free university education, free care for the elderly and now free prescriptions for Scots.

www.gm.tv, 20 November 2007

Role of local representatives

The role of **local representatives** varies depending on the structure of the local government and the level at which they work. The table below shows how this role differs depending on local authority level.

Salary

Councillors are part-time and are paid relatively low salaries. Some people suggest that increasing councillors' levels of pay would attract a higher calibre of candidate and encourage more citizens to apply.

THE ROLE OF LOCAL REPRESENTATIVES			
	Town or parish councillor	Councillor within a single tier (unitary) authority	Councillor within a two tier authority
Number of citizens represented per councillor	500–600	Approx. 2000–3000 (three councillors per ward of 7,000–10,000)	Varies depending on district or county level
Length of time between elections	4 years	4 years	4 years (on alternate years to unitary elections)
Salary	Unpaid – work is on a voluntary basis	Part-time salary £7,000	Part-time salary £7,000
Role	To represent the views of those living in their town or parish on plans by authorities, i.e. house building, public transport links	To represent the interests and views of the citizens in their ward to the local authority	To represent the interests and views of the citizens in their ward to the local authority

The retired or independently wealthy tend to be over-represented in local government because they can more easily afford to dedicate the time and resources required.

Some believe the role of a councillor is important, complex and demanding and should warrant an improved salary as it seems unfair that a citizen should have to suffer financially in order to serve their community – although, if a councillor is appointed to a leadership role their salary does increase. Town and parish councillors are unpaid and volunteer their time to serve their community and speak for the citizens in their ward.

However if salaries were increased, professional politicians would be more likely to take roles as local councillors and force out local residents with a more genuine focus on improving the local area. Allowing local people to represent their own community is an important vehicle for democracy.

Communication

Local councillors communicate with their constituents in a number of ways: these include using local newspapers, radio stations or by posting notices in the local area. Local councils must consult their citizens in a number of ways (set out in guidelines by central government). They do this via citizens' juries, focus groups, visioning conferences, opinion polling, citizens' panels and local referenda.

6 What is the impact of the EU on life in the UK?

What is the EU and what does it do?

The EU was created in the aftermath of the Second World War with the objective of bringing peace, prosperity and security to Europe. Its aim is to bring countries closer

ACTIVITY 4

Do you know who your local representatives are?
1) Look at the research you have undertaken into the representatives for your area.
2) Are any of the councillors affiliated to a particular political party?
3) Do you think councillors should be paid more?
4) How might the financial status, gender and age of councillors affect democracy at a local level?
5) What does your local councillor do to ensure that he or she understands how the community feels about certain issues?

together and bind them as members of a single organisation. It is thought that in this way, a repeat of the horror of the World Wars can be better prevented. It is also hoped that union of the European states encourages trade and helps to boost the economies of countries within Europe.

The union is based on a number of **treaties** and was established in 1951 when Belgium, Germany, France, Italy, Luxembourg and the Netherlands united in the European Coal and Steel Community (ECSC). This was a means of joining together the coal and steel production of all members, ensuring that no state would be able to use these resources to independently go to war with another. They further secured their commitment to a united Europe by signing the Treaty of Rome in 1957, which created the European Economic Community (EEC). This was a move to greater economic ties between the member states and in 1968 customs duties between the six countries were completely abolished. This made it much easier to trade goods between countries.

In 1965 the EEC became known as the European Community (EC) to reflect that it was evolving into a community no longer based purely on economic union. The UK, Denmark and Ireland joined the EC in 1973, bringing the total number of members states to nine – the UK had tried to join the Community twice before but had been **vetoed** by France.

The objective of the European Community then moved towards further enlargement (the inclusion of more countries) and a broadening of its powers. The Treaty of EU (also known as the Maastricht Treaty), signed in 1992, saw the creation of the EU, which merged European institutions and divided European policies into a three-pillar structure. The institutions of the EU have varying influence within these three areas of policy. However, the Treaty of Lisbon, signed in 2007 abolishes this structure in an attempt to simplify the working of the EU, if it is accepted by all member states.

The EU has now increased from its original six members to 27 member states in 2008 and further broadening of powers now means that the EU can create legislation that affects every aspect of the lives of citizens living within its borders. The EU consists of a mixture of **supranational** and **intergovernmental** bodies, but the laws that the union creates take precedence over the laws of the member nations.

Therefore central government within the UK (Westminster) must conform to the legislation created by the EU on certain issues. In exchange, the EU continues to offer its members a strong position in global affairs. Members achieve more power and influence within a large, united organisation of sovereign states than they would if they remained small, single states. It also offers membership of a single market that allows freedom of movement of people, goods and services, which means easier trade between member states. The introduction of the single currency (Euro) also removes barriers to trade by further facilitating trade between member countries. In 2009 the EU accounted for approximately 30 per cent of the world's gross domestic product.

European Union		
European Community (EC)	**Common Foreign and Security Policy (CFSP)**	**Police and Judicial Co-operation in Criminal Matters (PJCC)**
■ Customs Union ■ Common Agriculture Policy ■ Economic and monetary union ■ Trade policy ■ Social policy	Foreign policy ■ Human rights ■ Democracy ■ Foreign aid Security policy ■ Peacekeeping ■ European security and defence policy ■ EU battle troops	■ Drug trafficking ■ Weapons smuggling ■ Terrorism ■ Trafficking human beings ■ Organised crime

The three pillars of European Union policy

Institutions of the EU and their roles

European Commission

The role of the European Commission is to act as the executive arm of the EU, although it is the Council of the EU that bestows this power on it. The commission's interest is in the EU as a whole, and the decisions it makes are binding on member states as it has authority over them – it is therefore a supranational body. It consists of a college of 27 commissioners (one from each member state), including a president and approximately 22,000 officials. The commissioners are nominated by national governments but must swear an oath of independence, as they are not representing their nation. Each commissioner is responsible for a particular area of policy.

The president is appointed by the Council of Ministers but must also be approved by a vote in the European Parliament. The roles of the president are to provide leadership within the commission and allocate policy areas to commissioners. The president also has the ability to demand the resignation of a commissioner.

The commission's role is to propose new legislation (called legislative initiative) to the Council of Ministers and European Parliament – it is the only institution within the EU that has the right to do this. Within the UK parliamentary system, both the executive (government in power) and the legislature (Houses of Parliament) have legislative initiative, but within the EU this power is reserved for the commission only. The commission also ensures that EU legislation is implemented correctly and monitors the use of EU funds. Its officials function in a similar way to a national civil service, performing administrative tasks, although it has fewer staff than most nations' equivalents.

The Council of the European Union

The Council of the EU (sometimes known as the Council of Ministers) is the legislative arm of the EU, although it does share this role with the European Parliament. Government ministers from each member state sit on the council and negotiate, debate and then vote on issues in order to reach legislative decisions on areas such as: economic and financial affairs, justice, employment, health and education. It can therefore be described as an intergovernmental body.

Each member state takes it in turns to be president of the council and this presidency rotates every six months. The treaty of Lisbon will change this so that three states share the presidency for eighteen months. In this role member states must act as host and chair meetings, and set the focus for policy and act as spokesperson.

European Parliament

The European Parliament is the only directly elected institution within the EU. Its job is to amend, approve or reject legislation proposed by the Commission before it is passed into law. It shares this responsibility with the Council of EU in some areas. The European Parliament has the power to scrutinise and ultimately dismiss all European commissioners, but cannot disapprove the appointment of a single commissioner. The parliament also has joint budgetary authority with the Council of the EU and can ask for amendments to and veto the final budget. It is a supranational body.

Each of the 27 member states is divided into regions, which elect representatives to the European Parliament, based on the size of the population. These representatives are Members of European Parliament (MEPs) and take a seat in the European Parliament. Elections take place every five years.

EU MEMBER STATES AND THEIR SEATS IN THE EUROPEAN PARLIAMENT	
Member state	Seats in European Parliament (number of MEPs)
Germany	99
Italy	78
UK	78
France	78
Spain	54
Poland	54
Romania	35
Netherlands	27
Belgium	24
Czech Republic	24
Hungary	24
Greece	24
Portugal	24
Sweden	19
Austria	18
Bulgaria	18
Denmark	14
Slovakia	14
Finland	14
Lithuania	13
Ireland	13
Latvia	9
Slovenia	7
Luxembourg	6
Cyprus	6
Estonia	6
Malta	5
Total	785

MEPs do not sit in party groups as they would in their national parliaments but instead sit in larger political groups that broadly represent their political affiliations. There are eight political groups in all, including the Independence/Democracy group, which includes members from Britain's UK Independence Party. This is a political party whose objective is to cut economic ties with the EU.

The European Parliament does not hold the same authority as national parliaments because power is shared amongst the institutions of the EU. Unlike the UK Parliament, it cannot officially initiate legislation, as this is the role of the European Commission. Also, it does not have the power to independently approve legislation, as the UK Parliament can, because it shares this role with the Council of the European Union. The European Parliament does not have the same powers to interpret legislation as the House of Lords; this is the role of the European Court of Justice and the Court of First Instance.

Checks and balances

The EU is organised so that each of its institutions can provide checks and balances on each other. This means that power is shared between:

- citizens (via their elected representatives)
- national governments (via the Council of the EU)
- the EU as a collective organisation (via the European Commission).

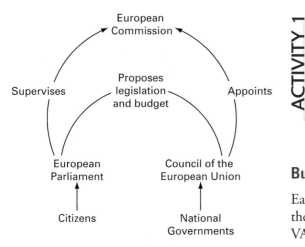

How power flows through the European Commission, European Parliament and Council of the EU

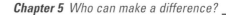

ACTIVITY 1

1) When did the UK join the EU (then the EC)?
2) What are the advantages to membership of the EU?
3) Which is the only institution to initiate legislation?

Budget for the EU

Each member state collects money on behalf of the EU to form its budget. This comes from VAT, a percentage of Gross National Income and from tax from other sources such as customs duties and agricultural duties. This money is then spent in a variety of ways.

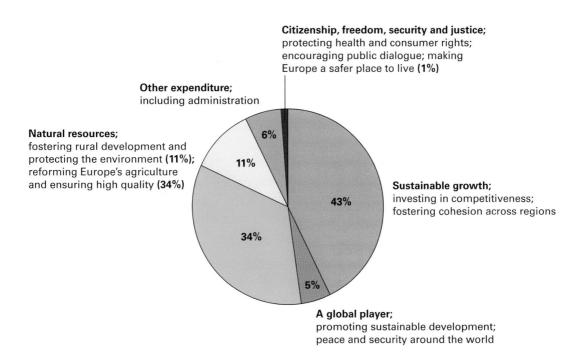

Citizenship, freedom, security and justice; protecting health and consumer rights; encouraging public dialogue; making Europe a safer place to live **(1%)**

Other expenditure; including administration

Natural resources; fostering rural development and protecting the environment **(11%)**; reforming Europe's agriculture and ensuring high quality **(34%)**

Sustainable growth; investing in competitiveness; fostering cohesion across regions

A global player; promoting sustainable development; peace and security around the world

6%

11%

43%

34%

5%

Pie chart showing the division of the EU budget 2007

EU BUDGET 2007 IN FIGURES		
Expenditure estimates for EU policies (in billion EUR)	Budget 2007	Change from 2006/%
Sustainable growth	**54.9**	**15.4**
Competitiveness, including:	9.4	18.6
Education and training	0.9	31.0
Research	5.5	3.1
Competitiveness and innovation	0.4	53.6
Energy and transport networks	1.0	32.9
Social policy agenda	0.2	8.6
Cohesion, including:	45.5	14.8
Convergence	35.3	16.8
Regional competitiveness and employment	9.0	11.5
Territorial cooperation	1.1	−11.7
Natural resources, including:	**56.3**	**1.0**
Environment	0.2	17.9
Agricultural expenditure and direct aids	42.7	0.6
Rural development	12.4	3.0
Freedom, security and justice (including fundamental rights and justice, security and liberties, migration flows)	0.6	12.8
Citizenship (including culture, media, public health and consumer protection)	**0.6**	**0.8**
EU as a global player, including:	6.8[1]	4.5[2]
Pre-accession	1.3	16.5[2]
European neighbourhood	1.4	11.1
Development cooperation	2.2	−5.4[3]
Humanitarian aid	0.7	3.1
Democracy and human rights	0.1	9.6
Common foreign and security policy	0.2	55.2
Stability instrument	0.1	143.6
Administration, including:	**6.9**	**5.1**
European Commission	3.3	5.3
Other institutions	2.6	4.8
Compensations to new EU countries[4]	**0.4**	**−58.6**
Total	**126.5**	**5.0**

(1) Including Emergency Aid Reserve.
(2) Excluding Bulgaria and Romania.
(3) Reduction due to the exceptional amounts allocated in 2006 to the post-tsunami, Afghanistan and Iraq reconstruction efforts.
(4) Amounts fixed by the accession treaties.

EXAMPLES OF BUDGET SPENDING

Sustainable growth:

- extra funding for less prosperous parts of the EU (especially rural areas)

- training for the EU's workforce

- research and investment in renewable energy sources.

Natural resources:

- managing fish stocks to prevent over-fishing

- creating new job opportunities for those living in rural communities

- promoting eco-friendly farming.

The EU as a global player:

- promoting human rights between countries

- tackling poverty in developing countries

- helping potential members get closer to the EU.

Freedom, security and justice and European Citizenship:

- help for EU countries with massive flows of refugees

- planning for public health crisis, for example flu pandemic

- border control for EU states.

ACTIVITY 2

In groups, discuss the distribution of the EU budget.
1) What kinds of activity does the EU spend its budget on?
2) Is there a category to which you think the EU affords too much funding? Explain your answer.
3) Which category do you think is the most worthy recipient of funding? Why is this?
4) What other suggestions do you have for useful ways in which the EU could spend its budget?

Impact of the EU

The main reason for Britain's initial reluctance to join the EU (or EEC as it was then) was the fear that it would result in a loss of power over its affairs of state. Britain's entry to the European Community meant that on some issues the EC (as it became known in 1965) would be able to create laws by which the UK must abide – thus undermining parliamentary sovereignty. Some people argued that Britain was a 'unique case' because it was a world 'player' in its own right, with special relationships with the US and the Commonwealth. By joining the EEC Britain would be tying itself to trade agreements within Europe that would prevent it from negotiating independently with other nations.

However as trade decreased with the Commonwealth and Britain's position in world affairs declined, the EEC became a more attractive prospect – especially as the union proved successful. Since the UK's entry to Europe however it has battled to negotiate its position in an attempt to retain sovereignty whilst still benefiting from an alliance with the EU – thus resulting in its reputation as an 'awkward partner'.

Sovereignty remains a contentious issue amongst those who feel that as the UK becomes more integrated into the EU it is losing control over its own legislature. The UK Independence Party (UKIP) was born out of this concern and now campaigns to replace EU political membership with a UK-EU Free Trade Agreement similar to non-EU Switzerland and Norway. It argues that the EU is too bureaucratic and expensive, and detracts from Britain's ability to govern itself effectively. UKIP has won seats in the European Parliament, highlighting similar feelings of many UK citizens. The term Eurosceptic is used to describe someone who is opposed to increasing powers to the European Union.

UKIP POLICIES IN BRIEF

- UKIP will leave the political EU and trade globally and freely. We will re-embrace today's fast-growing Commonwealth and we will encourage UK manufacturing so that we make things again.

- We will freeze immigration for five years, speed up deportation of up to a million illegal immigrants by tripling the numbers engaged in deportations, and have 'no home no visa' work permits to ease the housing crisis.

- We will have a grammar school in every town. We will restore standards of education and improve skills training. Student grants will replace student loans.

- We will radically reform the working of the NHS with an Insurance Fund, whilst upholding the 'free at the point of care' principles. We will bring back matrons and have locally run, clean hospitals.

- We will give people the vote on policing priorities, go back to proper beat policing and scrap the Human Rights Act. We will have sentences that mean what they say.

- We will take 4.5 million people out of tax with a simple Flat Tax (with National Insurance) starting at £10,000. We will scrap Inheritance Tax, not just reform it and cut corporation taxes.

- We will say No to green taxes and wind farms. To avert a major energy crisis, we will go for new nuclear power plants on the same existing site facilities and for clean coal. We will reduce pollution and encourage recycling.

- We will make welfare simpler and fairer, introduce 'workfare' to get people back to work, and a new citizens pension and private pensions scheme insurance.

- We will support our armed forces with more spending on equipment, military homes and medical care. We will save our threatened warships and add 25,000 more troops.

- We will be fair to England, with an English Parliament of English MPs at Westminster. We will replace assembly members like MSPs with MPs. And we will promote referenda at local and national levels.

- We will make customer satisfaction number one for rail firms – not cost cutting and will look seriously at reopening some rail lines that Beeching closed. We will make foreign lorries pay for British roads with a 'Britdisc' – and we will stop persecuting motorists.

- Last, but never least, we will bring in fair prices and fair competition for our suffering farmers, and restore traditional British fishing and territorial waters.

ACTIVITY 3

Read UKIP's policies. In groups, discuss the policies.
1) Do you agree with any of them? Give reasons.
2) Are there any that you do not feel would be beneficial to the UK? Why?
3) What might be the consequences of these policies?

Daily impact of the EU on UK citizens

In order to fully understand how membership of the EU affects citizens in the UK it is helpful to detail its impacts in relation to everyday aspects of our lives.

Food and drink

- The EU has introduced reforms to assist European farmers to produce better quality produce and trade it more easily. This encourages agricultural output in member states but also offers the consumer a better price in the supermarket, meaning citizens have more choice and can demand better value.
- Although fish and chips is a British favourite, the over-fishing of species such as cod has been a major concern as numbers were becoming dangerously low. Thanks to EU legislation, the amount and species of fish caught is monitored to protect against over-fishing.

Shopping and spending

- EU laws state that food must be labelled clearly and correctly and indicate if it contains any genetically modified (GM) ingredients.
- Health warnings on cigarette packaging now have to be 33 per cent of the size of the entire packet, as a result of an EU ruling.

- Mobile phone bills have been cut due to EU laws introduced to make calls made or received in an EU country up to 60 per cent cheaper.
- Tough policies have been put in place to ensure the consumer is able to have as much choice as possible, so that no single company can dominate a market and prevent the consumer receiving value for money.

Health warnings on cigarette packets have to be 33 per cent of the packet size, according to an EU ruling

Working life

- EU citizens are entitled to four weeks paid holiday every year, and with eleven hours of rest in every 24, as a consequence of the EU Working Time Directive. Many workers in the US are only entitled to two weeks' paid holiday by comparison.
- EU legislation also protects the rights of mothers and fathers to take time off from work after their babies are born – ensuring that they can return to the same job they left and are treated fairly if they need to take time off to care for their children.

Travelling

- As citizens holiday within Europe, they are likely to need to change currency only once as 15 member states now use a single European currency – the Euro.
- It's also likely that as they move through European countries, they will no longer have to undergo lengthy passport checks.
- Citizens can now take their pets with them much more easily because of the introduction of the pet passport.

Environment

- New EU legislation means member states are obligated to clean up their beaches – good for holidaymakers and the environment.
- The EU is also committed to cutting its energy consumption by 20 per cent by increasing the amount of energy produced by renewable sources.

Beaches in Britain that meet EU standards are awarded the 'blue flag'

---

50 reasons to love the European Union

As the EU celebrates its anniversary, _The Independent_ looks at 50 benefits it has brought, and asks: "What has Europe done for us?"

1 The end of war between European nations.
2 Democracy is now flourishing in 27 countries.
3 Once-poor countries, such as Ireland, Greece and Portugal, are prospering.
4 The creation of the world's largest internal trading market.
5 Unparalleled rights for European consumers.
6 Co-operation on continent-wide immigration policy.
7 Co-operation on crime, through Europol.
8 Laws that make it easier for British people to buy property in Europe.
9 Cleaner beaches and rivers throughout Europe.
10 Four weeks statutory paid holiday a year for workers in Europe.
11 No death penalty (it is incompatible with EU membership).
12 Competition from privatised companies means cheaper phone calls.
13 Small EU bureaucracy (24,000 employees, fewer than the BBC).
14 Making the French eat British beef again.
15 Minority languages, such as Irish, Welsh and Catalan recognised and protected.
16 Europe is helping to save the planet with regulatory cuts in CO_2.
17 One currency from Bantry to Berlin (but not Britain).
18 Europe-wide travel bans on tyrants such as Zimbabwe's Robert Mugabe.
19 The EU gives twice as much aid to developing countries as the United States.
20 Strict safety standards for cars, buses and aircraft
21 Free medical help for tourists.
22 EU peacekeepers operate in trouble spots throughout the world.
23 Europe's single market has brought cheap flights to the masses, and new prosperity for forgotten cities.

24 Introduction of pet passports.

25 It now takes only 2 hrs 35 mins from London to Paris by Eurostar.

26 Prospect of EU membership has forced modernisation on Turkey.

27 Shopping without frontiers gives consumers more power to shape markets.

28 Cheap travel and study programmes means greater mobility for Europe's youth.

29 Food labelling is much clearer.

30 No tiresome border checks (apart from in the UK).

31 Compensation for passengers suffering air delays.

32 Strict ban on animal testing for the cosmetic industry.

33 Greater protection for Europe's wildlife.

34 Regional development fund has aided the deprived parts of Britain.

35 European driving licences recognised across the EU.

36 Britons now feel a lot less insular.

37 Europe's bananas remain bent, despite sceptics' fears.

38 Strong economic growth – greater than the United States last year.

39 Single market has brought the best continental footballers to Britain.

40 Human rights legislation has protected the rights of the individual.

41 European Parliament provides democratic checks on all EU laws.

42 EU gives more, not less, sovereignty to nation states.

43 Maturing EU is a proper counterweight to the power of US and China.

44 European immigration has boosted the British economy.

45 Europeans are increasingly multilingual – except Britons, who are less so.

46 Europe has set Britain an example how properly to fund a national health service.

47 British restaurants now much more cosmopolitan.

48 Total mobility for career professionals in Europe.

49 Europe has revolutionised British attitudes to food and cooking.

50 Lists like this drive the Eurosceptics mad.

www.independent.co.uk, 21 March 2007

ACTIVITY 4

Read the article above.

1) Do you agree with all the reasons given to love the EU? Which ones do you think are not good reasons? Why?

2) Did you know that all of these issues were related to the EU? Which two surprised you most?

3) Which five reasons do you think are the most important? Why?

Web action

Use information from the websites below to create a poster, concept map/spider diagram or PowerPoint slide detailing the way in which the EU affects UK citizens.

- **www.europa.eu**: information on the EU in twelve simple steps and excellent factsheet-style publications.

- **www.news.bbc.co.uk**: easy to navigate facts and figures on the Institutions of the EU. Excellent resources on the social characteristics of member states.

- **www.europarl.org.uk**: useful breakdown of UK regions and incumbent MEPs.

Exam questions

SECTION B: MAKING A DIFFERENCE
Answer Question 4 and **either** Question 5 **or** Question 6.

This section carries 30 marks.

4 Read the extract below and answer parts (a) and (b) which follow.

> We must save the House of Commons. I never thought that, in writing such a sentence, I would be swimming against the tide of British public opinion, but people are so angry about the revelations of MPs' expenses that they seem not to care what happens to the entire institution.
>
> It matters, though, because it is ours. Its Members sit there only at our pleasure. We can – and I hope we will – throw out all those whose behaviour has incurred our displeasure.
>
> This crisis has revealed what is really wrong with Britain. *The Daily Telegraph* still has a great deal of interesting information to set before its readers. But after more than a week of its reports, we can say that – in scope, if not in every detail – we now know the worst.
>
> Eventually, it will be helpful to know the best as well. Once all the data are made public, voters can draw up lists of MPs who are without stain. Armed with computer discs about the good, the bad and the in-between, we shall be able to put pressure on parties, constituency associations and, of course, through the ballot box, to get the sort of MPs we want.
>
> ***The Daily Telegraph,
> 15 May 2009***

Your answers should refer to the extract as appropriate, but you should also include other relevant information.

(a) Identify two ways in which a citizen can take part in the democratic process.
(5 marks)

(b) Explain the role of elected Members of Parliament. *(10 marks)*

Either:

5 To what extent can multinational corporations be viewed as powerful?
(15 marks)

Or:

6 Assess the impact of the European Union (EU) on citizens in the UK. *(15 marks)*

SECTION 1: MAKING A DIFFERENCE

Chapter 6: How can I make a difference?

In this chapter we explore two main issues which examine the key question 'How can I make a difference?'

ISSUE 1: Playing your part: how the citizen can get involved and make a difference
This issue is explored through the following topics:

- what does 'taking part in the democratic process' mean?
- citizens and the electoral process
- do pressure groups improve the democratic process?

ISSUE 2: Citizenship in action: citizens working together to bring about change
This issue is explored through the following topics:

- how do citizens bring about change?
- what are the key factors in successful campaigning?
- the impact of campaigns on political decision making and political attitudes

---

ISSUE 1: PLAYING YOUR PART: HOW THE CITIZEN CAN GET INVOLVED AND MAKE A DIFFERENCE

In this section we explore the following three topics:

- what does 'taking part in the democratic process' mean?
- citizens and the electoral process
- do pressure groups improve the democratic process?

1 What does it mean 'taking part in the democratic process'?

The concept of democracy

In simple terms, democracy is a type of government based on the principle that all people are equal and collectively hold power. In practice, there are many forms of democracy – this topic establishes the key values behind the concept of democracy in the UK. It also examines the question 'how democratic is Britain?' and explores the barriers to democratic participation.

Not all world states adhere to the Western theory of democracy – arguably, this is the most difficult concept a new student of politics has to wrestle with. For those who have only experienced democracy as a system of government, it is almost inconceivable that a society can or should function without these principles – however it is important to remember that democracy and its variations are merely one of many theories of government. Other forms of government include:

- dictatorship – a single leader holds absolute power
- anarchy – no government at all
- monarchy – an individual who has inherited the role of leader and expects to pass that position to their heir.

In recent times democracy has been advocated by some Western states as a fundamental system that all other states should aspire to – delivering democracy was cited by the coalition of countries, including the UK and the US, as the main reason to invade Iraq in 2003.

Liberal democracy

Liberal democracy is the name given to a system of democracy through which the 'freedoms' of individuals are upheld and protected from government power – for example, freedom of speech and freedom to vote. However states that are defined as functioning under a liberal democracy may have varying degrees of individual freedoms. For example, in some states citizens may vote to elect their own government but may experience some curbs on their rights or freedoms.

Representative democracy

Representative democracy describes a system of democracy whereby citizens elect representatives to speak for them and to form a government. Although a state may adhere to the principles of democracy, it is obviously logistically difficult to consult every member of the public on every government decision. The UK, for example has a population of nearly 60 million – it would be impossible to get everyone around a table to discuss decisions and come to a consensus! Representative democracy therefore gives citizens the opportunity to elect someone to have those discussions and make the decisions that affect them – in theory with the best interests of citizens as a priority.

Direct democracy

Direct democracy describes a form of democracy whereby citizens are more closely involved in the process of democracy. Although representative democracy provides an effective means by which to debate and make decisions relatively quickly, it can be criticised for moving decision making a step away from the population and therefore creating a hurdle to true democracy – thus creating an indirect form of democracy. Citizens must rely on representatives to survey their opinions routinely and on a range of subjects. Also, they must rely on the fact that their views are accurately relayed by their representative –

some feel that a system of representative democracy therefore allows representatives too much power over decision making without being accountable enough to the public.

The most obvious way in which direct democracy can be achieved in a state with a large population is via a referendum. This enables an effective means by which to receive a clear answer from citizens on a particular topic. It allows an undiluted response directly from the entire population (or at least those that choose to participate) and can appease citizens' desire for democracy. However critics argue that citizens cannot feasibly be consulted on every single issue of government. Such questions could be endless:

- 'should the compulsory age of education be raised to 18?'
- 'should we agree to further integration into the EU?'
- 'should the legal age to buy alcohol be raised?'
- 'should the state be able to nationalise a high street bank?'

Asking constant questions of the public would make for very slow progression and delay in affecting change. Although direct democracy offers a more concentrated form of democracy it is argued that it would still have drawbacks because of the time wasted trying to consult all citizens.

Other means by which citizens could achieve direct democracy would be the ability to force the resignation of an elected representative by petitioning for a **recall election** – an option that some states in the US enjoy. US citizens are also able to petition for new legislation in some states – called **popular initiative**. The initiative allows the electorate to have a direct impact on legislature. Within a representative democracy the role of initiating legislature rests with the representatives elected by citizens.

ACTIVITY 1

1) In pairs discuss the advantages and disadvantages of representative democracy. Draw up a table detailing both.
2) Feed back your answers to the class and create a 'master table' of all the points.

Democratic values

The concept of democracy is a political system based on certain values – citizens' rights, freedoms and equality are seen as vital. These values are not only protected by a democratic system of government but they are required in order for a genuine democracy to function.

Rights

What exactly do we mean by 'rights'? Should we all *expect* rights? Does everyone have them or do we have to *earn* them? Are they moral or legal? Do they protect us or hinder us?

It is true that there is a set of 'human rights' enshrined in UK law and their breach can be challenged in court; so those rights, although derived from *moral* beliefs about the minimum requirement for human life and happiness, are in fact now *legally* protected. By asserting that citizens are entitled to those human rights, simply because they are human also means that all citizens must have equal *claim* to them.

Freedoms

Freedom itself is very difficult to define because it means different things to different people. Some people may see freedom as being able to do absolutely anything they wish, regardless of the consequences to others – but other people may see it as concerning freedom to advance economically and socially without government interference. In order to establish or strengthen democracy citizens must have certain freedoms.

For example, being free to discuss issues without fear of repercussions, freedom from discrimination so that all citizens can be equal or the freedom to join groups (such as political parties or pressure groups) in order to pursue the decisions they feel are best for society.

Equality

If democracy is ruled by the people then it is important that all people are able to have their voices heard. To ensure that all citizens' opinions are heard, equality is an essential value that democracy must uphold. Democracy can only be legitimate if it allows all people to be viewed as equal – if the opinions of some are favoured over others or one person's vote counts more than another, democracy becomes an empty concept. It can only be valid if all citizens within society are treated equally. There are of course many opposing views as to whether the UK achieves equality within its society, but it is essential to understand its place at the heart of democracy.

EXTRACT OF THE TRANSCRIPT FROM THE JON STEWART TONY BLAIR INTERVIEW

Stewart: [our President] is a big 'freedom' guy and he believes that if everyone was a democracy there'd be no more fighting.

Blair: Well, no two democracies have gone to war with each other.

See www.youtube.co.uk for full interview. This clip is available on the Daily Show website, www.thedailyshow.com and was screened on E4.

ACTIVITY 2

1) Divide the class into two groups. The first group must make a case for democracy. The second group must make a case against it. Hold a class debate to try to ascertain who has made the best case.
Think about the following:
- freedom
- equality
- participation
- why is democracy a good thing?
- how have democracies been successful?
- what are the possible problems for a democracy?
- what stops democracy from working?
- does the population always make the right decisions about what is best?
- could there be a better form of government?

Opportunities and barriers to citizen participation

Opportunities for participation

Within a representative democracy, participation is imperative because citizens are essentially bestowing their 'voice' to someone else – they must be certain therefore that the representative is the 'right person for the job'. Citizens have the opportunity to vote their representatives into office and, if they are not satisfied with their performance, or feel another individual could do better, they can vote them out of office. They also have the right to be able to meet their representatives and correspond with them on issues that concern them; within the UK, citizens may have representatives at local, regional, national and European level.

The UK system of government, although technically a representative democracy, does offer the opportunity for citizens to also be involved in direct democracy. Although rare, referendums are called in the UK – and political parties often promise them on certain issues in their manifestos.

Joining campaigns and pressure groups, signing petitions, protesting and attending public meetings are examples of ways in which citizens can be involved in civic participation.

Barriers to participation

If we hold that participating in a representative democracy is important and that not to participate would lessen citizens' ability to have their voice heard and steer their nation as they see fit – then why doesn't *everyone* vote? (see voter turnout figures on page 267). It is argued that for some groups in society there are barriers to participation, resulting in non-participation by some based on age, socio-economic status, ethnicity and gender.

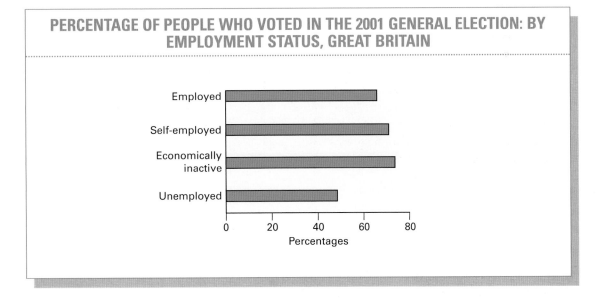

PERCENTAGE OF PEOPLE WHO VOTED IN THE 2001 GENERAL ELECTION: BY EMPLOYMENT STATUS, GREAT BRITAIN

ACTIVITY 3

1) In small groups analyse the data above and on page 258 discuss any trends you think are relevant.
2) What reasons can you think of to explain why certain groups are less likely to be involved in the examples of civic participation listed?
3) Are each of the examples activities that you think an individual should do regularly? Why?
4) Why might a citizen's employment status affect their willingness to vote?

PARTICIPATION IN CIVIC ENGAGEMENT AND VOLUNTARY ACTIVITIES AT LEAST ONCE A MONTH IN THE 12 MONTHS PRIOR TO INTERVIEW BY AGE, SEX AND ETHNICITY, 2007–08

Percentages

	Civic participation	Civic Consultation	Civic activism	Informal volunteering	Formal volunteering	Volunteering	Respondents
Ethnicity[1]							
White	3	2	4	35	28	49	8,036
All Asian	3	2	3	28	19	36	2,745
Indian	2	1	3	28	22	37	1,361
Pakistani	5	3	4	29	16	34	812
Bangladeshi	5	1	3	24	15	32	292
All black	2	2	5	38	27	48	1,672
Caribbean	2	2	6	39	27	49	808
African	2	2	4	36	26	46	818
Mixed race	4	2	6	42	27	52	479
Chinese/other	1	–	2	27	16	35	597
Minority ethnic groups	3	2	4	32	22	40	5,493
Sex							
male	3	2	4	31	25	44	3,854
female	3	2	4	39	29	51	4,946
Age							
16 to 24	3	2	4	41	24	52	727
25 to 34	3	2	4	36	22	45	1,319
35 to 49	3	2	5	37	29	51	2,449
50 to 64	3	2	5	31	29	46	2,084
65 to 74	3	2	6	35	31	50	1,148
75 and over	2	1	4	28	24	40	1,072
All respondents	3	2	4	35	27	48	8,804

[1] Ethnicity figures based on the combined sample, other figures based on the core sample.

CLG, *Citizenship Survey: 2007–08* (April 2007 – March 2008), England and Wales

Some people argue that education is key to understanding the relevance of participation and hopefully encouraging more young people to vote and become involved in civic participation. However other theories suggest that there is a general decline in interest in politics fuelled by a distrust of those in power and a belief that the opinions of ordinary people are being ignored in favour of the interests of politicians. It may also be the case that individuals are more likely to vote or try to affect change when they feel strongly about a particular issue. It has been asserted that if people are, in general, content with their lives they see less reason to act to change the status quo.

How democratic is the UK?

There are certainly challenges to democracy in the UK. As voter turnout drops in the UK, the result of any election – local, general or European – becomes less representative of the views of the population. In this sense democracy is weakened. There are also concerns about how representative local councillors, MPs and MEPs are of the citizens they act for. Middle aged, middle class, white males are considerably over represented and this is at the exclusion of other groups in society. The fact that elections also run up to five years apart means that, although convention says that representatives are accountable to the public, voters may have to wait some time to expel a representative from office.

However it is important to remember that Britain's liberal democracy does protect equality, rights and freedoms through its traditions, but also legally – such values are denied to many other citizens around the world. It is always wise to question whether they are being genuinely upheld and attempt to strengthen

How representative are our MPs?

democracy as far as possible. Moves towards more opportunities for direct democracy could prove vital in re-energising those that feel disengaged with democracy – in particular, referendum is a tool that could be integrated relatively easily into the UK political system.

ACTIVITY 4

1) Develop the arguments you made in Activity 3 to explore democracy in the UK. Create a list of evidence to prove that the UK is highly democratic and another to argue that democracy is not functioning effectively. Think about:
   - representation
   - participation
   - different groups in society
   - rights and freedoms
   - direct democracy
   - equality.

Web action

1] Use the website **www.freedomhouse.org** to research areas of the world that have varying levels of democracy.

2] Choose one country to research further. Try to find information and newspaper articles online with more information and other perspectives on issues of democracy, freedom and equality in your chosen country.

Note: Freedomhouse is a not for profit organisation that charts the freedom that citizens have in different states. Its Map of Freedom is a useful tool in assessing freedoms in different parts of the world.

2 Citizens and the electoral process

Citizens and elections in the UK

In order to vote in a parliamentary election in the UK an individual must:

- be on the electoral register
- be over 18 years of age
- be a British Citizen (or a citizen of the Irish Republic or a Commonwealth country)
- not be disqualified from voting.

Those people disqualified from voting include:

- members of the House of Lords (although they are permitted to vote in elections at local, devolved and European level)
- citizens of EU states (although they are permitted to vote in elections at local, devolved and European level)
- convicted prisoners serving a sentence
- anyone found guilty of corrupt or illegal election practices in the last five years.

In order to vote, an individual must first appear on the **electoral register**. This is a register of all eligible voters in each local authority area and is updated by local authorities. A citizen must ensure that they are on this register if they wish to vote, especially if they are moving house. On the day of an election (traditionally held on a Thursday) schools are often closed and used as polling stations where citizens can go to cast their vote. Each vote is secret and is cast in private, usually behind a screen, and then placed in a sealed ballot box. Individuals have a polling card sent to their address, which tells them when and where to vote and on arrival at the polling station, citizens tell the officials their name and address. These measures help to prevent electoral fraud, ensuring that each citizen can only cast one, anonymous vote.

Electoral process in the UK

Voting in an election may be the only time that many citizens take an active part in 'politics' and, for many, it is the single most important action a citizen can make within a democracy. This topic explores elections within the UK, different voting systems, participation, the impact upon the citizen and how the media is involved in the process.

Most citizens have the opportunity to vote in at least three different types of election:

- local (to elect local representatives)
- general (to elect Members of Parliament)
- European (to elect Members of the European Parliament).

- Depending on the region, citizens may also elect directly elected mayors and, in the case of London, members of a Regional Assembly. Citizens living in Scotland, Wales and Northern Ireland will elect members of their national Parliament or Assembly.

Elections are therefore an important part of the democratic process as citizens are electing the representatives they favour to make decisions on their behalf. Elections also allow citizens to select representatives that they feel best reflect their own personal beliefs and values, and choose those who have political policies that they prefer.

General elections

In the UK, 'general election' is the term used to describe the simultaneous election of all Members of Parliament for each constituency. Although political parties fight election campaigns by focusing on the policies the party would put in place should they form government, citizens are actually voting for the **candidate** that they wish to represent their constituency in the House of Commons. In effect they are electing a representative to speak for them on future legislation. If a Member of Parliament resigns or dies whilst in post, a **by-election** is called to elect a new representative.

There is a maximum of five years between general elections and the party in power decides the date on which the next election takes place. Under the advice of the incumbent Prime Minister the Queen must then suspend Parliament (known as the dissolution of Parliament) and election campaigning by political parties begins. This period of campaigning varies between three to eight weeks.

'First-past-the-post'

The system of voting used in UK general elections is known as 'first-past-the-post' (FPTP). In simple terms this means that the candidate with the greatest number of votes is declared the winner of the seat in the House of Commons. The party that occupies the greatest number of seats in the House of Commons then goes on to form the Government. The FPTP system is praised by some people, who feel it is the simplest, most efficient means of selecting a clear winner. However other people believe it to be unfair, as it does not provide representation to many who have voted for alternative parties/candidates. In some cases, the number of votes cast for the winner is outnumbered by the total of the votes cast against them. For example the total number of votes cast for the winning candidate in the Sittingbourne and Sheppey Constituency in the 2005 General Election was 17,051; however the total number of votes cast for other parties and candidates totalled 23,560. In this way, the majority of the constituency will not been represented in the House of Commons as the winner of the seat was in fact elected by a minority. In such cases, **proportional representation** is offered as a fairer voting system as it apportions seats based on number of votes cast and allows smaller parties with support spread nationwide to achieve representation in the House of Commons.

Candidate	Party	Votes
Derek Wyatt	Labour	17,051
Gordon Henderson	Conservative	16,972
Jane Nelson	Liberal Democrat	5,183
Stephen Dean	UKIP	926
Mad Mike	Young Rock 'n' Roll Loony Party	479

Local elections

The outcome of local elections arguably has a greater effect on the everyday lives of citizens, as local authorities are responsible for many of the facilities and services that people enjoy on a daily basis. Local authorities' structures differ across the UK and although they all serve four years in office, the proportion of representatives up for election differs for each authority. Some authorities may elect one third of their councillors at election time (i.e. one third of the council is elected each year for three years in a row, and then there is no election in the subsequent year). However other local authorities may elect the council in its entirety. The FPTP system is used in England and Wales, although some wards may have more than one candidate (size of population defines how many councillors a ward has) those candidates with the most votes win the council seats for that ward.

European Parliament elections

Electing Members of the European Parliament is in effect the citizens' opportunity to be represented at a European level. Although such elections may sometimes seem more distant to the electorate in terms of geography and relevance, they become ever more important as the remit of the EU grows and the issues dealt with by the EU have an increasing impact on the citizen. The UK is separated into twelve regions (one each for Scotland, Wales and Northern Ireland and nine for England) with a total of 78 seats in the European Parliament. Each region is then allocated a number of seats depending on their population size – the South East is the largest with ten seats.

The voting system for elections to the European Parliament is different from the FPTP system used for general and local elections – it operates using what is called a **closed party list**. This means that political parties decide on which candidates they wish to place on a party list and in which order. This list then appears on the ballot paper and the electorate votes for a party list rather than for a specific candidate. Seats are then allocated to each region according to parties' share of the vote. Candidates are selected according to their ranking on the list – so the greater a party's share of the vote, then the more candidates on their list are elected.

Scottish Parliament and National Assembly for Wales elections

Both the Scottish Parliament and the National Assembly for Wales use the **additional member system** of voting to elect their representatives (Members of the Scottish Parliament and Assembly Members). Under this system electors cast two votes; one for a candidate to represent them as their constituency member, and another for their preferred party on a party list (put forward by parties). Each constituency has a representative but this does not total all of the seats available. The remainder of seats is allocated proportionally according to the results of citizens' party list vote.

The votes cast for a single constituency member are counted using the FPTP system, but party seats are allocated proportionately using a formula called the d'Hondt formula. In this way if the number of winning single-member constituency candidates does not proportionately reflect the votes cast for them overall, their seats can be 'topped up' via the additional member system. The Greater London Assembly also uses this system but adds the proviso that parties have to have gained over five per cent of the vote in order to win additional member seats.

Northern Ireland Assembly elections

The Northern Ireland Assembly uses a **single transferable vote system** which allows voters to rank their preferred candidates (as opposed to simply choosing a party list) and to rank as many candidates as they wish. Candidates must reach a 'droop quota' of votes to be elected (calculated by dividing the number of votes divided by the number of seats plus one and then add one to that total). Any candidate that reaches this quota is elected but if not enough candidates have been elected to fill the seats, then surplus votes from the elected candidates are transferred to the others according to the voters' next preference. If there are still not enough candidates elected, then those with fewest votes are eliminated and their votes are transferred. This process continues until the required number of candidates is elected to fill the seats. This system is also used for local elections in Scotland and Northern Ireland.

Mayoral elections

Some regions are now able to select a directly elected mayor – don't forget these mayors differ from the ceremonial mayors or chairman of local authorities in other areas (see page 228). Directly elected mayors are elected by using the **supplementary voting system**. Under this system the electorate must identify their first and second choice of candidate on the ballot paper. If the winning candidate does not achieve 50 per cent of the first preference votes, then all but the leading two candidates are eliminated and the second preference votes are added to the first to determine the overall winner.

2008 MAYORAL ELECTIONS IN LONDON				
Candidate name	Party	1st choice votes	2nd choice votes*	Total votes
Boris Johnson	Conservative Party	1,043,761	124,977	1,168,738
Ken Livingstone	Labour Party	893,877	135,089	1,028,966

* On papers where the 1st and 2nd choice votes are for the top two candidates, the 2nd choice votes are not counted

Candidate name	Party	1st choice votes	1st choice per cent	2nd choice votes	2nd choice per cent
Boris Johnson	Conservative Party	1,043,761	43.20	257,792	12.86
Ken Livingstone	Labour Party	893,877	37.00	303,198	15.13
Brian Paddick	Liberal Democrats	236,685	9.80	641,412	32.01
Siân Berry	Green Party	77,374	3.20	331,727	16.55
Richard Barnbrook	British National Party	69,710	2.89	128,609	6.42
Alan Craig	Christian People's Alliance and Christian Party	39,249	1.62	80,140	4.00
Gerard Batten	UK Independence Party	22,422	0.93	113,651	5.67
Lindsey German	Left List	16,796	0.70	35,057	1.75
Matt O'Connor	English Democrats	10,695	0.44	73,538	3.67
Winston McKenzie	Independent	5,389	0.22	38,954	1.94

Areas counted	Votes
Electorate	5,419,913
Papers counted/turnout	2,456,990
Turnout	45.33%

Rejected votes *

1st choice	41,032
2nd choice	412,054

Rejected votes totals include:

Blank **(no votes cast)	13,034
No 2nd preference ***	407,840

'Rejected votes' refers to ballot papers where the vote has not been counted because the ballot paper has not been filled out correctly. This may be because the voter has marked more than one preference in one column, because the voter identified themselves on the ballot paper, if the voter's intention is unclear or if the voter has spoiled his or her paper in any way.

** 'Blank votes' refers to ballot papers where no 1st choice and no 2nd choice have been marked, and no vote has been counted. (This data is only available for 2008.)

*** No 2nd preference refers to ballot papers where voters have only made a 1st choice vote and no 2nd choice vote. The first choice vote has been counted. (This data is only available for 2008.)

www.londonelects.org.uk

ACTIVITY 1

Look at the table opposite and discuss the following in small groups:
1) By how many votes did Boris Johnson win the 2008 election?
2) Why might this be surprising?
3) What do you notice about the turnout figures?
4) What impact do you think this has on the overall result of the election?
5) How many rejected votes were there? Why do you think this was?

Standing as a candidate

To stand as a candidate in a UK parliamentary election an individual must be at least 18 years of age, be a British citizen (or citizen of a Commonwealth country or of the Irish Republic). Convicted prisoners serving a sentence of twelve months, certain employees of the Queen, people found guilty of certain electoral offences or members of the House of Lords are not eligible to stand as candidates. Nomination forms must be completed and ten other electors within a candidate's constituency must sign them. A candidate cannot stand in more than one constituency at a general election. Candidates can stand on behalf of a party or as an independent.

These conditions also apply in the case of local elections, although candidates must also be registered to vote in the local authority area (or, for the previous twelve months they must have lived, been the owner or tenant of land or premises or had their place of work within the local authority area). At a local election, council employees where election is sought and employees of connected organisations are disqualified from becoming a candidate. Also,

individuals who have served a prison sentence of three months or more within the last five years cannot stand as a candidate.

ACTIVITY 2

1) Create your own election. Find members of your class that you think have similar views and opinions to you and create your own political party. Decide as a class if you are participating in a local, mayoral, parliamentary, national or European election. Some amongst you may wish to stand as independent candidates.
   - What is your party's name?
   - What are your main policy points?
   - What does your party intend to do if it finds power?
   Be ready to present your ideas to the class.
2) As a class hold an election, following the appropriate voting system and ask an independent referee to count the votes. Disclose the winner and discuss why you thought that party won.
3) Extension task: Try running the election again with an alternative electoral system (either FPTP, supplementary vote, additional member system or closed list). Did it affect the result? How?

OVERVIEW OF VOTING SYSTEMS

	Voting system				
	First-past-the-post (FPTP)	Supplementary vote (SV)	Additional member system (AMS)	Party list (Closed list)	Single transferable vote (STV)
Examples	UK Parliamentary elections (general elections), local elections in England and Wales	Directly elected mayors	Scottish Parliament, National Assembly for Wales and Greater London Assembly	European Parliament elections	Northern Ireland Assembly, local government in Scotland and N. Ireland
How does it work?	Voters select one preferred candidate	Voters rank their two preferred candidates	Voters cast two votes, one for constituency member and one for party. Seats allocated to constituency members but leaves some seats remaining for 'top ups'	Voters choose a party list compiled by party managers. Single candidates not chosen	Voters rank candidates. Winning candidates must reach a quota to be elected. Preference votes are then transferred until all seats are filled
Advantages	• Voters are familiar with this system • Gives a clear result based on candidates with most votes	• Simple system • The second preference of those who voted for a minor party is not counted in deciding vote	• Top up of additional members allows for correction in proportionality • Electors retain a link with chosen constituency member	• Candidates allocated based on proportion of votes • Minority parties stand higher chance of election	• Minimises wasted votes • Votes cast for candidates not party lists • Quota based on majority number
Disadvantages	• Allows candidates to win seats by very narrow margins meaning majority of voters may not actually get desired representatives. • Small parties with support spread nationwide may be sidelined	• The winner may not necessarily have won the majority of the votes cast • Some voters find the system confusing and do not cast a second preference	• Creates members with no constituency • Party managers have control over additional member party lists	• No choice between candidates • Party managers have control over the order by which candidates are elected	• Based on multi-member election can be problematic to elect a new member at by-election • Seen as too complex

Participation

In topic 1 the issue of democracy was explored, and the importance of voter participation in maintaining a healthy democracy. If citizens do not turn out at election time then it is feared that groups with extreme views are more likely to gain power. In fact any small party is able to gain a disproportionate amount of representation if it can mobilise its supporters to vote whilst other voters stay away.

Typically local elections have a low turnout, as do European Parliamentary elections and general election turnout has declined considerably since the Second World War. Many reasons for this **voter apathy** have been discussed: some people believe that its root cause is a lack of faith in politicians; and a belief that representatives are not responding to their electorates' demands but instead pursuing their own interests. There are also those who argue that the inconvenience of voting, distance from

polling stations and the busy lives of citizens are all contributing to lower voter turnout. It is also the case that in some areas where certain parties have strongholds, many feel that a vote against that party is useless and therefore a waste of time. Tony Blair's government pioneered postal voting via pilot schemes, as a means of improving turnout and it appeared to be successful in raising turnout at local level. However, subsequent cases of postal voting fraud have meant that its worth as a tool for electoral reform has been questioned.

ACTIVITY 3

1) Look at the graph below. As a class try to brainstorm reasons why voter turnout has fallen since 1945. Think about:
   - modern lifestyles
   - levels of representation
   - political parties
   - polling stations
   - profile of representatives
   - education.

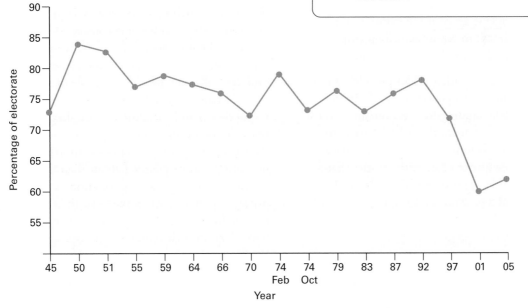

(Excludes votes deliberately or accidentally spoiled).
Graph showing the percentage of registered voters who actually voted at each election, 1945–2005.

Role of the media in elections

At election time political parties create **manifestos** to declare to voters their core beliefs and policy plans. In this way the voter can hold representatives to account if they stray from their manifesto whilst in office. To ensure that these manifestos and candidates' messages reach citizens parties utilise the media. TV is utilised before general elections as political parties are allocated broadcasts, according to the number of candidates they are putting forward. These broadcasts allow political parties to attempt to convince the electorate to vote for them and have become increasingly sophisticated.

As we have already explored in *'What is the influence of the media and how is power controlled?'* on pages 218–25 the relationship between the media and politicians is interdependent – the candidate needs the media to publicise their plans in order that they might be elected and the media can sell newspapers by reporting on political stories. At election time this relationship can become increasingly strained if the stories that the media choose to report actually prove detrimental to a political campaign.

In the UK, the independent press has an important role to play in scrutinising the individuals standing for election and also the plans and actions of the political party to which they belong. At election time the stance that a newspaper takes or the stories that a media outlet reports can be crucial to the success of a political campaign.

Opinion polls and focus groups

National newspapers often use opinion polls, which have been carried out by specialist organisations, to illustrate the respondents' voting intentions or opinions on specific

Carrying out an opinion poll. Do you think polls are a good indication of voter preference?

topics. Such polls are also of great interest to parties as they indicate the mood of the electorate and can prove a good gauge of how attractive their policies or announcements have been to voters. In this way they can react to the changing opinions of the electorate in order to improve their chances of election. A criticism of following such polls too closely is that political parties can become consumed by their results and fail to pursue a consistent message that is true to their original values. Also, opinion polls only provide a sample of popular opinion (approximately 1,000–2,000 respondents) and therefore cannot always be relied upon for an accurate representation of the electorates' voting intentions. Individuals may also be quite guarded about their voting intention, viewing such information as quite private – therefore when they cast their vote it may be for an alternative party to the one they have given in their opinion poll response.

Focus groups are similar tools in that they research the public's opinions on specific topics, but rather than one-to-one interviews they take place in groups where individuals can have more in-depth discussions with other members of a group. Focus groups are often used by government as part of their research into which of their policy ideas will be popular, or as a means of researching which issues are most important to the public.

Government departments will often use specialist research companies to organise opinion polls or focus groups.

ACTIVITY 4

1) In small groups try to list as many ways in which you think elections impact the citizen. You may want to discuss:
   - government policy
   - legislation
   - the media
   - participation
   - voting
   - standing as a candidate
   - representation.

Web action

1] Choose a newspaper and search online for articles on an election of your choice (general election, local election, mayoral election etc.).
2] Now choose a different newspaper and search for articles on the same election.
3] Do they report the election in the same way?
4] Are there any differences in the tone of the articles?
5] Do you think this newspaper supports a particular party or candidate over others?

www.timesonline.co.uk
www.thesun.co.uk
www.theguardian.co.uk
www.independent.co.uk
www.dailymail.co.uk

3 Do pressure groups improve the democratic process?

What is a pressure group?

A pressure group is a group of people with a common interest or purpose that try to influence the decisions made by those in power. The causes they pursue and the way in which they try to get their voices heard are varied. In this topic we explore the role and format of pressure groups, and the methods used to fulfil their objectives. We also examine whether pressure groups weaken or strengthen the citizen's ability to influence political decisions.

Pressure groups perform an important role in the democratic process because they allow the citizen to take action on specific issues and in some cases gain results more quickly than they might if they waited for an election in their area. However pressure groups can prove difficult to manage and the publicity that assists pressure groups can be difficult to attain.

It is hard to define common features of a pressure group, beyond their collective pursuit of a common cause, as they take many different forms. However they can be split broadly into two groups.

- Sectional or interest groups: whose main motives are the economic interests of their members, for example trade unions or professional bodies such as the British Medical Association (BMA).
- Cause or promotion groups: whose main aim is to raise awareness of an issue that is not within their own economic self interest (meaning they will not benefit financially from its objectives). Examples are Friends of the Earth and Campaign for Nuclear Disarmament (CND).

Membership of sectional groups is obviously based on a citizen's vested interest in an issue – so a citizen who does not work as a doctor would not be a member of the British Medical Association – but any citizen may become involved with a cause or promotional group. In fact a citizen could be involved with dozens of groups if they wished. In practice however, individuals tend to be actively involved with pressure groups linked to issues that they feel passionate about.

Pressure groups may be created in response to a specific problem, disbanding after that problem has been solved, or even in response to an issue that is unlikely to ever be resolved. For example, Oxfam is a charity that actively campaigns to make government do more about the issue of world poverty even though this problem is unlikely to be eradicated in the near future; as well as continually campaigning to ensure that areas are not allowed to return to poverty.

Pressure groups may be local, national or transnational, depending on the issue they are representing and the number of citizens to which that issue is relevant. A pressure group such as the Boston Bypass and Economic Growth Pressure Group (formed to tackle traffic in the area of Boston, England) is primarily concerned with influencing the decisions of local authorities and would therefore only be likely to receive the support of local residents. Alternatively, a national pressure group such as the Countryside Alliance (campaigns for the protection of the countryside and rural way of life), would potentially gain support from areas across the country, because it is relevant to many people. A group such as Oxfam has relevance worldwide because, unfortunately, poverty continues to be a huge problem across the globe. These groups are not mutually exclusive, for example transnational groups can include

smaller national groups committed to the same objectives and national groups can have regional branches.

Web action

Look at the websites of Oxfam, the Countryside Alliance and the Boston Bypass and Economic Growth Pressure group.
1] What are their main aims?
2] Are they local, national or transnational groups? Are any of them operating on several of these levels?
3] What sorts of activities are they involved in?
- **www.bbeg.org.uk** Boston Bypass and Economic Growth Pressure Group: includes updates of recent progress and copies of letters received from relevant authorities.
- **www.countryside-alliance.org.uk** Countryside Alliance: lists activities and regional groups.
- **www.oxfam.org.uk** Oxfam: details current campaigns.

Political parties and pressure groups

It may seem that citizens are using pressure groups in the same way that they may use political parties – to represent their opinions and beliefs in order that they are represented in political decision making. However political parties must function within the parliamentary system, putting forward candidates for elections as representatives within Parliament or local government, whereas pressure groups are not 'constrained' in this way. Pressure groups do not have to use the parliamentary system in order to raise awareness of their cause – although it is true that some independent candidates do win election on single issues such as local hospital closures. Pressure groups do not want to form a government of their own or create a manifesto covering an entire spectrum of policy – their focus is a single policy area or even a specific issue within that policy area.

Insider and outsider pressure groups

Pressure groups are arguably more successful if they work closely with government, although some choose to keep a distance from such 'conventional' methods of influencing political decision making. Some groups feel that to align themselves too closely with government is to lose the trust and support of members who are mistrusting of the 'establishment'. They may also feel that credibility is lost if they appear too close to government.

Other groups find themselves at a distance from government even though they would prefer to be in regular contact with them. Both can be described as **outsider groups**. Examples of outsider groups include Countryside Alliance and Fathers 4 Justice (campaigns for the rights of fathers).

Other groups are more successful in gaining the cooperation of government – even being consulted on policy issues as they are formulated. These groups are called **insider groups**. Examples of insider groups are the British Medical Association (protects the interests of doctors) and the Royal Society for the Prevention of Cruelty to Animals (animal welfare). Groups can operate as both insider and outsider in an attempt to try to be as effective as possible – consulting with government on some issues but continuing to carry out high profile protests or release information that embarrasses government.

In order for a group to be accepted as an insider group they must be willing to cooperate with policy makers, compromising on some issues in order to achieve their overall aims.

The power to disrupt the smooth running of the country is a tactic that both insider and outsider groups can use to get the attention of the public and government. Combined with public support this can prove a very powerful mixture and cause policy makers to pay greater attention to the demands of pressure groups.

ANIMALS IN RESEARCH – DIRECTIVE 86/609 BACK TO CURRENT CAMPAIGNS

The laws that regulate animal experiments in the European Union (EU) are being revised, and by acting now we can try to help change them for the better.

Scientists from the RSPCA's research animals department have already had significant input into the revision process at various stages and on a range of issues.

Find out more about animal experiments and the laws that govern them in the EU in our campaign facts.

Read about the sound science that backs our campaign.

Take action for lab animals
Now you too have a vital opportunity to have your say in reducing the use and suffering of animals used in research – so take action now!

Speak out for animals
Sign our online petition to call on the Government to improve the regulation of animal experiments.

Shout even louder
Lobby your MEP (Member of the European Parliament) at: www.giveanimalsavoice.org.uk

www.rspca.org.uk

ACTIVITY 1

Read the extract from the RSPCA website on page 271.
1) In which ways could the RSPCA be said to be functioning as both an insider group and outsider group?
2) What is the benefit to it in acting in this way?
3) In which ways does it ask citizens to 'get involved'?

Do pressure groups weaken or strengthen the ability of citizens to influence political decision making?

It is interesting to note that as voter turnout in the UK has decreased, membership to pressure groups has increased. This may be due to citizens' fading belief in existing political parties, and possibly their mistrust of politicians in general. Pressure groups offer individuals the ability to focus on trying to resolve injustices that they feel passionately about, or at least lend their support to campaigns. Arguably, political parties do not offer the same satisfaction. They do not focus on specific issues (with the exception of independent candidates standing for election on single issues). Instead they offer the citizen a broad range of policies on many issues – some of which citizens may not feel concern them at all.

Pressure groups offer citizens a very specific, concentrated dose of democracy. Citizens can attach themselves to a campaign they feel enthusiastic about without having to invest faith in another individual to represent them as they would have to by backing a candidate in a local or general election. Pressure groups remove the formality and third party representation offered by parliamentary politics, as like-minded citizens can organise themselves to allow their voices to be heard directly by government.

However there are many pressure groups constantly fighting for support, membership, funding and government attention and many are unsuccessful in creating a dialogue with government and so fail to achieve their overall aims. These groups fail to provide citizens a voice in decision making and weaken democracy.

How do pressure groups strengthen democracy?

- They give citizens a way to voice their opinions on specific issues and offer the possibility of affecting change outside of a slow moving parliamentary system.
- They allow for representation of citizens' views in between local and general elections.
- As citizens become more involved in pressure group activity, levels of active citizenship are increased and this encourages future participation.
- They offer a vital process of scrutiny, ensuring that the Government is fair and honest by carrying out alternative research and releasing objective information.
- They allow any citizen the opportunity to make change and have their voice heard, regardless of class, gender, ethnicity, disability or sexuality.

How do pressure groups weaken democracy?

- They deflect attention from election campaigns that are part of the legitimate and well regulated parliamentary system.
- There is a range of pressure groups all competing for citizens' attention and support – not all can be successful, leaving some citizens' voices unheard.
- Some pressure groups are more financially secure than others – this means they are at an advantage over other less influential groups as they have extra personnel and resources.

- If pressure groups enter into consultations with government there is a danger that important policy decisions are made behind the closed doors of Whitehall, without using the full democratic processes of parliament.
- The increasing use of more aggressive forms of direct action is irresponsible and dangerous.

- There is a risk that as pressure groups become more numerous, they begin to monopolise the Government's time and energy – thus leaving less chance for democracy to be achieved through the legitimate channels of the parliamentary system.

ACTIVITY 2

1) In small groups, find your own example of a pressure group. Create two lists like the ones above of the ways in which your choice of pressure group could be said to be both strengthening and weakening democracy.

ISSUE 2: CITIZENSHIP IN ACTION: CITIZENS WORKING TOGETHER TO BRING ABOUT CHANGE

In this section we explore the following three topics:

- how do citizens bring about change?
- what are the key factors in successful campaigning?
- the impact of campaigns on political decision making and political attitudes.

4 How do citizens bring about change?

In what ways can citizens campaign for change?

We have already discussed the function of pressure groups and their impact on the democratic process (pages 269–273). This topic builds on this knowledge to explore the kinds of methods that citizens can use to attempt to make changes within their local community and the wider nation, with or without membership of a pressure group.

The methods by which groups decide to achieve their aims are dependent on a number of factors: these include the overall objective of the group, the resources available, the number of people involved and their motivation. If the aim of a pressure group is to overturn or amend legislation, it is essential to try to establish contact with those in government that can realise this. It is also important to ensure their methods are legal in order to be viewed as responsible and legitimate to gain credibility. However pressure groups that attempt to use conventionally peaceful methods to gain cooperation may still fail to gain effective relations with government, even after years of campaigning. In these circumstances they may seek more active or radical forms of protest in order to raise public awareness and hopefully support for their cause. This sends the message that they can cause more disruption as an outsider group than they might as an insider group.

Direct and indirect action

The various methods that pressure groups use can be split into two categories:

- direct action
- indirect action.

Direct action refers to those activities that target individuals, organisations or political groups to seek immediate remedies, for example writing to MPs or local councillors, contacting key policy makers, **boycotting** firms or strike action. Indirect action is used to describe lower level activities, such as voting for sympathetic candidates in elections, distributing leaflets, raising awareness via the media or new technologies or staging peaceful demonstrations.

One form of indirect action is voting in general or local elections. The UK functions using a system of representative democracy so citizens are able to elect the representative at local and national level that they feel best understands their needs. More importantly perhaps, at election time the electorate can vote out an incumbent representative they feel is not performing. In theory, within a representative democracy an individual can protest against a local authority policy or legislation from Westminster by voting for an opposite candidate at election time or, indeed, by standing for election themselves.

However as elections can be up to five years apart, citizens may feel that their views are not being considered effectively in the interim and the changes they wish to see are not being

actioned. In this instance they may decide the direct action of joining or creating a pressure group to drive that change forward may be their best option. Achieving change may be difficult as many other groups compete for government attention. To successfully gain government attention and cooperation in policy development, pressure groups must possess some of the following qualities.

- Authority over its members – pressure groups may find that their own members can not agree on certain details, this does not present a united front and means government will be reluctant to deal with them.
- Expertise – government must be sure that pressure groups they consult are highly knowledgeable on their issue.
- Compatible with party in power – groups find that the political ideologies of the political party in power may define how they are received. For example, **trade unions** within the UK have traditionally been consulted on issues affecting workers and industry by Labour more readily than by Conservatives. This is due to Labour's history of protection of the rights of workers – although recently the changing priorities of the Labour party have altered this trend.
- Compatibility with public opinion – groups whose aims are contrary to the majority of public opinion are unlikely to be invited to discuss policy development. For example, a group that wishes to relax the laws on ownership of firearms would not be compatible with general public opinion and would thus be unpopular within government.
- Knowledge of the systems of government – a group with proven abilities to work well with government is likely to be consulted on future policy formation.

- Power to disrupt – in some cases pressure groups with the power to cause a great deal of disruption, for example hauliers that are threatening to protest over fuel prices, by striking or blocking vital highways, have the power to bring the country to a standstill. It may be wise in such cases, where groups have the potential to cause mass disruption, for government to enter into discussions with them.

Letter writing

In order to raise the profile of a particular issue, an individual acting independently, or as part of a pressure group, may use many methods to gain support for their cause. Letter writing may be the first step in this process – writing to MPs or local representatives is a simple way to bring attention to a particular issue, or simply to ask relevant questions. Letters to the press may also be an effective way of bringing people's attention to a particular subject – it can also be a great way to initiate public debate on an issue. Emails have become an increasingly popular way to contact MPs/MSPs/AMs and local representatives (see webaction on pages 236 and 281). Groups such as Amnesty use letters to protest against human rights abuse. By running campaigns encouraging citizens all over the world to write to those they believe have been unlawfully imprisoned, prisoners across the world can receive many bags of mail – highlighting to those detaining them the weight of support for their release.

Petitioning and leafleting

To successfully affect change it is important to contact those in positions of power. However proving to those in power that many other people also feel the same is key if a campaign is to be successful. Leafleting can provide a useful way of gathering this support – especially at a local level where the distribution area is smaller and costs can be minimised. This is a method that lends itself well to campaigns with greater funding as they have the ability to create the highest quality, eye-catching, persuasive literature and distribute it to the widest area.

Petitions can work in a similar way, as collecting signatures provides evidence that others support the cause. However petitions can prove very labour intensive as convincing power holders of their credibility means gathering hundreds or thousands of signatures. This can take time and effort to achieve, although the internet has proved invaluable at distributing petitions quickly and relatively effortlessly. Websites such as 10 Downing Street's petition site enable citizens to create and sign petitions, which can reach a huge audience – especially if links to then are sent in mass emails.

Demonstration

Although petitioning can provide clear documented evidence of support for a campaign, sometimes actually assembling people together 'in the flesh' can be hugely influential. Demonstration attracts attention and sends a clear visual message of the level of support behind a campaign. The march that took place through London in February 2003 to voice opposition to military action in Iraq proved to be one of the largest ever staged in the UK. Although it did not stop the Government from going to war in Iraq, it did allow British people a vehicle to very publicly announce their opposition. Demonstrations allow citizens to clearly state their feelings if government, elected to speak for the public, has been seen to fail.

This anti-Iraq war demonstration in February 2003 in London was one of the largest demonstrations staged in the UK

New technologies and democratic participation

Advances in technology have offered citizens new avenues through which to pursue democracy. The most obvious of these is the use of the internet. One of the main problems faced by campaign organisers is trying to contact large numbers of people, quickly and within budget. The internet has solved this problem and given campaigns a valuable tool by which to rally momentum behind a campaign relatively quickly. It also offers a space to collate large amounts of information on a topic in the form of a website, which interested parties can view at all times. Campaign groups can also contact their members easily with updates and newsletters via email and also gather support for petitions – gaining many signatures in a short space of time.

Contacting large numbers of people simultaneously has also changed the way in which demonstrations are organised. Mass congregations of people can assemble at a designated location, coordinated by email and text message to stage a protest. This was demonstrated recently by the impromptu demonstrations on the London tube system in protest against the legislation introduced to banning alcohol. Social networking sites such as Facebook and Twitter have also proved influential in this respect.

E-forums are also emerging as an opportunity for citizens to communicate about local issues and join together to affect change. By creating a forum, online communities can more easily discuss issues affecting them and organise campaigns to change those things they are dissatisfied with.

Web action

1] Explore **www.e-democracy.org.uk**: what sorts of issues are citizens talking about on their local forums in the UK?
2] Imagine you are starting an e-forum in your area:
   - what kinds of issues do you think citizens would want to talk about?
   - which issues do you think they should be discussing?
   - what difference might this make in your local community?

In recent years direct action has been favoured by groups that become frustrated with the slow progress they experience using indirect methods of campaigning and groups that seek maximum impact with the minimal resources available to them. Unfortunately, there have been cases of more extreme direct action involving dangerous behaviour and harassment or violence towards individuals.

Fathers 4 Justice (the pressure group campaigning against the bias of family courts towards the rights of mothers) entered the House of Commons in 2004, and threw purple flour at Tony Blair as a means of protest. This was a very visual way of gaining publicity as media outlets distributed footage across the country. Although this stunt raised awareness of the group's aims, it caused a great deal of concern about security measures within Parliament. It was also unlikely that Tony Blair's government would engage in serious talks with Fathers 4 Justice after it used such radical tactics.

A group of animal rights protestors took the use of direct action to its extreme, in their campaign to end experimentation on animals, by beating the Chief Executive of a company called Huntingdon Life Sciences (a company conducting animal experiments) using baseball bats. A court injunction had to be taken out to prevent the activists from going near any of the company's employees.

This was obviously an illegal and very violent way of taking action. It endangered the lives of other citizens as well as causing them undue stress and anxiety. Although such tactics attract media attention, this attention often proves negative for the activists involved.

Boycotts

As consumers become increasingly influential, the use of boycotts has become a powerful and well-utilised method of protest. By organising a mass boycott of a particular product or service, citizens can dramatically affect the profits or reputation of a particular organisation. They may also attempt to permanently change consumer habits or behaviour. A good example of this was the recent 'Chicken Out' campaign launched by Hugh Fearnley-Whittingstall and Jamie Oliver. By informing consumers of the realities of chicken farming in the UK they hoped to change their diets and their shopping habits, thus putting pressure on farmers to change their farming practices and government its legislation on chicken rearing. The power of the consumer can be very successful as it directly affects the profits of the organisations targeted.

The campaign that changed the eating habits of a nation

Boycott of battery chickens forces supermarkets to think ethically

Sales of factory-farmed chickens have slumped since a high-profile campaign raised awareness of the cruelty at the heart of the poultry industry and implored consumers to pay more to improve the animals' welfare.

In a victory for campaigners who have fought to expose the short and brutal lives of broiler birds, shoppers have bought millions more free-range and organic birds while leaving mass-produced chickens on the shelves.

Sales of free-range poultry shot up by 35 per cent last month compared with January 2007, while sales of standard indoor birds fell by 7 per cent, according to a survey of 25,000 shoppers by the market research company TNS.

Supermarkets have been stripped of free-range birds, prompting complaints from frustrated shoppers keen to embrace the movement away from intensive farming. *continued*

The rise in sales would have been even higher if poultry producers had been able to keep up with demand. Many suppliers in the £2bn-a-year poultry industry are now expected to convert cramped chicken sheds into more spacious accommodation.

Tesco, the country's biggest retailer, has doubled its order for higher-welfare chickens while Sainsbury's has been flabbergasted by the 'unprecedented' spurt in demand and forced to import free-range birds from France.

In the weeks after the chefs Hugh Fearnley-Whittingstall and Jamie Oliver launched a high-profile campaign on Channel 4, supermarkets had stated that sales of 'standard' chickens had held up, and even increased.

But the new national sales data suggests that shoppers' priorities have shifted dramatically. If the TNS data was extrapolated to the rest of the UK, it suggests sales of factory-farmed chickens dipped by 10 million, while shoppers bought 4.4 million more free-range chickens. Overall, chicken sales were down by 4.8 per cent, perhaps because many people, when faced with an absence of free-range chicken, simply bought no chicken.

The campaign against mass-produced poultry, of which a quarter have difficulty walking as a result of wading around in their own waste, is to be intensified. Fearnley-Whittingstall intends to produce a new television show on chickens later this year, updating viewers on the campaign and urging more people to join what he hopes will turn into a free-range revolution. 'We are going to keep the pressure up and we are going to do everything we can to make sure that this is not a flash in the pan,' he said.

During his Hugh's Chicken Run shows, residents of the Devon town of Axminster were invited to see free-range and intensive systems running alongside each other in a shed; many left in tears. According to separate polling by ACNielsen, half of the four million viewers who saw the shows said they would buy better chicken.

The cruelty inflicted on broiler birds was also exposed in secret footage from a farm, reported last month in *The Independent*. Earlier this month – to the disgust of the National Farmers' Union and animal welfare groups – Tesco announced a week-long offer of a £1.99 chicken. The move is believed by welfare campaigners to have been an attempt to shift unsold standard birds.

'If the growing consumer demand for free-range, organic and higher-welfare chicken continues, availability in store could certainly become an important barrier to consumer choice, at least in the short term,' said Maria Carrol, ACNielsen's consumer insight manager.

Compassion in World Farming, a campaign group which shot undercover footage inside a chicken shed in Herefordshire, was jubilant. 'It seems to me that there is a swath of people who have been moved by the programmes and it seems to be a lasting move, a definite move away from standard to free-range,' said its food policy officer Rowen West-Henzell. 'That's great. But what we need to do is to work with the people who still buy standard and we are 100 per cent committed to giving consumers the facts about poultry production and letting them make their own minds up. With the programme they were exposed to that reality.'

About 800 million chickens are bred in the UK every year. About 92 per cent of them are still of the 'standard' variety, despite the increase this year.

'I am thrilled but I am still a little bit cautious,' said Fearnley-Whittingstall. 'I am delighted we have helped create this change and I am delighted that, two months after the show, there appears to be no letting up.

'I just hope the British retailers and the industry are talking to each other, making sure that new free-range farms are built and new RSPCA Freedom Food farms are built to cater for a growing demand for high welfare chicken.'

Martin Hickman, *The Independent*, 28 February 2008

ACTIVITY 1

Study the article on pages 277–8.
1) How did Jamie Oliver and Hugh Fearnley-Whittingstall ask people to protest against battery farming?
2) What other methods did they use in their campaign?
3) Which factors do you think assisted the campaign?
4) What barriers to success were there?

High level/violent
Assassinations
Bombs
Use of letter bombs
Planned violence
Demonstrations – noisy and possibly violent
Denial of function/strikes
International collaborative action
Demonstrations with placards
Marches
Contact MPs/MEPs
Contact civil servants
Join action group
Write to papers
Advertising
Phone-ins
Contact councillors
Contact local government officers
Letters
Petitions
Low level activity/peaceful

Pressure group methods
Jones, B (2007) *Politics UK*, p257

Strike action

Citizens use strike action – refusing on mass to carry out their normal duties – especially when they wish to highlight the amount and value of the work they do. This type of action is often used in pay disputes. Strikes are usually associated with membership to trade unions and in the UK strike action must be approved by most members of a union for it to be legitimate. Recent strike action by postal workers, rail workers, teachers and firefighters have attracted much press attention for the disruption they cause to the population. For this reason they can prove very useful methods of forcing change – but are viewed as a last resort only after agreement cannot be reached through negotiation.

Strike action can also prove detrimental to the cause of a campaign if for example a union of workers wish to prove the worth of the service they provide but in actual fact services are either provided by someone else or manage to function with less manpower. In these instances, unions are left with little bargaining power. At the beginning of the twentieth century the Suffragette movement famously used hunger strike as a means of protest against the laws prohibiting women from voting. Hunger strike is an incredibly dangerous method of attempting to affect change yet is still used as a means of protest.

ACTIVITY 2

Study the diagram above.
1) In pairs discuss at which point on the diagram you believe pressure groups should not continue action.
2) Explain your reasons for choosing this point on the diagram.
3) Is it ever acceptable for pressure groups to use violence? Give reasons for your answer.
4) Analyse what the justification for violent action by some pressure groups might be.

Success and failure of campaigns

It is inevitable that of the many campaigns launched, some will be successful and others will fail. The two sources on pages 280–1 highlight this fact. The Save Stonehenge campaign was set up in response to plans to build a large road tunnel around the site of Stonehenge. The plans were scrapped and Save Stonehenge claimed victory. Conversely, plans to bypass through large areas of woodland around Newbury to ease traffic in the town were fought through direct action involving highly publicised demonstrations in 1996. This campaign was unsuccessful and the bypass was built regardless.

Newbury bypass ten years on – (ten years since work started – reunion)

On Saturday 7th January around 60 people gathered at Middle Oak to remember the resistance against the Newbury Bypass (A34), and reveal the huge traffic growth that's come since.

It's ten years on Monday since the destruction of around 10,000 trees began in earnest, or rather should have done – back then protestors scored an early victory by blockading the entrance to the security compound with scaffolding tripods, thus ensuring no vehicles could leave. The start of work heralded the most full-on phase of the '3rd Battle of Newbury', Britain's biggest ever road protest, which saw over thirty different tree camps set up to oppose the road and around one thousand arrests.

Ten years on and the same issues are still there. Research over recent years and in particular last year has shown that the Bypass has fuelled traffic growth of almost 50 per cent (compared with a national average of 5 per cent). Figures also show that local congestion is as bad at rush hour as it was before the building of the bypass – and that the new road encouraged more traffic.

Rebecca Lush from Road Block said in a statement:

'In 1995 we predicted the road would bring only short term relief, but even we did not anticipate that the traffic would rise again so quickly. Ten years on we are sad to see Newbury is still grid locked at rush hour, but has sacrificed its beautiful pristine countryside forever. The lessons must be learned, that building more roads generates more traffic. However the Government is still building roads and encouraging traffic growth. More roads mean more traffic, which means more climate change. We must change direction, and Newbury is an example of a failed twentieth century transport policy that must never be repeated'.

The A34 Newbury Bypass was Britain's most controversial road-building project. Local campaigners battled against the road throughout the 1980s, their efforts culminating in a public inquiry in 1988 (with a minor follow-up inquiry in 1992). When the public inquiry found in favour of the road, there followed a spectacular campaign from 1994 to 1998 that took in every form of protest, from mass letter writing and European lobbying to mass non-violent direct action and property damage.

The building of the road saw four Sites of Special Scientific Interest damaged or destroyed at Snelsmore Common, the River Kennet, the River Lambourn and the Kennet Flood Plains (previously home to the Desmoulin's Whorl Snail, discovered during the construction of the road); as well as this the road construction also damaged the site of the First Battle of Newbury in the English Civil War in 1643, and the North Wessex Downs Area of Outstanding Natural Beauty.

www.Indymedia.org.uk, 7 January 2006

Tunnel under Stonehenge scrapped

A plan to build a tunnel under Stonehenge has been axed.

The Department of Transport reviewed plans to build a 1.3 mile tunnel along with a bypass to the west of the monument.

But government ministers decided that the estimated £500 million bill for the scheme was too high.

Fleur de Rhe-Philipe, Wiltshire County Council cabinet member for the Environment, Transport & Economic Development, said: 'We are disappointed the Government has decided not to go ahead with the upgrading of the A303 at Stonehenge'.

Plans to improve the A303, one of the major arterial roads to the West Country, have been in the works for more than 20 years.

'After many years of discussion, a widely supported scheme had been developed which solved the traffic problems on the A303 past Stonehenge and improved the setting of the stones, but the opportunity has now been lost,' Coun Fleur de Rhe-Philipe said.

While many parts of the project attracted huge opposition, the proposal to route the A303 through a tunnel was the one bit of the scheme which received wide backing.

Bodies including the Council for British Archaeology, the International Council for Monuments and Sites and the National Trust, were among those advocating a longer tunnel to protect Stonehenge, a World Heritage Site.

Supporters of the tunnel argued that it would remove roads from the stones in Wiltshire which are believed to date back to 3,100 BC.

The decision to axe the road schemes was welcomed last night by Chris Woodford, spokesman for the Save Stonehenge campaign.

'On balance it is good news, because our fear is that they would press ahead with a comprehensive road scheme and that would have been the wrong thing to do.'

www.wiltshiretimes.co.uk, 6 December 2007

ACTIVITY 3

Compare the sources above. In small groups discuss the following.
1) Which factors affected the outcomes of the Save Stonehenge campaign and the campaign to save the Newbury Bypass? Why do you think one campaign was more successful than the other?
2) What do you think the Newbury campaigners could have done differently to improve their chances of success?

Web action

Using the work you did earlier in the topic on important problems or issues in your area – discuss as a class the issues you came up with. Decide individually on the issue you believe is the most pressing. Use the website **www.writetothem.com** to decide which of your representatives is best to contact in relation to this issue (local councillor, MP, MSP, MEP etc.) and draft an email or letter to them. You may want to include an overview and possibly recommendations or ideas on how to tackle it.

5 What are the key factors in successful campaigning?

What is required for a campaign to succeed?

We have explored pressure groups in depth and the ways in which citizens can bring about change. This topic looks at the many factors that affect the ability of a campaign to successfully achieve its aims.

Membership

Mass membership is not only useful in proving public support for a particular cause but also offers citizens a connection to an organisation outside of the parliamentary system. This provides an important democratic alternative for those who feel excluded or misrepresented by the traditional political system. It can also provide very public scrutiny of government – therefore strengthening democracy.

If a group has a large number of members it can prove a valuable tool in negotiations with government, which may in turn create a change in policy or legislation. Any administration within a representative democracy is beholden to its voters; when faced with a request for change by a number of the electorate it is therefore in its interest to listen, or at least be seen to be listening. Also, any group has the potential for support beyond its actual membership as friends and family may also be sympathetic to a cause although they are not fee-paying members of a pressure group. This means that groups, such as the RSPCA, can have a large membership but even wider support among the population as a whole. Such support can represent a surprisingly large proportion of the electorate and therefore valuable votes for any political party that appears to take their issues on board.

High profile members or supporters, such as celebrities, can also add weight to a campaign as they can raise awareness of issues through media coverage. Members of the public who admire a particular personality may be drawn to a cause that celebrity is associated with. The subject matter of the cause can also prove a factor in the success of a pressure group or campaign, especially if it is an emotive subject that garners large swathes of support from the public and incites passionate responses from them – for example the National Society for the Protection of Children. Such groups may find that not only are they more likely to find large scale support but they may also receive more consistent support. Even small pressure groups or campaigns can have a large impact if they have strong, well organised support.

Nature of the cause

Emotive causes can obviously rally huge support amongst citizens but there are other factors related to the nature of the cause that can positively and adversely affect its impact and ultimate success. A campaign that is at direct odds with government policy may struggle to achieve its objectives if they depend on government cooperation, unless it can convince those in power that their policy is unpopular with the electorate.

Any campaign may be adversely affected by the strength, public appeal and success of alternative campaigns, for example, smaller campaigns such as the campaign to save Hatfield Forest may struggle to gain the media attention and funding of the Campaign to Protect Rural England with the well-known author Bill Bryson as its president. It is also worth considering how powerful a campaign can prove if its subject is highly topical. Timing can also prove detrimental to the success of a campaign. For example, if a campaign's aims happen to clash with a newsworthy issue it may find it very difficult to achieve success – a group campaigning to relax gun licensing laws is unlikely to gain public support or government cooperation if there has been a recent increase in the number of gun related crimes.

It has been claimed that campaigns stand more chance of success if they appeal to those socio-economic groups with greater access to education and subsequent skills and funding to achieve a greater chance of success. Others dispute this claim and argue the existence of trade unions as proof of the ability to affect change regardless of wealth or social status.

Methods

The way in which a campaign chooses to achieve its aims and objectives can be key to its success. Groups may try to accomplish their goals by 'physically' attempting to put a stop to issues they are unhappy about – for example animal rights protesters lying in the road to prevent trucks transporting live animals from reaching their destination. In addition, if such action is quite radical it may also prove newsworthy and gain the added asset of media coverage. The dynamic tactics used by Greenpeace, such as boarding whaling ships and attempting to sabotage their expeditions, also exemplify a campaign which attempts to take the issue 'into its own hands' by taking direct action to stop the problem they are campaigning against.

The use of direct action can shape the success of a campaign both positively and negatively. If direct action attracts the public's attention, gathers support and achieves a change in government policy or legislation then it can obviously prove a worthy strategy. However if direct action takes a form that is dangerous, harmful to others or embarrassing to government it may negatively impact a campaign.

Greenpeace's campaigning methods often take the matter 'into its own hands'

Organisation of resources, strategies and supporters can be the difference between success and failure for many campaigns. If the message from a campaign's leadership is not clear, or a coherent plan of action is not in place then a campaign may not capitalise on opportunities to gather support, raise awareness or funding.

Finance

The amount of money or resources behind a campaign always plays a role in its success or otherwise. Creating campaign materials and websites, paying for staffing and events is expensive and can mean that campaigns often stall while they try to generate more funds. Conversely, other campaigns may have sizeable campaign 'pots' and as such be able to pay large salaries to attract expertise in marketing, fund raising and public relations – all of which can result in a high profile campaign that attracts maximum support. Greater funding allows new ways to contact citizens en masse that can raise awareness of a subject overnight – for example through mass mail shots or via email. A campaign with a large amount of capital behind it can also afford to pay **political consultancies** to lobby government proficiently and arguably with a greater chance of success.

Role of the media

The media can prove an essential aspect of a campaign's success as it can be a guarantee much needed exposure – a way of targeting a very large audience or even a very specific **demographic**. Campaigns may use the media effectively to advertise their objectives with the ultimate aim of encouraging donations of time or money; but also simply to gain support for their cause.

If a campaign can choose the type of media it uses and pays for cleverly, it can seek out the largest audience and target the social groups within society that it thinks will be most sympathetic to it. For example, there would be little point in funding a TV advertisement for a campaign that was trying to cut road traffic during a programme about sports cars – those people watching the show might not be the

---

NSPCC ads target child cruelty

Children's charity the NSPCC is launching a television advertising campaign to encourage people to act against child cruelty by donating time or money. The commercials, developed by Saatchi & Saatchi, includes two TV commercials called 'Caravan' and 'Marathon'. The first ad, which features a violent mother and complacent father, aims to raise awareness of the fact that every month the NSPCC needs 2,000 volunteers for its ChildLine service. The second spot, which features a young girl who is terrified when her father enters her room at night, pushes the message that the charity needs to raise £7m a month through fundraising and donations. The television ads, which break on Wednesday night, will be supported by press, posters, a new website, Bethefullstop.com, and viral activity. The campaign will steer visitors to the website to learn how they can help the NSPCC through volunteering, fundraising, campaigning and donating. 'Many people feel that child abuse is too big a problem for them to do anything about,' said John Grounds, the director of communications at the NSPCC. 'Each act adds up to ending cruelty to children. Everyone can be part of the human barrier against child abuse.' In May, the NSPCC turned to the web to distribute an ad aimed at 11- to 16-year-olds in a campaign against sexual abuse. The ad ran on a special website, Donthideit.com. Earlier this year the charity also ran a campaign featuring stars including Johnny Vegas, Christian Slater, Gillian Anderson and Bruce Forsyth that aimed to get the public to take part in its £10m Dream Auction run in partnership with eBay.

Mark Sweney, *MediaGuardian*, 13 September 2006

ACTIVITY 1

Read the source above.
1) How effective is TV in raising awareness for campaigns such as the NSPCC's 'Full Stop' campaign?
2) Would it be effective for all campaigns?
3) Which factors do you think would define its effectiveness? Why?
4) Select a different campaign and suggest an alternative media source by which to publicise it. Explain your choice.

most sympathetic to that particular cause. It is important for campaigns to be prudent and consider the best 'placing' for their media coverage, whether it is via radio, TV, newspaper or online as it requires the use of what are likely to be precious funds – thus having a lasting impact on the success of a campaign.

Media coverage is not always in the hands of those orchestrating a campaign and the way in which it is reported via the media can also affect how successful it proves. A media outlet's political bias affects its reporting. If a pressure group or campaign sits uncomfortably with the reporting media outlet's political affiliations it is unlikely to be portrayed entirely favourably. The newspaper or news channel will also be mindful of the profile of its typical reader/viewer and will have a clear target audience with regards to social class, race, age, gender and ethnicity. This affects the language and content of any report regarding a particular campaign; again affecting the image of that campaign.

The increased use of the internet also means that ordinary citizens can use web pages, video postings, blogs and social networking sites to raise awareness, support and funds for campaigns or even publicly criticise them. This form of media, more than any other, offers campaigns an exciting '**new media**' by which to increase the likelihood of success in achieving their aims. It also allows citizens many new forums in which to discuss campaigns without bias from large media outlets. Many charities and political groups now use social networking sites to pass on information and raise awareness

of new campaigns, following an upsurge of groups linked to social issues set up on sites such as Facebook and Bebo. For example, Amnesty International linked with social networking sites for a human rights campaign in 2007 as a direct result of observing a massive surge of interest in a Facebook group on human rights in Burma (Myanmar) earlier in the year.

Web action

1) In small groups, research a particular campaign – it may be local, national, global or even one you are involved with personally. Prepare a presentation on this campaign. It should include the following:
   - the ways in which that campaign uses new media to gain support, funding or raise awareness of its aims
   - suggestions on how you think this could be improved
   - the advantages of using new media
   - problems with using these forms of communication
   - a conclusion that outlines the factors that have affected the success or failure of the campaign.

6 The impact of campaigns on political decision making and political attitudes

This topic discusses three pressure group case studies:

- the Countryside Alliance
- Fathers 4 Justice
- Stop the War Coalition.

The aims of the groups, their methods and their impact on political decision making and attitudes are explored.

The Countryside Alliance

www.countryside-alliance.org

Aims

The Countryside Alliance was formed in 1997 by merging the British Field Sports Society, the Countryside Movement and the Countryside Business Group, in response to the Labour Government's plan to hold a free vote on whether hunting with hounds should be banned – a ban has since been passed via the Hunting Act 2004.

The Countryside Alliance aims are to protect the interests of those living and working in the countryside, and the countryside itself. It does this through lobbying government in order to influence policy and legislation. Typically it is difficult to make a clear distinction as to whether the Countryside Alliance is a cause or sectional group as some of its members may well have a financial interest in the aims of the pressure group (for example a supplier of feed or manufacturers/stockists of hunt wear have a financial interest in countryside pursuits). But those living in the country or those who are passionate about a rural way of life (opposing, for example, the closure of their local post office) also have cause to support the pressure group.

Methods

The Countryside Alliance uses both direct and indirect action, engaging in well organised, large scale demonstrations and lobbying government via traditional channels. They have also been linked to more controversial direct action (see article on page 287). They are funded through membership fees and donation.

Whilst the Labour party is in government it is likely they will remain an outsider group but this status may change if the Conservatives were to gain power as they have proposed to repeal the Hunting Act 2004. The Countryside Alliance's activity is wide ranging and involves issues relating not just to hunting but also countryside management, industry, wildlife protection, education, housing, farming and country pursuits (for example angling and shooting). Its website includes clear printable policy documents and links to relevant newspaper articles. The Alliance runs awards ceremonies to promote countryside retailers and other events to promote support for their causes.

Evaluation of effectiveness

A hurdle to achieving the aims of the Countryside Alliance has been the 'class' debate – with many people believing that the Alliance's cause revolves around protecting a distinctly upper class way of life, with no relevance to those living on low incomes in urban areas. Those supporters of the cause would argue that the countryside provides a vital function ecologically, along with providing food and green space to all citizens, regardless of where they live. They would also argue that a large proportion of the population lives in rural areas and therefore their voices should not be ignored. The Countryside Alliance has been successful in raising support (gaining over 100,000 members) and organising large scale, publicity generating marches. However it has been unsuccessful in preventing or repealing the Hunting Act 2004, which banned hunting with dogs, amongst other restrictions on hunting.

The Alliance is concerned with many other issues regarding the countryside which it provides regular and consistent support for, lobbies government and also attempts to maintain the public interest. However the hunting ban has been the most high profile of its causes and therefore it has not achieved its greatest and most controversial aim. It can be said however, that it has enabled a national debate on hunting issues and the moral concepts surrounding them, giving those advocates of hunting a strong vehicle through which to voice their perspectives and rationale.

Invasion of the Commons: Five protesters storm chamber

Ministers were last night considering a ban on demonstrations in Parliament Square and the introduction of armed police to guard the doors of the House of Commons in the wake of the most flagrant breach of parliamentary security in living memory.

Five protesters – members of the Countryside Alliance – with clear inside knowledge of the layout of the Commons, stormed the floor of the chamber at 4.20pm yesterday. The intruders had evaded armed police outside parliament and footmen in tights by donning construction suits and using back stairs.

Their entry route took them within yards of the offices of cabinet ministers, including the prime minister, Tony Blair, the foreign secretary, Jack Straw, and the home secretary, David Blunkett.

There were suggestions that a Tory MP's researcher may have been involved. Questions were also being asked why a door leading to the floor of the Commons that should have been locked had been left open.

The group of eight protesters took off their suits in a corridor above the Commons chamber, and then invaded the chamber, shouting at the rural affairs minister, Alun Michael: 'This is is not democracy. This is a denial of democracy.'

Three of the eight protesters, all under arrest last night, were stopped before they reached the chamber. They were arrested for uttering a forged instrument, burglary with intent to commit criminal damage, and violent disorder.

The invasion forced a 20-minute suspension of proceedings as stunned MPs assessed the violation of democratic debate. But the protest failed to stop mainly Labour MPs forcing through in one day a bill banning hunting. The vote was 356 to 166 at the bill's second reading. Mr Blair, a previous opponent of fox hunting, did not vote.

The Countryside Alliance's chairman, John Jackson, condemned 'these lawless activities which are selfish and self-indulgent. However appalling the behaviour of Alun Michael, people should not allow themselves to be provoked into activities of this kind which can only harm the cause for which thousands of their fellows are demonstrating peacefully'.

Conservative MPs also condemned the violence unequivocally.

Patrick Wintour and Peter Hetherington, *the Guardian*, **16 September 2004**

Countryside Alliance members stormed Parliament in September 2004 as part of their campaign

Read the article on page 287.

1) In groups, discuss the advantages and disadvantages of the protests undertaken by the Countryside Alliance on this occasion.
2) Did the protest achieve its aims?
3) Why might this form of protest have been criticised?
4) Why do you think the chairman of the Countryside Alliance condemned them?

Fathers 4 Justice

www.fathers-4-justice.org

Aims

Fathers 4 Justice is a pressure group founded by Matt O'Connor after he struggled to obtain satisfactory custody of his two children after divorce. He and other members believe that family law is biased in favour of mothers and neglects the rights of fathers. Its aim is to achieve reform of the closed family court system with a more open system, possibly involving judgement by an individual's peers. They believe that within the family court system mothers and fathers should have equal rights when determining how family disputes are settled. They also suggest mandatory **mediation** for couples as a first step before they can take a family dispute to court and an emphasis, through legislation, on joint parenting as opposed to awarding a parent sole custody.

Its proposals for a more open system of family law are criticised by those who believe such a change to law would breach children's right to privacy, something that hearing family cases in a closed court protects. Fathers 4 Justice could be viewed as a cause group as those involved have an interest based on improving the visitation or custody arrangements of their children, but that isn't a precursor to membership as any individual who felt that family laws is in need of reform could join – they would not necessarily have to be a father to become a member.

Methods

Fathers 4 Justice is funded through membership fees and donations. The methods used by Fathers 4 Justice can certainly be described as examples of direct action although they claim their intention is to be satirical and **subvert** the system. The very public 'stunts' staged by the group are intended to cause disruption and attract wide scale publicity. These have centred around the theme of 'Superheroes' with fathers climbing cranes dressed as Spiderman, gaining access to the Queen's balcony at Buckingham palace dressed as Batman and throwing purple flour at the Prime Minister whilst he spoke in the House of Commons.

Groups using such dynamic tactics struggle to be accepted as an insider pressure group as their actions either embarrass government or undermine its power – flour-bombing the Prime Minister is not a likely means of creating open discussion with government. However such strategies are incredibly successful in gaining press attention and publicity, which may garner support and create increased membership that may in turn prove useful in strengthening the campaign. Ensuring media coverage when undertaking the kinds of stunts that Fathers 4 Justice use is essential, as this allows optimum impact. It is also beneficial to arrange radio and TV appearances as a way of maintaining attention on the issues of inequality in family law.

This Fathers 4 Justice publicity stunt is certainly an example of direct action

Evaluation

Fathers 4 Justice has been highly successful in focusing attention on the difficulties fathers experience when going through custody or maintenance disputes following divorce. However it has also faced criticism by those that believe its methods are irresponsible, especially as many of their 'stunts' are illegal. They also risk setting a negative example to children who may emulate them. Climbing cranes and buildings is also dangerous and this is seen by some as irresponsible behaviour for a parent, as they risk being hurt or fatally injured. Those who defend Fathers 4 Justice's methods argue that they are setting a positive example for their children as they prove just how desperately they wish to play a larger role in their lives.

Leadership is an important factor in the success of Fathers 4 Justice and its leader, Matt O'Connor, has been heralded as the driving force behind its high profile. With many public appearances on TV and radio Matt O'Connor is a charismatic persona able to communicate the aims and motivation behind the Fathers 4 Justice group. Such a figurehead is a useful tool and helps the group to gain public support and understanding. The topic of parenting is perhaps one of the most emotive for many people and for this reason the cause itself is likely to gain attention as increasing numbers of families experience divorce.

Fathers 4 Justice's claim that its impact on decision making has been to force the Government to 'advance proposals to open up the secret family courts to greater scrutiny and propose tougher enforcement of contact orders.' However government would be unlikely to concede that the actions of such a dynamic pressure group has had any impact on their proposals – not least because it would set a dangerous precedent for future pressure groups, possibly encouraging them to undertake disruptive direct action as the main method of achieving their aims.

ACTIVITY 2

Read the article on page 290 on the protest that members of Fathers 4 Justice undertook on top of Harriet Harman's home.
1) Why might they have chosen Harriet Harman's home specifically?
2) Why might this protest have been criticised?
3) In which ways was it successful?

Fathers 4 Justice campaigners climb onto Harriet Harman's roof

Two Fathers 4 Justice campaigners have climbed onto the roof of Labour Party deputy leader Harriet Harman, Scotland Yard said.

It is the second time in little over a month the group has staged a protest at Ms Harman's home in Herne Hill, south London.

A Scotland Yard spokesman said police were called at 6.22am and officers are in attendance. It is not known if Ms Harman was at home when the incident began.

The pair were dressed as superheroes, with one in a Batman costume and the other dressed as Spiderman.

Last month two protesters, Jolly Stanesby and Mark Harris, both from south Devon, scaled the roof of Ms Harman's home in similar costumes.

Mr Stanesby spent more than 24 hours on the Cabinet minister's roof in a protest that began on June 8 and ended the next day.

The pair were bailed by police until July 16 pending further police inquiries.

The group said at the time it wanted to highlight the fact that fathers were being made redundant emotionally in the courts, and now biologically in the new Human Fertilisation and Embryology Bill.

Last month's protest forced Ms Harman, Minister for Women and Equality, out of her home.

www.telegraph.co.uk, 9 July 2008

Stop the War Coalition

www.stopwar.org.uk

Aims

The Stop the War Coalition was formed in September 2001 in response to what it describes as the US's 'war against terrorism'. The core belief of the group is that this war, constituted by conflicts in Iraq and Afghanistan, is unjust, illegal and initiated for reasons other than those presented to the public. It was formed after a large group of people met to discuss the impending conflict in Iraq and can be described as an example of a cause group, as its members do not benefit financially from membership. Anyone who agrees with the group's aims and objectives is able to join the pressure group. The Stop the War Coalition has agreed that its aims may be amended so that it can adjust to developments in the war against terrorism. Although it is agreed that members are free to organise their own protests, the aim of the Stop the War Coalition is to allow easy organisation of the many groups that oppose war. By creating one 'umbrella' group it can efficiently organise mass demonstrations that achieve maximum impact.

Methods

Financed through membership fees and donations, an important strategy used by the Stop the War Coalition is the use of inclusive and open local groups. This allows more effective forums for discussion and delivery of information/lectures etc. The Stop the War Coalition has encouraged groups that agree with its aims to affiliate with them, such as the Campaign for Nuclear Disarmament and the Muslim Council of Britain, this allows it to gain strength of support and influence. Its website is used successfully to relay news and video clips of recent speakers and events to all individuals and affiliated groups. Direct action is used in the form of peaceful demonstrations or marches. An example of indirect action – writing an article or letter that features in a newspaper – can be seen in the national newspaper article written by the Chairman of the Stop the War Coalition. The group also counts sympathetic academics, MPs and high profile figures such as Tony Benn amongst its supporters – all of which help to articulate and publicise the case for opposition to war. The group is likely to remain an outsider group as long as the administration that took Britain into war remains in power. However should those who sympathise with the cause find power or influence they could possibly gain insider status.

Evaluation

Such a huge collective action by citizens cannot fail, in some respect, to affect decision making by government. However by not halting the Government's movement to war many felt the group had failed. The demonstration staged by the Stop the War Coalition in February 2003 was the largest in British history and as such the group can boast success in mobilising an historic mass turnout. A well publicised mass march on the scale of that organised by the Stop the War coalition also provides citizens with a very clear alternative viewpoint to that being presented by the Government. This is a vital component to effective democracy and a definite influence on the political attitudes of citizens. It might be argued that the future of such a pressure group is limited in the face of mighty opposition from a super power such as the US, and all the time

the US and its allies remain in Iraq and Afghanistan their existence seems futile. However the Stop the War Coalition remains the most unified voice of opposition to the war and this is an important way for those citizens who disagree with the war to sustain pressure to end the occupation of Iraq. The group also allows debate and raises awareness of racism and incursions on civil liberties that have occurred as a result of the war.

Stop the War Coalition protest in February 2003

We didn't stop that war, but may have stopped the next

Five years ago, the biggest political protest in our history served to explode the myth of public apathy

Five years ago this week most readers of this newspaper were making plans to go on a demonstration. More surprisingly, just as many *Daily Telegraph* readers were getting ready for the same event. For most of those who marched against the Iraq war on February 15 2003 it was the first time they had ever demonstrated for or against anything in their lives. It was a protest such as Britain had never seen before, all-embracing in its diversity and imposing in its unity of purpose.

While there are always arguments over the size of demonstrations (the 2 million-or-so figure we claim is supported by considerable polling and photographic evidence), there is no dispute that this was not merely the country's biggest political protest, but the biggest by a substantial order of magnitude.

Two things are obvious about the demonstration to 'stop the war'. First, the millions on the march were right. Not just right on balance, but right on every single aspect of the question. There were no weapons of mass destruction, Iraq did turn into a bloodbath, the invasion did not help resolve the crisis in the Middle East, and it did damage the cohesion of our own society and imperil our civil liberties while not making us one whit safer from terrorism. So the people were smarter than the politicians.

Second the demonstration did not stop the war. Our hope had been that mass protest could drive the British Government out of its aggressive alliance with Bush and that the latter, isolated internationally as a result, would come under intensified domestic pressure. We came very close, as Donald Rumsfeld made clear. In the wake of February 15, Washington told Blair he could stand down our army if he wanted to.

The prime minister ignored that offer and the people he represents alike. However, failing is not the same thing as making no difference. February 15 has cast a long shadow over British politics since, and contributed to Blair's departure from office under circumstances – in public odium and with an exasperated party – scarcely of his choosing. What war have we stopped? The next one, perhaps.

The demonstration was the apex of a broader movement which touched almost every part of society in 2003. This included the greatest-ever engagement of British Muslims in active politics, thousands of school student walkouts, peaceful civil disruption in towns across the country, local authorities coming out against the war, and train drivers declining to move munitions for the invasion.

It was a movement entirely outside the established structures which normally mediate the relationship between people and power. It was organised by the Stop the War Coalition (with CND and the Muslim Association of Britain as our partners), a campaign not 18 months old and run on a shoestring.

Hundreds of thousands of trade unionists joined the demonstration, while the TUC – its eyes on its ministerial connections, not its members – maintained a frigid indifference. Labour and Tory party members protested against their leaders, while Liberal Democrats dragged their hierarchy to the demonstration behind them. Marching at the head of the demonstration, I missed what may have been the most telling sight of the day – Piccadilly blocked by people without a single banner among them. This was the march of the unmobilised.

It was also a march against Murdoch and his mendacious press, exploding the myth of his political omnipotence. Rupert said war, the people said no. All Alastair Campbell's strategy of controlling opinion through appeasing *The Sun* in vain!

The demonstration, and the movement around it, exploded the notion that society is slumped in a consumer-sodden apathy, and incapable of political engagement. The country's biggest mass movement followed a general election with the lowest turnout in modern times, and preceded one in which participation was scarcely improved. The problem is the system, not the people.

So perhaps the biggest lesson of February 15 is that it embodied the failure of representative democracy. It highlighted a gap between the electorate and the elected, a gap several hundred thousand lives have slipped down as a result.

The anti-war movement has lived under the shadow of that immense mobilisation too. But it was followed the next month by the biggest demonstration against a war British troops were actually fighting, by the biggest-ever weekday march (against the Bush visit to London later in 2003), by an unprecedented movement of military families against the war, and by a dozen further marches – including one which will mark the fifth anniversary of the war itself, on March 15. Opposition to empire has been put at the heart of politics as never before.

Emily Churchill, a Birmingham school student at the time, described the experience as 'trying to steer the course of our country with our own hands'. Of course in 2003 other, American, hands were on the wheel. But the lesson of February 15 is that we can and we will.

Andrew Murray has been chair of the Stop the War Coalition since 2001.

Andrew Murray, *the Guardian*, 13 February 2008

ACTIVITY 3

Read the article on pages 292–93 on the Stop the War Coalition.
1) How is the march described as being successful – what did it achieve?
2) How might it be viewed as unsuccessful?
3) What does the author of the article say was the 'biggest lesson' of the march?

Web action

1) Research another pressure group that interests you. It may be helpful to start with a topic you are interested in and then to research associated pressure groups. The list below may provide some prompts:
   - environmental issues
   - welfare
   - human rights
   - animal rights
   - local area issues
   - health
   - sport
   - crime
   - transport.
2) Write a report to:
   - explain the main aims and methods of the group
   - evaluate how effective it has been in achieving its aims and its impact on political decision making and attitudes
   - analyse the reasons for its success or failure
   - describe how its work is continuing.

Exam questions

SECTION B: MAKING A DIFFERENCE
Answer Question 4 and **either** Question 5 **or** Question 6.

This section carries 30 marks.

4 Read the extract below and answer parts (a) and (b) which follow.

In the North West, set to return eight MEPs on June 4, one fewer than last time, there are fears that disenchantment with mainstream politicians will result in an all-time low turn-out in a region which returns the lowest polls in Europe. In this atmosphere, UKIP candidates could fill their boots, and Nick Griffin, of the British National Party (BNP), could win a platform in Brussels.

Paul Nuttall, the cheerful Scouse chairman of UKIP, travelled to Blackpool on Friday to officially welcome Frank Carson, the comedian, into the fold. This week the party will unveil 176 billboards demanding British jobs ahead of migrant workers.

On the leafy streets of Dodleston, Mr Williams knocked on the door of a mother of two young girls who told him that, no, she would not be voting this time around.

"It is just with everything going on at the moment – my husband is being made redundant and all you read about is how wealthy MPs are. Well, we are not. Not voting feels like all I can do."

The Times, **18 May 2009**

Your answers should refer to the extract as appropriate, but you should also include other relevant information.

(a) Identify two reasons for the decline in voter turnout in recent years. (*5 marks*)

(b) Why should citizens be concerned about the decline in voter turnout? (*10 marks*)

Either:

5 Assess the ways in which citizens can bring about change.

(*15 marks*)

Or:

6 To what extent do pressure groups strengthen democracy? (*15 marks*)

ASSESSMENT GUIDANCE

Chapter 7: Active citizenship – skills and participation

Some ideas on where to start …

The AQA specification requires students to complete an active citizenship profile, on which they also answer questions in their Unit 2 examination. This is a really important way of getting real experience of some of the issues studied during the AS course. The profile itself is separated into three sections.

1 The informed citizen: gathering or researching information on an area of Citizenship Studies.
2 The participating citizen: discussing, evaluating or planning, using knowledge acquired.
3 The active citizen: the process of organising change in this area, based on information, discussion and planning in stages 1) and 2).

Under each of these headings, students log examples of activities that fall within these three areas. It could be the case that information gathered and applied in sections 1) and 2) then formulates an activity that can be logged in section 3). This could be completed in one whole school/college exercise or throughout the course.

However it could be the case that students log unrelated activities in each section. For example, a student may log activities involving research into case studies of human rights abuse in section 1) and discussions around the extent to which human rights are abused in the UK in section 2), but they may also regularly attend school council meetings, affecting change in areas unrelated to the human rights agenda – this could still be logged in section 3).

It may be the case that schools or colleges decide to task their citizenship classes with a specific activity – for example, organising school council elections. They would then have to research elections, organise the election process and then execute the election (fulfilling all three aspects of the *active citizenship profile*).

However, students may undertake a discrete active citizenship project, researching a particular area of interest to them, discussing it with their peers and relevant parties, creating an action plan and then attempting to affect change.

If students choose to undertake an active citizenship project in this way, they may find the following process useful.

Research and write reports on existing examples of active citizenship

Having studied Unit 1 of Citizenship Studies, students may already have particular examples of active citizenship they wish to explore – examples of active citizenship in their school, college, or possibly national or international examples of active citizenship.

This research could be turned into a report, detailing the process of this active citizenship and an evaluation of what it achieved and possible ways it could have been improved.

It may also be useful to then create an 'active citizenship display' of this information somewhere within school or college as a means of informing other students about active citizenship and its potential for positive change.

Discussion

Students could present information on their chosen examples to the rest of their group. In this way students are able to share many examples of active citizenship. It may also be productive to let this inform discussion about which examples students found most interesting and why. From these discussions students may also begin to identify areas that they themselves are interested in. It may also be useful to have class discussions to identify issues that students

are unhappy/dissatisfied with as a means of highlighting areas to research further in preparation for an active citizenship project.

Such discussions may also give students the opportunity to give ideas and advice to their peers on sources of information or action planning.

If students are struggling to identify areas of interest to them, it may be useful for teachers to have constructed some active citizenship tasks that students can be given, for example being asked to arrange the student council elections or improvement of facilities within school or college. However such projects are only likely to be enthusiastically pursued by students if the motivation for them originates with the students themselves.

In order to allow plenty of time for students to work on their projects it may be practical to begin planning them early in the academic year. This gives more time for students to work through their projects, improves the chances of them achieving their aims and allows maximum benefit from reflection. It is likely that those students working in groups will need to organise meetings outside of lesson time in order to allocate tasks, keep each other updated and maintain momentum.

Decisions on detail

Should students conceive an active citizenship project of their own, it can be very useful to hold 'think tank' sessions as a class in which students can assist each other with useful ideas for others' projects – possibly identifying new strategies and also possible hurdles to success. They should also identify which areas of the curriculum their project relates to. It's obviously key that students offer supportive and useful advice and learn how to offer constructive criticism.

Action planning

It's important that students plan their projects and regularly meet to report on progress; this ensures that students understand the time restrictions on their project – for example a reply to a freedom of information request should take 20 working days, but students should appreciate that the time this request might spend in the post could add another week and answers to requests may be unsatisfactory and demand an internal inquiry or additional inquiries until the student has the information they may need in order to continue. They should also appreciate the possible delays in trying to organise a meeting or debate, or the time it may take to research or gather information.

It might be useful to use a planning frame similar to the one below. It could be very useful to post such a plan on school or college intranet sites as a means of continuing a constant progress report between students and teachers. This can be a useful way to encourage and motivate students who may become disillusioned if they suffer setbacks. AQA gives details of the Active Citizenship Profile it suggests students take into the exam with them on its website www.aqa.org.uk. This could be used instead of the frame below, or completed as a summary exercise in preparation for the exam.

Overview of project				
Aims				
Activity	Content area	Target completion	Date completed and reflection	Evidence

Examples of active citizenship projects

- Organisation of a campaign (within school/college and/or within the wider community) involving raising awareness through petitions (online and hard copy), meetings or organised debates.
- Use of school council or learner voice forum to change a school/college policy.
- Campaign for a change in the local area. This could encompass any number of examples, for example a new pedestrian crossing or a campaign against a local decision or government policy.
- Campaign for improved local services.
- Organisation and implementation of events or services for a group in the community.
- Organisation and implementation of elections for school/college council or even creation of a school/college council.

Web action

www.citized.info: information on funding for active citizenship projects.
www.post16citizenship.org/alevel/: examples of possible active citizenship projects.
www.aqa.org.uk: guidance from AQA on the active citizenship requirement of the course in the Citizenship 'teacher resources' section.

ASSESSMENT GUIDANCE

Chapter 8: About the examination

This section is intended to assist you in preparing for the two written papers that comprise the assessment package for GCE AS Citizenship Studies.

The two modules or assessments are formally known as CIST 1 and CIST 2.

- CIST 1 is about identity, rights and responsibilities.
- CIST 2 is about democracy and active citizenship participation.

Three of the four elements within two examination papers follow a common structure; the fourth component assesses your understanding and involvement in active citizenship activities.

- CIST 1 requires that you answer two source based questions and two essay questions. This paper is equal to 40 per cent of the total AS assessment. CIST 1 lasts 1 hr 15 mins and the total mark for the paper is 60.
- CIST 2 requires that you answer one source based question and one essay question and a three part question regarding active citizenship. This paper is equal to 60 per cent of the total AS assessment. CIST 2 lasts 1 hr 30 mins and the total mark for the paper is 90.

Both of the AS examination papers are available in January and June of each year.

What do the questions look like?

Question paper	Source based two part question	Mini essay questions (choose one)	Active citizenship four part question	Total marks for the paper	Time allowed
CIST 1	Q1 and Q3	Q2 or 3 and Q5 or 6		60	75 minutes
CIST 2	Q1	Q2 or 3	Q4	90	90 minutes

Source based questions

These are based upon a short source; this may be a short piece of text, a table, graphs or statistics. This question is based upon either of the two key questions:

- Q1 CIST 1 What does it mean to be British?, or Are we all equal citizens?
- Q3 CIST 1 What are my rights and responsibilities?, or How are my rights protected and supported?
- Q1 CIST 2 Who can make a difference?, or How can I make a difference?

Between the sources based question and the two essay questions both of the key questions are assessed.

The source based questions have a part a) and b), worth 5 and 10 marks respectively.

The part a) question relates closely to the source and asks a candidate to 'Briefly explain'; this implies both extracting information from the source and adding some clarification. Candidates must take note of the phrase, 'briefly'. It is easy to write too much for this response and thereby lose marks later in the paper due to running out of time.

Part b) for 10 marks requires a fuller response and is often better answered as a structured response, i.e. an answer that has a clear structure containing several points which are drawn together with some concluding comments.

Mini-essay questions

Candidates must only answer one of these questions. The mini-essay is worth 15 marks so candidates should spend a reasonable amount of time on this question.

These questions are aimed to encourage responses that contain a reasonable degree of analysis and evaluation. The trigger words to watch in these questions are phrases such as 'assess', 'critically assess' or 'evaluate'. For these questions it is important to ensure that you have a clear plan to your response as they require both a range of knowledge to be outlined as well as the ability to place the evidence you present in context and draw out evaluative comments that lead to a well developed conclusion.

Remember that for CIST 1 you only have about 35 minutes to complete the source question and your chosen mini-essay question, leaving you 5 minutes to read over your responses to check for any errors or to add any additional comments.

The Active Citizenship question – CIST 2

One of the requirements of this course is that you become involved in and understand the nature of active citizenship participation. This element of the course is assessed in CIST 2, Q4.

You are allowed to take into the examination room your active citizenship profile in order to assist you when answering question 4. This is not compulsory but being able to recall events or activities you have been involved in will be helpful when answering this question. The profile will be collected at the end of the examination and retained by your centre until the results are published.

As candidates will have a range of varying active citizenship experiences the questions asked will need be able to allow all candidates to answer the questions.

The course develops three levels of active citizenship involvement as follows.

- the informed citizen: how a person becomes informed and knowledgeable about an issue.
- the participating citizen: the skills a person needs to be able to take part in contemporary society.
- the active citizen: using both knowledge and citizenship skills to make a difference.

The questions develop candidates' understanding of these phases of active citizenship. Candidates are expected to draw upon their own experiences when answering the questions.

The four part question awards part A 5 marks, B 15, C 15 and D 25. The marks to be awarded should clearly indicate to candidates that part D should take up the longest amount of time.

As in other questions, the 5-mark part A response doesn't need to be over-developed.

In regard to part C an additional short source appears on the paper to provide a framework. Candidates need to ensure that they incorporate the evidence they find in the source into their response.

In regard to part D candidates are expected to write a traditional essay-style response. The trigger words for this question could be 'critically assess' or 'critically evaluate'. The response should have a clear opening paragraph deconstructing the key elements of the question. Several distinct points need to be made regarding the evidence being presented. The conclusion, like the introduction, should bring together the main points evaluating their relative importance.

The key to success in regard to question 4 is the ability to integrate into your response relevant elements from your own active citizenship experiences, hence the importance of having completed your active citizenship profile to assist you.

What are examiners looking for?

When marking your work examiners have to work within the parameters of an agreed mark scheme.

Mark schemes are designed to enable examiners to award marks fairly in relation to any response. Mark schemes are written to meet the assessment needs of the subject. In regard to GCE Citizenship at AS there are three assessment objectives that examiners have to assess as follows.

- AO1 Knowledge and understanding.
- AO2 Analysis and evaluation.
- AO3 Communication and action.

Each of these assessment objectives is given a weighting within the AS course as follows.

- AO1, 30 per cent.
- AO2, 20 per cent.
- AO3, 50 per cent.

The two question papers are designed to deliver responses that together are in line with the weightings of the assessment objectives.

Therefore for some questions examiners are making more then one decision about your answer and then adding marks together for the assessment objectives to arrive at a total for the question.

The following grids show how the marks are awarded by assessment objective across the papers.

By understanding how the assessment objectives are weighted across the various questions you can then think about the balance of the structure of your response to each question.

The other component part of the mark scheme is the indicative comment, whereby examiners are given potential content in regard to each response.

The mark scheme is divided into three levels. So the initial decision the examiner makes is into which level does each the response fit in regard to each assessment objective. Therefore it is possible to achieve a high mark for assessment objective 1 and a low mark for assessment objective 2.

Maximum marks available	Assessment objective 1 Knowledge and understanding	Assessment objective 2 Analysis and evaluation	Assessment objective 3 Communication and action
5-mark questions	5		
10-mark questions	4	3	3
15-mark questions	6	5	4
CIST 2 Part B Active citizenship Q4 b and c 15 marks		3	12
CIST 2 Part B Active citizenship Q4 d 25 marks			25

	Level 3	Level 2	Level 1
Assessment objective 1 Knowledge and understanding	Highest mark	Mid range	Lowest mark
Assessment objective 2 Analysis and understanding	Highest mark	Mid range	Lowest mark
Assessment objective 3 Communication and action	Highest mark	Mid range	Lowest mark

Key terms and concepts

Chapter 1

Bias – favouring one side over another or at the expense of another.

British – name given to citizens of the UK (Great Britain and Northern Ireland).

Citizen – belonging to a nation. A key feature of being a citizen is belonging.

Citizenship – participation in a community and the nature of belonging as a citizen. The relationship between rights and responsibilities of a citizen.

Communitarian or **communitarianism** – the idea that a unified society requires participation by citizens and the strength in unity comes from active citizenship.

Culture – the usual customs and beliefs or values of a group of people with a shared heritage or history.

Democracy – political system based on the principle that government should serve the interest of the people, effectively allowing the people to collectively hold power.

Emigration – moving out of a country to another country, sometimes called 'out migration'.

Ethnic integration – different ethnic groups becoming part of a culture having been from a different ethnic background, often from another country.

Ethnicity – someone's racial, religious or national grouping. Most advanced, modern cultures, such as British culture, are multi-ethnic – they have various ethnic groups making up the culture as a whole.

European Union – collection of 27 countries in Europe that cooperate by sharing social, cultural, political and economic systems and decisions.

Gender – grouping according to sex. Associated with identity of different sexes – male (masculine) or female (feminine). Socially expected behaviour and identity of males and females.

Identity – an individual's self awareness; features of a person which make them distinct from others.

Immigration – moving into a country from another country, sometimes called 'in migration'.

Individualistic – promoting your own interests at times at the expense of others.

Labelling – tags or names given to behaviour and/or groups of people. A process of categorising and naming groups or actions.

Mass media – the organisations that produce news and entertainment for a mass (very large) audience.

Migration – moving away form one place to another.

Models of media influence – theories about how media images affect citizens.

Multicultural – where culture comprises a variety of different ethnic groups. The uniting of various cultures or ethnic identities into a collective culture.

Nature – things we are born with such as our sex which shape our character or identity.

Net migration – the difference between those immigrating and those emigrating, the 'in' and 'out' figures.

Norms – socially expected behaviour, normal actions.

Nurture – socially constructed identity shaped through processes of socialisation.

Peer – someone of your own generation that you associate with – peer group.

Peer group pressure – pressure or an expectation that you conform to and follow or mirror the behaviour patterns of your peers. It is a pressure to do what your friends or the group you are involved with expect of you; this can be an influence on your beliefs and values as well as your actions.

Responsibilities (duties) – things citizens are expected to do, such as follow the law. Other responsibilities may include parenting and concern for fellow humans. Many responsibilities are encouraged or expected but are not legal requirements.

Rights – benefits of being a citizen. The rights of citizens have evolved over the centuries from basic civil or human rights to political rights and more recently social or welfare rights.

Social class – a grouping or category in society depending mainly upon type of job and educational background. Working class is associated with manual work and practical not necessarily academic skills. Middle class is associated with academic and organisational responsibilities. Some argue these terms are becoming less reliable as culture and society develops more equality and mixing between communities and social class groups.

Social diversity – differences and variations in the social make-up of a community or society.

Socialisation – process an individual goes through learning how to fit into and understand their culture's beliefs and customs. Primary socialisation is the first stage and normally takes place in the family. Secondary socialisation occurs outside the home, for example at school.

State – the organisations responsible for running the country and services at both local and national level.

Stereotyping – over simplification of a group's identity or behaviour. A generalised impression of a group or individual held by another group or individual. Often used in media to typify some characters or groups however they are often generalised impressions.

Values – things we consider important, that underpin our norms (normal) behaviour.

Welfare state – a government (or state) which prioritises the welfare of its citizens. Associated with national services for welfare such as a national health service, benefits system, education and housing services. Believed to have developed after Second World War where the Government took prime responsibility for the welfare of its citizens.

 Chapter 2

Abuse – causing harm to others can be physical or psychological, could involve neglect, maltreating other people. Has various uses –

individuals could use abusive language, organisations can abuse workers by neglecting their rights, states could abuse human rights. Sometimes refers to misuse of information or position, for example abusing your position of responsibility.

Anti-discrimination policy – laws and actions designed to challenge discrimination and prejudice. Could be part of a school policy or a council policy or government policy.

Antilocution – rather like bullying, sometimes called speaking behind someone's back or 'hate speech' which causes bad feeling and produces the climate for discrimination.

Bullying – singling out individuals or small groups to abuse or intimidate. Takes many forms, most associated with schools but could occur in the workplace, home or in the local community.

Disadvantage – something stopping you taking opportunities; lack of opportunities compared to others.

Discrimination – acting on prejudiced beliefs, such that people or groups are treated differently. Discrimination can be positive, negative, direct or indirect.

Equal opportunities legislation – laws directly intended to challenge specific types of discrimination.

Equality of opportunity – the notion that all citizens have similar chances to succeed and operate in an environment without discrimination or unfairness.

Equality and Human Rights Commission – government funded organisation responsible for promoting the interests of all citizens, challenging discrimination and promoting fairness and equal rights. Checks through laws and creates proposals on equality issues and supports or advises on citizens' claims to unfair treatment.

Genocide – the deliberate or systematic destruction of an ethnic, religious or national group. Usually carried out by a state or large organisation. It is a crime under international law.

Heterosexism – discrimination against gay and lesbian people by heterosexual (straight) men and women.

Homophobia – prejudiced attitudes against homosexuals.

Institutionalised racism – racial prejudice (beliefs) which have become part of the language and daily actions of an organisation. Not always intentional, it causes discrimination because the daily routines, actions and systems of an organisation are racist or insensitive and unaware of the needs and concerns of all ethnicities. All public organisations had to review their systems and actions in light of the issue of discreet prejudice which had become the norm in them.

Islamophobia – the prejudiced and discriminatory attitudes and actions against Islamic beliefs/faith and people (Muslims).

Life chances – opportunities available to different citizens and groups of citizens.

Meritocracy – the idea that society rewards effort and hard work. The deserving are rewarded with, for example, better jobs, choices or higher quality of life.

Physical abuse – causing physical harm by assault or neglecting basic necessities for living, for example food, water, clothing, shelter.

Poverty – not having enough to provide basics. Absolute poverty sees the basics as simply enough food and water, shelter and clothing to remain alive without ill health. Relative poverty sees the basics to include things expected in a normal life (non-essentials) such as TV, mobile phones etc..

Prejudice – beliefs that one group or aspect of identity is better or worse than another.

Racism – unfair and unlawful treatment against people of different racial groupings. The belief that some races are superior (or inferior) to others.

Sexism – discriminating against men or women because of their sex.

Underclass – a group in society who, over generations, are excluded from normal society because they are either unable to break the poverty cycle or are vulnerable and isolated or are criminal. The group may be caused by the society and prejudice/discriminations in it or by its own actions. The concept has been used by various social scientists from various political persuasions.

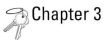 Chapter 3

Absolute duties – a duty that does not have a corresponding right – for example, the duty that all citizens have to not break the criminal law.

Advocacy – the role of representing a person or a view. In a legal context it usually refers to representing a client in court and putting across the client's case to the court or tribunal.

Alternative Dispute Resolution – (usually abbreviated to ADR) a method of settling a dispute between two or more parties by mediation, conciliation or arbitration, i.e. by a means other than litigation in the traditional courts.

Barristers – a branch of the legal profession. Barristers are regulated by the rules of the bar council. They provide advice on litigation and other issues, and advocacy in all courts (when instructed by solicitors).

Civil law – the area of law that deals with disputes between one individual (ie either a human person or a 'legal' person ie a limited company) and another. It is included in the area of law often referred to as 'private law' because the state is not usually involved in the proceedings. The purpose of the civil law is often to enable an individual to achieve a particular purpose (eg to make a will or a contract) or to obtain compensation from another individual who has caused a loss or an injury.

Constitution – the rights of a citizen, recognised by the state, which cannot easily be changed or withdrawn. The word is often used to designate the document in which these rights are set out.

Criminal law – the area of law where the state brings proceedings against an individual to punish the individual for a breach of the law. It is included in the area of law often referred to as 'public law' because it involves the state brining proceedings to punish behaviour that has been deemed to be so serious that punishment is considered the only way of dealing with it.

Defendant – the person against whom a civil action is brought. It is also increasingly used to identify the person against whom a criminal prosecution is brought, although such a person is more accurately described as the 'accused'.

Employment tribunal – official body that settles disputes relating to employment matters in a less formal way than in a court. Tribunals follow and apply the same principles of natural justice as the courts and provide a forum for a fair hearing of issues.

Information Commissioner – an independent person responsible for the operation of the Freedom of Information Act 2000. One of the duties of the Information Commissioner is to deal with complaints against public authorities that have failed to deal properly with a request for information.

Information tribunal – a tribunal set up under the Freedom of Information Act 2000 to hear appeals against decisions of the Information Commissioner.

Jural correlative – the term used by Hohfeld to express the legal position of the person against whom someone else has a 'right'.

Jural opposite – the term used by Hohfeld to express what a person claiming to have a particular right cannot have, at the same time as the right being claimed.

Legal Aid – a system of state funded legal help for those requiring legal services but who do not have the resources to pay for it. It is usually means tested (i.e. only given to those who can demonstrate financial need) and it is often merit tested too (i.e. only available where the issue involved is of particular importance and/or there is a significant likelihood of success).

Legal representation – acting on behalf of others in legal matters.

Ombudsman – an official appointed to investigate complaints against public authorities, government departments, and a variety of other bodies such as solicitors and estate agents.

Plaintiff – the name given to the person who brought a civil action against another person before 2000. The Civil Procedure Rules 1999 changed the name of the person bringing a civil action to 'claimant' (see below).

Relative duties – a duty that has a corresponding right – for example, if the lender has a right to claim the repayment of a debt, the borrower has the relative duty to repay the debt.

Residual freedoms – liberties enjoyed by UK citizens that have not been removed or restricted by statute or by the decisions of the courts.

Rights – privileges, liberties, powers and immunities that are recognised by law and which may be exercised in certain circumstances. Rights can be seen as the building blocks that form the basis of a legal system.

Solicitors – the largest branch of the legal profession. Solicitors are regulated by the rules of their professional body, the Law Society. They provide legal advice and conduct most of the litigation in the magistrates' and county courts.

Solicitor-advocates – solicitors who have the right to appear as advocates in all courts.

Sovereignty of Parliament – the principle that the UK Parliament is the supreme law maker so that (i) the laws made by Parliament take precedence over laws from all other sources, and (ii) Parliament can make whatever laws it wants to make, without legal constraint.

Statute – a law made by Parliament (also known as an 'Act' or as an 'Act of Parliament').

Statutory obligation – a duty imposed by an act of Parliament.

Success fee – the extra fee, in addition to the standard fee, paid to a solicitor and/or barrister who have successfully represented a client under a conditional fee arrangement in which neither would have been paid any fee had they lost the case. They receive this additional fee, when successful, to compensate them for the risk that they have taken in agreeing to represent the client. The success fee is usually one third of the standard fee, but can be more in particularly difficult cases.

Tribunal – the name given to the official body that hears a number of specialist cases, usually related to claims made by citizens in respect of various benefits under the welfare state. The Employment tribunal (*see above*) is one of the best known examples of the tribunal system.

Chapter 4

Advocate – a person who represents the interests of another. In a legal context it usually refers to a barrister or solicitor who appears in court on behalf of a client.

Barristers – a branch of the legal profession. Barristers are regulated by the rules of the bar council. They provide advice on litigation and other issues, and advocacy in all courts (when instructed by solicitors).

Caution – as used in the text, a caution is a formal warning given to a person accused of a crime instead of bringing a prosecution in court. A second, and quite different meaning, is a warning given to a person on arrest about his or her rights. The wording of this caution is 'You do not have to say anything, but it may harm your defence if you do not mention when questioned, something that you later rely on in court. Anything you do say may be given in evidence'.

Citizens' Advice Bureau – a state funded organisation that offers free advice on a range of topics to all who need it.

Claimant – the person who brings a civil action in court.

Conciliation – one of the forms of alternative dispute resolution. A neutral third party helps to resolve the dispute by bringing the parties together and actively helping them to resolve their differences.

Conditional fee agreement – an agreement under which a solicitor agrees to undertake a case on the condition that if the client loses the case no fee (or a reduced fee) will be charged, but if the client is successful, the solicitor will be entitled to an enhanced fee to recompense them for the risk taken in accepting the chance that no fee would be earned at all. Such an agreement is often referred to as a 'no win, no fee' agreement but that is not technically accurate.

County court – the court that hears most civil actions. It can hear cases involving personal injuries up to the value of £50,000.

Crown Prosecution Service – a body set up under the Prosecution of Offences Act 1985 to provide a prosecution service for England and Wales. It is run by the Director of Public Prosecutions who in turn reports to the Attorney General. As well as prosecuting offenders, the CPS makes the final decision on who should be prosecuted and what they should be prosecuted for.

Defendant – the person against whom a civil action is brought. It is also increasingly used to identify the person against whom a criminal prosecution is brought, although such a person is more accurately described as the 'accused'.

Duty Solicitors – there are two duty solicitor schemes: 1) the Duty Solicitor in the Police Station scheme (where independent solicitors in private practice provide a service to anyone in police custody) – they will give free advice to detainees and will, if the clients wishes, be present with the client during police interviews; and 2) the Duty Solicitor in the Court scheme (where independent solicitors attend all criminal courts on a rota basis to provide advice, and, where appropriate, representation in court, for defendants who do not have their own solicitor).

Fixed penalties – a system, mainly applied to motoring offences, under which offenders are given the option of accepting a standard form of punishment, usually involving the payment of a fine and the imposition of points on the offender's driving licence.

High Court – a civil court that hears important and/or large cases. It also has the right to supervise all lower courts and other bodies with a judicial responsibility.

Human Rights Act 1998 – a statute which came into force in October 2000. Under this statute the terms of the European Convention on Human Rights (the ECHR) became part of English law. It allowed UK citizens to use the UK courts to enforce rights under the Convention which they had previously had to take to the European Court of Human Rights.

Judicial Review – a process which allows the High Court to oversee the decisions of public bodies.

Lay people – a lay person is anyone who is not a member of a particular profession. Thus when a doctor refers to lay people, he or she means anyone who is not a doctor. In a legal context it therefore means anyone who is not legally qualified, i.e. anyone who is not a barrister or a solicitor.

Legal Aid – a system of state funded legal help for those requiring legal services but who do not have the resources to pay for it. It is usually means tested (i.e. only given to those who can demonstrate financial need) and it is often merit tested too (i.e. only available where the issue involved is of particular importance and/or there is a significant likelihood of success).

Legal executive – a member of the Institute of Legal Executives who has been trained to do much of the work that would otherwise be done by solicitors. Legal executives are trained to a similar level as solicitors, but in a narrower range of legal topics.

Legal Services Commission – the body responsible for managing both the Community Legal Service and the Criminal Defence Service

Litigants – the general term used to describe any party in legal proceedings.

Means test – the test applied to persons who apply for a financial benefit (in the legal context this is usually some form of legal aid) to ensure that the applicant is not able to afford to pay for the service out of his or her own capital or income.

Merits test – the test applied to persons who apply for support from the Community Legal Service to decide if the case the applicant wants the CLS to support is important enough to justify spending public money on and that there is a reasonable chance of it succeeding.

Natural justice – the concept that some basic rules (for example, that both parties in a case have the right to be heard) are fundamental to any decision making process. Any decision reached in a case where one of these fundamental rights was ignored would not be allowed to stand.

Negotiation – a discussion between the parties to a case or between their legal representatives, with a view to agreeing the terms on which the dispute might be settled without having to go to a hearing in court.

Police – there are 43 police forces in England and Wales. Scotland and Northern Ireland have their own police forces.

Precedent – the process by which the decisions of higher courts are followed by courts lower in the hierarchy. The effect of this is that the decisions of the highest court (the Supreme Court) are followed by all courts and so become law.

Solicitors – the largest branch of the legal profession. Solicitors are regulated by the rules of their professional body, the Law Society. They provide legal advice and conduct most of the litigation in the magistrates and county courts.

Solicitor-advocates – solicitors who have the right to appear as advocates in all courts.

Stare decisis – a Latin expression which literally means 'let the decision stand'. It sets out the rules, based on the hierarchy of the courts, about which courts bind other courts by their decisions, and which courts are bound by the decisions of other courts.

Statute – a law made by Parliament (also known as an 'Act' or as an 'Act of Parliament').

Tort – a civil wrong (from the old French *tort* meaning wrong, crooked or not straight) committed by one individual against another where the defendant owed a duty to the claimant, was in breach of that duty and as a result caused loss or damage to the claimant – for example, defamation, negligence and nuisance all give rise to actions in tort.

Tribunals – a board, usually consisting of three people, set up by statute to deal with a narrow range of disputes in a particular area. Often, but not always, involving some aspect of the welfare state.

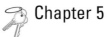 **Chapter 5**

Bureaucratic – term used to describe a system for controlling a country, company or organisation that is operated by a large number of officials who are employed to follow rules carefully.

By-election – An election held during a government term of office to fill a vacant seat.

Chancellor of the Exchequer – the cabinet minister responsible for government spending and setting levels of tax.

Democracy – political system based on the principle that government should serve the interest of the people, effectively allowing the people to collectively hold power.

Devolution – the transfer of powers from central government to localities.

Freedom of the press – the guarantee that ensures news is free to be reported without government restriction. However government does retain the power to keep any information confidential if it believes it puts the public at risk.

Globalisation – globalisation is the term used to describe the process by which countries are becoming more interdependent and interconnected – specifically via communication links and trade.

Inflation – a general, continuous rise in prices

Influence – the power to have an effect on people or events.

Interdependence – a situation in which countries are dependent on one another.

Intergovernmental – a process of decision making, within an internal organisation, in which all national governments meet and have equal influence.

Local representative – a person elected to represent the interests of citizens at a local level. Within local government this could be a councillor and/or elected mayor. Depending on the structure of local government within an area, a citizen may have several councillors, elected at various tiers of local authority, to represent their views/needs.

Mandate – the authority given to an elected group of people, such as government, to perform an action or govern a country.

Mass media – all forms of media, including TV, radio, newspapers, intended to reach a vast audience.

Mayor – the unelected member of a borough or city council (district councils have a chairman). Some larger areas may have lord mayors. Some local authorities may have a directly elected mayor – voted for by those living in the area, for example London.

Media – in its most basic sense, 'media' is the method by which something is expressed; but we have now commonly adopted this word to describe newspapers, TV, radio and the internet.

Policy – a set of ideas or proposals that result in a government decision.

Political bias – an inclination or prejudice toward a particular political viewpoint.

Referenda – votes in which citizens, within a country or region, are asked to answer 'yes' or 'no' to a single important political issue.

Sovereign – the highest power within a state/country.

State – the organisations responsible for running the country and services at both local and national level.

Supranational – a process of decision making, within an internal organisation, in which a particular institution has its own authority over single nations.

Treaty – a written agreement between two or more countries formally approved and signed by their leaders.

Veto – to veto something is to refuse to allow it. Members of the European Economic Community had the power to veto the entry of another state into the EEC.

Chapter 6

Additional member system – an electoral system whereby electors cast two votes; one for a candidate to represent them as their constituency member, and another for their preferred party. Candidate's votes are counted using the 'first past the post' system but votes for parties are allocated proportionately to a number of 'top up' seats.

Boycott – refusal to deal with a particular organisation, commonly by refusing to buy products or use services.

By-election – an election held during a government term of office to fill a vacant seat.

Candidate – a person putting himself or herself forward to be elected as a representative of citizens' interests, at various levels of government.

Closed-party list – an electoral system in which the electorate vote for a party list but have no choice between individual candidates.

Democracy – political system based on the principle that government should serve the interest of the people, effectively allowing the people to collectively hold power.

Demographic – a particular section of the population identified by specific characteristics, for example location, social class, age, gender.

Direct action – activity that focuses on individuals or organisations directly by groups attempting to influence political decision making.

Direct democracy – a form of democracy that more directly consults citizens, as opposed to a representative democracy that relies on a third party to act for citizens.

Electoral register – an official list of the people in a local authority area that are eligible to vote.

Indirect action – activity involving less immediate or aggressive methods, by groups attempting to influence political decision making.

Insider groups – pressure groups that do operate with the close cooperation of the Government, often being routinely consulted by the Government on new policies connected with their objectives.

Liberal democracy – a democracy in which certain freedoms are upheld e.g. freedom of speech, freedom of association etc..

Manifesto – a statement of the beliefs, aims and policies of a political party.

Mediation – a forum in which two separate people or groups involved in a disagreement try to agree or find a solution to their problems, with the help of a third party.

New media – forms of communication using computers or the internet, rather than traditional methods, such as radio, TV and newspapers.

Outsider groups – pressure groups that do not operate with the close cooperation of the Government.

Political consultancy – profit-making organisation that employs subject specialists and expert negotiators to lobby government. These consultancies are often employed by pressure groups, campaign groups or companies with an interest in a particular government policy.

Popular initiative – the process whereby a citizen can petition for the amendment of a particular legislation (used in some US states).

Proportional representation (PR) – a system of organising election results that allocates seats in government to political parties according to the proportion of votes achieved overall.

Recall election – a procedure by which US voters can remove an elected official before their end of term in office.

Representative democracy – a democracy in which representatives are elected to form government.

Single transferable vote system – an electoral system in which the electorate are able to rank the individual candidates on a ballot paper. Candidates must reach a quota in order to be elected and votes from all ballots are transferred to remaining candidates to ensure fairness.

Subvert – to try to destroy or weaken something, especially an established political system.

Supplementary voting system – an electoral system in which the electorate show their first and second preference candidate on their ballot paper. A winning candidate must secure over 50 per cent of the vote to be successful; if no candidate does so all candidates except the first two are disqualified and their votes transferred.

Trade union – an organisation that represents the people who work in a particular industry, protects their rights and discusses their pay and working conditions with employers.

Voter apathy – citizens' lack of action, enthusiasm or interest in the process of voting.

Index